Still the Greatest

The Essential Songs of the Beatles' Solo Careers

Andrew Grant Jackson

THE SCARECROW PRESS, INC.
Lanham • Toronto • Plymouth, UK
2012

Published by Scarecrow Press, Inc.
A wholly owned subsidiary of The Rowman & Littlefield Publishing Group, Inc.
4501 Forbes Boulevard, Suite 200, Lanham, Maryland 20706
www.rowman.com

10 Thornbury Road, Plymouth PL6 7PP, United Kingdom

British Library Cataloguing in Publication Information Available

Library of Congress Cataloging-in-Publication Data

Jackson, Andrew Grant
  Still the greatest : the essential songs of the Beatles' solo careers / Andrew Grant
Jackson.
      p. cm.
  Includes bibliographical references and index.
  ISBN 978-0-8108-8222-5 (cloth : alk. paper) — ISBN 978-0-8108-8223-2 (ebook)
  1. Beatles. 2. Lennon, John, 1940-1980. 3. McCartney, Paul. 4. Harrison, George,
1943-2001. 5. Starr, Ringo. 6. Rock musicians—England—Biography. I. Title.
  ML421.B4J33 2012
  782.42166092'2—dc23

                                                              2012007942

∞™ The paper used in this publication meets the minimum requirements of
American National Standard for Information Sciences—Permanence of Paper
for Printed Library Materials, ANSI/NISO Z39.48-1992.

Printed in the United States of America

To Barbara and Keira,

Out the blue you came to me
And blew away life's misery

Contents

Acknowledgments

$\mathcal{T}$his book draws upon two decades of reading about the Beatles, but when I formally began its writing in July 2010, three books were especially informative: John Blaney's *Lennon and McCartney: Together Alone*, Peter Doggett's *You Never Give Me Your Money*, and Simon Leng's *The Music of George Harrison: While My Guitar Gently Weeps*. Also essential were the two lengthy interviews that bookended John Lennon's solo career: Jann Wenner's 1970 *Rolling Stone* interview and David Sheff's 1980 *Playboy* interview (both with Yoko Ono).

Had I attempted this book in an earlier era, I would not have been able to hear many of the songs without endlessly searching record stores across the country. But since I'm lucky enough to live in the era of YouTube, this book has relied heavily on the countless anonymous fans who uploaded their bootlegs and out-of-print B-sides. Likewise, the book would have been much thinner without the ocean of information to be found on Wikipedia and "The Beatles Bible" (www.beatlesbible.com).

Priceless insights came from memoirs and biographies, including Paul McCartney's *Many Years from Now* (written with Barry Miles), Pattie Boyd's *Wonderful Tonight: George Harrison, Eric Clapton, and Me* (with Penny Junor), Chris O'Dell's *Miss O'Dell: My Hard Days and Long Nights with The Beatles, The Stones, Bob Dylan, Eric Clapton, and the Women They Loved* (with Katherine Ketcham), Bob Spitz's *The Beatles: The Biography*, Peter Carlin's *Paul McCartney: A Life*, Peter Shotton's *John Lennon in My Life* (with Nicholas Schaffner), and Peter Brown's *The Love You Make: An Insider's Story of the Beatles* (with Stephen Gaines). And yes—loathe though many Beatlemaniacs are to speak its name—Albert Goldman's *The Lives of John Lennon*.

Other very helpful tomes included Chris Ingham's *The Rough Guide to the Beatles*, Roy Carr and Tony Tyler's *The Beatles: An Illustrated Record*, Robert Rodriguez's *Fab Four FAQ 2.0: The Beatles' Solo Years, 1970–1980*, the

Beatles' own *Anthology,* Nicholas Schaffner's *The Beatles Forever,* Bob Woffinden's *The Beatles Apart,* and Tim Riley's *Tell Me Why: A Beatles Commentary.*

And I will always owe a great deal to three books that inflamed my passion for rock journalism all those years ago: Philip Norman's *Shout! The Beatles in Their Generation,* Greil Marcus's *Lipstick Traces,* and Nik Cohn's *Awopbopaloobop Alopbamboom: The Golden Age of Rock.*

Journalist Erick Trickey beat me to the punch many years ago by being the first person I ever heard of to make new Beatles CDs by intercutting solo tracks by the Fabs. He's been unfailingly supportive, enduring endless e-mails and pushing me to drill deeper. Rock journalist David Jenison read the whole book and gave me the bird's-eye view when I was lost in the forest. Writer David Lloyd went far beyond the call of duty with his meticulous copyediting and marketing expertise. Rockumentarian Jeff McCarty was always ready to see who could come up with the most obscure musical reference over a drink at Colombo's in Eagle Rock.

I would also like to thank the friends who generously read parts of the manuscript and gave thoughtful, much-needed feedback: Jeff Elbel, Thom Foley, Morgan Hobbs, Steve Kedrowski, Matthew Neelands, Ashley Sepanski, Foster Timms, and Michael Twigg.

I'm very grateful for the contributions of Aimee Baldridge, Jay Burnley, Chris Cantergiani, Jill Hesseltine, Topher Hopkins, Fred Kluth, John Koenigsberg, Dane Lee, Ethan Maile, Mary Patton, Rebecca Spring, Jamie and Jack Wheatley, The Book Doctors Arielle Eckstut and Dave Sterry, my mother-in-law, Aurora Clements, and the Dunlop family, the Van Dyke family, my cousin Jennifer Adams and the Adams family, my aunt Trudi Lawrence, and my aunt Vella DuPuis and the DuPuis family.

I was incredibly fortunate to connect with two music aficionados extraordinaire who agreed to take on the project: literary agent Charlie Viney and Scarecrow's senior acquisitions editor Bennett Graff. I am indebted to Charlie for his guidance and party mixes and to Bennett for his patience and vision. I am also extemely grateful for the immeasurable help of production editor Jessica McCleary. Thanks to artist Piper Wallis for her cover design, Amanda Kirsten for her diligent proofreading, Rowman & Littlefield's Sam Caggiula, Jared Hughes, and Rayna Andrews, and The Viney Agency's Sally Fricker.

I wish my parents were here to see the book. Its true genesis was the year I was born, when they played *Sgt. Pepper* and *Abbey Road* constantly while their hippie neighbor painted a psychedelic mural in their den. When my dad took my buddy and me to see *A Hard Day's Night* at a University of Michigan revival house, the packed theater's laughter and singing ensured Dad's Beatlemania was passed on to the next generation.

The book could not have been written without my wife, Barbara, the most beautiful, intelligent, insightful, artistic, strong, funny, and compassionate muse a man could hope for. She's also the finest mother imaginable to the best little girl in the world. I sang every Beatles song to Keira as I rocked and walked her, so we'll see what she thinks of them when she gets a little older. So far "Eight Days a Week" is her favorite.

Introduction

$\mathcal{T}$he magic of the Beatles was the interplay of four distinct personalities, an alchemy wherein the whole was greater than the sum of its parts. Lennon's anger, McCartney's melodicism, Harrison's spirituality, Starr's joie de vivre—interspersed with each other, they provided contrast and relief.

As a lifelong Beatles fan, I have endlessly replayed their '60s songs and craved more, but unfortunately they only released twelve studio albums during their eight years recording together as a unit. But the crème de la crème of their solo work stands proudly alongside their group efforts. Creating mixes that alternate the best solo tracks by John, Paul, George, and Ringo reveals that there is a fascinating and worthy second act to the Beatles' oeuvre.

The Solo Era has not received as much respect because the albums were spottier. When they were working together, Lennon and McCartney only had to come up with five tunes each per album, whereas once they broke up they had to come up with ten or twelve. Thus, they padded records with tracks that would not have made the cut during the Beatles' run. But now, thanks to iTunes and Amazon, we can cherry-pick the gems.

Still the Greatest spotlights the 182 finest songs by the Fab Four from 1970 to 2011. It offers in-depth information on each track—the musicians, the chart performance, the story of its creation, and the meaning of the lyrics. And it puts each song in the context of the foursome's remarkable journey musically, personally, and as a social phenomenon.

THE SOLO SEQUEL

The first two epic poems of Western literature are Homer's *The Iliad*—about Greece's Trojan War—and its sequel, *The Odyssey*, in which the hero, Odysseus, tries to find his way home. The story of the Beatles in the 1960s was an epic about a band that helped change the world by pushing back the bounds of conformity and then split up under the pressure. On their last album, they sang sadly that they no longer had a way to get home, because the band that was once their family had fallen apart.

The ex-Beatles' solo catalog can be seen as the *Odyssey* sequel, telling the story of what they did afterward to find their new homes. Their struggles along the way prompted them to write many of their strongest songs, as they dealt with the aftermath of their own intergroup feud, tumultuous marriages, career missteps and comebacks, the wrath of presidents and murderous reactionaries, and their own mortality.

Musically, they tried to carve out new identities for themselves by exploring new genres before circling back to re-embrace their Beatles-esque qualities. Later, when they came to accept that they were no longer players in the youth-oriented contemporary pop scene, they were free to make some of the best music of their careers, even as their Beatles' work enjoyed a remarkable resurgence in popularity.

THE MUSIC

When the Beatles broke up, their competition with each other spurred them to some of their finest work. Lennon brought a new level of soul-searing honesty to the singer-songwriter tradition, while McCartney filled the airwaves with lushly orchestrated mini–rock operas. Harrison synthesized Indian music, gospel, and Southern blues, mixed it with Phil Spector's Wall of Sound, and conquered the charts with paeans to the Lord while inventing the rock charity concert.

They delved deeper into genres they had explored as a group (fifties rock, folk, country, blues, music hall, and lounge music) as well as areas they hadn't yet tackled (protest songs, jazz, samba, calypso, soundtracks, and Scottish bagpipe music). Determined to stay contemporary, they continued to infuse their music with their take on the black music of the day, from Philly soul to disco, funk, and even reggae.

The late '70s and '80s saw a turn toward the synth-tinged light pop of the Michael Jackson era, and later the Big Drum progressive rock sound of Phil Collins and the Police. But starting in the late '80s, collaborators such as Jeff

Lynne, Elvis Costello, Don Was, and Mark Hudson convinced the survivors to stop chasing other identities and celebrate their inherent Beatles qualities, bringing the Fabs back to second-act highs.

McCartney continued to experiment with modern genres like electronica and trance even as he produced full-length symphonies and oratorios. When the death of his first wife and chaotic second marriage forced him to turn to music as catharsis, he produced music as emotionally raw as Lennon's early '70s work, surprising those who had written him off as a pop craftsman. Starr, too, confounded expectations by consistently releasing solid albums of sixties-esque jangle pop married to words of hard-won wisdom.

THE LYRICS

One of the Fab Four's greatest skills was in writing songs that expressed their own story yet remained open enough to apply to anyone. For those who are interested, their biography is present in the lyrics from the break-up of 1970 to today.

The songs explain how Lennon quit the group, how McCartney drove the others away, how business worries sundered them. Each of the four cracked at various points and recovered, and the music told their tales. Some events were too hot to write about except obliquely in songs like "Simply Shady," as when Harrison cheated with Starr's wife even as Eric Clapton did the same with Harrison's.

Their lives after the '60s brought the superstars down to earth from exalted heights. The angst of betrayal, critical derision, being dumped, aging, and losing their public all found their way into the tracks. But they did find their way home, as heard in McCartney's odes to country living, Lennon's idealization of his life with his wife and new son, and Harrison's hymns to his Friar Park estate.

Above all, they continued to write about love—romantic, brotherly, and parental—while crafting odes to their muses, both dark and light, from Linda to Yoko, Pattie, Olivia, Maureen, Barbara, May, and Heather.

THE TIMES

Like the English and Russian master novelists of the nineteenth century, the Beatles took in the scope of their century and tackled the themes of great literature: politics, religion, drugs, metaphysics, art, competition. In Dostoyevsky's *The Brothers Karamazov*, the characters debate various philosophical stances, and the brothers ex-Beatles did the same. Harrison espoused the spiritual underpinnings of all religions from Christianity to Hinduism, while Lennon encouraged people to imagine no religion, and McCartney groused that the others were too preachy.

They alternated between creating surrealist visions like the Romantics to capturing the era journalistically like Hemingway. But they went beyond just reflecting the times and actually changed them in a way few icons have done.

Technology allowed them to broadcast their songs on a scale previously unprecedented for minstrels and poets—and on a scale that will perhaps never be attainable again. In an era when the United States had only three channels and no Internet, 73 million people viewed the Beatles' first appearance on the *Ed Sullivan Show* when the total US population was 192 million.

Their fame gave them a first look at the myriad of lifestyle choices offered in the new era of the global village. When they tried on each new identity in search of the balanced life, they inspired others to do so as well. After the break-up, their solo music reflected their experiences with psychotherapy, drugs and alcohol, lawsuits, money, farming, and househusbandry.

They were simultaneously normal young guys, idealists, and "the biggest bastards on earth" (per John), who found themselves the spokesmen for a massive generational shift toward personal liberation, religious freedom, and nonviolence. Two of them were rebels, two were not, which was the secret to their universal appeal. Seeing the world change in their longhaired image gave the rebels messiah complexes despite the fact that they were definitely not saints, and they strove to be gurus, partly to atone for their abusive behavior. Both heroic and hypocritical, they struggled to rise above their flawed personas and use the power of their fame for both art and social progress.

As early as the mid-'60s, the Ku Klux Klan threatened to kill Lennon for saying the Beatles were more popular than Jesus. But it was primarily for the philosophical songs that Lennon and Harrison released *after* the break-up— "Imagine," "My Sweet Lord," and "God"—that they were shot to death and stabbed.

Ironically, the assaults came long after Lennon and Harrison had given up releasing overtly political or religious music and had joined McCartney and Starr in focusing on pure pop. But while it is fashionable to believe the Aquarian Dream failed, the war against the conformity of the '50s buzz-cut military industrial complex had actually been won. As the right to sex without marriage, long hair, and even drugs melded with the mainstream, the ex-Beatles could look around at the new, freer world and know they played a central role in birthing it.

When Lennon was killed and Harrison was grievously injured for expressing their religious beliefs, they paid the final price for asserting the freedom of speech in societies inclined toward witch hunts and fundamentalism. That makes their tale epic in scope, worthy of Shakespeare or Tolstoy, and they told it to us from the inside every step of the way, allowing us to experience vicariously the highest highs and the lowest lows. And it was a story that was only half told at the dawn of 1970.

HOW THE SONGS WERE SELECTED

The idea of the Beatles continuing as a group is not as unlikely as it may initially seem. McCartney and Lennon made their peace by the middle of the 1970s. Lennon got along better with McCartney than Harrison did, so since even Harrison and McCartney eventually reunited for 1995's *Anthology*, it's likely the group would've gotten back together sooner had a murderer's bullets not intervened.

But one can still get the Beatles album sensation just by intercutting the solo tunes. By the second half of the Beatles' recording career, actual songwriting collaborations between Lennon and McCartney were few and far between. After 1965, "A Day in the Life," "Baby You're a Rich Man," "Birthday," and "I've Got a Feeling" are practically the only songs that include lyrics written and sung by both artists within the same song.

In choosing the selections, I tried to imagine albums that could mirror the original Beatles canon. They had twelve (British) albums, including one double album.

1. *Please Please Me* (1963)
2. *With the Beatles* (1963)
3. *A Hard Day's Night* (1964)
4. *Beatles for Sale* (1964)
5. *Help!* (1965)
6. *Rubber Soul* (1965)
7. *Revolver* (1966)
8. *Sgt. Pepper's Lonely Hearts Club Band* (1967)
9. *Magical Mystery Tour* (1967)
10. *The Beatles* (aka *The White Album*) (1968) (double)
11. *Abbey Road* (1969)
12. *Let It Be* (1970)

The Beatles Albums That Should Have Been, 1970–2011:

1. *Year One* (1970)
2. *It Don't Come Easy* (1971)
3. *Gimme Some Truth* (1972) (double)
4. *Everest* (1973)
5. *Lost Weekends* (1974)
6. *Pizza and Fairy Tales* (1976)
7. *Other Plans* (1980)
8. *Borrowed Time* (1984)
9. *When We Was Fab* (1989)
10. *The Song We Were Singing* (1997)
11. *Never Without You* (2005)
12. *Ever Present Past* (2011)

All the Beatles albums through *Revolver* adhered to the British tradition of giving fourteen songs an album (certainly more value than the US standard of eleven songs). I've adopted that here—though, in reality, after songs grew longer in the late 1960s, technically it would not have been possible to fit seven tunes on each side if one of them was the length of "Isn't It a Pity." But for the sake of consistency, I've ignored that detail.

The overriding goal was to make the best album possible for that year. Which songs stood the test of time and could be listened to over and over again? What album collection would beat that year's competition, be it the Stones, Dylan, Bowie, Springsteen, or Prince? And what albums could hold their own against the Beatles' '60s work?

Sometimes that meant leaving out songs that were historically significant but just did not truly rate as the best, in my opinion—Michael Jackson duets like "The Girl Is Mine," for instance. In the epilogue I have listed the next tier of songs: ones that deserve mention for being big hits ("Ebony and Ivory"), ones that are terrific but had to be omitted due to space, and ones for fans only.

Many will say the endeavor is handicapped by Lennon's death in 1980, and it's true that 70 percent of their best work came during Lennon's era (which extends to 1984, as a number of his best songs were released posthumously on *Milk and Honey*). But the group had forty years to match the eight years of Beatles output. In the decades following Lennon's murder, Harrison and Starr stepped up and delivered some of the most amazing work of their careers, and McCartney had a third-act resurgence comparable to Bob Dylan's.

In many cases, the artists did not have a release on one year, but had an overflow of material from the previous year. For instance, Harrison released a triple album in 1970 (*All Things Must Pass*, which went six times double platinum), but did not release another album until 1973. In 1971 and 1973 McCartney released two albums each year, but none in 1972 or 1974. Lennon released an album every year until 1975, but then nothing until 1980. So in cases like these, some tunes from the previous year's release are used the following year if the artist hadn't released any new material to fill the slot. This is mainly to try to retain the classic *Revolver* balance of five Lennon tunes, five McCartney tunes, two to three Harrison, and one Starr, whenever possible.

To further justify this in "fantasy football–rock geek" terms, I refer to the precedent that many Beatles tracks were actually written and/or recorded many albums before they were officially released. Examples include: "The One after 909," "What Goes On," "Hot as Sun," "I'll Follow the Sun," "Yesterday," "Bad Boy," "Wait," "Michelle," "Across the Universe," "It's All Too Much," "What's the New Mary Jane," "Carnival of Light," "Hey Bulldog," "Not Guilty," "Mean Mr. Mustard," "Polythene Pam," "Look at Me," "Junk," "Teddy Boy," "Jealous Guy," and much of the *All Things Must Pass* album.

The general guideline was: if there was a new tune from that year that was Grade A, then use that; but if there wasn't anything else Grade A from that year, but there was some Grade A stuff from the previous year that did not fit before, then use that to make the best album possible, like when the Rolling Stones released 1973's "Waiting on a Friend" on 1980's *Tattoo You*.

THE DO-IT-YOURSELF BEATLES ALBUM CULT

I became a Beatles fanatic the first time I saw *Yellow Submarine* on TV when I was four or five. Next, reruns of the Beatles' Saturday morning cartoon permanently embedded their songs onto my brain's hard drive. At thirteen, I read J. P. Russell's music guide *The Beatles on Record* and Philip Norman's biography *Shout! The Beatles in Their Generation*. They established the twin ways in which the Beatles continued to blow my mind: both as musicians and as fascinating figures in a wild and epic soap opera that changed society. I've tried to reflect both aspects in this book.

At some point, I started musing about making mixes of their solo material as if they were Beatles albums, but my good friend Erick Trickey beat me to it when the ability to burn your own CDs came about.

With the explosion of the Internet, the debate over how to best make "new" Beatles albums out of the solo albums became something akin to fantasy football for music geeks. One well-known version was called *The Black Album: The Lost Album*. A writer named Stephen Baxter wrote a short story called "The Twelfth Album" in which two Beatles fans discover a Beatles album that was never recorded, *God*. Other fan sites presented faux-album covers of imaginary '70s releases. The "new Beatle album" game allows aficionados to ignore the fact that the group broke up at all and play a part by curating the avalanche of stupendous music the Fab Four continued to make over the last forty years. Here's one fan's take on the Beatles Albums That Should Have Been . . .

Abbreviations

B	Bass
BV	Backing vocals
D	Drums
G	Guitar
K	Keyboard
O	Organ
P	Piano
Rec.	Date recorded
Sax	Saxophone
V	Vocals

If the song was released as a single, the single's release date and chart performance is noted, along with the album on which it first appeared. If the song was not a single, the album on which it appeared is listed. The first time the album is listed, its release date and chart performance are included. Release and performance information can also be found in the discography.

UK 2/6/70 (5); US 2/20/70 (3) READS AS RELEASED IN THE UNITED KINGDOM ON FEBRUARY 6, 1970, PEAKING AT #5 ON THE UK SINGLES (OR ALBUM) CHART. RELEASED ON FEBRUARY 20, 1970, IN THE UNITED STATES AND PEAKING AT #3 ON THE BILLBOARD HOT 100 SINGLES (OR HOT 200 ALBUM) CHART

Recording location (usually studio), writer (if not the performer), producer, cover versions, film appearances, awards, and other honors are also listed.

Musicians who appear frequently are listed by their last name. Their full names are given below, with their instrument, the number of songs they performed on included in this book, and the Beatles for whom they played, abbreviated as L, M, H, or S. Most frequent collaborators are:

Jenkins, Arthur (percussion) 20 L
Keltner, Jim (d) 38 L, H, S
Laine, Denny (g, b, bv, co-composer) 32 M
Lynne, Jeff (producer, co-composer, v, g, b, k) 19 M, H, S
McCartney, Linda (bv, k, co-composer, producer) 53 M
Ono, Yoko (producer, vocals, co-composer) 36 L
Spector, Phil (producer) 33 L, H
Voormann, Klaus (b) 44 L, H, S

Artists who performed on ten to eighteen songs:

Ascher, Ken (p, k) 13 L
Clapton, Eric (g) 10 L, H, S
Cooper, Ray (percussion) 10 H
Davis, Jesse Ed (g) 13 L, H, S
English, Joe (d) 11 M
Hopkins, Nicky (p) 15 L
Keys, Bobby (sax) 15 L, H, S (including his work with Little Big Horns)
Levin, Tony (b) 12 L
Martin, George (producer, electric p) 10 M, H
McCracken, Hugh (g) approx. 18 L, M
McCulloch, Jimmy (g) 12 M
Newmark, Andy (d) 13 L, H
Preston, Billy (p, o, k, v) 16 L, H, S
Seiwell, Denny (d) 16 M
Slick, Earl (g) 11 L
Small, George (k) 11 L
White, Alan (d) 11 L, H
Wright, Gary (p, o, k, synthesizer) 11 H, S

Artists who performed on four to nine songs:

Badfinger: Pete Ham, Tom Evans, Joey Molland, Mike Gibbins (g, v, tambourine) 6 L, H, S
Barham, John (string arrangements, harmonium, vibraphone) 6 L, H
Casey, Howie (sax) 5 M
Douglas, Jack (producer) 8 L
Drake, Pete (pedal steel g, producer) 4 H, S

Dylan, Bob (v, g, harmonica, composer) 4 H
Edwards, Gordon (b) 4 L
Gilmour, Dave (g) 5 M
Godrich, Nigel (producer) 6 M
Gordon, Jim (d) 7 L, H
Horn, Jim (sax, flute, horns) 7 H, S
Hudson, Mark (producer, g, bv) 5 S
John, Elton (p, k, bv, co-composer) 4 L, H, S
Kahne, David (producer) 7 M
Laboriel, Abe, Jr. (d) 5 M
Linton, Rod (acoustic g) 4 L
Little Big Horns: Bobby Keys, Steve Madaio, Howard Johnson, Ron
    Aprea, Frank Vicari (horns) 5 L
McCullough, Henry (g) 6 M
Mottau, Eddie (acoustic g) 9 L
Paice, Ian (d) 5 M, H
Perry, Richard (producer) 6 S
Price, Jim (trumpet) 4 H
Radle, Carl (b) 5 H
Scott, Tom (sax, flute) 4 M, H, S
Spinozza, David (g) approx. 9 L, M
Stewart, Eric (bv, co-composer, g) 6 M
Weeks, Willie (b) 4 H
Whitlock, Bobby (p) 5 H
Wickens, Paul "Wix" (k) 4 M

Paul and Linda McCartney with sheepdog Martha on the McCartney farm at the Mull of Kintyre, Scotland, 1970. *Getty Images*

1970: Year One

Lennon and McCartney split but mirror each other by releasing their darkest, most stripped-down albums, while Lennon and Harrison share the same musical team.

At the end of 1969, Lennon and Yoko Ono issued a statement that 1970 would be called Year One A.P. (After Peace), "because we believe the last decade was the end of the old machine crumblin' to pieces. And we think we can get it together, with your help." But the Beatles couldn't get it together.

The Beatles may have started out as Lennon's band The Quarry Men, but McCartney got the most fans as "The Pretty One." This lit a competitive fire under Lennon, and for the first half of their recording career he dominated the group with singles and albums written and sung primarily by him.

Then, spurred on by the tremendous success of "Yesterday," McCartney began matching Lennon in output by releasing *Revolver*. As Lennon got weirder with songs like "Strawberry Fields Forever" and "I Am the Walrus," McCartney began writing universal anthems like "Hey Jude" and "Let It Be," and it began to seem like McCartney was the leader of the group. As McCartney became more of a perfectionist in the studio, Lennon began to feel like more of a sideman. Inexhaustible, McCartney drove the band to a backbreaking schedule, with barely a rest between albums. He also nagged them to get back out on the road, though touring was something Lennon and Harrison would avoid for the rest of their lives.

Meanwhile, their Apple Records label was hemorrhaging money due to the idealistic hippie chaos that defined its operation for a year and with many employees stealing. Lennon wanted to bring in manager/accountant Allen Klein to clean it up, since Klein had succeeded in getting the Rolling Stones the best record deal in the business. But Klein also ended up owning the copyrights to all the Stones' songs written before 1971, and McCartney didn't trust him. His wife's father, Lee Eastman, was a successful New York music lawyer, so McCartney pushed for him. But the other Beatles naturally did not want to be managed by McCartney's father-in-law. Why they didn't all choose a third, neutral manager is a tragic mystery. In the end, Lennon, Harrison, and Starr went with Klein, and McCartney went with his in-laws. (By the early '70s, Lennon, Harrison, and Starr would grow disenchanted with Klein themselves and file lawsuits to split with him.)

Increasingly, Lennon turned to Ono as his new collaborator, and the other Beatles resented her presence in the studio. Finally, in the summer of 1969, Lennon snapped and told the Beatles he was leaving. Klein was in the midst of negotiating a better contract for the group that would impact their future royalties, so he convinced Lennon to keep it a secret from the press. Thus the Beatles existed in a strange limbo for almost a year. Devastated, McCartney retreated to his Scottish farm and disappeared so completely the rumor spread that he was dead.

In April 1970, McCartney emerged from isolation with his first solo album, *McCartney*. In the press release accompanying the LP, McCartney stated that he no longer foresaw a time that the Beatles would record together, effectively announcing the end of the group. Lennon was enraged at McCartney "scooping" him on the demise of the Beatles, yet he admired his PR acumen in using it to hype his record release. However, the move backfired on McCartney, as he became known as the one who "broke up the Beatles."

In early 1970, a psychiatrist named Arthur Janov sent Lennon his book *The Primal Scream: The Cure for Neurosis*. Janov wrote how childhood trauma forced people to adopt defense mechanisms that blocked them from experiencing true happiness as adults. Janov's solution was to lead patients back to the memories that most haunted them and encourage the patients to react how they once did as a child before their defense mechanisms deadened their emotions. Often the clients would literally regress to infants sobbing and howling—that is, the primal scream. Janov wrote that once patients were no longer afraid to feel the intensity of their pure emotions, they could hope to attain catharsis and clarity.

Lennon and Ono underwent three weeks of therapy with Janov in England, and then traveled to Los Angeles in April to continue the treatment for four months. When Lennon's visa was revoked, he returned to England. In September, he recorded *John Lennon/Plastic Ono Band*, which chronicled the feelings unleashed by primal therapy. During the sessions, Lennon would sometimes break down crying, but he found the process to be one of the most empowering experiences of his life.

Ironically, Lennon's and McCartney's first solo albums shared many similar traits. They were both extensions of what the band had tried to achieve with the *Get Back/Let It Be* sessions, which had been inspired by Bob Dylan. In 1967 the orchestral grandeur of *Sgt. Pepper* had stunned the public, and most of the rock community slavishly attempted to imitate it. Dylan, however, went in an entirely different direction with *John Wesley Harding*, a rustic, folksy album that featured just him, a bassist, and a drummer. The Beatles realized they had lost connection with the raw power of their roots and made their own stripped-down album with *Let It Be*. Both *Plastic Ono Band* and *Mc-Cartney* continued this approach. *Plastic Ono Band* featured just Lennon, Starr, and Klaus Voormann on bass. McCartney went one better by playing every instrument on his album. Along with the stripped-down sound, both albums share a theme of isolation. But while Lennon was excited to face a new era, a heavy depression pervades *McCartney*. The album's cover features "life's cherries" scattered outside the bowl.

Released just half a year after *Abbey Road*, half of *McCartney*'s tracks are instrumentals since McCartney had not generated enough new songs to fill an album. Thus his album continues to receive mixed reviews, while Lennon's is now recognized as a classic, though it was mercilessly spoofed at the time by *National Lampoon* as "Magical Misery Tour."

In marked contrast to the minimalist Lennon and McCartney solo albums, Harrison stood out with the explosive bombast of his triple album set *All Things Must Pass*, just as he once stood out from the others through his use of Indian music. The Phil Spector–produced Wall of Sound was the perfect backdrop for a musician who had been ignored and was now determined to make as big a splash as possible. (Though Harrison would later regret using so much echo.)

Interestingly, one could almost make the case that a quasi-Beatles Mark II existed in the early '70s, in which Harrison and Lennon both fronted a band that regularly featured Klaus Voormann on bass, Jim Keltner on drums, and Billy Preston on keys, with Spector producing. Starr would use the same band with a different producer, Richard Perry. Other musicians would often fill in, but this was the lineup Harrison pushed for when he asked Lennon to reform a group with Starr and him called The Ladders in 1973.

Both Lennon and Harrison would stop working with Spector by 1973 but continued working with the other musicians throughout the decade, and in Keltner's case, until Harrison's death.

Lennon asked Voormann to play bass on "Cold Turkey" in 1969 after McCartney did not want to do the song, as it was overtly about heroin. In doing so, Lennon reached into the past for a bassist who had been there before the Fabs had made it. Voormann stumbled across the Beatles in 1960 when they were nobodies playing in Hamburg, Germany. After a fight with his girlfriend, Astrid Kirchherr, Voormann headed for the red-light district, where the Beatles were the house band for a strip club. Hooked by the group, Voormann became a regular and eventually brought Kirchherr and their buddy Jürgen Vollmer. In one sense, this wasn't the smartest move. Kirchherr promptly hooked up with the group's bassist, Stu Sutcliffe, who was Lennon's best friend. On the other hand, it intertwined Voormann with the Beatles for life.

Voormann was part of a clique dubbed The Exis, '60s Germany's incarnation of that ever-present subculture, The Pretentious, Depressed Kids Who Wear Black. They took their name from French Existentialists, philosophers like Sartre and Camus who would brood in cafes on Paris' Left Bank while pontificating that since there was no God, it was up to them to create their own reality, a philosophy Lennon would embrace in 1970.

Back then, the Beatles had affected the Gene Vincent–'50s rocker look. They wore leather jackets, leather pants, and greasy duck-assed hair like Elvis Presley. But when Kirchherr became Sutcliffe's lover, she gave him the artsy haircut Jürgen and Voormann sported, with washed bangs combed forward. Gradually, the other Beatles adopted the style—and the rest is history. Whereas their '50s rocker image was a bit of an anachronism even for 1961, soon the band was back in England sporting an exotic new continental look. The Beatles' early press was founded on their "outrageous" hair, which grew longer every year until the hippies took it even farther. Thus Voormann gifted the band with a haircut that garnered them a million headlines and helped undermine the militant conformism of post–World War II Britain and America.

When Sutcliffe left the band to stay in Germany with Kirchherr permanently, Voormann asked to take over on bass. He was informed that McCartney had already claimed the role since the band didn't need three guitarists. Still, Voormann made it to England in 1966, promptly joined the Manfred Mann group, and won a Grammy for his landmark *Revolver* album cover. (He'd later do the *Anthology* cover as well.)

After the Beatles split, Voormann ended up playing bass on all of Lennon's 1970s albums except *Mind Games*, four of Harrison's 1970s records, and four of Starr's. Other appearances included *Transformer* by Lou Reed, Harry Nilsson's *Nilsson Schmilsson*, and Carly Simon's "You're So Vain."

Tulsa-born drummer Jim Keltner was part of the Delaney and Bonnie group that Harrison briefly joined after the dissolution of the Beatles. Keltner ended up playing on five Lennon albums, eight Harrison albums, and five Starr records, as well as both Traveling Wilburys records. He also played on many Dylan records, including "Knockin' on Heaven's Door," and with many others, including Harry Nilsson, Randy Newman, Dolly Parton, Ry Cooder, Steely Dan, Joe Cocker, and Jackson Browne.

Billy Preston first met the Beatles in 1962 as part of Little Richard's band. After Preston sat in with the Beatles for the *Get Back* sessions, Harrison produced his next two albums. Preston would play on one Lennon record, four Harrison albums, and four Starr albums.

Phil Spector was the maestro behind a string of classic girl groups and Righteous Brothers singles in the early 1960s that—in Lennon's words—kept rock alive between the time Elvis went into the army and the year the Beatles arrived. A tiny man with a Napoleon complex, Spector created "little symphonies for the kids" via huge orchestras and innovative recording techniques.

The Beatles always played Spector hits in Hamburg and on the BBC. And the farsighted producer made sure he was on the plane when the Fabs took their first flight to New York for the *Ed Sullivan Show*. Spector's assistant, Sonny Bono, would fashion himself into an ersatz Starr. Bono hooked up with underage Cher (whose previous solo hit was named "I Love Ringo") and formed a successful folk rock duo.

Spector required his bodyguards to carry guns, guarded his castle with Dobermans, and became progressively unhinged with each passing year. In 1969, movie critic Roger Ebert prophesized his murderous streak in his script for Russ Meyer's camp classic *Beyond the Valley of the Dolls*. Ebert modeled the film's Machiavellian producer "Z-Man" after Spector. In the film's gory climax, Z-Man freaks out and starts chopping people's heads off and blowing them away. (It also turns out Z-Man has breasts, so the analogy breaks down at this point.) It is unsettling that the idealistic hymns "Imagine" and "My Sweet Lord" were crafted with the help of a man who would allegedly murder actress/waitress Lana Clarkson in 2003. Both Lennon and Harrison cut their ties with Spector after 1973, as he grew increasingly drunk, belligerent, and trigger-happy.

As Harrison was a guitarist, he didn't need an additional one as frequently, but the axe man who played most frequently with Lennon, Harrison, and Starr was Jesse Ed Davis. The Native American session musician first came into the Beatles' orbit through the Rolling Stones' 1968 *Rock and Roll Circus*. During the Concert for Bangladesh he was brought in to support Eric Clapton, who was transitioning off heroin onto methadone. Davis would become one of Lennon's most hard-partying drinking/drugging/fighting (and sometimes kissing) buddies during his Lost Weekend in LA. Born in 1944, his first break came touring with Conway Twitty in the mid-'60s. He then went on to play with everyone from Taj Mahal, the Monkees, Neil Diamond, John Lee Hooker, David Cassidy, Willie Nelson, Gram Parsons, Gene Clark, Leonard Cohen, and Steve Miller. One of his most famous guitar solos came on Jackson Browne's "Doctor My Eyes." He died from a heroin overdose at forty-three.

Other regulars on Lennon/Harrison/Starr recordings included Delaney and Bonnie's saxophone player Bobby Keys and trumpeter Jim Price, who would become integral components of the Rolling Stones' *Exile on Main Street*–era sound as well.

Many tracks feature the guys from Badfinger adding backing vocals, strumming acoustic guitars, and banging tambourines. Badfinger were the golden boys of the Beatles' Apple label, with both McCartney and Harrison producing some of their hits.

Although primal therapy inspired one of Lennon's greatest albums, he abandoned it at Ono's behest. When Janov pointed out that Lennon felt guilty for neglecting his son Julian, Lennon attempted to visit Julian, but Ono interrupted the reunion by threatening to commit suicide, as she feared Lennon would return to his ex-wife, Cynthia. Janov felt Lennon's relationship with Ono was unhealthy, but Janov was the one Lennon ultimately left.

A few days before the December release of *Plastic Ono Band*, Lennon sat down with the editor of *Rolling Stone*, Jann Wenner, for a nineteen-page interview. The session became legendary for its raw candor. Lennon relished burning his bridges to the Beatles and their extended family. Intent on demolishing the lovable mop-top image forever, he pulled the curtain back on everything censored over the previous decade: the groupies, whores, drugs, and bribery on tour, their gay manager, and the intergroup backbiting that had soured the previous two years. Calling his bandmates "the most big headed uptight people,"[1] Lennon vented that he did not forgive their treatment of Ono. Then, recalling all the incendiary things he said over the last hour or so, he laughed, "This is gonna be some fucking thing. I don't care, this is the end of it."

McCartney felt especially lacerated. Shortly after the magazine hit the stands, he started the court case to dissolve the Beatles' partnership.

INSTANT KARMA!—LENNON

REC. 1/27/70, ABBEY ROAD, LENNON/ONO/SPECTOR (PRODUCERS), LENNON (V, G, ELECTRIC P), HARRISON (G, P), VOORMANN (B, ELECTRIC P), PRESTON (O), WHITE (D, P), ONO (V), MAL EVANS (HANDCLAPS, CHIMES), ALLEN KLEIN (BV), APPROX. 12 UNKNOWN PEOPLE FROM NEARBY PUB (HANDCLAPS, BV), SINGLE: UK 2/6/70 (5); US 2/20/70 (3)

Inspired by the start of a new decade, Lennon came up with the concept "Instant Karma" and decided to embody its spontaneity in the song's execution. He told the press that he "wrote it for breakfast, recorded it for lunch," and was "putting it out for dinner." Actually, the song came out ten days later—still a remarkable turnaround. Lennon was an old hand at fashioning songs to order. When the Beatles were shooting *A Hard Day's Night* and the producer asked for a title song, Lennon banged out the tune that evening.

As would be Lennon's habit for the next two years, he recorded with at least one other Beatle. In this case it was George Harrison, who dug that Lennon was promoting the term "karma," a tenet of Harrison's Hindu religion. When Lennon called him, Harrison was talking with producer Spector about working together on Harrison's first solo album. Harrison suggested they bring Spector in on the "Instant Karma" session, too.

Spector was legendary for his command of huge orchestras, but Lennon did not want strings, preferring typical rock-and-roll instrumentation. Although Lennon had spent 1967 obsessing over the orchestration of "Strawberry Fields Forever" and "I Am the Walrus," he was now in the "back to basics" mind-set. Still, Spector managed to create a colossal effect. He directed multiple people to simultaneously play the same parts on different pianos, added titanic echo, and innovated a groundbreaking "gun shot" drum sound by laying towels on the drums and piling on the reverb.

Nevertheless, the most striking feature of the song is Lennon's voice itself. Even at the height of the mop-top era, Lennon's rasp sliced through all the bullshit with savage fury and desperation on tunes like "Money" and "No Reply." The '60s boasted a great pantheon of jagged-edged screamers, including James Brown, McCartney, Mick Jagger, and both Morrisons (Jim and Van)—but Lennon was second to none.

Now he was divorcing McCartney and the Beatles and was thrilled with the promise of a new identity—but also terrified of losing everything the Beatles' success had given him. Lennon's instincts had led him astray more than once. As a matter of fact, he would be the lowest seller of the solo Fabs throughout the '70s (though today's critics esteem Lennon's work the most). Even Starr had more number one hits!

Lennon faced his fear by diving into the maelstrom and howling at it from the pulpit of the Rock and Roll Church. His sermon excoriated us to overcome our own depressions and get back in the game. He knew pain, having endured the loss of his parents and the death of his best friend, Stu Sutcliffe, and it was this pain that was entwined with his universal appeal. Conquering his sadness through the catharsis of rock, his singing conveyed the rush of euphoric rebirth. The passion in his voice was a healing vaccine that transmitted his exhilaration to millions, making him one of his generation's greatest preachers.

MY SWEET LORD—HARRISON

Rec. May–October 1970, London, Harrison/Spector (producers), Harrison (v, slide g, bv), Starr (d), Clapton (g), Preston (p), Voormann (b), Gordon (d), Wright (electric p), Badfinger (acoustic g), Barham (string arrangement, maybe harmonium), Single: 1/15/71 UK (1); US 11/23/70 (1), Re-release: UK 1/02 (1); 1/02 US (94), Also on *All Things Must Pass*, Grammy nom. for Record of the Year

Both "My Sweet Lord" and Lennon's "Imagine" promote global unity beyond religious borders, but in opposite ways. Lennon encourages the listener to envision no religion, while Harrison encourages listeners to look beyond the surface differences between religions to find the core they all share.

Harrison begins by fervently strumming his guitar while singing about his desire to connect with his Lord. The backing vocalists sing "Hallelujah," as Harrison did when he was raised Catholic as a child. In the second part of the song, Harrison repeats his desire for union with God, but the backing vocalists switch to "Hare Krishna" before breaking into a long Hindu chant. "I wanted to show that Hallelujah and Hare Krishna are quite the same thing," he said. "All religions are branches of one big tree. It doesn't matter what you call Him just as long as you call."[2]

Millions of Christians bought the record in droves during the 1970 Christmas season. Did they miss the Hindu vocals or just ignore them? Or did they accept that Hare Krishnas just want to connect with God like Christians did, despite the cultural/language differences? Perhaps the song helped make some Westerners less alienated from an Eastern culture that began to encroach closer in a global village tied together by the media.

Despite its positive intentions, the song would impact Harrison's life in painful ways (see "This Song" and "Looking for My Life"). That was later, though; in 1971, it was a number one worldwide hit. A stunned and jealous Lennon cracked, "Every time I put the radio on it's 'oh my Lord.' I'm beginning to think there must be a God!"[3]

MAYBE I'M AMAZED—MCCARTNEY

Rec. 11/69–2/70, EMI's Number 2 Studio, McCartney (producer), McCartney (v, g, b, d, p, k), Linda McCartney (bv), Album *McCartney*: UK 4/7/70 (2); US 4/20/70 (1)

McCartney's wife, Linda, was destined to be a muse from an early age. Her father was a wealthy attorney to songwriters and commissioned the popular song "Linda" to be written for her when she was five years old. Ray Noble and Buddy Clark had a number one hit with the song in 1947. Charlie Spivak had a number six hit with it the same year.

Linda left the New York society scene to become a rock photographer. Having been through a divorce, she was wary of marrying McCartney. No doubt her reticence intrigued him. Above all, she was maternal and had a daughter with whom McCartney bonded (as he did with Lennon's son Julian, who inspired "Hey Jude"). Furthermore, Linda enjoyed marijuana as much as he did. Finally, he knocked her up.

McCartney and Lennon married within a week of each other at the same time their own friendship and partnership disintegrated. While Lennon turned to heroin, McCartney succumbed to an alcoholic depression. He later called it a nervous breakdown, saying he would lie in bed shaking.

Linda was the one who pulled him together. In "Maybe I'm Amazed," McCartney equates Linda hanging the wash on the clothesline with her help in drying him out from drinking by encouraging him to record a solo album on his own home equipment.

Most of the resulting *McCartney* album was recorded in his Cavendish Avenue home, but Macca knew "Maybe I'm Amazed" was a potential blockbuster so he returned to Abbey Road's Number Two studio to record it, playing all the instruments himself.

The despair of losing the group that meant everything to him soaks the bluesy guitar. He builds upon the burned-out, distorted sound he and Harrison developed with "She Came in through the Bathroom Window," "You Never Give Me Your Money," and "I've Got a Feeling." For all the talk about how McCartney was the sappy one, his guitar sound at the turn of the decade was earthy. The fact that he played all the instruments separately gives a halting rawness to the production, almost a demo sound with instruments sometimes out of sync. The live version from 1976 is tighter and became a 1977 top ten single. But it comes from a happy place. The 1970 original is an epic slice of blues and redemption from the supposedly lightweight Beatle with the rubber soul. You can hear him thanking God he has Linda to cling to as his identity elsewhere falls apart. Part of the song's initial inspiration came from "Amazing Grace," as he continued to explore "Let It Be" motifs, turning to spirituality in his time of strife.

Strangely, McCartney didn't release "Maybe I'm Amazed" as a single, though it received much airplay. Maybe he sensed the rest of the album wasn't quite up to snuff, and people would only buy the LP to get the standout tune—a trick that became commonplace in the album-oriented '70s and once again in the craven '90s CD era.

One of his solo tunes that can stand indisputably alongside his Beatles classics, McCartney said in 2009 that "Maybe I'm Amazed" was "the song he would like to be remembered for in the future."[4]

BEAUCOUPS OF BLUES—STARR

REC. 6/30/70 AND 7/1/70, NASHVILLE, BUZZ RABIN (WRITER), PETE DRAKE (PRODUCER), SCOTTY MOORE (ENGINEER), THE JORDANAIRES (BV), ALBUM MU-SICIANS INCLUDED CHARLIE DANIELS (G), JERRY REED (G), CHARLIE MCCOY (HARMONICA), D. J. FONTANA (D), SINGLE: US 9/5/70 (87), ALBUM *BEAUCOUPS OF BLUES*: UK 9/25/70 (DID NOT CHART); US 10/5/70 (65)

Judging by Lennon's and McCartney's music, 1970 was one of their darkest years emotionally. It wasn't the happiest time for Starr, either. With the Beatles dead in the water, Starr was at a loss. He wanted the group to get back together but in the meantime occupied himself by releasing two very different solo albums.

The first, *Sentimental Journey*, was a collection of old standards from the previous generation like "Bye Bye Blackbird" and "Night and Day." The album was produced by heavyweights like George Martin, Quincy Jones, and Elmer Bernstein. Starr did the album for his mom. These were the tunes the grown-ups would sing at the pub when Ringo was a little kid on the poor side of Liverpool. The LP was what it was, in the vein of the consciously schmaltzy "Goodnight" on *The White Album*. It wasn't a hit.

Starr's next album, *Beaucoups of Blues*, has a bit more cachet with the critics today.

Starr had always loved country and western music. Back in 1959, he joined an English group called the Raving Texans. He took the stage name Ringo not only because of the rings he wore but also in honor of "Johnny Ringo," a real-life cowboy involved in the Gunfight at the O.K. Corral.

When the Beatles and Rolling Stones barnstormed across America in 1964 and 1965, many parts of the United States only had country radio stations. The exposure deepened the bands' affection for the genre.

Coincidentally, at the end of 1964, *Bonanza* star Lorne Greene released an album called *Welcome to the Ponderosa* with a song about the gunfighter Johnny Ringo on it. Since this period was the height of Beatlemania, the label released it as a single. The song shot to number one by December even though it had nothing to do with Richard Starkey. It must have been a hilarious capper to one of the best years of Starr's life to hear cowboys atmospherically harmonizing "*Ring*-go" to the two-step beat coming out of the radio wherever he went.

Starr went on to cover country artist Buck Owens' "Act Naturally" on *Help!*, cowrote the country-inflected "What Goes On" on *Rubber Soul*, and wrote the country song "Don't Pass Me By" on *The White Album*.

Thus it was natural for Starr to share a rapport with Nashville guitarist Pete Drake during the *All Things Must Pass* sessions. When Starr broached the idea of doing a country album, Drake replied that everyone in Nashville would love to participate. Drake did hundreds of sessions a year and assured Starr they could complete the project in two days. With Starr's commitment, Drake rounded up his musician and composer friends and assembled a batch of songs for Starr to pick from.

Starr arrived in Nashville on June 22 and cut the tracks on June 30 and July 1. To keep Starr in tune, other vocalists sang just out of range of the microphone. For the album's title track, Starr selected a song by Buzz Rabin, a Nashville songwriter whose later credits included "If You'll Hold the Ladder (I'll Climb to the Top)," a tune used in the classic Robert Duvall country film *Tender Mercies*.

The incomparable Jordanaires provided the backing vocals. They backed Elvis for many of his classic songs, starting with "Heartbreak Hotel." They also sang for Ricky Nelson, among many others. Elvis's own guitarist Scotty Moore engineered, and Charlie "The Devil Went Down to Georgia" Daniels played guitar. With so many authentic country contributors, the song wasn't an odd pastiche like "Don't Pass Me By" but a bona fide Nashville production.

The album *Beaucoup of Blues* didn't make the UK charts and only reached number sixty-five in the US. For the next two years, Starr decided to focus on acting.

Today, *Blues* is often rated by critics alongside 1973's *Ringo* as the Ringed One's best solo album. It depends on whether you prefer country or slick '70s pop rock.

MAN WE WAS LONELY—MCCARTNEY

Rec. November 1969–February 1970, Abbey Road, McCartney (producer), McCartney (v, g, b, d, steel g), Linda McCartney (bv), Album *McCartney*

There are some minor gems on McCartney's first solo album aside from the perennial "Maybe I'm Amazed." McCartney took pains to restore the reputation of "Man We Was Lonely" by placing it on his *Wings: Hits and History* overview. He envisioned himself as Johnny Cash when he recorded it, as he envisioned himself as Ray Charles when he recorded "She's a Woman." In 1988, McCartney and Cash would be neighbors in Jamaica. McCartney suggested the pair do "Man We Was Lonely" as a duet on Cash's *Water from the Wells of Home* album, although they ultimately recorded McCartney's "Moon over Jamaica" instead.

Following the break-up, McCartney was the outcast, while Lennon, Harrison, and Starr stayed tight. You can hear the melancholy in the rippling steel guitar opening, which McCartney played on his Telecaster with a drum peg. In typical McCartney fashion, he mocks the depths of his feelings at the end by affecting a weird hillbilly voice—or maybe that's just what Englishmen did with country tunes, as the Stones did on "County Honk" from *Let It Bleed*. But then the sad guitar ripple returns to complete the tune, and the inescapable melancholy settles back in.

This was the last track recorded for the *McCartney* album. He and Linda came up with the chorus in bed, wrote the verse that afternoon, and McCartney laid it down on tape with a bass drum and three guitars the same day—shades of "Instant Karma." It was the first song the couple wrote together, presaging their partnership in Wings.

WHAT IS LIFE—HARRISON

R ᴇᴄ. M ᴀʏ–O ᴄᴛᴏʙᴇʀ 1970, L ᴏɴᴅᴏɴ, H ᴀʀʀɪsᴏɴ/S ᴘᴇᴄᴛᴏʀ (ᴘʀᴏᴅᴜᴄᴇʀs), H ᴀʀ-ʀɪsᴏɴ (ᴠ, ɢ, ʙᴠ), C ʟᴀᴘᴛᴏɴ (ɢ), G ᴏʀᴅᴏɴ (ᴅ), B ᴀᴅғɪɴɢᴇʀ (ᴀᴄᴏᴜsᴛɪᴄ ɢ, ᴛᴀᴍ-ʙᴏᴜʀɪɴᴇ), B ᴀʀʜᴀᴍ (sᴛʀɪɴɢ ᴀʀʀᴀɴɢᴇᴍᴇɴᴛ), B ᴏʙʙʏ W ʜɪᴛʟᴏᴄᴋ (ᴘ), R ᴀᴅʟᴇ (ʙ), P ʀɪᴄᴇ (ᴛʀᴜᴍᴘᴇᴛ), K ᴇʏs (sᴀx), S ɪɴɢʟᴇ: US 2/15/71 (10), A ʟsᴏ ᴏɴ *A ʟʟ T ʜɪɴɢs M ᴜsᴛ P ᴀss*

In the old days, Harrison was the dour one, often singing sullen, minor key songs that contrasted with the others' pop. Now, as his former gang descended into their respective isolations, Harrison became the standard bearer of uplifting Beatle happiness. With the joyous intro of fuzz guitar, the determined clang of a second guitar falling in, the Rolling Stones' horn section, Clapton's band Derek and the Dominoes, Badfinger on acoustic guitars, and Phil Spector's strings, Harrison constructed a slab of AM radio salvation.

The song was originally written for Billy Preston in 1969. As was often the case with Harrison's lyrics, the singer could be singing to his lover, to God, or to his fans. In the early days, Lennon and McCartney spoke directly to the Beatlemaniacs in tunes like "From Me to You" and "Thank You Girl." Now that Harrison was stepping out on his own, maybe he was doing the same thing by asking what his life would be without the listener's love.

While his former bandmates were now his rivals on the charts, Harrison also had a rival in love as well—his best friend playing on the song. Clapton had become obsessed with Harrison's wife, Pattie, in one of the most famous love triangles in rock history, which contributed to the fire lit in Harrison in 1970 and 1971. *All Things Must Pass* was recorded from May to September, and in August Clapton started recording his album full of odes to Pattie, *Layla and Other Assorted Love Songs*. Both records were released in 1970.

COLD TURKEY—LENNON

Rec. 9/28/69, Abbey Road and Trident Studios, Lennon/Ono (producers), Lennon (v, g), Starr (d), Voormann (b), Clapton (g), Single: UK 10/24/69 (14); US 10/20/69 (30)

Both Lennon and Keith Richards were addicted to amphetamines. To come down, they eventually became addicted to heroin in the late '60s. "Rain" and "Fixing a Hole" were both junkie slang. The orchestra rising to a crescendo in "A Day in the Life" could be mirroring the junkie's rush like the Velvet Underground's "Heroin." But it wouldn't be until *The White Album* that Lennon came definitively out of the heroin closet with "Happiness Is a Warm Gun" and "Everybody's Got Something to Hide Except for Me and My Monkey."

The rebel in Lennon resented that the Beatles were viewed as squeaky clean while the Rolling Stones were supposedly hipper and more dangerous, but he went along with their whitewashed image even as late as their authorized biography by Hunter Davies published in 1968. But in the second half of the year, he threw in his lot with Yoko Ono, whose entire reason for existence was to shock the middle class. Lennon became determined to shatter the mop-top straightjacket any way he could, whether by boasting about being a junkie or posing naked with Ono.

Aside from mounting business pressures on the Beatles—and John's preoccupation with Ono—the heroin shadow was the third major culprit in the darker feel that encroached into the Beatles' music in 1968, compared to the whimsy of the Summer of Love. In a sense, it was the final nail in the Beatles' coffin. "Cold Turkey" was slang for trying to kick heroin addiction.

Determined to overcome his addiction, Lennon had himself tied into a chair for three days, wrote about the agonizing experience, and wanted it to be the Beatles' next single. McCartney didn't want to do it.

Perhaps McCartney was afraid of being associated with heroin after Lennon and Harrison had both been busted for weed. Ironically, in the 1970s McCartney would be busted for marijuana possession more frequently than any of the others.

When the other Beatles declined to participate, Lennon began to see the group as too constricting. On September 13, 1969, shortly after wrapping *Abbey Road*, Lennon was invited to perform at the Toronto Rock and Roll Festival. He formed an impromptu band including Eric Clapton, Klaus Voormann, Alan White on drums, and Ono. At the concert he debuted "Cold Turkey." He was so exhilarated by performing without the Beatles that he decided to leave the group.

What if McCartney had agreed to record the song? Would the Beatles have stayed together?

On September 28, two weeks after the concert, Lennon recorded "Cold Turkey" with Clapton, Voormann, and Starr. For the first time, Lennon released a song with only a "Lennon" writing credit as opposed to "Lennon/McCartney." His previous solo single, "Give Peace a Chance," had still been credited to Lennon/McCartney though McCartney had not contributed.

In the song's extended fade-out, Lennon moaned and screamed, acting out the agony of withdrawal, drawing on the avant-garde records he'd already made with Ono that featured the couple howling weird noises at each other. Though few people have been inspired to seek out their joint recordings, the exercises expanded Lennon's technical palette, which would reach final flower with the climax of "Mother." In the long instrumental fade-out of the 1973 song "1985," McCartney bursts into a loving spoof of Lennon's agonized shrieking.

Shortly after the release of "Cold Turkey," Lennon returned the Most Excellent Order of the British Empire medal (more simply known as MBE) the Queen had awarded each Beatle in 1965 for creating an economic boom in music and fashion exports for England by sparking the British Invasion and Swinging London. Lennon's accompanying note to Buckingham Palace read, "I am returning this MBE in protest against Britain's involvement in the Nigeria–Biafra thing, against our support of America in Vietnam, and against 'Cold Turkey' slipping down the charts. With love, John Lennon of Bag." Bag was Lennon and Ono's latest shtick; at a press conference they took questions from reporters while hidden inside a white bag, explaining that it represented "total communication."

For all of Lennon's genius, PR was often his blind spot. Returning an honor from the queen as a political act while complaining about the preordained chart failure of a discordant song about heroin only served to increase the alienation that many in the mainstream audience felt for him. Such bizarre acts also contribute to the fact that we're still talking about him today.

JUNK—MCCARTNEY

REC. NOVEMBER 1969–FEBRUARY 1970, CAVENDISH AVENUE HOME STUDIO AND MORGAN STUDIOS, LONDON, MCCARTNEY (PRODUCER), MCCARTNEY (V, G, B, D, XYLOPHONE, MELLOTRON, PIANO), LINDA MCCARTNEY (BV), ALBUM *MCCARTNEY*

EVERY NIGHT—MCCARTNEY

REC. NOVEMBER 1969–FEBRUARY 1970, ABBEY ROAD, MCCARTNEY (PRODUCER), MCCARTNEY (V, G, B, D), ALBUM *MCCARTNEY*

It must have bemused McCartney to read about the "Paul Is Dead" hoax when that was actually how he felt. It was almost as if his millions of fans picked up on the morbid feelings emanating from his farm.

"Every Night" is the song of a guy who's lost his job, his dream, and his friends (who, incidentally, used to be the biggest pop group in the world). Not wanting to get out of bed, McCartney just wastes his time leaning on lampposts. The first two lines of the tune were written during *The White Album*, just as things started falling apart.

"Junk" was fully formed during *The White Album* but didn't make the cut for any of the Beatles' last three albums. For the first several listens it seems pretty slight, with McCartney's twee tendencies threatening to reach new heights. But the lyrics come to resonate, with the images of bicycles made for two and sleeping bags for two ("memories for you and me") rotting in the junkyard. A sign on a shop window reads, "Buy," but all the junk in the junkyard just makes the singer wonder, "Why bother?" As the singer looks at the detritus of a relationship long dead (ex-girlfriend Jane Asher, perhaps?), the melody's haunting, elegiac air perfectly encapsulates the despair of McCartney's "post-break-up" album.

MOTHER—LENNON

Rec. 9/70–10/70, Abbey Road, Lennon/Ono/Spector (producers), Lennon (v, p), Voormann (b), Starr (d), Single: US 12/28/70 (43), Also on *Plastic Ono Band*

Only six years after bouncy confections like "Eight Days a Week" and "I Feel Fine," "Mother" opens with the sound of church bells tolling to announce a funeral. The bells rang for the death of the Beatles, the death of Lennon's parents, for doom all around. Accompanied only by Starr, Voormann, and the stark finality of his pounding piano chords, Lennon's peerless voice launches into the most un-pop album of his career, *John Lennon/Plastic Ono Band*.

Lennon's mother, Julia, was an eccentric free spirit who "lived in sin" with Lennon's dad, Alf, and then proposed to him when her dad threatened to disown her. Alf, meanwhile, was vehemently opposed to religion as the opium of the masses. So it's not hard to see where Lennon's streak of nonconformity originated.

When Alf was away at sea as a merchant marine, Julia went out clubbing, leaving two-year-old John to wake in the middle of the night alone, screaming in the dark in futility.[5] Julia got pregnant by another man, but gave up the baby for adoption and dumped that father for a bon vivant who beat her.

Alf returned to Liverpool when Lennon was five and tried to get Julia and Lennon to go to New Zealand with him. When Julia refused, Alf told Lennon he must choose between his father and his mother. The confused boy initially chose his dad, then ran sobbing back to his mom, and Alf left town for good. Shortly thereafter, British Social Services decided it was unacceptable that Julia coslept with young John while she was living in sin. Julia gave young John to her sister Mimi to raise and didn't see him again until his teens. She only lived a few blocks way, but Lennon wasn't told.

Mimi was stern but loving, and biographers claim that Lennon sought the same domineering maternal relationship he had with Mimi in Ono. But Lennon was forever bitter that he had chosen his mom over his dad and then his mom had dumped him on his aunt. With such a strange family background in the conformist '40s and '50s, Lennon developed into a vicious wit and fighter, quick to go on the assault before anyone could make fun of him.

When Julia did reconnect with him in his teens, she taught him the rudiments of the guitar and shared his love for Elvis. She also delighted him with her off-kilter sense of humor (as Ono would later do), and the Beatles' early fame would derive in large part from their witty press conferences, a massive departure from monosyllabic predecessors like Presley.

On July 15, 1958, an off-duty policeman without a license was driving drunk and hit Julia, killing her instantly. After her death, Lennon descended into alcoholism, fighting, and shoplifting. A friend recalled finding him passed out drunk on the back of a local bus.

One person who understood what he was going through was Paul McCartney, who had lost his mother to breast cancer a few years earlier. Their early encounter with primal loss made them feel both the sorrow and euphoria of their favorite music more deeply than the average listener, and drove them to communicate it with an intensity few others could match.

Some have speculated that Lennon subconsciously drew upon his strange yearning for a mother who was half there and half not when he wrote all those sad love songs. At the peak of Beatlemania, it would be hard to imagine that a girl could hurt him as much as the ones in "Misery," "There's a Place," "Not a Second Time," "If I Fell," "I'm a Loser," "No Reply," "I'll Cry Instead," "I'll Be Back," "You've Got to Hide Your Love Away," and "Ticket to Ride." Perhaps he was drawing on that earlier well of pain.

Lennon explicitly linked the nonconformist Ono with his mother in *The White Album*'s "Julia," which alternated Lennon's mother's name with "Ocean Child," the translation of Yoko's name. Also, Lennon named his son Julian after his mother.

The flipside of his dreamlike yearning for Julia was Lennon's rage at the fact that she had abandoned him. During "Mother," he castigates his parents for letting him down and declares that he must tell them good-bye. At the climax, he regresses to the little boy forced to choose between both parents, screeching some of the most blood curdling howls ever put to wax. "Mama don't go, Daddy come home," over and over, louder and longer, until it sounds like his throat will rip. For all the talk during the era of punk that the Beatles were soft, who roared more harrowingly than this?

GOD—LENNON

REC. AUTUMN 1970, ABBEY ROAD, LENNON/ONO/SPECTOR (PRODUCERS), LENNON (V), VOORMANN (B), STARR (D), PRESTON (P), ALBUM *PLASTIC ONO BAND*: UK 12/11/70 (8); US 12/11/70 (6)

Lennon was always searching for "help!" to fix his pain, but as often as not, once he found "The Answer," he'd become disillusioned and reject it. After being burned by his parents, he rejected anything he was dependent on so it couldn't hurt him. Like Oedipus, Lennon needed to kill authority.

Lennon also suffered from a short attention span, with fame and money allowing for every whim to be indulged. Both a spoiled prince and journalist seeker, his desire to self-medicate and his intellectual curiosity synergized with the attention-whore's knowledge that he had to constantly reinvent himself to sustain public fascination. Before media maestros like Bowie and Madonna, the Beatles were the original quick-change artists—musically, fashion-wise, and philosophically. In "God," Lennon looked back on all the previous identities he had tried on and wiped his deck clean.

Lennon asked Billy Preston to sit in on piano to give the song a gospel tinge, an irony as the first lines declare that God is a mental construct we've created to deal with our pain.

Then Lennon launches into a litany of all the things that were supposed to save him but in which he no longer believes. Few would care about the disillusionment of a lone narcissistic acid casualty, but his search mirrored that of millions of baby boomers exposed to alternate religions and philosophies thanks to TV and other media.

First, Lennon dismisses the hippie standbys: magic, the I Ching, tarot, Buddha, meditation, Gita, yoga. The last three are all Hindu, remnants of when the group went to the Maharishi's camp in India in the spring of 1968. It was the Beatles' last moment of idyllic unity, the Indian summer of the hippie dream.

Next he topples his two biggest influences, Elvis and Bob Dylan (Zimmerman). Finally, he mournfully sings that the '60s dream is over. The dream was marijuana, sitars, competition with the Beach Boys, backward tapes, baroque strings, apocalyptic orchestras, surreal lyrics inspired by LSD and Lewis Carroll, and album covers exploding with colors in homage to San Francisco bands with unwieldy names. The Dream was ripping off the Merry Prankster's magic bus for *Magical Mystery Tour* and Timothy Leary's proclamation that "the Beatles are mutants. Prototypes of evolutionary agents sent by God, endowed with a mysterious power to create a new human species, a young race of laughing freemen. They are the wisest, holiest, most effective avatars the human race has ever produced. Tune in, turn on, drop out."[6]

The dream was hippies listening to Beatles albums as if the band members were oracles and the songs were prophecies, glass onions like crystal balls peeling off layers of meaning. (Unfortunately, one of those hippies was Charles Manson.) The dream was that you only needed love, community, music, and art to save the world.

One of the most strangely appealing aspects of Lennon was his megalomania. Second only to the hubris of his proclamation that the Beatles were more popular than Jesus was his declaration that the dream was over. Now all Lennon believes in is himself and Ono, and so he tells us that we'll just have to get along without him. Even Tupac and 50 Cent didn't have egos that big.

Lennon was still one step ahead, still moving on before things got stale. He knew the zeitgeist was dying, so he'd be the one to kill it and be reborn into the cold mist of a new decade with just his woman by his side. If the '60s utopia couldn't come to pass, then They Who Were the Sixties should implode as well, as perfectly as James Dean or the Sex Pistols.

ALL THINGS MUST PASS—HARRISON

REC. MAY–OCTOBER 1970, LONDON, HARRISON/SPECTOR (PRODUCERS), HAR-
RISON (V, G), DRAKE (PEDAL STEEL G), CLAPTON (G, BV), WHITLOCK (P, BV),
VOORMANN (B), STARR (D), GORDON (D), BARHAM (STRING ARRANGEMENT),
ALBUM *ALL THINGS MUST PASS*: UK 11/27/70 (1); US 11/27/70 (1), SIX TIMES
PLATINUM, ALT VERSION: *BEATLES ANTHOLOGY*, GRAMMY NOMINATION FOR
ALBUM OF THE YEAR

Harrison's euphoria at his freedom from the Beatles was palpable in each cut of *All Things Must Pass*, the most sprawling high-profile release until Guns N' Roses' *Use Your Illusion* quadruple album twenty years later. Determined to prove himself artistically and commercially, the quiet Beatle delivered no less than three discs of much-needed light to counter his former bandmates' dark-ness, under the tutelage of pop maestro Phil Spector.

Harrison brought in Delaney and Bonnie's backing group, and a dozen other musicians drifted in and out of the sessions. Determined not to be like McCartney, and not to dictate how his friends should play, Harrison allowed the musicians to contribute what they wanted. They would all remember the happy atmosphere of *All Things Must Pass*.

Harrison referred to the set as recovering from an "an eight-year dose of constipation," an appropriate description for the first triple album. Many of the songs had been composed over the previous four years but rejected by Len-non and McCartney for inclusion on Beatles albums. In 1966, Harrison got three songs on *Revolver* (his peak in per-album composition count), but "Art of Dying" and "Isn't It a Pity" were rejected. It was at this time that Harrison started stockpiling tunes, though many of his most accessible seem to have been composed after Harrison had his "Something"/"Here Comes the Sun" commercial breakthrough: "My Sweet Lord," "What Is Life," "Awaiting on You All," and "Ballad of Sir Frankie Crisp."

As George Martin said about *The White Album*, it would have been advis-able for Harrison to carve the collection down to one stupendous LP and dole out the best of the rest over the next year or two. As it was, his next studio release wouldn't come until 1973. With the third album composed of long studio jams, Harrison did seem to be pushing the limits of what a Beatle could get away with. Yet despite a hefty price tag, the album sat at number one for seven weeks in the United States and eight in the United Kingdom.

It would take Harrison eighteen years to come close to revisiting that level of success. In 1970 and 1971, however, it seemed that the younger brother had left his older siblings in the dust.

Harrison rehearsed the album's title track as early as the Beatles' *Get Back* sessions. The song falls in with Harrison's recurrent theme of looking to nature to remind oneself that suffering is transitory. Hold on through the dark times because winter or the night or the rain will soon pass (as in "Here Comes the Sun" and "Blow Away"). It's unclear whether Harrison was already yearning for the passing of the Beatles when he composed the song. Still, it must have bemused Harrison how perfectly it fit in the wake of the break-up. "All Things Must Pass" resonated in other ways, as well; while recording the album, Harrison's mother died from cancer.

GIVE PEACE A CHANCE—LENNON

Rec. 6/1/69, La Hotel Reine Elizabeth, Room 1742, Montreal, Lennon/McCartney (writers), Lennon/Ono (producers), Lennon (v, g), Ono (v), Tommy Smothers (g), Backing vocals: Allen Ginsberg, Dr. Timothy Leary, Petula Clark, Rosemary Woodruff, Derek Taylor, Murray the K, Dick Gregory, Abraham Feinberg, the Canadian chapter of the Radha Krishna Temple (hand drums, finger cymbals), unknown others, Single: UK 7/4/69 (2); US 7/21/69 (14), Re-entry: UK 1/24/81 (33), US 1/19/88 (91) as B-side to Jealous Guy, UK 12/13/99 (3) as B-side to Imagine

Across the United States, kids were furious about being drafted to defend a corrupt South Vietnamese government that exploited its own people. A vocal minority was garnering headlines by advocating the overthrow of the current political system. Lennon penned "Revolution," hoping to have it both ways. On the one hand, he wanted to scare the straights with the song's title and distorted guitar. Within the lyrics, however, he voted against revolution if it involved hate and destruction.

Ono, meanwhile, as the queen of happenings and performance art, was brimming with ideas. Together they decided that they should use Lennon's power to sell the concept of peace like Madison Avenue sells soap. For their honeymoon, the pair staged their first "Bed In." They reclined in bed, taped signs reading "Peace" on the windows, invited the press, and got the word "Peace" splashed all over the front pages. The media argued whether they were really doing anything or indulging themselves on a ridiculous scale, which only gave both them and the concept of peace more attention.

For the second Bed In staged in Montreal, Lennon decided to crystallize it with a new anthem. "In me secret heart I wanted to write something that would take over 'We Shall Overcome.' I don't know why. It was the one they always sang, and I thought, 'Why doesn't somebody write something for the people now, that's what my job and our job is.'"[7]

"Give Peace a Chance" was recorded live in the hotel room with a pretty amazing cast of characters: Lennon, Ono, Allen Ginsberg, Timothy Leary, Petula Clark, comedian Dick Gregory, DJ Murray the K, cartoonist Al Capp, Beatle publicist Derek Taylor, and Tommy Smothers, the latter joining Lennon on guitar. Lennon can be heard exclaiming, "Come together!" which started out as Timothy Leary's political campaign slogan and which Lennon would record as the opening track on *Abbey Road* the same month "Give Peace a Chance" was released.

While Lennon's attention span for movements (meditation, radicalism) was notoriously short, his impatience with long-winded claptrap melded with his genius in boiling things down to one-sentence slogans. Twenty years before the term "sound bite" was coined, and forty years before Twitter, he said whatever propaganda he wanted in a couple words: "Give Peace a Chance," "Power to the People," "Imagine." Soon the masses were singing his song on the Moratorium Day march in Washington, DC.

WORKING CLASS HERO—LENNON

REC. AUTUMN 1970, ABBEY ROAD, LENNON/ONO/SPECTOR (PRODUCERS), LENNON (V, G), ALBUM *PLASTIC ONO BAND*: UK 12/11/70 (8); US 12/11/70 (6), ALSO B-SIDE TO UK *IMAGINE* SINGLE 10/24/75

In Britain during the late 1950s, the "Angry Young Men" were working class writers with a rebellious spirit that infused a golden era of black and white British social realist films, dubbed "Kitchen Sink" cinema. The movies were the filmic equivalent of that echo-drenched harmonica sound heard on the Beatles' first albums. It was the sound of rainy British port towns, dance hall nights, and mornings after when the brooding Brando type realizes he knocked up the girl he never planned to marry (as Lennon, indeed, did).

Whereas earlier British movies fixated on the upper crust in drawing rooms, the late '50s and early '60s saw a rejection of class barriers and celebrated the salt of the earth. The "Angry Young Man/Kitchen Sink" movement helped pave the way for the Liverpudlian band.

Before the Beatles, Britain tried to manufacture its own versions of Elvis, but as critic Nik Cohn pointed out, it didn't work because, at that early stage, the '50s Brit rockers were like adults trying to learn a new language—in the same way that Vanilla Ice didn't cut it, but ten years later Eminem did. Cliff Richard tried too hard while the Beatles assimilated rock and roll in their early teens. They lived it for years, and then translated it to British terms instead of trying to ape Americanisms. In being specific to themselves, they ironically underscored a commonality between all countries: raw passion and the desire for transcendence.

At the turn of the '60s, the UK entertainment industry was exclusively centered in London. The Beatles were outsiders from the northern factory town of Liverpool, with scouse accents that sounded to the big city folk like thick New Jersey or Southern accents do to the rest of Americans. But the Beatles arrived in London at the moment when "working class" was hot. Pretentious was out, being real was in, and the Beatles' regionalism solidified their authenticity. McCartney would occasionally try to dilute his accent, but Lennon would shame him when he tried to put on airs. In truth, Lennon was the most middle class (if not affluent) of the group, growing up next to a golf club. Regardless, he loved to play the angry young man who took no shit.

The fact that Lennon actually was angry (deadbeat dad, dead mom with loose morals, dead friend, etc.) only heightened the Beatles' appeal. On the one hand, you had pretty McCartney smiling and deferring to the elders, assuring everyone that things were happy and normal—and that was essential because Lennon would never have made it alone with his borderline looks and self-destructive inclinations. At the same time, you had Lennon sulking as the true embodiment of Brando's Wild One, much more of a violent rogue than Elvis ever was.

When word of the group spread to the United States, the band's first in-depth profile on CBS focused on how sociologists were proclaiming them the authentic voice of the proletariat. But gradually the group's phenomenal success carried Lennon so far from his working class roots that by 1967 he was singing about being one of the beautiful people who only needed love.

Then, at the end of his decade, his affair with Yoko Ono brought down the scorn of the media and the persecution of the police, resulting in her miscarriage (see "Isolation"). Soon Lennon's songs began advocating the revolution he was once ambivalent about.

"Working Class Hero" offers no blueprint for how to change society, it only insists that it must be changed because it scares the individuality out of you when you're young and compels you to spend your life in the rat race backstabbing your fellow man, doped with religion, sex, and TV.

Accompanied only by his acoustic guitar and unmelodic, simple chords, Lennon uses a low, conversational voice. As it is such a contrast to his typical singing or screaming, the intimate tone achieves maximum effect. He sounds like exiled Vladimir Lenin conspiring with fellow comrades in the early days before the Revolution.

"Working Class Hero" was banned from many radio stations because Lennon tells us that we're still "fucking" peasants even though we think we've made middle class progress. US Representative Harley Orrin Staggers tried to have radio station manager Ken Sleeman thrown in jail for playing the song. But Sleeman defended himself by stating, "The People of Washington [DC] are sophisticated enough to accept the occasional four-letter word in context, and not become sexually aroused, offended, or upset."[8] The prosecution dropped the charges.

NOTES

1. Jann S. Wenner, "January 1971 *Rolling Stone* Interview with John Lennon and Yoko Ono," JannSWenner.com, www.jannswenner.com/Archives/John_Lennon_ Part1.aspx (October 10, 2011).

2. Subhamoy Das, "George Harrison and Hinduism—His Idea of God and Reincarnation," About.com, http://hinduism.about.com/od/artculture/a/harrison.htm (October 10, 2011).

3. Wenner, "January 1971 *Rolling Stone* Interview."

4. "The Song Paul McCartney Would Like to Be Remembered For," *Época Magazine* 2009, http://en.wikipedia.org/wiki/Maybe_I%27m_Amazed (October 10, 2011).

5. Albert Goldman, *The Lives of John Lennon* (London: Bantam, 1988), 24.

6. Phillip Norman, *Shout! The Beatles in Their Generation* (London: Elm Tree, 1981), 293.

7. Wenner, "January 1971 *Rolling Stone* Interview."

8. Guy Raz, "Radio Free Georgetown," WashingtonCityPaper.com 1999, www .washingtoncitypaper.com/articles/16638/radio-free-georgetown (October 10, 2011).

George Harrison, Ringo Starr, and guitarist Jesse Ed Davis perform at the Concert for Bangladesh at Madison Square Garden on August 1, 1971. *Getty Images*

• 2 •

1971: It Don't Come Easy

Harrison synthesizes his musical and spiritual interests to create his greatest album and invent the rock charity concert.

Nineteen seventy-one was one of the solo Beatles' richest years musically. Lennon unveiled his most definitive album (*Imagine*). McCartney produced one of his most ambitious and eclectic efforts (*Ram*). Starr came up with his signature single, with a little help from Harrison. And Harrison stole the show with the Concert for Bangladesh. It was the climax of his long climb out from under the shadow of his former bandmates.

One of the moments that crystallized the joie de vivre of the early Beatles was the opening scene of *A Hard Day's Night*. With that *claaaanng* of Harrison's twelve-string Rickenbacker guitar, the movie opens on Lennon, Harrison, and Starr running toward the camera, chased by a mob of fans. Suddenly Harrison trips and falls flat on his face. Starr topples over him while Lennon turns back and cracks up but keeps running. Harrison and Starr pick themselves up and start running again, laughing as well. You couldn't have faked a better opening. It shows how much the Beatles' phenomenon owed to luck and lightning in a bottle, and it also shows a bit of band psychology. McCartney isn't there—he's off on his own in the next vignette—and Harrison and Starr are Lennon's sidekicks, with Harrison as the little brother running and tripping behind.

Lennon was born October 9, 1940, and was two school years ahead of McCartney, born June 18, 1942. Though a grade ahead, McCartney was only eight months older than Harrison, born February 25, 1943. Still, he would forever refer to Harrison as his baby brother, which seems to have gotten Harrison's goat to no end.

McCartney knew Harrison at school and brought him into Lennon's group. Soon Harrison was always following Lennon around like his little disciple, exasperating Lennon's then-girlfriend Cynthia. Still, in the early days Harrison was more of an equal when they would play six to eight hour sets in Hamburg. It necessitated him taking a greater share of the vocal duties, as the BBC radio tapes confirm. But when Lennon and McCartney started cowriting, Harrison wasn't included.

So he started writing a song or two an album by himself. He penned minor key tunes to take the opposite track from Lennon and McCartney's happy pop confections, and affected a gruff downer persona, off-handedly arrogant and ambivalent. He wrote a couple of classics ("Don't Bother Me," "If I Needed Someone," "Taxman," "Long Long Long"), but was more influential as a key component of the Beatles' sound. The Byrds' Jim (Roger) McGuinn used Harrison's twelve-string Rickenbacker sound to invent folk rock, which freed Dylan to leave the folk ghetto. McGuinn copped the shimmering, chiming outro of "A Hard Day's Night" for the Byrds' "Bells of Rhymney," which Harrison in turn copped back for "If I Needed Someone" and "Nowhere Man."

Harrison then opened Western minds to world music after being enthralled by the Indian sitar during the filming of the Beatles' second film, *Help!* The film egregiously featured white actors portraying Hindus as human-sacrificing buffoons, but it inspired Harrison to incorporate Indian instruments into the Beatles' music. In translating the sitar's sound into the electric guitar, he also helped birth psychedelic rock.

He was trained by Ravi Shankar, in whose tradition music was seen as a way to commune with God. An ironic place for a young man to end up, considering his journey began in the red-light district of Hamburg (Germany's version of Vegas) when he was seventeen. Perhaps Harrison sought spiritual stability more than the others because he was the youngest and had to grow up the fastest, jaded by a life of decadence and splendor few would ever know at the age of twenty.

Harrison's example encouraged millions of baby boomers to look into alternate philosophies and lifestyles in reaction to the massive conformism of the 1950s. Of course, it also led to Hare Krishnas at the airport, which Harrison conceded made for a great joke in the spoof *Airplane!* Arguably he did more than any other public figure to make Western youth aware of Eastern religions and world music.

In the mid-'60s, Harrison focused mainly on the sitar and took time out from the guitar while Clapton and Hendrix and others competed to be the most technically impressive. He had been the bridge between the '50s rock guitarists like Carl Perkins and Elvis' Scotty Moore and the '60s guitar virtuosos, but he didn't relate to the new generation's showboating. Then, in late 1968, he visited Dylan and the Band during the latter's recording of *Music for Big Pink* (with tunes such as "The Weight"). There Harrison found kindred spirits ushering in a new, more restrained era where the musicians once again served the song itself, as opposed to using it as a backdrop for instrumental pyrotechnics.

Dylan and the Band respected Harrison as an equal, so when Harrison returned to London for the January 1969 *Get Back* sessions, he could no longer endure the condescending treatment he received from Lennon and McCartney (see "Wah Wah"). He briefly quit, then recalled how much better the guys had behaved when Clapton came into the studio to play on "While My Guitar Gently Weeps" the year before. He hit upon the idea of bringing his friend Billy Preston to flesh out the group's sound, since the climax of the *Get Back* sessions was going to be a concert on the roof of Apple Records. With Preston in tow, Harrison returned to the group.

Later that year he would produce an album for Preston and also one for Doris Troy (whose hits included "Just One Look"), both soul albums with heavy gospel influence. Working with the Edwin Hawkins Singers gospel choir (whose songs included the classic hit "Oh Happy Day"), he found the black American equivalent of the spirituality he felt in Indian music.[1] During this time, Preston recorded Harrison's song "My Sweet Lord," but it went unnoticed.

Harrison then learned how black music could be translated by Southern whites when he joined up with the husband-and-wife team Delaney and Bonnie Bramlett, who mixed soul, gospel, rock, blues, and country in a traveling revue called Delaney and Bonnie and Friends. The friends included no less than Eric Clapton, Duane Allman, Leon Russell, Rita Coolidge, Dave Mason, King Curtis, and the guy who would go on to drum with the solo Beatles more than anybody, Jim Keltner. The revue was also how other future regulars Bobby Keys, Jim Price, and Jim Gordon would come into the solo Beatles' orbits. When Harrison saw Delaney and Bonnie in concert on December 1, 1969, he yearned for the group's carefree camaraderie and asked if he could join.

On the tour, Harrison asked Delaney how to write gospel songs, and Delaney mentored Harrison on the slide guitar. Harrison would unveil his new bottleneck technique on an early take of "If Not for You" on Dylan's album *New Morning* (1971). Dylan ultimately did not use that take, but Harrison would do his own version on *All Things Must Pass* (and could be heard on Dylan's "Day of the Locust").

Harrison's new guitar style, coming as it did at the dawn of his new era as solo artist, was like a superhero giving himself a new costume. He incorporated techniques learned from his apprenticeship in Indian instruments and fused them with slide guitar techniques developed under Delaney's tutelage, emerging with one of the most distinctive sounds of the early '70s, heard on his own songs, Lennon's, Starr's, and Badfinger's. It was similar to the way Keith Richards crystallized his own unique sound in the late '60s with the secret recipe of open tunings and no sixth guitar string.[2]

Along the way Harrison had transformed his songwriting. When he had stalked out of the *Get Back* sessions, his songs were not the kind to burn up the hit parade ("For You Blue," "Old Brown Shoe," and "I, Me, Mine"). If he was going to tell McCartney and Ono to shove it, he was going to have to write his own hits to keep his forty-acre estate. Amazingly, he knocked two out of the park. For the first time, he penned the highlights of the latest Beatles album, just in time for their final LP: "Here Comes the Sun" and "Something." The latter became Harrison's first number one hit and Sinatra proclaimed it the greatest love song of the twentieth century.

Harrison worked on his voice, too. Whereas he'd sung with the surliest, thickest Liverpool accent of the bunch, now he lightened it up a notch, as he did with his melodies, fashioning them more warm and upbeat. Having been the "invisible voice" in the harmonies for ten years, he drew on what he'd learned from the others.

By the time he began the *All Things Must Pass* album, Harrison had a remarkable recipe: Indian music, gospel and soul, slide guitar, more accessible vocals, and hit songwriting—all set against Phil Spector's Wall of Sound. Lastly, the timing for his religious theme was impeccable.

The end of the '60s saw a huge spiritual revival as people looked for answers in the midst of massive social upheaval (civil rights movement, antiwar movement, feminist movement, gay rights movement, sexual revolution, drug revolution, etc.). While many explored Eastern religions, Christianity also saw a resurgence, Lennon's comment that it would "shrink and vanish" notwithstanding. "Jesus freaks" bridged the gap between hippies and Christians, and the airwaves swelled with biblical imagery. Songs with gospel themes included the Byrds' "Jesus Is Just All Right," the Youngbloods' "Get Together," Norman Greenbaum's "Spirit in the Sky," Simon and Garfunkel's "Bridge over Troubled Water," and Ocean's "Put Your Hand in the Hand." Harrison rode the wave higher than any of them with "My Sweet Lord," the best-selling record of 1971. After its release, two smash hit musicals in a similar vein would open in New York, *Jesus Christ Superstar* and *Godspell*.

Soon he had the opportunity to turn words into action. As recounted in Harrison's single "Bangladesh," Ravi Shankar came to him asking for help in raising emergency funds to aid the people of his homeland. Bangladesh, in the eastern section of Pakistan, was trying to secede and Pakistan's dictatorship was fighting to hold on through a genocidal civil war. Thousands of refugees fled to India, where they were hit by a cyclone, torrential rains, and flooding. Disease and starvation followed on a massive scale. Harrison released "Bangladesh" as the first charity single by a major recording artist, and then organized two benefit concerts held at Madison Square Garden on August 1, 1971. Starr, Dylan, Clapton, Preston, Badfinger, and Leon Russell were guests at what became the event of the season. The concerts raised $243,418 for UNICEF, the concert film raised an additional $10 million, and sales for the album and DVD continue to benefit UNICEF. After its delayed release, the live album won the Grammy for 1973 Album of the Year. *The Concert for Bangladesh* was the forerunner of Band-Aid's "Do They Know It's Christmas" single, Live Aid's "We Are the World," and all activist rock events to follow.

While Harrison emerged as the best-selling Beatle who created a new model for rock to fulfill its Woodstock-era idealism, Lennon and McCartney squabbled bitterly in open letters to each other via the music press.

McCartney had wanted the group to endure more than anyone, but neither Lennon nor Harrison wanted to work with him. Yet at the same time, they did not want to end the Beatles' company, Apple, because then they would each get taxed individually at a much higher rate. They wanted McCartney to stay stuck in Apple with them even though they didn't like him, release his albums by their schedule, and deal with their manager, Allen Klein, whom McCartney thought was probably crooked. McCartney never truly let loose in the press at Lennon because, as he admitted, he knew Lennon would verbally destroy him. Instead, he began a not-so-subtle assault through his music.

IMAGINE—LENNON

REC. 1971, ASCOT SOUND STUDIOS, RECORD PLANT EAST, NYC, LENNON/ONO/SPECTOR (PRODUCERS), LENNON (V, P), VOORMANN (B), WHITE (D), THE FLUX FIDDLERS (STRINGS), SINGLE RELEASE: US 10/11/71 (3), UK 10/24/75 (6) (B-SIDE TO WORKING CLASS HERO), UK 12/27/80 (1) (4 WEEKS AT NO. 1), UK 12/10/88 (45) (B-SIDE TO JEALOUS GUY, HAPPY XMAS), UK 12/25/99 (3) (B-SIDE TO HAPPY XMAS, GIVE PEACE A CHANCE), UK 12/12/03 (33) (B-SIDE TO HAPPY XMAS), HONORS: NAMED ONE OF TOP 100 MOST PERFORMED SONGS OF THE 20TH CENTURY BY BMI, NO. 23 ON YEAR 2000 LIST OF BEST-SELLING

UK SINGLES, NO. 3 GREATEST SONG OF ALL TIME PER *ROLLING STONE* AFTER "SATISFACTION" AND "LIKE A ROLLING STONE," VOTED GREATEST SONG OF THE PAST 100 YEARS IN 2005 BY CANADIAN BROADCASTING SYSTEM LISTENERS, NO. 30 SONG OF THE CENTURY WITH MOST HISTORICAL SIGNIFICANCE PER THE RECORDING INDUSTRY OF AMERICA, FILM APPEARANCES: *THE KILLING FIELDS* (1986)

"Imagine" was inspired by Ono's 1963 book *Grapefruit,* which often instructed the reader to imagine things like goldfish swimming across the sky or a thousand suns in Zen-like quasi-haikus. Lennon's work was always succinct, except for his Lewis Carroll/Dylan phase of "I Am the Walrus" and "Lucy in the Sky with Diamonds," but Ono's poetry pushed him even further toward simplicity.

The song was also inspired by a prayer book Dick Gregory gave him in the vein of the self-help phenomenon *The Secret.* Lennon described it as "the concept of positive prayer. If you want to get a car, get the car keys. Get it? 'Imagine' is saying that. If you can imagine a world at peace, with no denominations of religion—not without religion but without this 'my-God-is-bigger-than-your-God thing'—then it can be true."[3]

For his vision to have the most impact, Lennon realized he had to present it in a way most palatable to the masses. The ultra-mellow "Love" had been the most popular track on *Plastic Ono Band* even though it was not originally released as a single. The song was a stripped down variation on *Abbey Road*'s bucolic "Because," and Lennon again used this soothing template. To further sell it to the mainstream, he let Spector put his easy listening strings on it.

"Revolution" had criticized the radicals for not having a plan, but he himself offered none in "Working Class Hero." Finally, in "Imagine" he spelled out the Lennon doctrine of how to achieve world peace: No heaven, no hell, no religion, no countries to kill/die for, no possessions, no greed, and no hunger—just sharing.

Basically, Lennon was advocating socialism, communism, or, as the conspiracy theorists call it, One World Government—ideologies entwined with existential atheism. But while Lennon had an aversion to organized religion, he was not an atheist. In 1969, he told David Wigg, "God is a power, which we're all capable of tapping. We're all light bulbs capable of tapping energy. You can use electricity to kill people or light the room. God is that. Neither one nor the other, but everything."[4]

England was a socialist nation in which the King had broken from the Church. Therefore, Lennon's critique didn't seem as radical at home as it did in the United States, where big religion, big business, and big military were more pervasive.

The well-known irony of the tune is the fact that he sang of "no possessions" in his white mansion while playing his white grand piano. In later interviews, he admitted that he wanted to be rich, and he also wanted people to be looked after by a socialist system, and shrugged off any contradictions. But Mark David Chapman was enraged by his "phoniness" and "blasphemies" and shot Lennon in the back four times on December 9, 1980 (see "Watching the Wheels").

Back in 1966 Lennon had claimed, "Christianity will shrink and vanish," and the KKK threatened to kill him. Lennon could've simply shut up about organized religion, but he truly did seem to have a vendetta against it, and ended up a martyr for freedom of speech. He was on the vanguard of a generation that pushed back boundaries in a country often inclined toward witch hunts and fundamentalism. His bravery created the airspace for others to more freely say what they felt.

"Imagine" is perhaps the prime example of how the Beatles, like Dylan, were not just musical phenomena. They were descendents of the great romantic poets like Shelley, who once wrote, "Poets are the unacknowledged legislators of the world."

Jimmy Carter was quoted as observing that, in the 125 countries he and his wife had visited, "Imagine" was played almost as often as the national anthem. One YouTube video from 2003 shows Bill Clinton attending the eightieth birthday party for Israel's Prime Minister Shimon Peres. Teenage Israeli pop star Liel beckons Clinton onstage with eighty Israeli and Arab children to sing "Imagine." Clinton sings the lines about being a dreamer who wants everyone to live as one, though he smiles awkwardly during the "no religion/no countries" parts.

One can dismiss Lennon as an armchair dreamer, but then so was novelist Leo Tolstoy (*War and Peace* and *Anna Karenina*) when he articulated his philosophy of passive resistance in *The Kingdom of God Is Within You*. A young Indian activist named Mohandas Gandhi read the treatise and began a correspondence with Tolstoy that lasted for over a year until Tolstoy's death in 1910, in which the two discussed the real-world applications of nonviolence. Over the next thirty years, Gandhi would lead the Indians in taking back their nation from British imperialists and achieving national independence in 1948. Gandhi provided the model for another civil rights activist, Martin Luther King, to break the stranglehold of segregation in the United States.

IT DON'T COME EASY—STARR

REC. 2/18/70, 3/8/70, AND 10/70, ABBEY ROAD'S STUDIO 2, POSSIBLY TRIDENT STUDIOS, STARKEY/HARRISON (WRITERS), HARRISON/MARTIN (PRODUC-

ERS), STARR (V, D), HARRISON (G), VOORMANN (B), STEPHEN STILLS (P), RON
CATTERMOLE (SAX, TRUMPET), BADFINGER'S HAM AND EVANS (BV), MAL EVANS
(TAMBOURINE), SINGLE: UK 4/9/71 (4); US 4/16/71 (4)

Harrison had a habit of offering his best tunes to his friends. He originally gave
"My Sweet Lord" to Billy Preston. He gave a song called "You Gotta Pay
Your Dues" to Badfinger, although they turned it down.

So Starr took a crack at "You Gotta Pay Your Dues" during his *Sentimental Journey* sessions. George Martin produced and Stephen Stills was on
the piano, but after thirty takes on February 18 and 19, 1970, it still wasn't
coming easy.

So Harrison sang a demo himself with Badfinger on backing vocals, in-
structing them to chant "Hare Krishna!" during the instrumental. In the final
version of the song you can still hear it, low in the mix.

Starr tackled the song again on March 8, this time with Harrison producing. It sat in the can until October, at which point Harrison added sax and
trumpet like he had once added horns to *The White Album*'s "Savoy Truffle."

In mid-April 1971, Harrison's haunting guitar intro finally drifted across
the airwaves. Its arresting sound came courtesy of the Leslie speaker cabinet.
The cabinet was originally built for the Hammond organ but had been adapted
for guitar and vocals. It housed a rotating bass speaker and a pair of horn speak-
ers that spun around in different directions, making the guitar sound as if it
was swirling under the ocean. Lennon ran his vocals through the Leslie for
1966's "Tomorrow Never Knows," and Harrison had used it in 1969 when
he wrote "Badge" with Clapton for Cream; in fact, the "Badge" instrumental
break sounds pretty close to "It Don't Come Easy." Harrison was always a
master at recycling—or should we say, developing further. Thus the outro of
"A Hard Day's Night" became the intro to "Ticket to Ride."

The Leslie effect became one of the most distinctive sounds of the late
'60s and early '70s, gracing songs including Harrison's "Something," Badfinger's "No Matter What," the Grateful Dead's "Casey Jones," Three Dog
Night's "Mama Told Me Not to Come," The Hollies' "Air That I Breathe,"
the Eagles' "Hotel California," and Boston's "More Than a Feeling."

Badfinger's soaring backing vocals, Stills's pounding piano, Starr's perfect
drum fills, and the horns build an epic momentum behind Starr's exhortation
to stay resilient in the face of hardship. The lines about paying dues to pay the
blues probably wouldn't have worked with Harrison singing; the guy came
from a stable family and was a superstar before he was twenty. But Starr was
born into an inner-city house without a toilet, fell into a coma from appendicitis at age six, then was confined to a sanatorium for two years at age thirteen
due to tuberculosis, before dropping out of school altogether.

In Beatles tradition, the lyrics challenged the listener to be peaceful. It was a sentiment that could apply on any scale, though it might have been aimed at McCartney, who was taking the others to court at the time. Yet with a reunion increasingly unlikely, the song actualized Harrison's and Starr's determination to carve out a career for themselves independent of the Lennon and McCartney gravy train.

Starr preaches with such confidence that you wouldn't know he was filled with doubt about the direction of his life. Perhaps his determination to transcend his fears is what fills the performance with its enduring power. Forty years later, Starr still opens every show with it. The song shot up the charts, passing Lennon's "Power to the People," Harrison's "What Is Life" (both reached number eleven), and McCartney's "Another Day" (number five), all the way up to number four, settling just beneath the Rolling Stones' "Brown Sugar" at number one. It was the first of three top ten hits Harrison cowrote or produced for Starr. The success stunned those who had assumed Starr couldn't cut it on his own.

WAH-WAH—HARRISON

REC. 8/1/71, MADISON SQUARE GARDEN, HARRISON/SPECTOR (PRODUCERS), HARRISON (V, G), STARR (D), CLAPTON (G), PRESTON (K, V), VOORMANN (B), KELTNER (D), LEON RUSSELL (B, K), DAVIS (RHYTHM G), BADFINGER (G, TAMBOURINE, BV), DON PRESTON (G, BV), RADLE (B), THE HOLLYWOOD HORNS: HORN, ALLAN BEUTLER, CHUCK FINDLEY, JACKIE KELSO, LOU McCREARY, OLLIE MITCHELL, BACKING VOCALISTS: DON NIX, JO GREEN, JEANIE GREENE, MARLIN GREENE, DOLORES HALL, CLAUDIA LINNEAR, ALBUM *THE CONCERT FOR BANGLADESH*: UK 1/10/72(1); US 12/20/71 (2), GRAMMY WIN FOR 1973 ALBUM OF THE YEAR

In *The Beatles Anthology*, Harrison recalled, "There used to be a situation where we'd go in (as we did when we were kids), pick up our guitars, all learn the tune and chords and start talking about arrangements. But there came a time . . . when Paul had fixed an idea in his brain as to how to record one of his songs. . . . It was taken to the most ridiculous situations, where I'd open my guitar case and go to get my guitar out and he'd say, 'No, no, we're not doing that yet.' . . . It got so there was very little to do, other than sit around and hear him going, 'Fixing a hole . . . ' with Ringo keeping the time."[5]

Lennon would allow Harrison to weave guitar hooks into his compositions, but McCartney would remove Harrison's guitar solos on songs like "Another

Girl," "Penny Lane," and "Hello, Good bye." Throughout the '70s, guitarists for Wings would quit after realizing they would have almost zero input on what they played or did not play. Which is fine; McCartney's a musical genius and should be able to hire who he wants to do what he wants. But Harrison didn't need or want to be a faceless session man getting paid on the clock.

Harrison was also losing Lennon, the big brother and mentor with whom he had gone through every phase from rockabilly to acid, to Ono. Lennon recounted to *Rolling Stone*, "And George, shit, insulted her right to her face in the Apple office at the beginning; just being 'straightforward' you know, that game of 'Well, I'm going to be upfront because this is what we've heard and Dylan and a few people said she's got a lousy name in New York, and you gave off bad vibes.' That's what George said to her and we both sat through it, and I didn't hit him. I don't know why."[6]

A terrible argument erupted between Lennon and Harrison on January 10, 1969. "See you 'round the clubs," Harrison said as he stalked out of the *Get Back* sessions.

Back at his home in Esher, he began writing "Wah-Wah." The group and the public had made him a star, but Eastern mysticism had shown him he could enjoy inner peace if he just got all the Beatles drama out of his life. While he would briefly return to the group, next year "Wah-Wah" would be on his first solo album.

The live performance of the song on *The Concert for Bangladesh* has the edge. On *All Things Must Pass*, Spector's monolithic wall of noise stays at the same level throughout the song without any dynamic shifts—as opposed to starting more subtly and building to a crescendo—and thus seems overlong. The live version is a notch slower, and the cleaner mix allows breathing room to hear the space between the instruments. And more importantly, there's the euphoria of the performance itself.

The rumor had been that the Beatles would reunite for the Bangladesh benefit. There was such a traffic jam outside of Madison Square Garden that the police insisted the box office open twelve hours early, at which point it sold out almost immediately. But Ono was not invited to perform, so she fought with Lennon and he bailed. McCartney said he'd only play if they dissolved the legal partnership, and Harrison refused.

The band included Starr on drums alongside future Wilbury Keltner, Clapton, Russell, Preston, Voormann, and Badfinger. They only had a day's rehearsal, but when they launched into the commanding riffs of "Wah-Wah," Starr kicked in with one of his patented fills, the gospel chorus started clapping, a serious-looking Harrison leaned into the groove, and twenty thousand people roared in delight upon seeing a Beatle for the first time since 1966.

Harrison's stoicism belied his nervousness at being the front man for the first time. But by the time the horn section started grooving in step, Harrison did his sideways kick shuffle from the Beatlemania days, and his exhilaration at being free from his domineering ex-bandmates was palpable. Turning around to look at the huge ensemble pulsating all around him, he grinned, singing how good life can be with no more crying.

When he grew serious to concentrate on the opening of "Here Comes the Sun," everyone cheered and you could see the unaffected surprise in his smile, just as you could see his lack of ego when he stepped back to support the other headliners of the day: Starr (who forgot the words to "It Don't Come Easy" but kept going), Clapton, Preston, and Russell.

And then Bob Dylan came out after having been in seclusion since 1966, blowing everyone's mind with "A Hard Rain's A-Gonna Fall," which could have been written for Bangladesh, his voice strong and reedy. After Altamont, the concert was perhaps the last stand of the Woodstock dream.[7]

In the rehearsal the night before, Dylan wavered on whether he'd actually show. Harrison protested that it was he (Harrison) who hadn't played solo before! In the end, their bond was real, as the Traveling Wilburys twenty years later would demonstrate, and Dylan delivered for his friend. As the two stood together singing "Just Like a Woman" with Leon Russell, no one cared where Lennon and McCartney were.

As he wrapped the show up with "Something" and a ringing "Bangladesh," it might have been Harrison's finest moment, transcending the wah wah that once held him back.

UNCLE ALBERT/ADMIRAL HALSEY—MCCARTNEY

REC. 11/70–12/70, COLUMBIA STUDIOS, NYC, A&R STUDIO, 1/71 (ORCHESTRA), MIXED AT SOUND RECORDERS STUDIOS, LA, 2/71–3/71, PAUL/LINDA MCCARTNEY (PRODUCERS), MCCARTNEY (V, B), SEIWELL (D), MCCRACKEN (G), LINDA MCCARTNEY (BV), THE NEW YORK PHILHARMONIC ORCHESTRA, MARVIN STAMM (FLUGELHORN), SINGLE: US 8/2/71 (1), ALSO ON *RAM*, COVERS INCLUDE: BUDDY RICH, GRAMMY WIN FOR 1971 BEST ARRANGEMENT ACCOMPANYING VOCALISTS

One of McCartney's most successful mini–rock operas, "Uncle Albert/Admiral Halsey" has been dismissed as free association whimsy, but the case can be made for a coherent subtextual narrative.

After his do-it-yourself, rough-hewn debut album received mixed reviews, the auteur was determined to pull out all stops and wow everyone with another *Sgt. Pepper* or *Abbey Road*. He employed New York City's top session players, and for this song reunited with George Martin. The old-time Britannia orchestration recalls Martin's instrumental soundtrack to the *Yellow Submarine* feature. With its naval theme and sound effects, the song is almost a sequel to that Beatles touchtone, which benefited from Martin's experience producing comedy and sound effect albums.

"Uncle Albert" has twelve different sections and is a precursor to "Band on the Run" with its slow, restrained opening, which bursts into cathartic transcendence. It's raining as the song begins, and McCartney's apologizing to his Uncle Albert for, apparently, blowing him off. McCartney did have an Uncle Albert whom he was fond of, a gent known to read aloud from the Bible when he got drunk. Uncle Albert wants something, but McCartney can't get motivated, weighed down by the melancholy that infused his previous album.

Session guitarist Hugh McCracken picks out a delicate, wistful melody. (In an unusual freedom granted by McCartney, McCracken was allowed to come up with his own guitar lines.) Soon actual rain sounds accompany the guitar. Assistant Armin Steiner was sent to stand at the edge of a cliff during a thunderstorm to record it for the track. Then the New York Philharmonic, under the direction of George Martin, glides in as well.

McCartney lackadaisically assures his uncle he'll call if anything happens, then, as a "highpass filter" telephone effect is added to his exaggerated English accent, he defiantly concedes he hasn't done anything all day—in marked contrast to the overachieving ambition that drove him throughout the sixties. As Linda's ghostly harmonies swirl and swoop around him, he admits that he's easily distracted from doing much of anything. McCartney then sings a yearning, plaintive "ooooooo," like someone weary of their depression and wishing for escape.

Suddenly, Martin's strings become more insistent. Galvanizing piano keys begin pounding and jazz trumpeter Marvin Stamm bursts through the clouds with a flugelhorn solo. A flutter of *Pepper*-esque atonal effects—four French horns, whistling, sea birds chirping, and wind blowing—bring to mind the image of *Yellow Submarine*'s Captain Fred, or rather, Admiral Halsey, arriving to spirit McCartney and Linda away as their exhilarating vocals soar.

Admiral Halsey says it's time to get out to sea. Though the singer remains ambivalent, more interested in his tea and pie, the call to action's tempo is permanent now.

Who is Admiral Halsey and why is he there? McCartney said later that he was referring to American Admiral William "Bull" Halsey, who commanded the South Pacific during World War II. Halsey was played in movies by James Cagney and Robert Mitchum—but probably the most relevant portrayal came in the film *Tora! Tora! Tora!* released at the end of September 1970, just before McCartney started recording *Ram*. In the film, Halsey says that, after the war, the Japanese language will be spoken only in hell. *Ram's* opening number, "Too Many People," originally included the lines "Yoko took your lucky break and broke it in two." Put together, these seem more than a coincidence.

As a boy, when McCartney was mad at his parents, he wouldn't lash out directly. Rather, he'd sneak into the living room at a later time and subtly rip the bottoms of their beloved curtains. While McCartney was otherwise not racist (writing "Blackbird," "Ebony and Ivory," etc.), Ono seemed to have brought out some bigoted anger in him, having "stolen" his best friend and partner. For Lennon, one of the moments that crystallized his alienation from McCartney came when he and Ono were staying at McCartney's place. For some reason, McCartney left a note on his mantle one morning for them that read: "You and Your Jap Tart Think You're Hot Shit." In 1980, McCartney would also release a tune called "Frozen Jap," although that was four months after he spent nine days in prison after a Tokyo pot bust.

In this context, perhaps the chorus of "hands across the water" is a mutation of the cry "all hands on deck!" which rang out on battleships. McCartney always thrived on competition, and he used his rage and resentment against Ono and Lennon to fuel himself out of despondency and challenge them for dominance of the record charts.

In the final segment of the song, McCartney exhorts himself to be a gypsy and get back on the road. He had spent months imploring the other Beatles to perform live. Now that he didn't have their dead weight anymore, what was his excuse for not doing so by himself? Perhaps his procrastination was part of the indolence of the first half of the song. Soon he would put his money where his mouth was and assemble a touring band.

The song was the seventh biggest hit of the year, innovative for the day's AM radio, though it divided people then and now. It was the closest thing any of the solo Beatles released that captured the baroque fantasia of the band's middle phase, with the brass bands and French horns that enchanted young kids and hooked them for life. This had always been primarily McCartney's forte in songs ranging from "Penny Lane" to "For No One."

It was a rousing synthesis of old-time music and surrealism about a man struggling to shake off his black and white doldrums and reactivate the Technicolor kaleidoscope Beatles magic. Soon McCartney would leave the safety of his farm for the open sea and sky, and attempt to conquer the world once more.

JEALOUS GUY—LENNON

REC. MAY–JUNE 1971, ASCOT SOUND STUDIOS, RECORD PLANT EAST, NYC, LENNON/ONO/SPECTOR (PRODUCERS), LENNON (V, ACOUSTIC G), VOORMANN (B), KELTNER (D), JOHN BARHAM (HARMONIUM), WHITE (VIBRAPHONE), BADFINGER (ACOUSTIC G, TAMBOURINE), THE FLUX FIDDLERS (STRINGS), ALBUM *IMAGINE*: UK 10/7/71 (1); US 9/9/71 (1), SINGLE: UK 11/18/85 (65), RE-ENTRY TO PROMOTE *IMAGINE: JOHN LENNON* DOC.: US 1/19/88 (91) (B-SIDE TO GIVE PEACE A CHANCE), UK 1/28/88 (45) (B-SIDE TO IMAGINE), COVERS: ROXY MUSIC (UK 1980, NO. 1), OVER 90 OTHERS

Some Lennon fans ignore his dark side, while others are fascinated with how frequently he switched from hero to antihero. He had an eerie, vampiric gift to pen perfect illusions that people (especially women) wanted to hear—from "If I Fell" to "Julia"—as if he were the gentlest, most sensitive soul, while rampaging like Mr. Hyde through London after midnight.

When the Beatles were in India in spring 1968, the Maharishi gave a talk regarding the "son of the mother nature." Afterward, McCartney wrote "Mother Nature's Son" and Lennon wrote "Child of Nature," with a melody not dissimilar from "A Day in the Life." After the trip, the group reconvened at Harrison's home in May to record demos and decided that of the two, McCartney's song would go on *The White Album*. Lennon continued tinkering with "Child of Nature" during the *Get Back* sessions. Then, at some point over the next two years, he scrapped the lyrics altogether and used the gentle melody, paradoxically, to express remorse at his darkest nature.

Lennon had overtly threatened his woman in "Run for Your Life" (1965). Some say the lyrics in "You Can't Do That" (1964) about leaving the girl "flat" are suspect, as well. He directly admitted he was prone to domestic abuse in "Getting Better" (1967), though McCartney sang lead on the song. He told *Playboy*, "I used to be cruel to my woman, and physically—any woman. I was a hitter. I couldn't express myself and I hit. I fought men and I hit women. That is why I am always on about peace, you see. It is the most violent people who go for love and peace. Everything's the opposite. But I sincerely believe in love and peace. I am a violent man who has learned not to be violent and regrets his violence. I will have to be a lot older before I can face in public how I treated women as a youngster."[8]

While dating his first wife, Cynthia, he was so enraged when he saw her dancing with another guy that he confronted her the next day in the school bathroom and slapped her, knocking her head on the pole behind her.[9]

Girlfriend May Pang recounted that a drunken Lennon attempted to strangle her one time when he thought she was trying to block him from a bottle of alcohol, and he had to be stopped by Harry Nilsson.[10]

No doubt the fact that he was dependent on amphetamines and a terrible drunk exacerbated the situation. The sad truth was that many rock stars of the day (and men from every walk of life) were guilty of domestic violence.

In that respect, Ono was a brave lion tamer, confronting him on his male chauvinism, forcing him to grow up, and helping him channel his anger toward more deserving opponents (such as the military industrial complex).

The lyrics of "Jealous Guy" do not go into the extremes of his jealousy. The words are vague enough so that the listener assumes that he's made the woman cry with harsh words and nothing more. Phil Spector's studio wizardry gives the delicate piano a gorgeous, crystalline sheen, and Torrie Zito's strings almost make you feel sorry for the guy, who only lashed out because he was scared. Lennon's skill as a performer is such that you can visualize him trying to gently tilt a sobbing Yoko's chin, imploring her to forgive him.

It's the quintessential song for domestic abusers and narcissistic vampires everywhere, the fragile depths of the singer's own remorse and pain so convincing that the woman is seduced into staying, even though part of her knows it will happen again.

The rise of female equality, *The Burning Bed*, and Lorena Bobbitt would put an end to the silent acceptance of Stanley Kowalski brutes flipping out on their wives and then sobbing, "Stella!" like little boys and being indulged. Today it's hard to picture Chris Brown coming out with such a self-pitying track when millions of Rihanna's fans tweet in outrage each time she considers forgiving him. Lennon was lucky to never be taped like Mel Gibson during one of his drunken rants.

Ono would exile him in 1973, and when she let him back home in 1975, it appears he had put the hitting behind him.

ANOTHER DAY—MCCARTNEY

REC. 11/70–12/70, COLUMBIA STUDIOS, MIXED AT SOUND RECORDERS STUDIOS, LA, 2/71–3/71, PAUL AND LINDA MCCARTNEY (WRITERS/PRODUCERS), MCCARTNEY (V, G, B), SEIWELL (D), SPINOZZA OR MCCRACKEN (G), LINDA MCCARTNEY (BV), SINGLE: UK 2/19/71 (2); US 2/22/71 (5)

Though it was written and previewed during the *Get Back* sessions, "Another Day" sounds like a continuation of McCartney's 1970 depression tunes. Now, however, the (female) protagonist is forcing herself to take a shower and go to the office, accompanied by a deceptively peppy melody and sophisticated production and instrumentation. One of his many songs told in the third person like "She's Leaving Home" and "Lady Madonna," the protagonist is basically Eleanor Rigby twenty or thirty years earlier. She tries to plow optimistically through the nine-to-five routine, but despite the coffee, finds it hard to stay awake. The sadness kicks in as she remembers the man who spends the night with her but then leaves; apparently she's just a booty call to him. By the end of the song, while her smile is glued on her face for the office, inside she's feeling suicidal.

Perhaps subconsciously the emotions of the song were informed by McCartney's feeling abandoned by Lennon. Maybe he was secretly wishing Lennon would come back.

As McCartney finished the sessions for *Ram*, it became time to choose what would become his first official post-Beatles single. This would mean that the song would be left off the album so fans weren't forced to pay for the same thing twice. For this momentous decision, McCartney asked Assistant Studio Engineer Dixon Van Winkle to pick. Van Winkle loved "Another Day," and McCartney said okay.

Van Winkle mixed the song. The next day, he was shocked to hear on the radio how high he had mixed the bass, causing it to pump much more than the regular radio fare of the day.[11] But McCartney never complained, perhaps because EMI had been famously weak in the bass department, mixing his pioneering bass work so low that, compared to James Brown's records, it hardly seemed present. Listening to the song today after the hip-hop revolution, it's hard to understand what Van Winkle was concerned about.

It was a strange single to lead with. Songs like "Instant Karma" and "My Sweet Lord" were anthemic statements of liberation from the Beatles' yoke. McCartney was the spurned partner who cried, "It's over!" to the world, but the singles show Lennon and Harrison psyched to be free and McCartney despondent. In the United States, "Uncle Albert/Admiral Halsey" would later be released as a single. That song might have seemed like a more ambitious statement to lead with.

Still, much of the world could relate to "Another Day," secretaries or otherwise, and it became a hit. Predictably, *Rolling Stone* and *Creem* loathed the song. With the draft going on and the National Guard shooting kids at Kent State, the rock intelligentsia expected "Let It Be" or "Hey Jude." In his song "How Do You Sleep," Lennon would sneer that McCartney's first single was Muzak and he was all washed up. There was no sympathy for a guy who was just trying to get back on his feet.

IT'S SO HARD—LENNON

REC. 1971, ASCOT SOUND STUDIOS, RECORD PLANT EAST, NYC, POSSIBLY ABBEY ROAD, LENNON/ONO/SPECTOR (PRODUCERS), LENNON (V, G), VOORMANN (B), GORDON (D), KING CURTIS (SAX), THE FLUX FIDDLERS (STRINGS), ALBUM *IMAGINE*, ALSO B-SIDE TO IMAGINE

It must have been difficult for even Lennon himself to truly know how much he was deeply unhappy and how much he was feeding on his angst for the songwriting mill. Psychiatrist Arthur Janov did once say that Lennon carried more pain than anyone he had ever worked with. Also, because of his traumatic youth, Lennon became addicted to self-medicating. As every addict knows, one's tolerance keeps going up while the medicating high keeps going down. Before long, the addict feels the original pain plus the drag of the new addiction.

Even for listeners who didn't share his troubles, "It's So Hard" is a funny rant about life that anyone who hasn't slept enough before another day at work can make his or her own. The pain of love had been trod to death by other songwriters, but here Lennon moans about how hard it is to even eat and drink. It's why Lennon was the perfect frowny face to McCartney's "Silly Love Song" face. As banal as it is, no one before had kvetched in such a humorous way about how hard it was just to function as a human being. Everywhere you turned, it was just more inescapable responsibilities to live, love, be somebody, feel something, worry, run, share, hide, and keep your woman satisfied, on and on.

Sometimes it's all too much, and Lennon feels like going down. But by the time of the chorus, Lennon remembers that when it's good, it's really good. Holding his woman in his arms, he feels like going down, but in a different kind of way, and the "hard" of the title takes on a new meaning in Beatles pun tradition.

The song's primitive blues rock recalls *Plastic Ono Band* but is fleshed out and lightened by saxophone and strings. It's not far removed from McCartney's "Oh Woman, Oh Why" or "Oh! Darling," actually demonstrating how close the two still were musically. Lennon recorded the song during the sessions for "Power to the People." On the same day, he also did "I Don't

Want to Be a Soldier" and a cover of the 1958 doo-wop hit "Well (Baby Please Don't Go)" by the Olympics. The sax on the songs was played by King Curtis, who had played on everything from the Coasters' "Yakety Yak" (1958), his own "Memphis Soul Stew" (1967), and the original theme to the TV show *Soul Train*.

Plastic Ono Band had done well with the critics but commercially did not make much of a splash. Lennon was determined to have a hit for his second solo record. Spector produced again, but this time Lennon let him bring in his bag of orchestral tricks to "sugar coat" it, and the overall mood was not as angry. The tracks were recorded at Lennon's Tittenhurst Park home (Ascot Sound Studios), though the strings and King Curtis's sax were added in New York City. "It's So Hard" would be chosen as the B-side to the "Imagine" single, underscoring the difficulty in attaining utopia when everyday life could be annoying drudgery.

A month before the release of the album, junkies stabbed King Curtis to death in front of his New York apartment. Curtis fought back and stabbed them as well, but it did not save him. Jesse Jackson was the minister of the funeral, at which Aretha Franklin and Stevie Wonder performed.

OH WOMAN, OH WHY—MCCARTNEY

REC. 11/70–12/70, COLUMBIA STUDIOS, NYC, MIXED AT SOUND RECORDERS STUDIOS, LA, 2/71–3/71, PAUL AND LINDA MCCARTNEY (PRODUCERS), MC-CARTNEY (V, G, B), SEIWELL (D), SPINOZZA OR MCCRACKEN (G), LINDA MC-CARTNEY (BV), B-SIDE TO ANOTHER DAY: UK 2/19/71 (2); US 2/22/71 (5)

The rock snobs were underwhelmed by the cute and seemingly nontortured "Another Day," but had they listened to the B-side they would have realized that the son of Little Richard was still in possession of his shredding rock-and-roll vocal range. McCartney slips back into the mode of "I'm Down," "Oh! Darling," and the climax of "Hey Jude," while the slide guitar sounds like he's riffing off the country blues of *Led Zeppelin III*'s "Bron-Y-Aur Stomp" or "Hats off to Roy Harper," released three months earlier. McCartney was always trying to keep pace with the guitar virtuosos; after seeing Jimi Hendrix, he wrote the guitar for "Sgt. Pepper's Lonely Hearts Club Band." "Helter Skelter" was his attempt to outdo the Who's live sonic assault. Basically, "Oh Woman" is "Why Don't We Do It in the Road" with lyrics and a full band backing him. McCartney would dig the song's drummer, Denny Seiwell, enough to bring him into Wings later in 1971.

In the song, McCartney's woman shows up with a gun to shoot him down. He pleads with her to tell him what he's done wrong. Naturally, it's his cheating ways. Perhaps it's a flashback to the night his pre-Linda girlfriend Jane Asher came home to London earlier than expected. The Apple Scruffs (see next entry) saw her arriving and tried to warn McCartney, who was with girlfriend number two, Frannie Schwartz. He scoffed, "Ah, pull the other one," until suddenly Jane was standing there glowering. Hopefully, McCartney had gotten philandering out of his system by the time he was with Linda; no gossip has yet come to light.

The main attraction of the song is McCartney's voice, a freak of nature every bit as powerful and rough as Kurt Cobain's or any who have come down the pike since. This song should be played for people who associate McCartney solely with soft pop like "The Girl Is Mine."

It is also the first in a distinguished tradition of great B-sides by McCartney, which have not been consistently available and are thus overlooked. Hopefully they will be collected in a comprehensive box set like Springsteen's *Tracks*— preferably while he's still touring, so he can bust out these lost nuggets.

APPLE SCRUFFS—HARRISON

REC. 5/70–8/70, ABBEY ROAD, MIXED 8/70–9/70, TRIDENT STUDIOS, HARRISON/SPECTOR (PRODUCERS), HARRISON (V, G, HARMONICA), ALBUM *ALL THINGS MUST PASS*

In the early '60s, girls used to stand in line for three hours before the Beatles' daily Cavern Club shows, sometimes clawing Starr's future wife, Maureen, out of jealousy. In the late '60s, when the group no longer played live, there was a clique of hardcore female fans who would permanently hang around outside Apple Records or Abbey Road Studios, regardless of the weather, in the hopes of getting to chat with the Fabs. They'd come by in the morning for a while, then go to their day jobs, then return in the evening. Collectively, they were known as the Apple Scruffs.

Since McCartney lived in town, they also loitered outside his gates. "She Came in through the Bathroom Window" from *Abbey Road* talks about when they snuck into his house and swiped some pants, which they all traded off wearing. They also took a photo, but gave that back when McCartney asked. Although they could get on the group's nerves, the Beatles also invited two of them (Lizzie Bravo and Gayleen Pease) to sing backing vocals on the first version of "Across the Universe." The song was given to the World Wildlife

Fund charity and is now on *Past Masters, Volume 2*. One night, McCartney sang his new song "Blackbird" to them from his window.

Harrison always had a grumpy relationship with his fans. His first composition was entitled "Don't Bother Me," apropos for a guy who would later be stabbed by a crazed stalker. Philip Norman, author of the epic *Shout!* Beatles biography, says Harrison would sometimes kick at the Scruffs when they'd block him from going into the studio, though it should be noted that Norman seemed determined to diminish everyone's reputation except Lennon's.

During the early "Longest Cocktail Party" days of Apple, before all the Beatles grew to hate their own label, Harrison and publicist Derek Taylor considered doing a musical about the place, at which point Harrison started composing Apple-related tunes. One of them, "Not Guilty," would be rejected for *The White Album* and resurface eleven years later on *George Harrison*. Another was "Apple Scruffs," which he finished for his first solo album.

If he was once ambivalent to his fans, in the early days of going solo he seemed to be trying to shore up his base with this wistful love letter. Perhaps he sensed that he'd never again experience such unwavering devotion. One of the scruffs, Carol Bedford, later wrote in her memoir, *Waiting for the Beatles*, that George came home with her once but didn't make a move because he was scared of venereal disease. (After all, the band got the clap multiple times in Hamburg.) Mainly, Bedford just ended up warning him to quit smoking, which turned out to be advice he should have heeded, as Harrison died from cancer.

Harrison's evocative lyrics describe the Apple Scruffs waiting on the steps in the fog and the rain with flowers in their hands. His wavering voice momentarily veers toward good-natured exasperation, but the Dylan-esque harmonica makes the overriding mood one of nostalgia for days already fading.

OH YOKO!—LENNON

Rec. 6/23/71–7/5/71, Ascot Sound Studios, Lennon/Ono/Spector (producers), Lennon (v, g, mouth organ), Voormann (b), White (d), Hopkins (p), Spector (bv), Rod Linton (acoustic g), Andy Davis (acoustic g), The Flux Fiddlers (strings), Album *Imagine*, also B-side to Jealous Guy: UK 11/18/85, Film appearance: *Rushmore* (1998)

Lennon believed in the romantic songs he sang in the Beatles' early days. Starting in 1962, he began composing love songs that still resonate, though perhaps the real love affair was the one between him and his audience, whose adoration he certainly craved "Eight Days a Week." In his personal life, however, he hadn't found someone with whom he shared that intensity. He had it with his first wife, Cynthia, in the early days of their relationship, and there was a bond of warmth and security between them, but not passion. Despite some reported liaisons with folk singer Joan Baez, journalist Maureen Cleave, and *Help!* actress Eleanor Bron, there has been no single woman posited as the muse for those early classics.

By 1967, the euphoria of Lennon's love with the public had worn off. "A Day in the Life" found him sunk in a near-catatonic depression (likely accelerated by rampant substance abuse) in which reading about a friend's death in the newspaper drives him to despair. Though he sang mournfully, "I'd love to turn you on" (à la Timothy Leary's "Turn On, Tune In, Drop Out"), Lennon needed someone to turn *him* on. He imagined a dream woman coming to save him in "Lucy in the Sky with Diamonds." Amazingly, she did come to him that year, although it would take him a year to realize it.

Lennon had circumvented the globe numerous times, and Ono was the most unique woman he'd ever met. Lennon had a thing for big breasts, and since his trip to the Far East in 1965, he also had an Asian fetish. Ono combined both. Lennon had envisioned himself the ultimate "Bad Boy," but Ono was a bad girl more extreme than he had ever dared to be. She was an exhibitionist artist from New York who'd done time in a mental hospital and who might have been the prime instigator in their joint plunge into heroin. Ono also strove to be a "people teacher" who wanted to change the world for good. She was a glass onion on acid.

His earlier songs were not just "made to order" odes to puppy love; they expressed an ideal vision of love he'd been waiting to live out. In Ono, Lennon was electrified to discover that he had at last found his Juliet, and he sang it from the rooftops in the *Let It Be* film with "Don't Let Me Down."

The final song of the *Imagine* album, "Oh Yoko!" is another song that captured the intensity of his love, though from a more childlike and joyful angle. The proclamation that his love will turn her on echoes "A Day in the Life" and underscores his salvation since that tune. If he felt 100 years old then, he sounds like a little boy here, even bringing his harmonica back out from the cobwebs to express a joy he hadn't felt since the triumphant early days in songs like "I Should Have Known Better."

Still, there is a haunting and indefinable tinge of loneliness to Nicky Hopkins's sparkling piano. Perhaps Lennon chose it because it expressed the mood of two needy children who had pushed the rest of the world away from their vast estate. After living in the spotlit fishbowl for two years, they now had to face each other truly alone for the first time, and the deal she made with the devil became clearer. In return for fame beyond her wildest dreams, she had to live with a guy who could be a moody nightmare. Lennon sensed her growing reservation and tried to tap back into the little girl in her who wanted to be innocently and passionately in love. Soon the couple would abandon the estate for the myriad distractions of New York.

Despite the fact that Lennon used Ono's name in the title—which wasn't a common Western name like "Rhonda," "Cathy," or "Sheila"—EMI wanted Lennon to release "Oh Yoko!" as a single. He declined, calling it too "pop." This seems odd from a guy who was determined to get a "sugar-coated" hit. Maybe it was just too vulnerable.

EARLY 1970—STARR

REC. OCTOBER 1970, ABBEY ROAD, HARRISON (PRODUCER), STARR (V, ACOUS-TIC G, P, D), HARRISON (SLIDE G, B, BV), B-SIDE TO IT DON'T COME EASY

Perhaps inspired by Lennon's self-referential musical documentary "The Ballad of John and Yoko," Starr decided to sketch a portrait of the Beatles during their strange limbo at the turn of the decade when Lennon had secretly quit and McCartney was incommunicado.

Originally entitled "When Four Knights Come to Town," the song describes one charming bandmate who lives on a sheep farm. Starr wonders aloud whether the old friend will play with him when he comes to town.

Then the good-time piano kicks in, mirroring the camaraderie Starr feels as he thinks about another bandmate. This one's lying in bed with his Japanese mama watching *Sesame Street*, screaming and crying and getting free (i.e., going through primal scream therapy). Starr knows this friend will always play with him.

Finally, there's the longhaired guitarist who can always be counted on to hang out. His jolly slide guitar answers and duets with Starr's vocals in the way Harrison had wanted to on "Hey Jude" before McCartney squelched him.

It's the same group dynamic depicted at the beginning of *A Hard Day's Night*—Lennon, Starr, and Harrison laughing and having a blast, and McCartney the loner in the distance. Now the loner was instituting legal proceedings to allow him to leave the gang permanently.

Starr and Lennon recorded the song during the *Plastic Ono Band* sessions in October 1970, and Harrison added his slide guitar later. Klein deviously encouraged Starr to invite McCartney to play on the song; if McCartney played with the Beatles it would negate his lawsuit to break up with them. McCartney didn't take the bait.

THE BACK SEAT OF MY CAR—MCCARTNEY

Rec. 11/70–12/70, Columbia Studios, NYC, 1/71, A&R Studio, NYC (orchestra), Mixed at Sound Recorders Studios, LA, 2/71–3/71, Paul/ Linda McCartney (producers), McCartney (v, b), Seiwell (d), Spinozza or McCracken (g), Linda McCartney (bv), The New York Philharmonic Orchestra, Single release: UK 8/13/71 (39), Also on *Ram*

On January 14, 1969, during the *Get Back* sessions, McCartney played this song to the others Beach Boys style. Later early takes recorded for the *Ram* album almost suggest *Abbey Road*'s "You Never Give Me Your Money." In some ways, this song can be seen as the optimistic sequel to the earlier song's account of the Beatles' disintegration. "You Never Give Me Your Money" presents the Beatles mired in negotiations for "funny paper," which McCartney prophesized would degenerate into courtroom investigations. Given the sack by Lennon, he's out of money with nowhere to go. But the flipside of the situation is the "magic feeling" of having no more work or pressure. With his woman beside him, he jumps in the car, hits the gas, and gets the hell away from Apple and the other Beatles.

"Back Seat" opens with a couple flying down the highway digging the lights. Maybe they'll drive all the way to Mexico City, like Jack Kerouac and Neal Cassady in the climax of *On the Road*. The idea that the song is a direct sequel breaks down at this point, because the couple is haunted by the girl's father's admonitions that making love is wrong. But presumably doing just that in the backseat of the car, they know their love is right.

The song represents a subgenre of McCartney songs in which he vehemently proclaims that he can't be wrong—or alternatively, that he is right. From "Get on the Right Thing," also recorded during the *Ram* sessions, to 1984's "No More Lonely Nights" and beyond, asserting that he is indeed correct has been a lyrical preoccupation for McCartney. The proclivity dates back to "The Fool on the Hill," at least. That titular fool was modeled after the Maharishi in the early days of the Beatles' infatuation with him. The character also may have represented how McCartney felt after being barraged by bad press for admitting to the media that he took LSD. Lennon took most of *Ram* to be a direct attack against him, assuming that McCartney and Linda were singing that they believed that they couldn't be wrong at him. Lennon snapped back in an interview, affecting a very proper British accent, "Well, I believe that he could possibly *be* wrong."[12]

Wrong or not, musically the song was a sumptuous climax to an album designed to answer the critics who felt he hadn't pushed himself with *McCartney*. He was so into orchestration at the time that he also released an instrumental/ lounge version of the entire record under the pseudonym Thrillington.

ISN'T IT A PITY—HARRISON

REC. 5/70–8/70, ABBEY ROAD, MIXED 8/70–9/70, TRIDENT STUDIOS, HAR-RISON/SPECTOR (PRODUCERS), HARRISON (V, SLIDE G, BV), STARR (D), PRESTON (K), VOORMANN (B), WRIGHT (K), BADFINGER (ACOUSTIC G), BARHAM (OR-CHESTRAL ARRANGEMENT), TONY ASHTON (PIANO), SINGLE: US 11/23/70 (1) DOUBLE A-SIDE TO MY SWEET LORD, ALSO ON *ALL THINGS MUST PASS*

Some accounts maintain that Harrison wrote "Isn't It a Pity" during *The White Album* period. Others say that three years earlier, Lennon and Harrison had debated whether to submit it to Frank Sinatra, before Lennon shot it down. The song is in the vein of Harrison's tunes from 1966 through 1968, wherein he used Indian instruments while expressing Eastern pieties. Harrison laments how we break each other's hearts and take without giving back, blind to the beauty all around us. Like church, you've heard it before, but it's good to be reminded.

What makes it great is the way Spector's magisterial strings and horns meld with Harrison's slide guitar. Everything proceeds with deliberate slowness, building to a hypnotic climax of almost cosmic grandeur. Falsetto voices singing, "What a pity," are countered by otherworldly "ommms" at the end of each bar, as if intoned by the transparent faces of solemn, planet-sized gods. The indistinct, eerie droning would eventually influence generations of indie rockers, including the "Phil Spector of the South," producer Mitch Easter. Easter used this unintelligible reverb technique to exemplary effect on songs from R.E.M.'s classic first album *Murmur* (1983) including "Pilgrimage."

The effect in "Isn't It a Pity" is accentuated by the song's unending repetition, clocking in one second shorter than McCartney's "Hey Jude." It so happened that "Hey Jude" was just ten seconds shorter than "MacArthur Park," the groundbreaking Richard Harris single written by Jimmy Webb that became a smash during the recording of *The White Album*. The Beatles' competitive nature ensured that they would make "Hey Jude" just as long.

With "Isn't It a Pity," Harrison goes toe-to-toe with the tune McCartney wouldn't let him embellish.

HAPPY XMAS (WAR IS OVER)—LENNON

Rec. October 1971, Record Plant East, NYC, Lennon/Ono (writers), Lennon/Ono/Spector (producers), Lennon (v, g), Ono (v), McCracken (g), Keltner (d, sleigh bells), Hopkins (p, chimes, glockenspiel), Chris Osbourne (g), Teddy Irwin (g), Stuart Scharf (g), The Harlem Community Choir (bv), Single: US 12/1/71 (did not chart), Re-entry UK: 11/24/72 (4), 1/4/75 (48), 12/20/80 (2), 12/19/81 (28), 12/25/82 (56), 12/24/83 (92), 12/22/84 (92), 1/28/88 (45) (B-side of Imagine), 12/20/03 (33) (B-side of Imagine), 12/13/99 (3)

And now the story of how an unsaintly thug with a hang-up about organized religion and a Messiah complex wrote a perennial Christmas classic.

During the holidays of 1969, Lennon bought billboards in major cities that proclaimed in stark black and white: "War is over! (If you want it) Happy Christmas from John and Yoko"—most pointedly across the street from the Marines recruitment center in Times Square. Perhaps the phrase was inspired by Phil Ochs' 1968 song "The War Is Over," or the Doors' "Unknown Soldier," in which Morrison cries out at the end, "War is over!"

Always recycling, Lennon decided during October 1971 to turn the phrase into a holiday song. The Beatles had often created Christmas singles especially for their fan club (the most memorable of these being the almost-song "Christmastime Is Here Again"). Of all the Beatles, the one who had recently proclaimed that God was a mental construct would seem the least likely to attempt a yuletide carol. Maybe that was why Lennon was among the first recording artists to simply refer to the holiday as "Xmas" in the song's title, although that may have been to also fit "(War Is Over)" on the label as well.

Always canny, Lennon knew the best way to slip in a message was through sugar. He was also as sentimental as the rest of the Fabs, regardless of his agnostic flip-flops. With the most dysfunctional family of all of the Beatles, perhaps he felt particularly emotional around the holidays. At any rate, Lennon's Christmas composition was destined to outshine Harrison's phoned-in "Ding Dong Ding Dong" and McCartney's trifling "Wonderful Christmastime"—the latter of which seems to have achieved perennial status more due to radio's need to fill airtime than because of inspiration. Starr, incidentally, would record an entire album of Christmas songs called *I Wanna Be Santa Claus*.

Spector's over-the-top tendencies were put to good use. Chimes, glockenspiel, sleigh bells, a dozen guitars, and thirty kids from the Harlem Community Choir were all included. Ono and Lennon opened the tune by whispering, "Happy Christmas," to their kids, Kyoko and Julian. Lennon then began a melody taken from an old folk song about a racehorse called "Stewball." Musing that another year has gone by, he asks us pointedly what we've accomplished. It was a heavy question to lay on a listener at the beginning of a holiday song. Despite his extreme hedonism, Lennon was driven by a Protestant work ethic that seems unmatched in rock history (except, perhaps, by McCartney and Prince). As always, he was singing to both himself and to his audience. Did we do anything to make the world a more peaceful place?

The song appropriates Sly and the Family Stone's "Everyday People," referring to white, black, yellow, and red folks. Ono can barely wait to start trilling out the chorus, but the Harlem Community Choir is undeniably touching as they sing, "War is over if you want it." It dovetails with an image that would be burned into baby boomers' minds the following June, when AP photographer Nick Út and NBC cameraman Le Phuc Dinh would film sobbing children fleeing their village while it was being napalmed.

"Happy Xmas (War Is Over)" was released in the United States too close to Christmas to gather much steam in 1971. Maybe the US audience didn't want to hear children singing a song against the war it was fighting. (Such a release would be unimaginable in World War II.) It wasn't issued in the United Kingdom at all that year, but it would place in the British charts repeatedly in the holiday seasons to follow.

NOTES

1. Simon Leng, *The Music of George Harrison: While My Guitar Gently Weeps* (London: Firefly, 2003), 59–62.
2. Keith Richards and James Fox, *Life* (New York: Little, Brown and Company, 2010), 241–42.
3. David Sheff, "January 1981 *Playboy* Interview with John Lennon and Yoko Ono," John-Lennon.com, www.john-lennon.com/playboyinterviewwithjohnlennonandyokoono.htm (October 10, 2011).
4. David Wigg, "May 1969 BBC Radio-One 'Scene and Heard' Interview," The Ultimate Experience Beatle Interview Database, www.beatlesinterviews.org/db1969.0508.beatles.html (October 11, 2011).

5. The Beatles, *The Beatles Anthology* (San Francisco: Chronicle Books, 2000), 316.

6. Jann S. Wenner, "January 1971 *Rolling Stone* Interview," JannSWenner.com, www.jannswenner.com/Archives/John_Lennon_Part1.aspx (October 10, 2011).

7. Nicholas Schaffner, *The Beatles Forever* (New York: McGraw-Hill, 1978), 148.

8. Sheff, "January 1981 *Playboy* Interview."

9. Cynthia Lennon, *John* (New York: Three Rivers Press, 2005), 37.

10. Goldman, *The Lives of John Lennon*, 590.

11. John Blaney, *Lennon and McCartney: Together Alone* (London: Jawbone, 2007), 41.

12. Ron Schaumberg, *Growing Up with the Beatles* (New York: Pyramid, 1976), 129.

John Lennon in the "I Don't Wanna Be a Soldier Mama" segment of the promotional film for *Imagine,* filmed in 1971. *PhotoFest*

1972: Gimme Some Truth

*McCartney mirrors Lennon by bringing his wife onstage as Lennon and
Ono hurtle toward the biggest train wreck of their career.*

The solo Beatles were all exhausted in 1972. The year saw only the release
of Starr's hit "Back off Boogaloo," Lennon's disastrous bomb *Some Time in
New York City*, and three McCartney singles, only one of which stands the
test of time as more than a curio. However, the previous two years saw such
an abundance of riches that it takes a double album to house the remaining
grade-A material. Collectively, the quality of the output perhaps surpasses *The
White Album*, as the solo Beatles had more to prove and pushed themselves as
hard in 1970 and 1971 as they did in 1968. But many listeners were alarmed
to see a second Beatle partnering with his nonmusician wife.

Originally, it seemed to be a ploy for money. In the early '70s, McCartney's earnings from his solo albums were held in receivership by EMI until the
legal details of the Beatles' split were finalized. Since McCartney needed cash,
he tried to get around the money holdup by naming Linda as his cowriter.
That way, even though half the new songwriting royalties would go to the
record label and be stuck in limbo, half could go to Linda, allowing the couple
to maintain their earthy ramshackle farm lifestyle. Fans and critics howled at
the arrangement, but Linda did bring a distinctive sound to *Ram* with her
vocal harmonies, which were quite strong and beautiful. Maybe the fact that
McCartney could sing with her is one of the factors that attracted him in the
early days of their courtship.

McCartney was also itching to get back on the road and wanted to put
a full band together. *Ram*'s drummer Denny Seiwell signed on, but guitarist
Hugh McCracken passed, and guitarist David Spinozza had butted heads with
the McCartneys. (The two guitarists would go on to work on Lennon albums;

Spinozza on *Mind Games*, during which he would begin an affair with Ono; and McCracken on *Double Fantasy* and *Milk and Honey*.)

In searching for a guitarist, McCartney recalled Denny Laine, a good-looking Roger Daltrey–type born Brian Hines in 1944, the son of a boxer. He'd been a tap dancer until he heard the guitar of "That'll Be the Day." After he started playing in groups, he switched his name in honor of jazz artist Cleo Laine. He fronted the Moody Blues in the early days and sang their first hit, the classic "Go Now," strikingly sophisticated for 1964 when the year's other big hits included "Do the Freddie." He became friends with McCartney hanging out at the hip nightspots of swinging London. However, the Moody Blues stagnated for the next couple years, so Laine quit in 1966, just before the Moodys reinvented themselves with "Nights in White Satin." Laine had never topped "Go Now," so when McCartney called him to join in 1971 he leapt at the chance.

Laine got on well with Linda, too, who had been a fan of his and encouraged his inclusion in the group. He and Linda would be the only permanent fixtures of Wings over the next decade. In a way, he was McCartney's next Harrison, a friend with a high-quality voice that almost seemed invisible when blended with the other members' harmonies, and a songwriter who would have his own track or two per album. Unlike Harrison, however, he and McCartney cowrote together occasionally; their song "Mull of Kintyre" became the biggest noncharity UK single of all time. Laine was a pretty normal Northern guy, not an India-influenced visionary, and he didn't chafe under McCartney's dominance.

Laine was a bit taken aback when he learned that McCartney planned to have Linda, a novice musician, play keyboards. It would have struck Stu Sutcliffe as an ironic move, had he been alive. McCartney had resented it when Lennon insisted his nonmusician best friend, Sutcliffe, play bass in Hamburg.

Poor Linda didn't want to be in the band, either. But Paul McCartney was a very stubborn man and also probably the only rock star this side of John Lennon who could have foisted his wife on the public so that she could be there in the background as his security blanket.

It's intriguing that both of the principal Beatles brought their wives on stage with them (women who had both gone to Sarah Lawrence College, though at different times). Perhaps something about the Lennon-McCartney bond made them permanently codependent. Was McCartney trying to beat Lennon at his own "Johnandyoko" game? "Anything your wife can do mine can do better."

Lennon perhaps wanted to drive "squares" away to give him some breathing room. Also, perhaps having their wives on stage (and on album covers) was a way to create a force field against temptation. If their wives were with them at all times, it would be harder for groupies to fling themselves at them. By all accounts, the McCartneys' marriage stood the test of time and produced well-adjusted kids.

The high-water mark for Lennon harmonizing with Yoko was 1971–1972. Yoko's vibrato on "Happy Xmas" is a bit distracting, but she acquits herself well in some tunes from the *Some Time in New York City* album, such as the surprisingly catchy "Sisters O Sisters," which sounds like a bouncy predecessor to Shonen Knife. But when the album stiffed, Lennon never sang with her again.

Lennon abandoned vocal harmony to a large degree all together. Harrison would multitrack his own voice. But the Paul/Linda/Denny Laine harmonies would become Wings' signature sound for the next ten years. Perhaps harmonizing was most integral to McCartney because his father had taught him and his brother to harmonize at a young age.

McCartney's money really must've been tied up, because his Scottish farm had no hot water and they had to grow their own vegetables. It was here he created Rude Studios, where he'd rehearse and record demos all the way until 2001's *Driving Rain*. In August 1971, McCartney, Linda, Laine, and Seiwell started their first album there as a band. McCartney was determined to do it like Dylan had done *New Morning* (1970), all in one or two takes per song, the opposite of the meticulous *Ram* approach and one that would get the product out faster. Simultaneously, McCartney gave Linda lessons on keyboards and drilled her on harmony—while she was eight months pregnant.

In September, Linda gave birth to their second daughter (her third), Stella. The birth was difficult and both Linda and Stella almost died. As McCartney prayed feverishly at the hospital, he had an image of wings. Upon learning that his wife and daughter were okay, he named the band Wings in gratitude.

For the band's first single, McCartney would follow Lennon's lead by issuing a protest song, decrying the Bloody Sunday massacre with "Give Ireland Back to the Irish." In 1971 and 1972, Lennon, Harrison, and McCartney each used their status to release records that were really political editorials. Lennon, of course, had been doing so since "Give Peace a Chance" and "Power to the People." Harrison followed with "Bangladesh." All the songs featured impassioned vocals and instrumentation but did not transcend their context to bear repeated listening.

That would be the fatal flaw of Lennon's 1972 album *Some Time in New York City*, where his radical messiah persona finally jumped the tracks. No doubt anyone in the Beatles' position would have courted megalomania and delusions of grandeur. Lennon was joking about it as early as 1964, when he sieg-hieled the more than 35,000 people who turned up outside the Beatles' hotel in Australia. Despite his irreverence, by autumn 1965, Lennon was lost, grappling with what to do with his power as he sat in his country club mansion, literally playing with his train sets in the attic. That year he had met his childhood idol, Elvis, and knew he didn't want to end up in a directionless existence like him.

A couple of weeks after expressing his confusion in "Nowhere Man," Lennon teamed up with McCartney to write "The Word." Drawing on the Bible's Gospel of John ("In the beginning was the Word, and the Word was with God, and the Word was God"), they sang they had seen the Light and their mission was to get everyone to love their fellow man. It was the first time they dealt with love in a nonromantic sense, and a precursor to their peace songs. Paradoxically, it was shortly thereafter that Lennon made his infamous comment that the Beatles were more popular than Jesus and that Christianity would shrink and vanish.

Soon bonfires of Beatles albums were set ablaze across the Bible Belt. Lennon didn't help matters when the group released an American album, *Yesterday and Today*, covered with butchered baby dolls and said, "It's as relevant as Vietnam." The anti-Beatle backlash scared the Beatles out of touring. Lennon got further into LSD and encapsulated his peace philosophy in his first slogan song, "All You Need Is Love."

After returning from the Maharishi's camp in India in 1968, Lennon went on an acid binge and stayed up for days without sleeping. He came to the conclusion that he was the Second Coming and called a meeting of the other Beatles to inform them. No doubt used to acid casualties from the Summer of Love, the others didn't try to argue with him. Whether or not he still believed he was the Second Coming after getting a good night's sleep, in 1969 he took to wearing all white and affecting the longhaired, bearded look of the West's conception of Jesus. For an artist who thrived on rebellion, he may have been trying to annoy conservatives by looking like Jesus while espousing his message of peace against an American war.

But there was no doubt he believed in peace. He felt a need to atone for both his domestic abuse of women and the many fights he had been in over the years. In the most notorious fight, in 1963 Lennon put the DJ of the Cavern Club in the hospital. When the DJ teased Lennon for going to Spain with his gay manager while his wife gave birth to their son Julian alone, a drunken Lennon had to be restrained from beating the guy with a shovel.

In 1969, Lennon and Ono originally tried to sell peace via good-natured put-ons like Bed Ins. But as the media scorned them, the law persecuted them, and the Beatles' break-up turned nasty, Lennon's peace anthems turned angry. All-white suits and Jesus hair was out; short hair and Che Guevara army fatigues were in. Lennon also said he became a radical because he felt guilty for being rich.

Soon Lennon was using his media power to bring the Black Panthers and Yippies (Youth International Party) into American living rooms on *The Mike Douglas Show*. To share his new agenda, he changed back to the friendly charmer he had been in the early days of Beatlemania. He urged people to vote for Democratic presidential candidate George McGovern and planned a tour that would raise funds to beat President Nixon and climax with a concert across the street from the Republican National Convention.

Alarmed, the Nixon administration began a deportation campaign against Lennon. They had his phone bugged, had him tailed, and transcribed all his TV appearances. Everything was documented in 281 pages of FBI files that were eventually released to the public in 1991.

In the end, Nixon did not need to fear Lennon. Nixon slaughtered McGovern in one of the biggest landslides in American history, having convinced the heartland that McGovern represented "acid, amnesty, and abortion."

The nail in the coffin of Lennon's political era was the universal disdain that greeted his 1972 double album *Some Time in New York City*. Elephant's Memory rocked as hard as any band that ever backed Lennon, but the record was undone by topical protest lyrics that were boring at best and ridiculous at worst. In "Attica State," he and Ono demanded that all prisoners everywhere be freed, because all they needed was love and care. Years later, Mark David Chapman would serve his life sentence in Attica. Every time he would come up for parole, Ono would write the parole board to block his release.

The album and its single "Woman Is the Nigger of the World" were the biggest chart failures of his career. The wipeout shook his confidence and he never performed live again (except for a few numbers with Elton John). He stopped trying to innovate or push the boundaries. He'd soon retreat to a cover album of rock oldies.

On March 23, 1973, Lennon was told to leave the country in thirty days. On April Fool's Day, he held a press conference in New York with Ono in which they proclaimed themselves to be the ambassadors of the country Nutopia. It was the incarnation of his song "Imagine," with no land, boundaries, or passports, "only people" (a track on *Mind Games*). Waving the white flag of Nutopia, he requested diplomatic immunity to allow them to stay in the country.

But when all is said and done, he had used his fame to go on *Dick Cavett* and *The Mike Douglas Show* to talk about things that much of America wanted to sweep under the carpet. Like Norman Lear and Phil Donahue, he was part of the evolution of American TV in the 1970s.

HI HI HI—MCCARTNEY

Rec. 1972, Morgan Studios, London, Paul/Linda McCartney (writers), McCartney (producer), McCartney (v, b), Linda McCartney (keyboard, bv), Laine (b), Henry McCullough (g), Seiwell (d), Single double A-side with C Moon: UK 12/1/72 (5); US 12/4/72 (10)

When Wings' first single, "Give Ireland Back to the Irish," was banned in the United Kingdom, McCartney responded by releasing a nursery rhyme set to music, "Mary Had a Little Lamb," which seemed to suggest that after ten years of unrelenting activity he was perhaps getting a little slap happy. On one hand, McCartney put it out as an ironic comeback to the BBC ban. "Oh, the Irish single was too hot for you? Do you think you can handle a nursery rhyme?" He also had a stepdaughter named Mary and a farm of sheep. (During the *Ram* sessions he had recorded the strangely haunting "Little Lamb Dragonfly" about an errant member of his flock.) "Mary Had a Little Lamb" was bizarrely catchy and featured nice mandolin by the newest addition to Wings, lead guitarist Henry McCullough. It made the British top ten, but the dudes in Wings must've started to wonder what sort of band they'd gotten into.

McCartney finally gave them something to sink their teeth into with "Hi Hi Hi," a solid rocker and perfect opportunity for McCullough to show off his slide guitar. Another fleshed-out descendent of "Why Don't We Do It in the Road," it celebrates McCartney's favorite things: music, sex, and weed. He meets his woman at the station where she's waiting with a bootleg record and they go back to his place to get high, blast the music, and do it all night long.

Perhaps trying to remind people that he was an adult after "Mary Had a Little Lamb," he sang excitedly of his woman lying down on the bed getting ready for his "body gun." When the BBC banned *this* record, he said what he had actually sang was "his polygon." But if you believe that, you believe "Lucy in the Sky with Diamonds" doesn't stand for LSD. The BBC also took issue with his "sweet banana" and "getting hi hi hi."

The second ban helped his rock-and-roll image—but he then became the third Beatle to get busted for weed when a nosy cop found pot plants on his farm. McCartney said that a fan had mailed him some seeds so he just planted them to see what they were, similar to his "polygon" defense. Unfortunately, the bust would keep him out of the United States and Japan for quite some time.

POWER TO THE PEOPLE—LENNON

Rec. January–February 1971, Ascot Sound Studios, Lennon/Ono/Spector (producers), Lennon (v, g, p), Voormann (b), White (d), Preston (p, k), Keys (sax), Rosetta Hightower (bv), unknown others (bv), Single: UK 3/12/71 (7);US 3/22/71 (11)

Lennon was a sponge, and when he came under the influence of a strong figure he turned their philosophy into fodder for his songs. The day after being interviewed by Tariq Ali, a writer for the Marxist revolutionary newspaper *Red Mole*, Lennon lifted one of the Black Panthers' slogans, "All Power to the People," composed a song to go with it, and called Ali up to play it to him over the phone. Then he got in touch with Phil Spector.

Spector took the "Instant Karma" template and refashioned it into one of Lennon's hardest yet funkiest tunes. As befitting a Black Panther slogan, this time the sound was overtly gospel, like an angry version of *The Jefferson's Theme*. The backing vocalists were led by Rosetta Hightower, a member of the popular girl group the Orlons in the early '60s, whose hits include "The Wah Watusi." Spector had everyone march their feet, which sounded like a political rally but also became the rhythm. Then Lennon came roar-snarling in, his voice echo-Spectorized into the sonic equivalent of giant posters of that other famous Lenin, while Bobby Keys's sax made you want to go dancing in the streets while you overthrew the government.

In "Revolution," Lennon said to count him out if there was destruction involved, but now he howls that it's time to revolt right away on behalf of the millions of workers getting paid nothing. He puts the fat-cat capitalists on notice that the hordes are coming into town to take ownership of the businesses and society. It was one of his most contemptuous vocals to date, a further development of the surly persona still simmering that he'd been cowed into apologizing for the "More Popular Than Jesus" faux pas.

Under Ono's influence, Lennon then turns his attention to his "comrades," reminding them to treat "their" women as equals. Years later, the film *Forrest Gump* would also address the contradictions of the radical movement in which the men called for equality yet expected the women to stay quiet, do the dishes, and accept being smacked around.

Lennon told *Red Mole*, "We can't have a revolution that doesn't involve and liberate women. It's so subtle the way you're taught male superiority. It took me quite a long time to realize that my maleness was cutting off certain areas for Yoko. She's a red-hot liberationist and was quick to show me where I was going wrong, even though it seemed to me that I was just acting naturally. That's why I'm always interested to know how people who claim to be radical treat women."[1]

For years after its release, the song was out of style, with Hunter S. Thompson disparaging it as "ten years too late" and Lennon saying that it was "embarrassing" and "didn't really come off." But in the wake of the global economic recession, it became the name of his 2010 compilation, and the workers are still working for nothing.

BACK OFF BOOGALOO—STARR

Rec. February 1972, London, Harrison (producer), Starr (v, d), Harrison (g), Voormann (b), Wright (k), Single: UK 4/1/72 (2); US 3/17/72 (9)

Starr didn't rush to maximize the success of "It Don't Come Easy." Instead, he decided to direct a rockumentary of the current king of the UK music scene, his buddy Marc Bolan of the band T. Rex. T. Rex started out as a folk rock band in the Donovan/Middle Earth mode. Then, like David Bowie, T. Rex made the switch to androgynous glam rock, one of the first major movements of the post-Beatles era. Named *Born to Boogie*, Starr's film captured the brief heyday of "T. Rexstacy." It also marked the beginning of Lennon and Starr's habit of frequently shouting "Boogie!" in their songs. (With corny "booo gie" pronunciation, this was perhaps one of the indicators that they had ceased being 100 percent cool.)

Over dinner one night, Starr was struck by how many times Bolan used the term "Boogaloo." Later that evening while drifting off to sleep, the beat and then the song floated into Starr's head. As there had only been two or three other tunes that had floated in over the last ten years, he rushed to find a tape recorder, but found them all to be broken or with dead batteries. Luckily he found some batteries in one of his kid's toys and preserved the idea.

In the lyrics, he castigates himself to finally write a "tasty" song. But at the same time, he was probably castigating McCartney. His alienation from Macca began when McCartney's perfectionism drove Starr to temporarily quit during *The White Album*, then boiled over one very bad day in 1970.

On March 31, Lennon and Harrison learned that the album *Let It Be* had to be released in April to coincide with the film's premiere. Unfortunately, that was when McCartney was slated to release his *McCartney* solo album.

Without discussing it with McCartney, Lennon went ahead and told EMI to push back *McCartney*'s release to June 4. Instead of talking to him directly, Harrison wrote him a letter.

> *Dear Paul,*
>
> *We thought a lot about yours and the Beatles LPs—and decided it's stupid for Apple to put out two big albums within 7 days of each other (also there's Starr's and Hey Jude)—so we sent a letter to EMI telling them to hold your release date till June 4th (there's a big Apple-Capitol convention in Hawaii then). We thought you'd come around when you realized that the Beatles album was coming out on April 24th. We're sorry it turned out like this—it's nothing personal. Love John and George. Hare Krishna. A Mantra a Day keeps MAYA! Away.*

Then he stuck it in an envelope marked "From Us, To You," and called a messenger. It echoed the same bravery the Fabs demonstrated when they gave Brian Epstein the job of firing Pete Best.

But Starr decided it wasn't cool to have a courier relay the news, so he took the letter and went over to McCartney's place. When Starr told McCartney that he felt the plan made sense, McCartney "went crazy; he was crazy, I thought," Starr said in the court case later. "He just shouted and pointed at me. He was out of control, prodding his finger toward my face. He told me to get my coat on and get out. I got brought down, because I couldn't believe it was happening to me."

Lennon said, "He attacked Starr and he started threatening him and everything, and that was the kibosh for Starr."[2]

In the end, McCartney was allowed to go ahead with his original release plan, but Starr was still pissed off almost two years later. When McCartney started bagging on the group on the *Ram* album, Starr finally joined Lennon and Harrison in bitching about Macca on vinyl. Referencing the "Paul Is Dead" hoax, he calls McCartney a meathead and tells him to quit pretending he's dead and finally put out some decent music.

It's not quite in the same league as Tupac hissing to Biggie that he slept with his wife on "Hit 'Em Up," but the genuine anger no doubt helped make the tune a staple of football and soccer matches with its marching band drums. As he did on Lennon's anti-McCartney diatribe "How Do You Sleep," Harrison joins in with his ubiquitous slide guitar in Allman Brothers mode. The song remains a highlight of Starr's live act and has been appropriated by everyone from glam metal Warrant for their hit "Cherry Pie" to indie rockers Franz Ferdinand for "Take Me Out."

In the video, the Frankenstein monster stalks Starr, but in the end the two hug and dance together, as thankfully, he and McCartney eventually did, leading to many more collaborations over the next forty years.

AWAITING ON YOU ALL—HARRISON

REC. 5/70–8/70, ABBEY ROAD, MIXED 8/70–9/70, TRIDENT STUDIOS, HAR-
RISON/SPECTOR (PRODUCERS), HARRISON (V, G), CLAPTON (G), VOORMANN
(B), PRICE (TRUMPET), KEYS (SAX), RADLE (B), GORDON (D), ALBUM *ALL
THINGS MUST PASS*

In many of his songs over the course of his career, Harrison would talk about
falling off the path and struggling to get back on. Here, he sings that if you've
gotten yourself into a mess, all you need to do to get yourself clean and forget
your cares is chant the name of the Lord. Harrison maintains you don't need
churches, temples, rosaries, books, or love-ins, echoing Martin Luther's insis-
tence that people could study the Bible and commune with God without the
church as the middleman. In fact, Harrison slips in a critique at the Catholic
Church he was raised in, claiming they're keeping the masses down while
owning 51 percent of General Motors' stock. Two months after the song was
released, the Vatican felt compelled to tell *Time* in the January 25, 1971, issue
that its portfolio was worth only approximately $140–500 million.[3]

Matching the scope of Harrison's theme was the cacophony devised by
Spector for this and many of the tunes on *All Things Must Pass*. Several drum-
mers, bassists, pianists, and percussionists would play live simultaneously for
multiple takes. Spector would direct Badfinger to strum four acoustic guitars
and then bury them in the mix so they could be felt but not heard. Harrison's
voice would be overdubbed multiple times to create a heavenly choir. Horns
and strings would be layered and made even more titanic through echo and
reverb. But once Spector showed how it was done, Harrison ended up producing much of the album himself since Spector was drinking so much.

LOVE IS STRANGE—MCCARTNEY

REC. AUGUST 1971, ABBEY ROAD, BAKER/VANDERPOOL/SMITH (WRITERS),
PAUL/LINDA MCCARTNEY (PRODUCERS), MCCARTNEY (V, B), LAINE (G), SEI-
WELL (D), LINDA MCCARTNEY (K, BV), ALBUM *WILD LIFE*: UK 11/15/71 (8);
12/6/71 (10)

After an extended vacation in Jamaica, McCartney and Linda decided to do
a reggae version of the 1956 Mickey and Sylvia hit "Love Is Strange," which
had also been recorded by Bo Diddley, Buddy Holly, and Peaches and Herb.

It was one of the few highlights on *Wild Life* and was originally slated to be their first single, perhaps to show off McCartney's new group's mastery of the new hot genre of the '70s—the genre his old group couldn't grasp.

One of the biggest cracks in the Beatles appeared when McCartney ran them through endless retakes of "Ob-La-Di Ob-La-Da" because they just couldn't get a grip on the ska groove. (In Starr's defense, Zeppelin's John Bonham had a hard time getting the reggae beat in 1973's "D'yer Mak'er" and the rest of the group made fun of him for it.) One of the reasons McCartney dug seasoned pro drummer Denny Seiwell was the fact that he had the reggae feel, and here his taut drumming melds with McCartney's bass mixed to the fore. The song is basically a workout of bass, drums, and guitar stretched out to give each player lots of space to show their chops, a vehicle to appreciate how tightly they interlock with each other. Linda's offbeat harmonies meld impressively with McCartney's reggae accent.

NEW YORK CITY—LENNON

Rec. March 1972, Record Plant East, NYC, Lennon/Ono/Spector (producers), Lennon (v, g), Keltner (d), Elephant's Memory: Stan Bronstein (sax), Gary Van Scyoc (b), Adam Ippolito (p, o), Richard Frank Jr. (d, percussion), Album *Some Time in New York City*: UK 9/15/72 (11); US 6/12/72 (48)

Ono missed Greenwich Village, where she had been an artist in the early '60s, so on August 31, 1971, she and Lennon moved there, first to the St. Regis Hotel on 5th Avenue, then to 105 Bank Street.

Fueled by methadone and B12 speed shots, they hired an army of workers to crank out art pieces for Ono's next show and befriended Yippie leaders Abbie Hoffman and Jerry Rubin. The duo had been famously on trial with the rest of the Chicago Seven for contributing to chaos in the streets during the 1968 Democratic Convention, where antiwar protestors clashed with the National Guard. Another frequent visitor to the Lennons' pad was A. J. Weberman, a radical who regularly combed through Dylan's trash in the attempt to prove that Dylan was a junkie.

Until 1972, Lennon and Ono would record their songs at the same time but issue their material on separate, parallel albums. Thus, Ono had a *Yoko Ono/Plastic Ono Band* record. But for their 1972 release they decided to do an LP together and found their backing band in Elephant's Memory. The group had been featured on the *Midnight Cowboy* soundtrack (in the scene where the protagonist does acid in the Warhol-esque loft party). Carly Simon had once been a member, but even so they rocked fiercely. (Lennon produced their own album around the time they backed his.)

The theme song of the Lennons' new album, "New York City," was the latest installment of "The Ballad of John and Yoko." Like the earlier tune, it journalistically related their latest exploits, but this time it rocked out with a distorted Chuck Berry riff and the full power of a large but tight band.

Like the earlier song, it is hyperspecific, but here it works toward capturing a snapshot of a wild city overflowing with life. He name-checks Max's Kansas City, a nightclub restaurant that served as the epicenter of hip until 1981. Originally a hang out for abstract expressionist painters, it was taken over by Warhol and the Velvet Underground and became the home to glam rock's New York Dolls, with frequent appearances by David Bowie and Iggy Pop. Patti Smith and gay photography icon Robert Mapplethorpe hung out there before they made it, Aerosmith was discovered there, Bob Marley opened for Springsteen there, and the vanguard of punk made their name there. Lennon also celebrates the Apollo, the Fillmore East, and folk-punk artist David Peel. Reveling in the fact that no one hassles them in the blasé Big Apple, Lennon and Ono vowed to make it their home whether "the Man" likes it or not. He wouldn't.

C MOON—MCCARTNEY

Rec. 1972, Morgan Studios, London, Paul/Linda McCartney (writers), McCartney (producer), McCartney (v, p, marimba), Linda McCartney (percussion, bv), Laine (b), Henry McCullough (d), Seiwell (cornet, xylophone), Single: double A-side with Hi Hi Hi

McCartney was the most middle of the road of the Beatles. He hung back for months after the others started taking acid, never following Lennon into heroin. In the song "How Do You Sleep," Lennon languidly taunted him for living with straights. In the press, Lennon scoffed that both McCartney's music and lifestyle were conventional and safe, while he and Ono were true artists living on the edge.

Now, within the last year, McCartney had been busted for pot twice and banned by the BBC twice for songs about sex, drugs, and politics. He made one album brimming with symphonic innovation and one in which half the songs were recorded on the first take. What the hell did he have to do to be considered hip by Lennon and *Rolling Stone*? The true answer was—"not care." But, exasperated, he released this statement of laid-back defiance to the hip police.

Jazz musicians used the term "square" to refer to close-minded people who thought "inside the box." The 1965 classic "Wooly Bully" by Sam the Sham and the Pharaohs coined the term "L7" as a code word for square, since if you laid an L next to a 7 you'd make a square. McCartney wanted to come up with something that conveyed the opposite of square, and realized if you put a C and a half moon together you could make a circle . . . hence, "C Moon."

To further underscore his cool cred, "C Moon" was reggae in the same year reggae broke in the West. Jimmy Cliff's feature film *The Harder They Come* was produced, and Johnny Nash had a hit with Bob Marley's "Stir It Up." It was a year before the Stones went to Jamaica to record *Goat's Head Soup* and Zeppelin did "D'yer Mak'er," and two years before Clapton's "I Shot the Sheriff" further introduced Marley to the West. Though "C Moon" was a bit more of a hybrid than the pure reggae "Love Is Strange," with xylophone and understated horns processed to interesting effect. As befits the title, the song is in the key of C.

McCartney also threw in a verse about a young couple living together, a very hip new thing for young people to be doing during the sexual revolution, though the lady in the song is stressed out because she hasn't told her dad about it.

But his statement of coolness was complicated by a promotional film featuring a somewhat awkward Linda McCartney front and center banging a tambourine. Linda was a wonderful mother, a strong singer, even more of a reggae fan than McCartney, and could smoke spliffs like nobody's business, but she was not "intimidatingly-cooler-than-thou" like Stones women Anita Pallenberg or Marianne Faithfull. (Of course, Pallenberg ended up in bed with a seventeen-year-old who blew his brains out while her ten-year-old son was downstairs—who needs cool?) In the video the band performs on stage, and Linda does not try any sinuous slinky moves, but rather does a little hop at the end of each chorus, probably like she did with her daughters when they recorded the tune, as their little girls' voices can be heard on the recording, giving Wings a whiff of the Partridge Family. It's undeniable that Linda accelerated McCartney's tendency toward occasional dorkiness, like in the beginning of the song when she giggles indulgently as he misses his cue and hams it up. One of the things McCartney lost in the break-up was having Lennon around to cut his corny tendencies, like on *Anthology 3* when Lennon starts mocking McCartney's twee "Teddy Boy" mid-song.

But by putting his wholesome wife front and center and his stepdaughter on the backing vocals, he was defiantly saying, "Yes, I am a family man, and actually, that *is* cooler than wearing a military jacket and making films about flies crawling over naked bodies." By not being afraid to be uncool, he was actually cooler. Around and around in a circle—ahh, c moon. Over the years, he would do many songs for animated children's films.

Since the A-side "Hi Hi Hi" was banned, "C Moon" got played a lot instead and became a top five hit in its own right.

In the video, he sported the mullet that Bowie would as Ziggy Stardust; cousin to the shag popularized by David Cassidy, Florence Henderson, and Rod Stewart. It almost looks cool in those early days, but when McCartney added the mustache it started edging out of "C Moon" territory.

I FOUND OUT—LENNON

REC. AUTUMN 1970, ABBEY ROAD, LENNON/ONO/SPECTOR (PRODUCERS), LENNON (V, G), VOORMANN (B), STARR (D), ALBUM *PLASTIC ONO BAND*

Another prime cut borne of primal therapy, "I Found Out" is in the minimalist "Cold Turkey" vein with the main instrument being Lennon's voice. Plumbing new depths of snarling bitterness, he launches into his parents for not wanting him and does the same thing to his father in real life the year he recorded the song.

Depending on whom you believe, Lennon's dad, Alf, dropped out of Lennon's life till Lennon became famous—or, he made sporadic attempts to reconnect but had always been rebuffed by the mother's side of the family. Either way, in the mid-sixties he turned up on Lennon's doorstep and would thereafter occasionally hit his son up for money. He even recorded some old-fashioned easy listening songs and snagged a teenage wife (he looked a lot like his son, if his son had lived sixty years with one foot in the gutter and lost his teeth).

But in 1970, Alf had the misfortune of dropping by during the same period Dr. Janov was guiding Lennon into reliving his childhood trauma. Lennon went berserk on Alf, denouncing him for all the agony he'd caused. Lennon took back the little house he'd given Alf and threatened to have his father shot if he told the press. Terrified, the old man fled and they never saw each other again, though Lennon did send him flowers from America on his deathbed in the mid-seventies.

Because of his parents' failure, Lennon was forever searching for the key to fix his pain, and in "I Found Out" Lennon lists all the ways he tried to self-medicate. In a scathing companion piece to "God," he rues how stardom, sex, heroin, cocaine, and religion (Christianity and Hinduism) are all just traps in the long run. He also denounces the hippies who pretend they're his brothers but are just out to use him.

He sings that ultimately the only answer is to have the courage to feel the original pain caused by your childhood dysfunction instead of constantly running from it into the arms of a new illusory crutch. By confronting the pain and working through it, you can one day learn to get beyond it.

And disillusionment has its benefits. When one discovers that everyone, from parents to gurus, are phony or inadequate, then you know you don't have to believe anyone when they say you can't do something. Once you get your head clear, no one can really hurt you but yourself (unless they have a gun, that is).

MONKBERRY MOON DELIGHT—MCCARTNEY

REC. 11/70–12/70, COLUMBIA STUDIOS, MIXED AT SOUND RECORDERS STUDIOS, LA, 2/71–3/71, PAUL/LINDA McCARTNEY (WRITERS/PRODUCERS), McCARTNEY (V, B, P), SEIWELL (D), SPINOZZA OR McCRACKEN (G), LINDA McCARTNEY (BV), ALBUM *RAM*

Backed by what sounds like a villainous circus organ from a creepy 1930s cartoon, McCartney lurches in with a voice that has gone beyond Little Richard into demented Screamin' Jay Hawkins territory. In Hawkins's seminal hit "I Put a Spell on You" (1956), he shrieked, gargled, cackled, and guffawed like an unhinged black Vincent Price. Onstage he would rise from a coffin bearing voodoo props. Later, Tom Waits would take up his growling, guttural mantle.

In his incendiary *Rolling Stone* interview, Lennon expressed surprise at McCartney's first album, saying he expected more from him. At the dawn of 1971, McCartney found himself in the position of being dismissed by the critics while Lennon—and Harrison!—were heaped with praise. Pelted with tomatoes in his mind, he realized he must catch up or be left behind.

He goes to the piano in the attic while the wild wind howls. He's getting older, his hair's a mess, he's in his pajamas, his stomach is in knots from the bad reviews, and the rats are in the walls (both real farm rats and the ex-bandmates in his mind).

But then he sees Linda giving the kids their milk and it inspires him to get back in touch with his own absurd inner child. "When my kids were young they used to call milk 'monk' for whatever reason that kids do—I think it's magical the way that kids can develop better names for things than the real ones. In fact as a joke, Linda and I still occasionally refer to an object by that child-language name. So, monk was always milk, and monkberry moon delight was a fantasy drink, rather like 'Love Potion No. 9,' hence the line in the song 'sipping monkberry moon delight.' It was a fantasy milk shake."[4]

Linda echoes his words like a gum-smacking, seen-it-all, hand-on-her-hip New York moll. Her singing gilds the razor's edge of flatness with surprising defiance, as coached meticulously by her perfectionist husband. Finally, he degenerates into eerie howling and spastic mumbling.

Hawkins would go on to release "Monkberry Moon Delight" as a single in 1973.

REMEMBER—LENNON

REC. AUTUMN 1970, ABBEY ROAD, LENNON/ONO/SPECTOR (PRODUCERS), LENNON (V, P), VOORMANN (B), STARR (D), ALBUM *PLASTIC ONO BAND*

Hammering the piano staccato and relentlessly like a ticking bomb, Lennon recalls how when he was young it seemed the outlaw heroes always escaped. Perhaps he is thinking how different it is now, in the aftermath of being busted and Ono losing their baby. He segues into remembering the earliest authorities in his life: narcissistic, phony parents who forced him to do whatever suited them.

The beat cuts to half time as Lennon's vocal soars, exhorting himself not to regret what he's done. Perhaps he's thinking of all the bridges he'd burned in the last two years: to his band, to his first wife, to the UK establishment. Thinking clearly thanks to the catharsis of primal therapy, he tells himself to remember this moment of respite in the future, when life will no doubt threaten to drive him crazy again. Then the relentless pounding resumes, in a stunning display of how to milk power out of the most minimal accompaniment, until he screams to remember November 5 and an explosion ends the song.

On that date the English commemorate the death of Guy Fawkes. In 1605, Catholics realized King James was not going to grant them religious tolerance, so Fawkes joined a movement called the Gunpowder Plot to kill the king. Fawkes was put in charge of blowing up Parliament but was captured. Before the authorities could hang him, he leaped to his death. The Guy Fawkes Mask would be popularized by the film *V for Vendetta* and the Occupy Wallstreet Movement.

Lennon said he just ad-libbed the "Remember the 5th of November" line. Afterward, the take degenerated into him goofing around and becoming unusable, so "I cut it there and just exploded, it was a good joke . . . I thought it was just poignant that we should blow up the Houses of Parliament."[5] That fall he would blow up the House of the Beatles with his *Rolling Stone* interview. The song carries all the fear and conviction of a man who left the golden nest for an uncertain future because he wanted to be free.

HEAR ME LORD—HARRISON

REC. 5/70–8/70, ABBEY ROAD, MIXED 8/70–9/70, TRIDENT STUDIOS, HARRISON/SPECTOR (PRODUCERS), HARRISON (V, G), GORDON (D), CLAPTON (G), WRIGHT (P), PRESTON (K), WHITLOCK (O), RADLE (B), PRICE (TRUMPET), KEYS (SAX), ALBUM *ALL THINGS MUST PASS*

Originally presented to the other Beatles by Harrison during the *Get Back* sessions, "Hear Me Lord" is a prayer song in the vein of *Godspell*'s "Day by Day" (which it predates). Harrison implores the Lord to forgive him for ignoring Him and asks for His help in rising above desire. Gary Wright's piano riff gleams as Harrison's guitar slices through Preston's moody organ chords. Spector multitracks Harrison's vocals to create a choir.

WOMAN IS THE NIGGER OF THE WORLD—LENNON

REC. MARCH 1972, RECORD PLANT EAST, NYC, LENNON/ONO/SPECTOR (PRODUCERS), LENNON (V, G), KELTNER (D), THE INVISIBLE STRINGS, ELEPHANT'S MEMORY: STAN BRONSTEIN (SAX), GARY VAN SCYOC (B), ADAM IPPOLITO (P, O), WAYNE "TEX" GABRIEL (G), RICHARD FRANK JR. (D, PERCUSSION), SINGLE: US 4/24/72 (57), ALSO ON *SOME TIME IN NEW YORK CITY*

The inspiration for the slogan came to Yoko through her struggles in three male-dominated milieus: 1950s Japan, the New York art scene, and the London rock clique. When she did an interview with the British radical/intellectual woman's magazine *Nova* in 1969, she said the phrase and they put it on the cover.

Always ransacking commercials and posters for slogans, Lennon did a demo version of the song then filed it away, but over the years the phrase kept popping up in his mind when he would argue with Yoko about his inherent sexism.

Their love affair was unique in its time in many respects, especially in how she forced him to confront his own chauvinism. The struggle for civil rights inspired the antiwar movement, but in both movements, the men continued to treat women unequally. By the end of the 1960s, the women's liberation movement broke off to become its own separate force, working to stop discrimination, pay inequality, and sexism.

Seeing the title of the song today, most people assume it was the moment Lennon truly jumped the shark. But a number of Beatles books have said that—beyond its abhorrent title—it was one of his greatest vocal performances and one of Spector's finest production jobs. *Fab Four FAQ 2.0* maintains that if the music and passionate singing were used for any other song it would have been one of his greatest.[6]

Lyrically, it revisits many of the techniques the oppressors use to keep the masses down as described in "Working Class Hero": Women are attacked, whether they're too smart or too dumb, to undercut their confidence and make them scared to be free. Yet women have it even worse than the men. They're told they're only qualified to take care of the home and children (this was written back in 1972), and then when they get older their husbands leave them for someone younger.

Elephant's Memory lays down a thunderous backing dominated by a terrific sax sound that later generations would primarily associate with the *Saturday Night Live* band. In the climax, Spector's strings advance like a lumbering stalker looming ever closer as a manic Lennon works himself into a demented rant, howling, "We make her paint her face and dance!" over and over again. It brings to mind the manic scene from the classic feature film *I Am Cuba* in which the shantytown girl must take a job as a dancer in a bar filled with rich Americans who run her ragged around the room.

Countless painted women had danced for Lennon in the last ten years, from the ladies of the night he knew in Hamburg to the "slags" on his tours. He recalled, "Derek [Taylor, publicist] and Neil [Aspinall, road manager]'s rooms were always full of junk and whores and fuck knows what . . . such a heavy scene it was. They didn't call them groupies then, they called it something else. But if we couldn't have groupies, we'd have whores and everything, whatever. Whatever was going . . . Derek and Neil, that was their job, and Mal, but I'm not going into all that."[7]

The book *Ticket to Ride* tells of a young journalist's experience on the first American tour and says that Lennon even bought hookers for the press corps that followed them around the country.[8] *Paul McCartney: A Life* recounts Lennon ordering in call girls to the band's hotel suite for an orgy and throwing dollar bills on them, crying, "It's on me!"[9]

Inevitably the song was banned from the radio, but Lennon hustled like crazy to try to explain himself. He put the *Nova* issue in which Yoko had originally proclaimed the statement on the cover of the single. At a press conference with reporters from black magazines *Jet* and *Ebony*, Lennon said the slur was used as a metaphor and not meant to insult people. *Jet* put Lennon and Ono on the cover with their friend, black comedian Dick Gregory, with the headline, "Ex-Beatle tells how black stars changed his life."

He performed the song on *The Dick Cavett Show*, for which ABC insisted Cavett apologize in advance. In the interview with Cavett, Lennon maintained, "Obviously there's a few people who reacted strangely to it but usually they were white *and male!* All my black friends feel I have quite a right to say it because they understand."[10]

Many assumed he was just trying to give himself license to get off saying the worst word possible by cloaking it in a moral feminist critique. The live version on the *Lennon Anthology* is weirdly embarrassing. He gamely tries to get people to scream along, but no one does.

Lennon called radio stations and did interviews to get them to play it, but the stations would play the record in the studio while they interviewed him but not broadcast the song over the air. The same week Sammy Davis Jr.'s "The Candy Man" was number one, the song limped to number fifty-seven, Lennon's worst showing in his lifetime.

TOO MANY PEOPLE—MCCARTNEY

Rec. 11/70–12/70, Columbia Studios, mixed at Sound Recorders Studios, LA, 2/71–3/71, Paul/Linda McCartney (producers), McCartney (v, b), Seiwell (d), McCracken (g), Linda McCartney (bv), Album *Ram*, also B-side to Uncle Albert/Admiral Halsey

No song by McCartney captures the loneliness and anger of the Beatles' feud as intensely as "Too Many People," in which all his vitriol spewed out like an infected zit. The lyrics read as the anti-Beatles version of Starr's "Early 1970." McCartney is getting pushed around by Lennon going underground and letting himself be a mouthpiece for Communist party radicals. One of them, Yippie A. J. Weberman, even took a break from harassing Dylan to stage a protest in front of Linda's father's Park Avenue residence on Christmas Eve 1970.[11] McCartney also slams Lennon for sinking into heroin with Ono, losing weight, and just eating cake, as junkies have a notorious sweet tooth.

Not only was Lennon preachy politically, Harrison was religiously preachy to the max as well. And all of them were trying to grab McCartney's cake: under the groups' contract, all the profits of each ex-Beatles' albums go to the company and then the total is divided among them. (Although, truth be told, Harrison was the biggest seller at the moment, so the set up benefited McCartney in 1971.)

McCartney vows that he's not going to hold back his feelings anymore, though he did temper the opening line. Originally it was "Yoko took your lucky break and broke it in two," but he changed "Yoko" to "you."

The performance opens with a malevolent groan that could either be an effects-treated guitar, a harmonium, or far-off horns. The sense of physical space in the recording conjures the dread of walking into a deserted mausoleum in a horror film, underscoring the "lucky break" taunt. No doubt it is meant to instill the unease in Lennon and Co. that they will never be able to measure up in the future without McCartney. It perfectly captures the eerie foreboding when partners are divorcing, with one wondering privately if he is making a mistake even while trying to scare the other that he will regret it. When Lennon heard it, did he have an inkling that he would only have one more number one record in his lifetime? McCartney whips himself into a war dance, dancing around Hugh McCracken's guitar pyrotechnics with falsetto shrieks and whoops, banging the floor tom drum.

Lennon would counter on his next album with "How Do You Sleep," which would also be magnificently played and produced. But it is so overtly about McCartney that its subject can't be separated from the performance, making it difficult to enjoy beyond the context of Lennon's character assassination. By being lyrically just vague enough and played within an arresting sound scape, "Too Many People" transcends the backdrop that inspired it.

GIMME SOME TRUTH—LENNON

Rec. 1971, Ascot Sound Studios, Lennon/Ono/Spector (producers), Lennon (v, g), Harrison (lead g), Voormann (b), White (d), Hopkins (p), Andy Davis (acoustic g), Rod Linton (acoustic g), Album *Imagine*, Covers: Jakob Dylan with Dhani Harrison, Primal Scream, Travis, Billy Idol, Matthew Sweet and Susanna Hoff, Pearl Jam

An acoustic demo of this song was recorded during the *Get Back* sessions in January 1969. McCartney chimes in on the chorus, and as can be heard on YouTube, the song is almost cheerful, miles away from the nauseous despair of the final version.

It would be interesting to know whether at that point the song already had the lyrics denouncing paranoid egomaniacs or they were an addition from 1971 aimed at a certain ex-bandmate. Also, no doubt all the scorn heaped upon Lennon and Ono between 1969 and 1971 turned the song darker.

Yet despite the rage, there's vengeful joy in his performance, the catharsis of a brilliant wordsmith at the height of his powers unleashing a hilariously cynical barrage of bile. There's spiteful glee in the perfectly phrased proto-raps of bitterness he spits out against a "short hair" establishment utterly beneath contempt. It's as sharp as Dylan's "Subterranean Homesick Blues," though Lennon's songs were almost always succinct whereas Dylan's luxuriated in precedent-smashing length.

Unlike the political songs that would follow in 1972's *Some Time in New York City*, this is one of his most timeless because it is unspecific—as relevant to the Iraq Invasion in 2003 as it was in 1971. Most essentially, it's witty. He can't decide whether to spend his money on dope or rope, and we don't know if the rope is to lynch the politicians or to just give up and hang himself. With humor as black as could be, he spoke for every guy of draft age deciding whether it was time to run through the jungle or run for Canada.

In high school, the schoolmaster regularly caned Lennon. In his twenties, his records were burned in the South. Now, he called out "Tricky Dicky" by name and brought down the wrath of the US government, immersing himself in a quagmire of deportation court battles for the next four years. Eventually, his big mouth got him killed.

The song carries the righteous indignation of "I Found Out," but unlike that stark and primitive track, here Harrison perfectly compliments the vitriol with the desolate beauty of his distorted and chiming slide guitar. Harrison stopped by to play on half of *Imagine*, and Lennon later exclaimed it was the best Harrison had played in his life. As Harrison harbored the desire for a McCartney-less Beatles, he was proving to Lennon what he could still bring to the table.

DEAR BOY—MCCARTNEY

Rec. 11/70–12/70, Columbia Studios, NYC, mixed at Sound Recorders Studios, LA, 2/71–3/71, Paul/Linda McCartney (writers/producers), McCartney (v, b, p), Seiwell (d), Spinozza or McCracken (g), Linda McCartney (bv), Album *Ram*

The Beatles' greatness was due in no small part to their competitors who kept them on their toes as they all strove to be the kings of the '60s. Dylan kept them lyrically innovative. The Stones prodded them to be ever more rebellious, the Who more instrumentally anarchic. The Motown hit factory challenged them to compose soulful pop masterpieces. But for melodicist McCartney, there was no finer rival than the Beach Boys' Brian Wilson, whose shimmering *Pet Sounds* pushed the Beatles to top it with *Sgt. Pepper*.

Now bereft of his partner, McCartney went back and listened to the other musical contemporary who taught him the most. *Ram* is McCartney's most sustained homage to the Beach Boys, especially "The Back Seat of My Car" and "Dear Boy." The songs are rife with layer upon layer of lush bass and falsetto harmonies, swirling "doo doo doos," and other trademarks of the Wilson brothers.

McCartney's lone partner in *Ram* was someone who didn't realize she was being drafted into the enterprise until it was too late—his wife. "God, I tell you I worked her on the album," McCartney said. "Because she hadn't done an awful lot, so it was a little bit out of tune. I was not too pleasant to live with, I suppose, then. She was all right; she took it. She understood that it had to be good and you couldn't let any shit through. I gave her a hard time, I must say, but we were pleased with the results; it just meant we really forced it."[12]

"Dear Boy" was inspired by Linda's first marriage to her college sweetheart, Joseph Melvin See Jr. They were wed in June 1962 and daughter Heather was born six-and-a-half months later. In 1965, the anthropologist/ geologist See wanted the family to move out of the country, but instead they divorced. McCartney sings about how amazed he is that See didn't realize what a great woman he had in Linda and goes on to credit her with saving him when he was down and out. Years later, McCartney commented that he was glad that he never actually told See that the song was about him, since See shot himself in 2000.[13]

Lennon, meanwhile, thought that *he* was the boy who blew it with the girl who was "just the cutest thing around." Apparently Lennon jumped to that conclusion because McCartney had long been known as "The Cute Beatle." The Beatles had changed the sex of their song models before; Lennon turned Peter Fonda into a woman for "She Said She Said." But it's pretty bizarre to think of McCartney pounding the piano and going on about how he's so cute.

In the tradition of earlier Beatles deep-cut classics like "I'm Looking through You," the song is so short and tight (two minutes, fifteen seconds), it's over before you barely have time to appreciate what an inventive minor gem it is, an example of a man creating a piece of art with the muse who saved him.

CRIPPLED INSIDE—LENNON

REC. 1971, ASCOT SOUND STUDIOS, LENNON/ONO/SPECTOR (PRODUCERS), LENNON (V, ELECTRIC G), HARRISON (DOBRO), VOORMANN (B), WHITE (D),

HOPKINS (P), TED TURNER (ACOUSTIC G), ROD LINTON (ACOUSTIC G), JOHN TOUT (ACOUSTIC G), STEVE BRENDELL (UPRIGHT B), ALBUM *IMAGINE*

Lennon's uncle encouraged him to draw. By the time he was in high school, he was compiling his poetry, cartoons, and stories into *The Daily Howl*, the precursor to his mid-sixties books *In His Own Write* and *A Spaniard in the Works*. (Even at that early age, *The Daily Howl*'s title reflected his penchant for puns by being a howl of laughter and of angst. It also revealed he was primal screaming from the beginning and was another apparently coincidental Beat Generation reference, like their band name.)

Frequently his sketches were of deformed people. His friends reported that Lennon wasn't above making fun of the handicapped as a drunken youth on the bus, due to a cruel streak of humor and his phobia of them. One of the quirkiest aspects of Beatlemania was how he'd pull Quasimodo faces at the cameras, hunching up, sticking his tongue in front of his bottom row of teeth, and twisting his hands like a cripple.

In the footage from the Beatles' first concert in America after the *Ed Sullivan Show*, it's initially confusing, then bizarre, to see Lennon making fun of the handicapped people seated in the front row by stomping his foot and clapping his hands like a "spastic." While shock rappers like Eminem do similar things in their music, it would be hard to imagine Eminem actually making fun of the crippled kids in the front row.

Parents would bring their children in wheelchairs to see the Beatles backstage in the hope that their presence might somehow rejuvenate the kids, perhaps even heal them. Thus the jerk who had mocked the afflicted was now surrounded by them. Instant karma, indeed. It no doubt contributed to his Jesus complex.

The music of "Crippled Inside" seems to have originated from a *Get Back* jam session based on the old folk tune "Long Lost John." Lyrically, it is in the tradition of "I'm a Loser" and "Nowhere Man," as Lennon both attacks himself and others who try to hide their psychological problems behind the pleasant mask of conformity: going to church with combed hair, shined shoes, suit, tie, and a smile. (It could also be in response to McCartney's "3 Legs," in which he called the other Beatles a three-legged dog.) Unlike those earlier tunes, however, Lennon adds humor to the mix. In sarcastic counterpoint to the dark theme, the music and vocals have a jaunty, old-time country feel, as if Lennon's doing the old soft shoe on a Mississippi riverboat.

Voormann plays the stand-up bass and Harrison plays the Dobro, a brand of resonator guitar that was the missing link between acoustic and electric guitars. In the old dance hall days, the drums and horns would drown out the acoustic guitars, so they put metal cones under the strings instead of the regular wood to make the sound resonate more. Even after electric guitars were developed, bluegrass and blues artists continued to use the resonator guitars because of their unique sound.

RUN OF THE MILL—HARRISON

Rec. 5/70–8/70, Abbey Road, mixed 8/70–9/70, Trident Studios, Harrison/Spector (producers), Harrison (v, g), Wright (p) Gordon (d), Bobby Whitlock (o), Radle (b), Price (trumpet), Keys (sax), Album *All Things Must Pass*

Maybe Lennon and McCartney didn't perceive Harrison's growth because they saw him all the time. Maybe by taking him for granted, they actually spurred on his musical maturation. Perhaps the others didn't want to acknowledge that he was improving because they didn't want to give up space on the albums.

"Run of the Mill" is a portrait of Harrison's final year in the group. He sings that each day is a chance for them to realize how he's grown—or disregard him again—and he doesn't have much hope that his position will improve. As disrespect, Allen Klein, Ono, and heroin drive their wedges through the group, Harrison is stunned that he's lost the others' friendship, but he can see it in their eyes. He debates whether to speak up and fight for his place in the band or just leave the group with their blessing.

Such personal musings would be irrelevant to anyone but the biggest Beatles fans if Harrison hadn't so artfully written the words to be open-ended and applicable to anyone. The haunting soundscape is lonely like *The White Album*'s "Long Long Long," but with the grandeur of mournful horns, strings, trumpet, sax, and organ. A touching work of maturity by a little brother who saw more clearly than the others, realizing that he loved them but it was time to move on.

ISOLATION—LENNON

Rec. Autumn 1970, Abbey Road, Lennon/Ono/Spector (producers), Lennon (v, p), Voormann (b), Starr (d), Album *Plastic Ono Band*

From Lennon to Springsteen, the biggest winners like to pretend they're losers, underdogs in the movies of their minds. Lovers with a taste for drama like to think of themselves as Romeo and Juliet persecuted by ignorant and malevolent fools. Lennon and Ono also saw themselves as just a little boy and girl out to save the world.

Neglected kids often get into trouble because any attention is better than none. The parentless Lennon picked fights and got into trouble at school. And while no one deserved the abuse heaped on the couple, it's hard to imagine a lover Lennon could have picked who would have antagonized conservatives more than Yoko Ono. (Unless he picked her alter ego in the Beatles spoof *The Rutles*, a Nazi.) Not only was she "foreign," she was pretentious about performance art.

He picked a partner he knew would annoy people, shoved her into everyone's face twenty-four/seven through the media, and then cried that he was in pain because the world didn't accept her. So how much of a poser was Lennon?

In psychology, a person with a martyr complex desires the feeling of suffering from being persecuted because of his moral superiority. It's a complex related to masochism, the desire to feel pain. Hence, Lennon's near-celebration in "The Ballad of John and Yoko" is that they're going to crucify him.

After being condemned by the Bible Belt for having the delusional megalomania to mention himself and Jesus in the same breath, he affected the image of Jesus as a sort of bizarre revenge. A twentieth-century noncelibate Jesus, but one who chose as his mate someone who further underscored his integrity by symbolically reminding people that all Asian people were not faceless Viet Cong or Japanese war enemies.

Lennon got plenty of flak from the British public because he left his wife and got Ono pregnant. There was also the racism element, no doubt heightened by the fact that the United States was at war with an Asian country. Then Lennon and Ono released the nonmusical, avant-garde album *Two Virgins* with themselves displayed in full frontal nudity on the cover. The British police decided he'd gone so far outside public decency they no longer had to give him the "MBE" treatment and busted the couple for weed. They dragged Lennon and the pregnant Ono to jail, and then forced them to return to court and push their way through a mob of more than three hundred. The ensuing stress contributed to Ono's miscarriage.

The couple recorded the last heartbeats of the stillborn John Ono Lennon and included them on their second avant-garde LP *Life with the Lions*. It was a pun on the name of a popular British TV show, but it really referred to how the Romans would entertain themselves by throwing the Christians to the lions. The album jacket featured them surrounded by the mob outside the courthouse.

For the song "Isolation," Lennon added an organ to the stark Voormann-Starr rhythm section. With a candor few other performers possessed back then, he admits he fears everyone. The highlight is the middle eight, another example of his habit of appropriation/homage. It's remarkable that it wasn't another lawsuit, as it is clearly lifted from "Oh I Apologize," the B-side of Barret Strong's "Money," which the Beatles had definitively covered on their second album.[14] Lennon revises Strong's words to berate the closed-minded provincials by singing that he knows they'll never understand how much they've hurt him because they're just victims of an insane society.

As Voormann's bass drops out to leave just Starr's laid-back swing, Lennon's double-tracked voice rings out at the masses, McCartney, the cops, and the media in one of the most arresting moments of his career, panning from one side of the stereo to the other. Pink Floyd's Roger Waters called it one of his all-time favorite songs, which makes sense as he went on to be the auteur of the epic of isolation, *The Wall*.

DEAR FRIEND—MCCARTNEY

Rec. August 1971, Abbey Road, Paul/Linda McCartney (writers/producers), McCartney (v, p), Seiwell (d), Linda McCartney (bv), Album *Wild Life*

Ram's back cover included the subtle snapshot of one beetle screwing another. The front featured McCartney holding a ram by horns, so for *Imagine* Lennon inserted a postcard in which he holds a pig by the ears, grinning. He and Harrison pilloried McCartney in the blistering "How Do You Sleep." Lennon also continued to be a loose cannon in the press. He sent an open letter to McCartney via the music mag *Melody Maker* in which he wrote that McCartney had said to him, "'Ringo and George are going to break you John' . . . Who's the guy threatening to 'finish' Ringo and Maureen, who was warning me on the phone two weeks ago? Who said he'd 'get us' whatever the cost? As I've said before—have you ever thought that you might possibly be wrong about something?" He then slagged off McCartney's father-in-law.[15]

Obviously, fighting with the vicious Lennon in public was like dancing around gasoline with a match. And while Lennon forgot the fact whenever convenient, to McCartney they had been best friends, which was why he had overreacted and botched the whole "dealing with Yoko" thing in the first place.

McCartney began working on the song that would become "Dear Friend" during the *Ram* sessions. For many critics it was the sole redemption of the *Wild Life* album. It was the record's last song, showing the continued primacy of the feud in his life, as "Too Many People" had been the first song on *Ram*.

The disconsolate piano brings to mind a man walking through a dark cavern, as McCartney faced the precarious decision of whether to up the arms race of mutually assured destruction. His voice strains at the high end of his register, like a guy who has been bullied but knows he must speak up though he's also afraid. He can't believe they've come so close to the edge, and he's shocked it all means so much to Lennon. Perhaps he's referring to the money and how they were forcing McCartney to stay in the company to avoid paying higher taxes. Perhaps he's referring to Lennon's need to yell his side of the story through the press at everyone else's expense.

The song is famously known as a conciliatory make-up song. With surprising honesty, McCartney sings that he's in love with his friend and wishes him the best with his marriage. But McCartney also asks Lennon if he's a fool and if he's afraid, which sounds like a bit of a provocation, even as his voice is timid in the gloom, a passive-aggressive Gemini as always. Probably it was hard for McCartney to be the guy stepping back saying, "I don't want to fight," even though he had been the one who started it.

McCartney plays the same ruminating piano chords for almost six minutes, mirroring the emotional obsession he couldn't shake. But he uses what he learned on the Thrillington instrumental album to sustain interest through a subtle build in accompaniment with forlorn strings and foreboding horns until everything recedes except the quiet, lonely piano, and then it finally stops as well.

Wild Life was released in the United Kingdom in November 1971 and in the United States in early December. At some point, McCartney called Lennon, and shortly afterward Lennon sent McCartney a Christmas gift, a bootleg of the group's audition for Decca Records. A little after Christmas, the McCartneys dropped by Lennon and Ono's Greenwich Village home, and the former bandmates stopped attacking each other in public. Eventually, the postcard in *Imagine* was changed to one of Lennon playing the panpipes.

Compared to later rap feuds, it was pretty mild. By the end of 1971, the ex-group had made it out of the war zone. There was at least the possibility they could be friends again.

BEHIND THAT LOCKED DOOR—HARRISON

REC. 5/70–8/70, ABBEY ROAD, MIXED 8/70–9/70, TRIDENT STUDIOS, HARRISON/SPECTOR (PRODUCERS), HARRISON (V, G), PRESTON (O), VOORMANN (B), WRIGHT (P), WHITE (D), PETE DRAKE (PEDAL STEEL G), ALBUM *ALL THINGS MUST PASS*, COVERS: OLIVIA NEWTON-JOHN

All Things Must Pass is split between the Spector bombast and the country/folk sound of Dylan, the Band, and Nashville guitar player Pete Drake.[16] The songs that fit into the latter category include "I'd Have You Anytime"

(cowritten by Harrison and Dylan), "If Not for You" (Dylan), "I Live for You" (belatedly released on the 2000 remastered version), "Apple Scruffs," "Ballad of Sir Frankie Crisp," and "Behind That Locked Door."

The Beatles met Dylan at the end of 1964, the night the Bard famously got them all properly stoned for the first time. Though Lennon and Dylan seemed to hit it off the most initially, by the end of the decade it was Harrison whom Dylan was closest to. They shared a deep spirituality (despite their worldly vices) that transcended their Judaism or Hindu denominations, whereas Lennon had a more bipolar relationship with organized religion and New Age beliefs.

Harrison and Dylan wrote "I'd Have You Anytime" when Harrison stayed with Dylan and the Band at the end of 1968. And Harrison was inspired to write "Behind That Locked Door" after seeing Dylan perform at the Isle of Wight Festival in 1969. It was Dylan's first performance since he had retired from the road at the end of 1966. He had been on the go for five solid years and wanted to spend time with his family. The conventional wisdom is that this song is Harrison asking Dylan to come back out from isolation. But the truth is, Dylan had been recording albums consistently even though he didn't tour. Regardless, it's a halcyon tune reminding us to stop crying and start smiling, with fine steel guitar and organ interplay in Dylan's *Nashville Skyline* mode.

Really, it was Harrison who was coming out from behind that locked door. He was the Dave Grohl of his day, rising from the ashes of a group in which he was a secondary member to dominate the charts with statements that he never could have made from within his former band. On the cover of *All Things Must Pass*, he sat calmly on the front lawn of his estate, stone dwarves toppled beside him like the annoying guys he had left behind.

HOW?—LENNON

REC. 6/23/71–7/5/71, ASCOT SOUND STUDIOS, RECORD PLANT EAST, NYC, LENNON/ONO/SPECTOR (PRODUCERS), LENNON (V, P), VOORMANN (B), WHITE (D), HOPKINS (P), BARHAM (VIBRAPHONE), THE FLUX FIDDLERS (STRINGS), ALBUM *IMAGINE*

Alongside Woody Allen and *Peanuts* creator Charles Schulz, Lennon may have done the most to popularize psychotherapy. While in the 1950s manly men with military industrial buzz cuts didn't talk about the skeletons in their closet, by the 1970s more and more people were trying to get in touch with their feelings in group therapy, thanks in no small part to Lucy's psychiatrist booth and Woody's jokes about his shrink. TV specials like *Free to Be You and Me* featured football players like Rosie Greer singing, "It's All Right to Cry" to little Gen Xers. "How?" is an anthem for all sensitive men learning how to feel.

When Lennon frets that he doesn't know how to feel, it seems odd, as his work over the previous ten years had run the manic-depressive gamut of just about every human emotion. He might actually have been one of the most accomplished "feelers" of the twentieth century, introducing new colors of emotional expression in ambiguous songs like "Strawberry Fields Forever."

A typical example of blind self-pity follows when Lennon wonders how he can give love when love is something he has never had. In reality, there are probably only a scant handful of figures in history who were more beloved in their own time than the Beatles. He goes on to ask how he can have feelings when his feelings have always been denied—this from the guy who got to do everything except fly to the moon in a space shuttle. Despite his riches, he was terminally bound up by a childhood in which he was left alone in the crib while his mom went out partying.

But "How?" is a brilliant song if you forget the specifics of Lennon's life. In the end, it was his very blind spot of narcissism that allowed him to tap into the universal feelings of everyone else. Someone with a more mature view of his fortunate position in life would never allow himself to feel such self-pity, which means we would have been denied many great songs.

When he asks how he and his partner can go forward when they don't know where they're going, it fits any relationship at that scary moment when it's come time to make a commitment or not. The warm string arrangement by Sinatra-vet Torrie Zito commiserates with John like the sympathetic birds of Disney movies. Whether the listener is in a high school romance or debating whether to buy a house, it's the aural equivalent of the theme of the novel *The Unbearable Lightness of Being*: the angst of never knowing if the choice you're making is the right one or not.

Lennon commiserates with everyone who's been depressed by a heavy struggle, feeling the world just may be too tough for him after all. It's the opposite of the raging Lennon; it's the scared little boy who gulps, "Oh no"— a performance that took him many takes to get just right.

RAM ON—MCCARTNEY

REC. 11/70–12/70, COLUMBIA STUDIOS, NYC, A&R STUDIO, 1/71, MIXED SOUND STUDIOS, 2/71–3/71, PAUL/LINDA MCCARTNEY (WRITERS/PRODUCERS), MCCARTNEY (V, P, K, UKULELE), LINDA MCCARTNEY (BV), ALBUM *RAM*

Paul Ramon (or Ramone) was a pseudonym McCartney used in the Beatles' early days when they toured Scotland opening for Johnny Gentle. (The punk band the Ramones took their name from his alter ego in homage.) McCartney later revived the identity when he contributed to a Steve Miller album in 1969. Also, by 1971 he had a farm with rams and sheep. And, as the Beatles always loved dirty puns, *Ram* had that aspect to it. Most importantly, the album title expressed McCartney's resolution to plow forward with his life and smash his way out of the Beatles as a business entity so he could be free. Now that he was recovering from his post-break-up devastation, he was committed to seeing the happy side of life again.

Hypnotic, ghostly harmonies swirl around McCartney as he strums a ukulele and exhorts the listeners to ram on and give their hearts to somebody right away, intermittently accompanied by an electric piano with just a hint of distortion. It's almost as if he had taken the "Can You Take Me Back" fragment from *The White Album* and developed it into a stripped-down music hall piece that treads the line between major and minor key, vaguely haunting and uplifting at the same time.

For the album, he revived the *Sgt. Pepper* trope of reprising the theme at the end, something he'd continue to do on many of his ensuing albums over the years—either a trademark or a way to fill up the album sides, your call.

ANGELA—LENNON

REC. MARCH 1972, RECORD PLANT EAST, NYC, LENNON/ONO (WRITERS) LENNON/ONO/SPECTOR (PRODUCERS), LENNON (V, G), KELTNER (D), ELEPHANT'S MEMORY: STAN BRONSTEIN (SAX), GARY VAN SCYOC (B), ADAM IPPOLITO (P, O), RICHARD FRANK JR. (D, PERCUSSION), ALBUM *SOME TIME IN NEW YORK CITY*

Between 1971 and 1972, Lennon, the Rolling Stones, and Bob Dylan all released songs of solidarity with the Black Panthers. McCartney had already released his hymn to the civil rights movement on *The White Album* with "Blackbird." Dylan released his as a nonalbum single called "George Jackson," recorded in November 1971.

When Black Panther Angela Davis was imprisoned, the "Free Angela" campaign asked Lennon to contribute, so he refashioned a song with which he'd been tinkering. It started out as "JJ," about a lady who "couldn't get laid at all," then morphed into a peace song named "People." With Ono he molded it to suit Davis's story, calling her a political prisoner in an era before Amnesty International popularized the term.

They praise her as a teacher and comfort her with the idea that the love and hope of freedom fighters is a wind that never stops moving around the world, albeit slowly. Even though Davis is behind bars, her brothers and sisters are breathing together with her and soon she will be returned to them. (The themes of wind and breathing show this to be a predominantly Ono composition.) When Lennon and Ono sing that the world watches her, they quote the famous phrase civil rights marchers would chant when Southern racists would attack them with clubs, hoses, or guard dogs. The images were captured by TV cameramen, exposing the brutality to millions of viewers and turning the tide of public opinion against the Southern whites.

Spector's strings and Elephant's Memory paint a suitably strong mid-tempo backdrop. The highlight is a sumptuous organ that sounds akin to Steely Dan's "Dirty Work," also from 1972. Ono's voice duets nicely with Lennon. Her vibrato is a touch ostentatious, but it's her nicest singing on his albums.

The Stones' Angela Davis tribute, "Sweet Black Angel" from *Exile on Main Street* has the edge, however, assuming one isn't offended by Jagger's imitation of a stereotypical black sharecropper circa 1933. You have to read the lyrics on the Internet to understand what he's saying, which makes the song more accessible by making it basically meaningless to the 99 percent of the listeners who, forty years later, have no idea who Angela Davis is. The fact that they made it the B-side to "Tumbling Dice" also shows they were confident they'd captured a unique, earthy country-blues groove.

In the end, perhaps the most poignant aspect of "Angela" is when Ono and Lennon sing about how "they" shot down Angela's man, never suspecting what their own future would hold.

MAMA'S LITTLE GIRL—MCCARTNEY

Rec. March 1972, Olympic Sound Studios, mixed in 1987 by McCartney and Chris Thomas, AIR Studios, London, McCartney (v, b), Linda McCartney (bv), Laine (g, bv), McCullough (g), Seiwell (d), Single: B-side of Put It There: UK 1/29/90 (32); US 5/1/90 (failed to chart)

An acoustic ballad like "Mother Nature's Son" from a father's perspective, the song is a gentle portrait of McCartney's daughter playing on the side of a mountain and singing. One lyric gives a touch of ambiguity when he says his heart needs some time to take it all in. Perhaps he's hinting at the growth required in becoming a parent and how it necessitates moving beyond the preoccupation with self.

Originally recorded during the *Red Rose Speedway* sessions, he performed it for his 1973 TV special *James Paul McCartney*, but it did not make the final cut, just as it did not make the album, though substandard dross did. Almost twenty years later, it was released as the flipside to "Put It There." The A-side was a tribute to McCartney's father, so it made for nice symmetry.

OH MY LOVE—LENNON

REC. 6/23/71–7/5/71, ASCOT SOUND STUDIOS, LENNON/ONO (WRITERS), LENNON/ONO/SPECTOR (PRODUCERS), LENNON (V, P), HARRISON (G), VOORMANN (B), WHITE (D, TIBETAN CYMBALS), HOPKINS (ELECTRIC P), ALBUM *IMAGINE*

Lennon wrote this around the same time he composed 1969 the classic "Don't Let Me Down." In both songs, he proclaims that he is in love for the first time in his life, which may be why he picked one for the Beatles' single and set the other aside for two years. But whereas "Don't Let Me Down" had an edge of desperation, "Oh My Love" celebrates the blissful peace he shared with Ono in their finest moments together.

Harrison's gentle guitar work tastefully sets the mood then harmonizes with Lennon's Steinway as Nicky Hopkins joins them on a second piano. In one of his most delicate vocals, Lennon marvels that his eyes are wide open and can see for the first time. Coming from the visionary whose kaleidoscope eyes had already traveled across the universe, such lyrics might sound like hyperbole. But Lennon's ability to articulate this vision of inner peace creates the experience in the listener's mind, or at least suggests it as a possibility to envision and perhaps somehow to achieve.

"Oh My Love" was cowritten by Ono, and her hallmarks are apparent in the lyrics, as they celebrate just looking at the wind, trees, clouds, and sky, with mind wide open. Everything for once clear in his heart, all the emotions of life pass through—sorrow, love, dreams—but do not disrupt the overall equanimity. Though written before the primal era, it suggests the tranquil state of being that was the ultimate goal of the therapy. The song is the inner peace counterpart to the world peace envisioned in *Imagine*'s title track, symbolically accentuated with Alan White's Tibetan cymbals.

BALLAD OF SIR FRANKIE CRISP (LET IT ROLL)—HARRISON

REC. 5/70–8/70, ABBEY ROAD, MIXED 8/70–9/70, TRIDENT STUDIOS, HARRISON/SPECTOR (PRODUCERS), HARRISON (V, G), PETE DRAKE (PEDAL STEEL G), VOORMANN (B), WHITE (D), PRESTON (O), WRIGHT (ELECTRIC P), WHITLOCK (P), ALBUM *ALL THINGS MUST PASS*

The most spiritual Beatle possessed a split personality like Lennon. While Harrison chanted to the Lord, he also lived in a titanic mansion and indulged in drugs and extramarital sex. But while he would eventually try to clean up the sex and drugs, he would always love Friar Park, a massive Victorian-Gothic manor house in Henley-on-Thames, an hour-and-a-half west of London. Its 35 acres and 120 rooms would cost Harrison 200,000 pounds when he bought it in 1970, just in time to be featured on the cover of *All Things Must Pass.*

Built in the nineteenth century by an eccentric lawyer named Sir Frank Crisp, it would have been a good place for Harry Potter to hang out, as bloggers have noted. The outside featured turrets, gargoyles, and stone dwarves; the inside housed light switches made to look like monks' skulls. The living room was three stories high with a balcony overlooking it. The multilevel artificial lake with waterfall held stepping-stones just under the surface so you could cross it and look like you were walking on water. (How apropos for the guru posers.) There were also labyrinthine tunnels that required the use of a boat to navigate.

Over the years, Harrison would find Zen maintaining the extensive gardens with the help of ten workers including both of his older brothers. Gradually, he'd spend more time gardening than playing music, returning to the drudgery of promoting albums to pay for the garden. He dedicated his autobiography to gardeners everywhere.

Delighted with his new home during the making of *All Things Must Pass,* he wrote "Ballad of Sir Frankie Crisp" in tribute to it, one of the catchiest and most haunting songs on the record. Spector said the melody was so strong many artists would cover it if Harrison changed the lyrics so they were about something more universal than his cool estate. But Harrison left the lyrics as they were, a cinematic recreation of a day in the life at the manor.[17]

Nashville guitar master Pete Drake contributes, but the effect isn't country. It was more magical folk rock with a hint of that echoey gloom Harrison had employed on "Long Long Long," but here held in check by up-tempo piano, drums, and cathedral-sparkling organ. Low-pitched backing vocals murmur indecipherably in the distance, like the gargoyles and dwarves looming in the mist, another example of the sound that would influence next-generation indie rockers like R.E.M.

HOLD ON—LENNON

REC. AUTUMN 1970, ABBEY ROAD, LENNON/ONO/SPECTOR (PRODUCERS), LENNON (V, G), VOORMANN (B), STARR (D), ALBUM *PLASTIC ONO BAND*

Another admission of emotional fragility, Lennon sings about how when you have no one else but yourself you just gotta tell yourself to hold on. Though he mentions his own name and Ono's, it doesn't detract, as the feelings of being overwhelmed are universal.

The band tested various tempos and genres for thirty-two takes before Lennon discovered a gentle tremolo guitar style that matched the soothing reassurance of the lyrics. To further cheer himself up, in the middle of the song he calls out, "Cookie!" à la the Cookie Monster of *Sesame Street*, which had recently premiered on PBS in November 1969. (Lennon could no doubt relate to a muppet with a bottomless appetite to consume the object of his addiction. He also probably dug Oscar the Grouch.) After the session, he took a rough mix of the song home and decided to leave it as is.

TOMORROW—MCCARTNEY

REC. AUGUST 1971, ABBEY ROAD, PAUL/LINDA MCCARTNEY (WRITERS/ PRODUCERS), MCCARTNEY (V, P), LAINE (G), SEIWELL (D), LINDA MCCARTNEY (BV), ALBUM *WILD LIFE*

This true gem of Wings' first album spotlights the gorgeous harmonies of McCartney, Linda, and Laine. The loneliness of the Beatles' break-up still lingered in the melancholy tinge of McCartney's fragile vocal, but there was a growing light at the end of the tunnel. Determined to move on from "Yesterday," he flipped that song's piano chords around to become "Tomorrow."[18] A more tentative yet still hopeful variation on "Good Day Sunshine," he looks forward to a lazy Sunday in the shade beneath the trees, running his fingers through Linda's hair, breathing the country air. It's still possible it will rain, but he's praying for sunny skies and looking forward to leaving his sorrow behind.

NOTES

1. Robin Blackburn and Tariq Ali, "*Red Mole* Interview with John Lennon," John Lennon Interviews, http://homepage.ntlworld.com/carousel/pob99.html (October 10, 2011).

2. Peter Doggett, *You Never Give Me Your Money* (New York: HarperCollins, 2009), 121–22.

3. "Finance: Diversification at the Vatican," *Time*, January 25, 1971, www.time .com/time/magazine/article/0,9171,904684,00.html (October 10, 2011).

4. John Blaney, *Lennon and McCartney: Together Alone* (London: Jawbone, 2007), 47.

5. Jann S. Wenner, "January 1971 *Rolling Stone* Interview with John Lennon and Yoko Ono," JannSWenner.com, www.jannswenner.com/Archives/John_Lennon_ Part1.aspx (October 10, 2011).

6. Robert Rodriguez, *Fab Four FAQ 2.0: The Beatles' Solo Years, 1970–1980* (Milwaukee: Backbeat Books, 2010), 278.

7. Wenner, "The *Rolling Stone* Interview."

8. Larry Kane, *Ticket to Ride* (Philadelphia: Running Press, 2003), 77–79.

9. Peter Ames Carlin, *Paul McCartney: A Life* (New York: Touchstone, 2009), 95.

10. "John Lennon on Dick Cavett (Complete show) 2nd Appearance with Live Performance," YouTube, www.youtube.com/watch?v=31qVGN1gKOE (October 10, 2011).

11. Nicholas Schaffner, *The Beatles Forever* (New York: McGraw-Hill, 1978), 151.

12. Blaney, *Lennon and McCartney: Together Alone*, 44.

13. Blaney, *Lennon and McCartney: Together Alone*, 46.

14. Peter Doggett, "John Lennon and Money," *Beatles Blog by Author Peter Doggett*, June 2, 2010, http://peterdoggettbeatles.blogspot.com/2010/06/john-lennon-and -money.html (October 10, 2011).

15. Doggett, *You Never Give Me Your Money*, 184.

16. Schaffner, *The Beatles Forever*, 142.

17. Simon Leng, *The Music of George Harrison: While My Guitar Gently Weeps* (London: Firefly, 2003), 94.

18. Chris Ingham, *The Rough Guide to the Beatles* (London: Rough Guides Limited, 2009), 115.

Ringo Starr points to a button promoting his most successful album, 1973's *Ringo. Getty Images*

· 4 ·

1973: Everest

The solo Beatles hit their peak in chart domination.

Everest was an original candidate for the title of *Abbey Road*, as it was engineer Geoff Emerick's favorite cigarette brand. The year 1973 was the peak for the solo Beatles collectively, the last time in which all four were still formidable presences on the singles and album charts within the same year.

In the United States their number one singles included "My Love," "Give Me Love (Give Me Peace on Earth)," and "Photograph," and two songs from their 1973 albums would go to number one in 1974: "Band on the Run" and "You're Sixteen." Other top ten hits included "Live and Let Die," "Oh My My," and "Jet." "Beatles Mafia" member Billy Preston also topped the charts with "Will It Go Round in Circles."

McCartney's *Red Rose Speedway* was knocked from the number one position by Harrison's *Living in the Material World*, which no doubt gave the other Fabs some chuckling satisfaction. On the US album charts, Harrison held the number one spot for five weeks. Ironically, the soundtrack to Starr's film *That'll Be the Day* kept Harrison out of the number one spot in the United Kingdom. Most surprising, Ringo's self-titled 1973 album would hit number two, and at the end of the year McCartney released what would be 1974's blockbuster, *Band on the Run*.

As the original leader of the group, Lennon must've felt strange that his *Mind Games* album just barely made the US top ten, with the single peaking at number eighteen in the United States. The era saw a replay of the Beatles' story in which early dominance by Lennon gave way to McCartney's increased assurance. Still, *Mind Games* was a recovery from *Some Time in New York City*, with some strong songs for fans of his work.

When bootleggers released a four-album Beatles greatest hits package, Allen Klein quickly released the retrospective collections *The Beatles 1962–1966* and *1967–1970* (more commonly known as the *Red Album* and *Blue Album*), and they hit the top of the charts as well. A publicity photo of the lads from 1963's *Please Please Me* adorned the first volume. The second volume featured a 1969 shot of the four taken from the same angle at the same council estate, originally planned for the aborted *Get Back* album. Their shoulder-length hair and beards reflected the long, strange trip they'd taken in only seven years, during which time they helped shake the walls of Western civilization.

In the three years since their break-up they had already collectively released fourteen albums (one being a double album, and one being a triple)—strange to think in this age when chart toppers from Gwen Stefani to the Killers take off years at a time to maximize sales potential.

Lennon and Harrison would cut ties with both Allen Klein and Phil Spector in 1973. Spector's accelerating madness had alienated them both, and they had both learned enough to produce their own albums by themselves by now.

McCartney continued to innovate through mini–rock operas. The Who released the first mini–rock opera with 1966's "A Quick One While He's Away," a song made up of six distinct parts that told a story. The always-competitive Beatles tried to trump them with the concept album *Sgt. Pepper*, in which songs segued into one another and the theme was reprised at the end. They would return to a segue suite in *Abbey Road*. Following the success of "Uncle Albert/Admiral Halsey," McCartney continued with a string of multisegmented singles like "Live and Let Die," "Band on the Run," and "Venus and Mars/Rock Show." The *Band on the Run* album cover would feature many celebrities, like *Sgt. Pepper*, and also a thematic reprise at the end. McCartney pulled out all the stops in promoting it and at last had a bona fide commercial *and* critical juggernaut on his hands. The critics who had berated him for squandering his potential finally lined up to praise his return from the wilderness.

The biggest surprise was that in 1973 Starr was as commercially successful as McCartney, with not only a hit album but also a hit film (in the United Kingdom) called *That'll Be the Day*, the British counterpart to the nostalgia-drenched *American Graffiti*.

The Stones had a number one smash with "Angie" and Dylan released "Knockin' on Heaven's Door." Led Zeppelin was the era's greatest concert draw, with the theme song of the decade, "Stairway to Heaven." David Bowie pointed the way to the future evolutions of punk and New Wave, and Elton John and the Eagles were shaping up as the era's biggest pop stars. But the solo Fabs were still major players to the young generation.

LIVE AND LET DIE—MCCARTNEY

Rec. October 1972, AIR Studios, London, Paul/Linda McCartney (writers), Martin (producer), McCartney (v, p), Linda McCartney (k, bv), Laine (b, bv), Henry McCullough (g), Seiwell (d), Single: UK 6/1/73 (9); US 6/18/73 (2), Cover version: Guns N' Roses, Academy Award nom. for Best Original Song, Grammy win for Best Arrangement Accompanying Vocalist, nom. for Best Pop Vocal Performance and Best Original Score

Britain was badly wrecked by the Nazis' blitzkrieg during World War II. Though the Allies won the war, money was a lot tighter in England than it was in the untouched United States. That difference manifested itself in the alternate versions of Beatles albums on either side of the Atlantic. Britons purchased albums with fourteen songs. None of them were repeats of the current single. US fans bought records with eleven songs, which included the singles. The Beatles' soundtrack albums in the United States were even more of a racket, with only seven Beatles' songs. The other tunes were background instrumentals. The consolation for hardcore Beatles fans was the fact that these instrumentals were performed by the George Martin Orchestra—and thus pretty groovy if you happened to dig sixties-period soundtrack music.

In 1973, Martin was hired to create the soundtrack to the latest Bond film, *Live and Let Die*. McCartney had always loved Bond. He envisioned himself as a sort of a Bond himself during the heyday of Beatlemania, when he would carouse London until the early morning going to the casinos in his sharp suits. This was echoed in *A Hard Day's Night*, though in that film the boys only pop in to the casino to retrieve McCartney's errant grandpa.

If McCartney was going to do a Bond song, this was a pretty good movie for it. The plan was for it to be "Bond meets blaxploitation in the Caribbean," which meshed well with the McCartneys' love of reggae. Supposedly, Linda came up with the song's reggae middle section.

With movie score veteran Martin's help, McCartney came up with one of his tightest, most dynamic mini–rock operas. It opens with a verse of regret as the singer mourns the idealistic pacifism of his youth. Then thunderous explosions of doom compel him to morph into the killer he must be to survive the dangerous real world, at which point the song launches into the pounding orchestral equivalent of an action-packed chase scene. The flourishes are not far removed from the *Help!* instrumentals, as that film had been designed to spoof the Bond pictures. The song suddenly turns on a dime to nonchalantly stroll along in the reggae break—before whirling around like McCartney shrieking and swinging an axe to your gut.

It was custom-made for the fireworks that would forevermore accompany the tune during McCartney's stage show. No doubt, the orchestrated version of *Ram* developed under McCartney's Thrillington pseudonym had given him added chops he was happy to flex. Here McCartney's technique of stringing tunes together evolved to serve the purpose of different Bond plot points. It pointed the way to "Band on the Run," where the different elements melded into a cohesive narrative.

Movie producer Harry Saltzman thought McCartney's demo was okay, but he wanted a black lady to sing it, as it was "blaxploitation Bond." Shirley Bassey had done well with "Goldfinger" and "Diamonds Are Forever." The Old Hollywood Rat Pack Generation still didn't really get the '60s generation. But McCartney said he would only allow use of the song if he sang it and if it was in the iconic opening credit sequence, with the silhouettes of Bond whirling and shooting his gun. *Live and Let Die* had a pretty slick opening, including silhouettes of hot black ladies making multicolored voodoo fire. Saltzman had passed up the chance to produce *A Hard Day's Night*, so the guy wised up and met McCartney's demand. "Live and Let Die" was the first Bond theme to be nominated for an Oscar for Best Original Song.

Rolling Stone criticized McCartney for doing such a nonhippie thing as a glitzy Bond movie. Subsequent generations have synthesized the Establishment and counterculture and don't have such hang-ups. "Weird Al" Yankovic wanted to spoof it as "Chicken Pot Pie." Although Yankovic performs the parody in concert, McCartney said no to an album version because he's a vegetarian.

McCartney continues to recycle "Live and Let Die" on various live recordings because the song provides an especially good spotlight for the tightness and dexterity of his band.

Though he and Lennon had made their peace, perhaps with this song McCartney was still exorcising the bad vibes of the feud. Perhaps he was looking back with sadness at how the band had once been united in their utopian hippie vision before degenerating into a horrible court battle where McCartney had to kill off the Beatles' business entity. But he couldn't worry about that because he had a job to do. *All right, guys, you don't want to be in a band with me, then I'm going to clobber you on the charts.* It's the sound of McCartney recovering his killer instinct. It must have jolted Lennon, licking his wounds from *Some Time in New York City.*

MIND GAMES—LENNON

Rec. Summer 1973, Record Plant East, NYC, Lennon (producer), Lennon (v, g), Keltner (d), Spinozza (g), Gordon Edwards (b), Ascher (k), Single: UK 11/16/73 (26); US 10/29/73 (18), Also on *Mind Games*

Many great artists do the "one for them, one for me" two-step, in which they create the commercial work they know the public wants, then tackle the borderline-indulgent, truly personal work that they want to do. *Some Time in New York City* was unquestionably "one for him" (no one else wanted it), so Lennon did one for the public next. "Mind Games" the song was in some respects "Imagine Part 2," a low key, piano-based ode to abstract cerebral idealism.

Musically, it was livelier. Lennon said, "The seeming orchestra on it is just me playing three notes on a slide guitar. And the middle eight is reggae. Trying to explain to American musicians what reggae was in 1973 was pretty hard, but it's basically a reggae middle eight if you listen to it."[1]

"Mind Games" actually predated "Imagine." During the *Get Back* sessions, one of the latest "found media" phrases magpie Lennon planned to use was "Make Love, Not War." The *Lennon Anthology* includes a version of him singing that phrase to the bittersweet melody that would become "Mind Games." There's a piercing yearning to his vocals, but the catchphrase was too played out. Lennon set the song aside.

In 1972, a book was published called *Mind Games: The Guide to Inner Space* by Robert Masters and Jean Houston. It consisted primarily of exercises for groups of people to do to increase their visionary thinking and intuition. (Lennon would also write a song called "Intuition" for his 1973 album.) The book was part of the bourgeoning Consciousness or Human Potential movement, later rebranded New Age. Like the Beatles, the baby boomers were busy exploring countless new paths in the pursuit of happiness: cults, therapy, psychology, Rolfing, Scientology, Est, Moonies, MDMA, the occult—you name it. Lennon used his old "Make Love, Not War" melody to celebrate his generation's search for higher knowledge—or, as he sings, the Grail.

In the 1960s, Lennon believed in everything from the I Ching to astrology to his technology guru, Magic Alex. In 1970, he believed in nothing. In 1973, he believed in magic again. Lennon gently chides himself for his endless quest, knowing it's all a mind game, but accepts the game as necessary. He comes to terms with the idea that there may be no final key, just the ritual of the search to see behind the veil.

In his 1980 *Playboy* interview, Lennon recounted that when he was little:

I always was so psychic or intuitive or poetic or whatever you want to call it, that I was always seeing things in a hallucinatory way. It was scary as a child, because there was nobody to relate to. Neither my auntie nor my friends nor anybody could ever see what I did. It was very, very scary and the only contact I had was reading about an Oscar Wilde or a Dylan Thomas or a Vincent van Gogh—all those books that my auntie had that talked about their suffering because of their visions. Because of what they saw, they were tortured by society for trying to express what they were. I saw loneliness.

Playboy: Where you able to find others to share your visions with?

Only dead people in books. Lewis Carroll, certain paintings. Surrealism had a great effect on me, because then I realized that my imagery and my mind wasn't insanity; that if it was insane, I belong in an exclusive club that sees the world in those terms. Surrealism to me is reality. Psychic vision to me is reality. Even as a child. When I looked at myself in the mirror or when I was 12, 13, I used to literally trance out into alpha. I didn't know what it was called then. I found out years later there is a name for those conditions. But I would find myself seeing hallucinatory images of my face changing and becoming cosmic and complete. It caused me to always be a rebel. This thing gave me a chip on the shoulder; but, on the other hand, I wanted to be loved and accepted. Part of me would like to be accepted by all facets of society and not be this loudmouthed lunatic musician. But I cannot be what I am not. Because of my attitude, all the other boys' parents, including Paul's father, would say, "Keep away from him." The parents instinctively recognized what I was, which was a troublemaker, meaning I did not conform and I would influence their kids, which I did. I did my best to disrupt every friend's home I had. Partly, maybe, it was out of envy that I didn't have this so-called home. But I really did. I had an auntie and an uncle and a nice suburban home, thank you very much. Hear this, Auntie.[2]

The counterculture revolution would show that there were many more who thought like Lennon.

Having hit the wall politically the year before, Lennon turns inward and switches from political guerrilla to "mind guerrilla." In a sense, he's making excuses for his radicalism, implicitly saying it was all a "mind game" like the Maharishi and everything else. Still, he believes that people can continue to push barriers and plant seeds for the next generation. Most importantly, he has hope that people can finally let go of whatever was hanging them up so much that they had to go on the "mind game" search to fix themselves in the first place.

GIVE ME LOVE (GIVE ME PEACE ON EARTH)—HARRISON

REC. OCTOBER 1972–JANUARY 1973, LONDON AND FRIAR PARK, HARRISON (PRODUCER), HARRISON (V, G), VOORMANN (B), KELTNER (D), WRIGHT (O), HOPKINS (P), SINGLE: UK 5/25/73 (8); US 5/7/73 (1), ALSO ON *LIVING IN THE MATERIAL WORLD*, COVER VERSION: DAVE DAVIES

The United Nations gave Harrison and Ravi Shankar The Child Is Father to the Man Award for the Concert for Bangladesh, but the experience ultimately depressed and frustrated him. Harrison had tried to convince the artists and record companies to donate the royalties to the people of Bangladesh, but the US and UK governments wouldn't waive their taxes. Ultimately, he had to cover a million pounds of tax personally. Also, *New York* magazine accused Allen Klein of pocketing some of the money. Klein slapped them back with a $100 million libel suit, which was later withdrawn. The concerts raised 15 million pounds, but the business aspect dragged on for two years, another business nightmare for Harrison, like the Apple fiasco.

The experience made his next album somber, but he pushed his disillusionment aside for the lead single and captured the essence of what he had set out to do with the concerts—and what the Beatles had tried to do in their most idealistic moments. "Give Me Love (Give Me Peace on Earth)" stands alongside "All You Need Is Love," "Let It Be," and "Imagine" as the purest expression of the Aquarian Age dream.

Harrison's voice may not have possessed the raw power of Lennon's or McCartney's, but the way he strains to hit the notes perfectly suits the yearning of his finest plea to God. Asking God to take hold of his hand and help him cope with his heavy load, Harrison expresses the core of why people turn to religion. It's not a theme commonly found on pop radio, although in the early 1970s it was a bit more frequent. The hippie-gospel-showtune "Day by Day" from *Godspell* hit number thirteen the previous year, the same year Cat Stevens reached number six with the Christian hymn "Morning Has Broken."

"Give Me Love" seems perfectly constructed for a hip church's choir, save for one unusual lyric in which Harrison asks God to keep him "free from birth." It harkens to his Hindu belief in reincarnation, in which you have to be continually reborn until you perfect yourself spiritually, at which point you no longer have to return to the material world to learn.

Musically, the song is a gentler take on the God-rock of *All Things Must Pass*. Harrison produced it by himself in his own home, with no Spector echo or hordes of musicians. It opens with just an acoustic guitar and the sparing use of his trademark slide to accompany his plaintive vocals. The fine arrangement accentuates the entrance of a lilting piano. Drums wait until the second verse to take the energy up a notch.

On the back of the LP was the symbol for OM, the über-mantra of Hindu meditation representing the primordial sound at the root of all things before the beginning and after the end. Meditators chant OM in their quest to merge with the higher spiritual plane, and Harrison chants it in the middle section. Ironically, this hymn might have started out as a slowed down version of Dylan's worldlier "I Want You."

I'M THE GREATEST—STARR

Rec. 3/13/73, Sunset Sound Recorders Studio, LA, Lennon (writer) Richard Perry (producer), Starr (v, d), Lennon (p, bv), Harrison (g), Voormann (b), Preston (o), Album *Ringo*: UK 11/23/73 (7); US 11/2/73 (2), platinum, Alternate version: *John Lennon Anthology* (Lennon lead v)

Following the *Ed Sullivan Show* in 1964, the Beatles met with underdog boxer Cassius Clay to take some publicity photos for their mutual promotional benefit. Unfortunately, the session involved the Fabs lying prone on the floor while Clay roared and shook his fists triumphantly above them, and gags like a fake Clay punch to Starr's head, which knocked into Harrison's, then into McCartney's, then Lennon's. For an egomaniac like Lennon, it must've been murder. To top it off, Clay picked on Starr for being short and underweight.

Throughout his career, Clay would often say to someone, "You know, you're not as dumb as you look." When he said it that day, Lennon replied, "But you certainly are."[3]

Legend diverges at this point. Some accounts say Clay glared at Lennon and Lennon glared back. Everyone got tense, until Clay laughed and everyone else laughed. Afterward, the furious Beatles sulked all the way home. Other accounts say Lennon's reply broke the ice and everybody had fun.

Either way, Clay defeated Sonny Liston a week later and unleashed one of his legendary rants: "I shook up the world, I'm the king of the world. You must listen to me. I am the greatest! I can't be beat!" Soon afterward, he would rename himself Muhammad Ali.

Whatever the truth, Lennon couldn't have loathed him too much because one of the catchphrases he appropriated in 1970 was "I'm the Greatest." In the midst of primal therapy, he stumbled across *A Hard Day's Night* on the TV and seeing it gave him a boost. He penned a song about how when he was a little boy his mom called him the greatest, then when he got older his friends called him the greatest, then his girlfriends called him the greatest, then he was in the greatest show on earth, and now his wife and kid call him the greatest. Lennon knew he might make everyone sick if he was so honest about his healthy self-regard, so he passed the tune to Starr.

In 1973, Starr resolved to finally take a swing at a regular pop album, as opposed to one that was so niche-targeted he didn't have to feel bad if it flopped. One of the producers on *Sentimental Journey* had been Richard Perry, a whiz who started out producing Captain Beefheart and Tiny Tim. Improbably, he was soon handling über-divas Barbra Streisand, Diana Ross, and Carly Simon. More importantly, he produced Starr's good buddy Harry Nilsson's smash album *Nilsson Schmilsson* and its sequel *Son of Schmilsson*. Starr asked for Perry's help. In March, they began.

Lennon and Ono dropped by the Los Angeles studio to work on "I'm the Greatest." Harrison called up in the midst of the session, having arrived in town and learned that the guys were hanging out. Immediately, Lennon exhorted him to come down and help him work out the guitar part.

Billy Preston and Klaus Voormann set up the wry, light-hearted tone. Harrison contributed his *Abbey Road*–sounding descending guitar notes. Lennon harmonized. They tweaked the lyrics so that Starr could revisit his "Billy Shears" persona, and Perry had the *Sgt. Pepper* audience cheering again. By the song's end, Starr was ranting like Ali that he was the greatest, and we'd better believe it, baby! Ringo had broken his "album block."

Other friends appearing on the record included Marc Bolan, Nilsson, The Band—and the one ex-Beatle who couldn't make it to Los Angeles because of visa problems due to pot busts. As a consolation, McCartney played kazoo on "You're Sixteen." He also contributed the heartfelt ballad "Six O'Clock," in which the singer apologizes to his wife for not treating her as well as he knows he should.

With its *Pepper*-like cover, the record had the feel of a Beatles reunion, spawned three hit singles, and went platinum. If 1970 had been Harrison's year, 1973 was Starr's, between the album and his movie *That'll Be the Day*. Lennon sent a telegram reading, "Congratulations. How dare you? And please write me a hit song."

Lennon later recounted that Harrison and Billy Preston asked him to form a group after the "I'm the Greatest" session. Harrison wanted to call themselves "The Ladders" and feature Lennon, Starr, Harrison, Preston, and Voormann. Lennon declined and the session would remain the closest thing to a Beatles reunion until "All Those Years Ago" in 1981 and *The Beatles Anthology* in 1995.

HELEN WHEELS—MCCARTNEY

REC. 1973, EMI AND ARC STUDIOS, LAGOS, NIGERIA, MIXED AT KINGSWAY STUDIOS, LONDON, MCCARTNEY (PRODUCER), MCCARTNEY (V, B, D), LINDA MCCARTNEY (K, BV), LAINE (GUITAR, BV), SINGLE: UK 10/26/73 (12); US 12/12/73 (10), ALSO ON *BAND ON THE RUN*

Now that he had his new band put together, McCartney finally actualized the dream he'd harbored since the *Get Back* days, when he tried to talk the other Beatles into playing out-of-the-way places where they could warm up and get tight outside of public scrutiny. On February 8, 1972, the Wings' van pulled up to the Nottingham University and the group asked the head of the student union if there was a place they could put on a show. The confused young person said they could use the lunchroom. That evening, a select group of Northerners had their minds blown by Paul McCartney playing their commissary with his new group.

The only problem was they ran out of material early; playing Beatles songs was too painful for McCartney, so Wings mainly stuck to Elvis Sun sides and *Wild Life*.

They drove across Northern England with their wives, kids, and dogs. They performed ten university shows in two weeks, charging between $1.25 and $1.75, until word got out and people started expecting Wings to turn up. Then they switched to small European gigs where no one spoke English and there wasn't much pressure.

The band got a double-decker bus. They covered the upper deck with mattresses and hung out up top with the kids getting a tan and the wind blowing back their shag mullets.

"Helen Wheels" (a pun on the phrase "Hell on wheels") was the name of McCartney's land rover. The song name-checked the towns McCartney would pass during the drive from his farm to London. In a more general way, the song also captured McCartney's euphoria at being back on tour, carburetor blasting, seeing the signs go by like long lost friends, remembering all the crazy tours of his youth with the Beatles as they crisscrossed England.

With a very un-rock-and-roll mentality, he celebrates not drinking and telling the driver to slow down so they stay alive and make the journey last. It was a philosophy that would allow him to keep touring more than forty years later.

A sped-up variation on the blues of "Hi Hi Hi," he would revisit the groove again with "Junior's Farm." The song was a single and not included on the UK edition of *Band on the Run*. In the United States, Capitol pushed McCartney into putting it on the album. Fortunately, it fit the vibe thematically.

BRING ON THE LUCIE (FREEDA PEEPLE)—LENNON

Rec. SUMMER 1973, RECORD PLANT EAST, NYC, LENNON (PRODUCER), LENNON (V, G), KELTNER (D), SPINOZZA (G), GORDON EDWARDS (B), ASCHER (K), SNEAKY PETE (PEDAL STEEL), RICK MAROTTA (D), SOMETHING DIFFERENT (BV), ALBUM *MIND GAMES*: UK 11/16/73 (13); US 11/2/73, FILM APPEARANCE: *CHILDREN OF MEN* (2006)

Started in 1971 as "Free the People," "Bring on the Lucie (Freeda Peeple)" was one of only two political songs on *Mind Games*. The public had definitively told him he needed to drop politics (as they would tell Harrison to drop religion), but he was still weaning it out of his system.

In the spoken-word intro, Lennon assumes the tongue-in-cheek persona of a World War II sergeant leading his troops into battle, then a Harrisonesque slide guitar kicks in like a drunken, weaving sidekick. As Gordon Edwards vamps on the bass, the music takes on the wooziness of a cartoon character who just got bopped on the head and is staggering around. It is vaguely akin to Funkadelic's "Back in Our Minds," that group's classic about trying to regroup after the devastation of an inner-city riot.

Backing himself in the chorus, Lennon sounds either facetious, drunk, exhausted, sick of politics, or all of the above. It sounds as if he just wants to sleep while someone drags him to another protest march: "Yeah yeah, free the people, sure, right." Maybe he doesn't care any more, maybe he's slaphappy after having been battered by the previous year, or maybe he's taking a piss. And in turn, it becomes one of his most appealing protest songs because, like "Gimme Some Truth," it incorporates his humor.

The tossed-off quality of the lyrics underscores his ambivalent attitude as he sneers at Nixon and his cronies for thinking they are cool while "jerking each other off" and sliding down a hill covered in the blood of the people they've massacred.

Lennon concedes the radicals got slammed in the presidential election, but as the drum rolls lock in with the fluid bass, Lennon gets his second wind and reminds his brothers and sisters not to despair but to keep demanding an end to the killing in Vietnam. He tells Nixon his name is 666 (mark of the Beast, and the inverse of Lennon's favorite number 9) and that his time is up. Nixon's time actually was up—on May 17, 1973, the Senate Watergate Committee began its nationally televised hearings.

Strangely, Voormann did not appear on this album, maybe because he was working on Starr's *Ringo* album in LA. In his place was Edwards, a black guy who was later in the jazz-funk band Stuff. Edwards vamped more flamboyantly than Voormann, like McCartney when he had to play on a Harrison track, but Voormann was back for Lennon's subsequent album, *Walls and Bridges*.

YOU'RE SIXTEEN—STARR

Rec. 3/5/73–4/30/73, Sunset Sound Studios, LA, Bob/Dick Sherman (writers), Richard Perry (producer), Starr (v, d), McCartney (kazoo),

Linda McCartney (bv), Voormann (b), Harry Nilsson (bv), Hopkins (p), Vini Poncia (g), Jimmy Calvert (g), Single: UK 2/8/74 (4); US 12/3/73 (1), also on *Ringo*

Every generation has a twenty-year nostalgia cycle. That's about the time one generation comes of age and rediscovers what their parents played in the background when they were babies. The 1970s nostalgia cycle was particularly acute, as there were few decades in which the culture went through such spasms of evolution as in the 1960s. The conventional wisdom says the storm of the sixties started when Kennedy was shot, and that it kicked into gear when the Beatles arrived in America four months later. The press and the kids were looking for a distraction from talking about the assassination and the Beatles were in the right place at the right time. Since the girls liked the band's long girly hair, the cool boys emulated it to get girls. The rebellious boys emulated it to piss off their parents and teachers. Blind allegiance to the military industrial complex began to waver. But by 1973, people were wrung out after more than ten years of civil rights marching, draft card burning, *Roe vs. Wade*, LSD, riots, and the usual litany of sixties tumult. They started to look back at the calm before the storm.

In 1973, George Lucas's mega-smash *American Graffiti* came out, featuring Ron Howard. ABC soon built a '50s situation comedy called *Happy Days* around Howard, malt shops, and cars with big tail fins, featuring a certain leather-jacketed hood named the Fonz played by Henry Winkler. A few years later Robert Stigwood had John Travolta bring his disco moves to the '50s stage musical *Grease*.

Though the Beatles were the ones who had killed the '50s, they came of age then and loved that era of rock more than any other musical style. Happy to jump on the nostalgia bandwagon, Starr released a cover of "You're Sixteen," a hit from 1960 by rockabilly cat Johnny Burnette featured on the *American Graffiti* soundtrack. The song was written by the Sherman Brothers, who also wrote the *Mary Poppins* soundtrack. Starr's version was recorded in September 1973, a month after *American Graffiti* was released. McCartney contributes a kazoo solo and backing vocals along with Harry Nilsson—though presumably their backing vocals must have been recorded on different continents, as McCartney still couldn't get a visa to the United States. Starr's singing really takes off, possessing none of the lugubrious clunkiness that weighs down some of his other work. Released as a single in December, by January it was, remarkably, Starr's second number one.

Today, YouTube cranks argue about whether it's appropriate for Starr to escort a sixteen-year-old into his car. But back when the tune was originally written, Jerry Lee Lewis had married his thirteen-year-old cousin and Elvis was dating a fourteen-year-old Priscilla in Germany.

American Graffiti's success bankrolled Lucas's next film, an obscure little flop about a galaxy far, far away. That film's star Carrie Fisher appeared in a Starr video promoting "You're Sixteen" made five years later in 1978 to promote Starr's greatest hits and his TV special.

Starr also rode the nostalgia boom by starring in the feature *That'll Be the Day*, a big hit in the United Kingdom that didn't make such a splash on American shores. Written by journalist Ray Connolly, it was inspired partly by the story of John Lennon's rise, as well as Harry Nilsson's autobiographical song "1941," about a father abandoning his son. (That song was one of the first things that drew Lennon to Nilsson, as it matched his life as well.) The movie took place in the late 1950s and featured singer David Essex ("Rock On") as a young man working at a summer resort who befriends the streetwise Starr and becomes a rock star.

Starr's role was supporting but large. He played a Teddy boy, English cousins to greasers who wore velvet-collared jackets instead of the leather variety. Starr brought the same naturalistic, low-key charm to the part that he had brought to *A Hard Day's Night*. After the flops of his first two genre albums, Starr had concentrated on films and finally got to the point of making an undeniably good movie. Had he continued performing in well-written indie films he could've really made it as an actor. But just then, his record career kicked back in, so after this his most notable film was, alas, 1981's *Caveman*. A sequel was made to *That'll Be the Day* called *Stardust*, in which Essex's and Starr's characters go through the decadent, psychedelic sixties. Starr demurred and let Keith Moon replace him in the role.

MY LOVE—MCCARTNEY

Rec. 1972, AIR Studios, London, Olympic Studios, or Abbey Road, Paul/Linda McCartney (writers), McCartney (producer), McCartney (v, electric p), Linda McCartney (bv), Laine (b), Henry McCullough (g), Seiwell (d), unknown full orchestra, Single: UK 3/23/73 (9); US 4/9/73 (1), also on *Red Rose Speedway*

McCartney cut his teeth as a balladeer covering show tunes like "Till There Was You" and movie themes like "A Taste of Honey," then moved on to composing his own classics like "And I Love Her," "Michelle," and "Here, There and Everywhere." Like "Maybe I'm Amazed," "My Love" was another tribute to Linda, but it came from a happier, more stable place in his life. With no emotional baggage or dark edges, the song indicated that McCartney was back in the sunshine, celebrating Linda's cooking and loving in a lyrical variation on "My Guy." Marvin Hamlisch would swipe the "my love does it good" line for Carly Simon's hit "Nobody Does It Better," the theme to the 1977 James Bond smash *The Spy Who Loved Me* (starring Starr's future wife, Barbara Bach).

The track is soothing, comfortable, and on the edge of complacent but redeemed for rockists by McCullough's unexpected guitar solo. Though still within the bounds of Easy Listening, the solo sparkles with distortion. McCartney usually had each detail of his songs worked out to specification, and this was especially true for "My Love," as it was being recorded live in the studio with a full orchestra. The canny McCullough waited until the last minute to go for a change-up. McCartney recalled, "I'd sort of written the solo, as I often did write our solos. And he walked up to me right before the take and said, 'Hey, would it be alright if I try something else?' And I said, 'Er . . . yeah.' It was like, 'Do I believe in this guy?' And he played the solo on 'My Love,' which came right out of the blue. And I just thought, fucking great. And so there were plenty of moments like that where somebody's skill or feeling would overtake my wishes."[4] Harrison and the members of Wings who ultimately left would dispute that, but "My Love" was lifted out of the Muzak comfort zone. McCullough also displayed some cool guitar hero moves in the song's promotional video—until the smoke machine made him vomit over the side of the stage.

ONLY PEOPLE—LENNON

REC. SUMMER 1973, RECORD PLANT EAST, NYC, LENNON (PRODUCER), LENNON (V, G), KELTNER (D), SPINOZZA (G), GORDON EDWARDS (B), ASCHER (K), SNEAKY PETE (PEDAL STEEL), MICHAEL BRECKER (SAX), SOMETHING DIFFERENT (BV) ALBUM *MIND GAMES*

When Lennon and Ono cohosted *The Mike Douglas Show* for a week in January 1972, they brought in friends ranging from radical political figures to Chuck Berry. When Lennon performed "Imagine," he made the comment, "Only people can save the world." With "save" switched to "change," the phrase would become the chorus for this *Mind Games* track and be printed on the album's inner sleeve.

The ebullient melody reflects the hopeful little boy part of Lennon's personality in the same vein as tunes like "I Should Have Known Better" and "Oh Yoko!" With its skipping, folk/R&B swing, it almost sounds like something that could have been sung by the Brady Bunch or *Sesame Street* kids. As

Lennon was adept at finding inspiration for songs in commercials, it would be unsurprising to learn that the song owed something to the famous "I'd Like to Buy the World a Coke" commercial from 1971, helmed by *Medium Cool* director Haskell Wexler. The commercial made such a splash that the New Seekers ("Georgy Girl") quickly released it as a hit single refashioned as "I'd Like to Teach the World to Sing." Coke allowed the proceeds to go to UNICEF.

"Only People" was certainly Lennon's least threatening attempt to use pop to sway the masses. For the ultraconservatives who wrote books like *The Beatles, LSD, and Communism,* no doubt this would have struck them as one of Lennon's most insidious propaganda pieces, refashioning a Coke commercial for socialism.

Bouncing back from Nixon's 1972 landslide, Lennon commiserates with his fellow idealists. He concedes they've cried a lot of tears, but now they're wiser and ready to start again. He throws in his usual feminist reminder that if man and woman work together they are unstoppable, and vows to resist the Pig Brother scene, conflating the "Big Brother" that had put him under surveillance and slang for the cops.

Whooping like a cheerleader before a clapping gospel chorus, Lennon finished his final political song. He and Ono would mirror their generation by transitioning into apathetic hedonism, and by the end of the decade, Ono would transform herself into an economic wheeler-dealer like the yuppies.

But while it would be easy to slam the sixties idealists for selling out, they had won the war against conformity. The right to liberated sex without marriage, promiscuity, long hair, freedom of expression, and drugs progressively melded with the mainstream throughout the decade. The ex-Beatles could look around at the new, freer world and know they had played a central part in changing it.

JET—MCCARTNEY

REC. 1973, ABBEY ROAD AND AIR STUDIOS, LONDON, McCARTNEY (PRODUCER), McCARTNEY (V, B, G, D), LINDA McCARTNEY (K, BV), LAINE (GUITAR, BV), HOWIE CASEY (SAX), SINGLE: UK 2/15/74 (7); US 2/18/74 (7), ALSO ON *BAND ON THE RUN*

"Jet" is the sound of McCartney with his swagger back, with badass horns, fuzz bass rumbling like *Air Force One* on the tarmac, and Linda and Denny soaring behind him like vapor trail loop-de-loops. Perhaps it was inspired by riding atop their double-decker tour bus with the wind in their hair.

On first listen, the unusual mention of "suffragettes" sounds like it could be a "Blackbird"-esque song of encouragement to the nascent feminist movement. Then there's something about a girl's family being shocked when she tells them she's getting married. Presumably this story is not from McCartney's own experience; Linda's music lawyer father must have been overjoyed at hearing her daughter was marrying the most profitable composer of the twentieth century. In actuality, the inspiration for the tune came from the McCartney's black Labrador puppy named Jet. In other words, it was "Martha My Dear" part two, starring a little puppy stalking around to the tasty horns. As for the suffragettes, it rhymes with Jet, and Bowie's "Suffragette City" came out the year before. McCartney often left his words obtuse so listeners could project onto them whatever they wanted. While Harrison and Lennon were concrete in their lyrics, McCartney was the opposite, slapping down whatever came to his head like an abstract expressionist. If subconscious patterns revealed themselves later, that was a bonus.

The harmonies are some of McCartney's finest since "Lucy in the Sky with Diamonds" and "Dear Prudence," while the density of the song's hum gives the tune a foreboding power. Engineer Geoff Emerick said the sound came about because the oxide on the recording tape was bad and the particles literally started to fall off. Emerick didn't want to break it to McCartney after he'd laid down such good takes, so he copied the tracks to another tape. The disintegration plus the second-generation transfer created a happy sonic accident. The saxophone came courtesy of Howie Casey, whose old group Derry and the Seniors used to play the Cavern Club the same era the Beatles did.

The single's cover featured a topless woman with her nipples airbrushed off. Very un-suffragette, unless it was after she burned her bra.

DON'T LET ME WAIT TOO LONG—HARRISON

REC. OCTOBER 1972–JANUARY 1973, LONDON AND FRIAR PARK, HARRISON (PRODUCER), HARRISON (V, G), STARR (D), VOORMANN (B), KELTNER (D), WRIGHT (K), HOPKINS (P), ALBUM *LIVING IN THE MATERIAL WORLD*: UK 5/30/73 (2); US 5/30/73 (1)

In 1967, while staying at a house in Los Angeles, Harrison waited impatiently for a friend to arrive. To distract himself, he wrote "Blue Jay Way," named after the street the house was on. Six years later, Harrison was again sitting around with his guitar waiting for someone to show up. This song, however, is a much happier affair. During the same *Living in the Material World* sessions,

Harrison also wrote the similarly joyful acoustic ditty "Miss O'Dell," about waiting for his assistant to show at his place in Malibu. At least Harrison was productive when the various flaky people in his life were late.

Whoever the woman of "Don't Let Me Wait Too Long" is, you can't blame him for being anxious. She cheers him up when he's crying and turns the bed into heaven. Vocally, the song shares the upbeat, plaintive yearning of "Give Me Love," with the same acoustic and pedal steel guitar interplay and only a slightly more insistent tempo. Some have said Harrison may have been influenced by an English band named McGuiness-Flint, whose hits like "When I'm Dead and Gone" have a similar sound. This may be why Harrison didn't release this tune as a single, even though it would have been a natural successor to "Give Me Love."

Harrison revisited the formula with a slick cover of the standard "True Love" on his 1976 album *Thirty-Three and a Third*. Harrison scholar Simon Leng contends "Don't Let Me Wait Too Long" influenced Electric Light Orchestra's 1976 hit "Livin' Thing." ELO's main man, Jeff Lynne, would later be the producer who brought Harrison back to the top with the *Cloud Nine* album.

OUT THE BLUE—LENNON

REC. SUMMER 1973, RECORD PLANT EAST, NYC, LENNON (PRODUCER), LENNON (V, G), KELTNER (D), SPINOZZA (G), GORDON EDWARDS (B), ASCHER (K), SNEAKY PETE (PEDAL STEEL), SOMETHING DIFFERENT (BV), ALBUM *MIND GAMES*: UK 11/16/73 (13); US 11/2/73 (9)

The night presidential candidate McGovern garnered only 37 percent of the vote in the 1972 election, Lennon was stunned by how out of touch he was with the masses. Shock quickly turned to snarling rage aimed at Ono, Jerry Rubin, and Abbie Hoffman as the latest gurus who had misled him. He was doubly angry because he assumed Nixon would now be able to definitely boot him out of the country.

At the "party" to watch the election returns, Lennon got wasted and started insulting Ono, calling her the Japanese "Mrs. Miller" (a singer famous for her horrible voice) while she wordlessly did cocaine. He started ranting about how stupid he'd been to believe in the Revolution, and how he wanted to join the radical group the Weatherman and shoot a cop. Then he made out with Rubin's roommate in front of Ono and took her to another room to have sex. Rubin's roommate said she couldn't do it with Lennon's wife in the next room, but Lennon said they were getting a divorce. Soon everyone in the party could hear the sex going on in the next room. When Lennon emerged, he wordlessly motioned for Ono to follow him, and they left. Their relationship would limp on for another six months, but in June 1973 they would separate right before the sessions for *Mind Games* began, fried from five and a half years of being drugged-out workaholics in the public fishbowl. Ono was sick of Lennon's emotional abuse and was anxious to have an affair with their guitarist, David Spinozza (who had also worked on *Ram*).

Lennon didn't want to believe they were through, and many *Mind Games* songs were apologies and tributes to Ono: "Aisumasen (I'm Sorry)," "You Are Here," and the best of them, "Out the Blue."

In one of his finest arranging jobs, he keeps the song continually interesting through the gradual introduction of each element: first just guitar, then piano/steel guitar/bass/and drums, then Beatles-esque backing harmonies. His impassioned vocal becomes a touch rawer, then leads into a fiery piano solo. With each piece making its own entrance, the listener can appreciate the new color it adds to the whole more clearly than if they had all been playing together right from the beginning.

Lennon fiercely pins his survival on Ono, singing that he was born just to get to her. A reformed chauvinist, he thanks both the Lord *and* Lady that he survived long enough to marry her. He sings that she came to him like a UFO out of the blue *and* cast out the blue that had been depressing him with the romance that rocked their world. A UFO is an apt metaphor, for it's hard to think of any other woman who could have been more surprising to find on Lennon's arm than Ono back in 1968. One has to give him points for originality. Lennon himself was an alien to much of the conventional world, so naturally he adored someone who had a similar power to confound the small-minded.

Lennon uses all his power to express how much Ono means to him to sway her to stay. The song comes close to being a standard that could serve as the traditional first dance in a wedding, though Lennon's intensity and offbeat lyrics are too much for that context.

Ono still said it was over. Lennon half-sacrificed his career for his woman, just like he once sacrificed the Beatles' chance to back Billy Fury because he insisted his nonmusical best friend, Stu Sutcliffe, play bass. Now that they had both flopped, she didn't have patience for him anymore. But he couldn't say that she was just a user, because he was abusive and knew he deserved to be shut out.

He designed the cover of *Mind Games*. A very small Lennon walks away from a mountain that is Ono's profile, as if she's lying in a sarcophagus.

PHOTOGRAPH—STARR

Rec. May 1973, Sunset Sound Studio, LA, Starkey/Harrison (writers), Richard Perry (producer), Jack Nitzsche (orchestral and choral arrangements), Starr (v, d), Harrison (12-string acoustic g, bv), Voormann (b), Keltner (d), Hopkins (p), Vini Poncia (rhythm g), Jimmy Calvert (rhythm g), Keys (sax), Lon Van Eaton (percussion), Derek Van Eaton (percussion), Single: UK 10/27/73 (8); US 10/5/73 (1), also on *Ringo*

The rousing, sing-along quality of this classic belies its sadness. A picture of a lover's face torments the singer, and he finds he can't handle living in their old place alone now that she's gone. He realizes that he actually does want to live out the ideal of marriage with her—to have and to hold, till death do they part . . . but she's not coming back, and all he can do is cry.

The song matched the tumultuous marriages of its writers, Harrison and Starr. And in a vague way, it suggested the nostalgia Starr and the public felt for the Beatles, as if their reunion would help recapture the optimism of a better time.

Between the strings, horns, and Bobby Keys's terrific sax break, it sounds like a Spector tune, and it was arranged by a producer who had served as Spector's righthand man in the early 1960s, Jack Nitzsche. Nitzsche had worked with the Stones (circa 1966–1967) and Neil Young before moving primarily to soundtracks, winning the Oscar for cowriting "Up Where We Belong" for 1983's *An Officer and a Gentleman*. Like his mentor Spector, Nitzsche knew how to give Starr an epic backdrop. Starr sang the tear jerker for all the baby boomers as they neared the age they once vowed never to trust, thirty. It's one of the best vocal performances of his career, without any "Ringo" flatness that could sometimes distract—just pure, solid singing to serve the song.

It topped the charts in the States and was perhaps Starr and Harrison's finest moment together. Thus it was doubly tragic that their friendship would fall apart for a number of years due to a shocking betrayal by Harrison later in 1973.

BAND ON THE RUN—MCCARTNEY

Rec. August–September 1973, EMI Studios, Lagos, Nigeria, mixed at Kingsway Studios, London, McCartney (producer), McCartney (v, b, g, d), Linda McCartney (k, bv), Laine (guitar, bv), Single: UK 6/28/74 (3); US 4/8/74 (1), also on *Band on the Run*

Bored with recording in England, McCartney checked out a list of EMI's international recording studios and discovered one in Lagos, Nigeria. Dreaming of new African rhythms to be discovered, he made plans for his band to travel there with former Beatles engineer Geoff Emerick.

Tension had been growing between McCartney and guitarist Henry McCullough. In performances, McCullough prided himself on always improvising something new. McCartney believed the crowd wanted to hear it how they expected it. As Harrison had learned long ago, there wasn't a lot for McCullough to add to McCartney's tunes since Macca wanted them recorded exactly as he envisioned them. The low pay rankled, and Linda got on McCullough's nerves. Finally, he turned in his notice a few weeks before the trip to Lagos. McCartney was surprised but figured they could make do without him.

The night before they were set to fly, drummer Denny Seiwell also quit, having lost faith that McCartney would ever give him a raise from $175 a week. McCartney decided, screw 'em both, Wings would record the album as just a trio. He had already played drums on *The White Album* when Starr walked out, and then on *McCartney*. He figured it'd be easier taking over the drums himself than trying to explain what he wanted to a Nigerian. Seiwell noted later with irritation that McCartney mainly re-created all the drum parts Seiwell had worked out in advance.

It's interesting that McCartney made perhaps his greatest album immediately after two-fifths of his band split—in particular, an album built around a song celebrating the camaraderie of bands. Perhaps having lost his second band in three years, McCartney had a vendetta to make an album so good they'd regret leaving.

McCartney's previous hit "Live and Let Die" had introduced a more cinematic, action-oriented mind-set, and now the adrenalin of a very unique set of circumstances poured into "Band on the Run." There was the life-threatening chaos of Lagos (see "Mrs. Vanderbilt"). Also, McCartney's persistent busts for marijuana had made him feel that the authorities were turning musicians into outlaws simply because they wanted to substitute herb for booze. The strands combined to make "Band on the Run" the greatest of his rock operas.

The song begins with the group stuck in jail for life, harmonizing like inmates in old prison movies. McCartney ruminates about what he'd do "if I ever get out of here," a line Harrison uttered during one of the interminable Apple board meetings.

Suddenly, guitars and orchestra rev and roar like dynamite blasting a hole through the wall. The gang runs for the fences as the debris falls like the sound of the acoustic guitars strumming, embodying light and freedom as McCartney's vocals echo. As the band runs toward the sun, one of them turns to the others and wryly cracks that he hopes they're having fun. No other line captures the exhilaration and terror the Beatles must've felt being chased by the fans who nearly tore them limb from limb. Beatlemaniacs would drop down onto the tops of the limos and nearly crush the group inside so frequently that it became necessary to transport them in armored vehicles.

The song crystallizes McCartney's nostalgia for old friends sharing the eye of a hurricane together, a time never to return, and simultaneously reflects his steely determination to capture the excitement again anyway. Even if Mc-Cullough and Seiwell had bailed out, he'd do it with his wife and Denny. McCartney's vision of escape became the best-selling album of 1974, and the seventh best-selling album of the 1970s. Soon he would conquer America and the rest of the globe again in his 1976 Wings over the World tour.

It would have been nice to be a fly on the wall the first time Lennon, Harrison, and Starr heard the song. Perhaps they smiled a little, remembering the blood stone days. Hard nut Lennon sang the album's praises. A month after the single "Band on the Run" hit the US number one spot, Lennon went into the studios to record *Walls and Bridges* and finally came up with his own number one, "Whatever Gets You thru the Night." Soon, he'd be talking with McCartney about meeting in New Orleans to record together.

The poisonous feud and its aftermath were over. McCartney had forgiven the others and let it go. He was now healed and complete on his own, even as he nostalgically looked back at his old mates and celebrated them, echoing that moment from *A Hard Day's Night* when the four banged open the theater door and ran down the fire escape with Ringo's cry, "We're out!"

NOTES

1. David Sheff, "January 1981 *Playboy* Interview with John Lennon and Yoko Ono," John-Lennon.com, www.john-lennon.com/playboyinterviewwithjohnlennon andyokoono.htm (October 10, 2011).

2. Sheff, "January 1981 *Playboy* Interview."

3. Buzz Fleischman, "Ferdie Pacheco, Cassius Clay, and the Beatles at the 5th Street Gym on Miami Beach, a Back Story," *Miami Pop Culture Examiner* 2009, www .examiner.com/pop-culture-in-miami/ferdie-pacheco-cassius-clay-and-the-beatles -at-the-5th-street-gym-on-miami-beach-a-back-story (October 10, 2011).

4. Tom Doyle, "Starting Over," *Mojo*, no. 203 (October 2010), 76.

Singer-songwriter Harry Nilsson and an unidentified man restrain John Lennon from attacking a photographer in the parking lot of West Hollywood's Troubadour club, after Lennon had been thrown out for heckling the Smothers Brothers comedy duo, on March 12, 1974. *Getty Images*

· 5 ·

1974: Lost Weekends

Lennon and McCartney jam again, but Harrison betrays Starr.

One of the earliest manifestations of Beatles nostalgia was the May 1974 opening of the British musical *John, Paul, George, Ringo . . . And Bert* by Willy Russell. In September, the first Beatlefest convention would be held in New York. In November, the theatrical revue *Sgt. Pepper's Lonely Hearts Club Band on the Road* made its debut.

With the success of the quasi-reunion *Ringo* album and Allen Klein out of the picture, there were growing indications that the Fabs would consider getting back together, including a late-night jam session in Los Angeles with Lennon and McCartney. But the foundation was cracked anew when Harrison pursued an affair with Starr's wife.

That Harrison could so easily seduce Starr's wife probably has a lot to do with the fact that one of his other best friends, Eric Clapton, was doing the same thing to his own wife, Pattie. But Pattie's vulnerability to Clapton's overtures can almost entirely be laid at Harrison's feet. She recalled, "George was fascinated by the god Krishna who was always surrounded by young maidens. He came back from India [in 1968] wanting to be some kind of Krishna figure, a spiritual being with lots of concubines. He actually said so."[1]

When Clapton broke up with model girlfriend Charlotte Martin in 1968, Pattie invited her to stay with her and Harrison, which wasn't the wisest move, as Harrison and Martin quickly had a fling. No doubt that added an element of revenge to Pattie and Eric Clapton's subsequent affair, though Pattie stayed with Harrison for another half-decade. Clapton tried to woo her by composing classics like "Layla," "Bell Bottom Blues," and "I Looked Away," and even confessed one night to Harrison in front of a mortified Pattie that he loved her. Harrison was enraged and demanded to know whom Pattie was

111

going home with. She stayed with Harrison; it was hard to leave the palace for someone without a stable family or much schooling, accustomed to the finer things in life.

Still, their semi-secret affair persisted, with Harrison ambivalent to their liaison. Pattie wrote about the time Clapton came by and Harrison wordlessly challenged him to a duel by handing him a guitar and an amp in lieu of swords. An emotional Harrison tried to go for musical pyrotechnics, but Clapton stayed cool and Pattie thought he won the match.[2]

As the seventies progressed, Harrison would go on cocaine-fueled binges at his estate, then vow to get clean through religious chanting. When he chanted he would isolate himself from Pattie and withdraw. She couldn't win either way. The irony was that Harrison had begun to alienate many fans with the solemn spirituality of his albums even as he was carousing like a decadent vampire behind the scenes. To his credit, he owned up to it on songs like 1974's "Simply Shady." Most likely, he was preaching to himself, articulating a purity he strove for but could only sporadically attain. In the meantime, he'd ask Apple manager Neil Aspinall to swap wives, or go off on holiday with Ron Wood's wife, Krissie. In retaliation, Pattie had a fling with the carefree Wood.

Finally, just as his good friend Clapton had cuckolded him with his wife, Harrison did the same to Starr with his wife, Maureen. Starr also ignored his wife and partied and cheated to excess. But it's still mysterious why Harrison went for Maureen. Perhaps the only women to make much of an impression on rockstars beyond the role of disposable groupie were the wives of their friends, since they were the only women who got to stick around when the sun came up. Perhaps the only thrill left was the thrill of taboo. Later, when asked why, Harrison would only shrug, "Incest."

Pattie first became aware of their affair when she discovered some photos of Maureen hanging out at the Harrison Friar Park estate during a weekend Pattie had left to see her mother. Also, Harrison gave Maureen a necklace and she began to wear it in front of Pattie.

Then came the day Pattie discovered them locked inside Harrison's bedroom. She pounded on the door, but Harrison just laughed that Maureen was tired so she was lying down. Enraged, Pattie lowered the "OM" flag that flew atop the mansion's turret and replaced it with a skull and crossbones.

Maureen grew bolder, turning up at midnight to listen to Harrison and the other musicians recording in the home studio. When Pattie said she didn't like it, Maureen replied, "Tough." Pattie would pointedly ask her where her children were at that hour, but when Pattie would wake up in the morning, Maureen would still be there.

Pattie called Starr to tell him and he was furious, but Harrison denied it and acted like Pattie was paranoid. Financially dependent, Pattie didn't leave.

At Starr's New Year's party when it turned 1974, Harrison told Pattie he wanted a divorce. To cheer her up, Starr offered her a job as set photographer for his ill-fated spoof, *Son of Dracula.*

Finally, at dinner at Starr's one night later that year, Harrison got drunk on wine, strummed his guitar and suddenly confessed to Starr, Pattie, Maureen, and Apple assistant Chris O'Dell that he was in love with Maureen. Maureen went red and just shook her head as Starr stalked off, quoting Lennon over and over: "Nothing is real. Nothing is real." Pattie locked herself in the bathroom and soon afterward dyed her hair red, to do *something.*[3]

In July 1974, Clapton left for the United States. Pattie told Harrison she was leaving for LA to be with family there and, presumably, Clapton. Sadly quiet, Harrison sat on the bed and said, "Don't go." But she finally left Friar Park, to a whole new mess of problems with Clapton. Through it all, Clapton and Harrison remained friends. Harrison would later attend Pattie and Clapton's wedding.

Maureen did not want to divorce Starr, but they officially split on July 17, 1975. Maureen tried to kill herself by driving her motorcycle into a brick wall and had to have facial reconstruction.[4]

As inbred as royalty in eras past, the rockstars' mate swapping seemed like a self-created soap opera, a cross between *Less Than Zero, Dangerous Liaisons, Melrose Place,* and John Updike's 1968 novel *Couples.*

Perhaps because Clapton had done it to him, Harrison didn't feel it was as egregious as it would seem to normal people. Perhaps it didn't seem like such a betrayal to him because he knew Starr was no saint.

Starr left Maureen and England for Los Angeles. Having split with Ono, Lennon was there producing the next album of one of Starr's best buddies, Harry Nilsson. Back in 1968, Nilsson was writing songs for the Monkees and Glen Campbell when he first came to the Beatles' attention via his tune "1941." Also on Nilsson's first album was a cover of Lennon's "You Can't Do That," which skillfully interwove snatches from twenty-two other Beatles lyrics into the song. Both Lennon and McCartney proclaimed Nilsson to be their favorite artist in their press conference announcing the formation of Apple. Lennon ended up listening to Nilsson's album *Pandemonium Shadow Show* for thirty-six hours straight and invited him to his Tittenhurst estate to hang out. Nilsson hit the big time with his immortal cover of "Everybody's Talkin'" when it became the theme to the Best Picture of 1969, *Midnight Cowboy.* Nilsson's streak continued with hits like "Without You" and "Coconut."

Lennon figured the best way to make sure they could get to Nilsson's *Pussy Cats* album sessions on time was if they lived together, so the gang moved into a beach house in Santa Monica: Lennon, Nilsson, Starr, and

Who drummer Keith Moon—the perfect crowd with whom to pursue a punctual work ethic. Another pal on the scene was Mick Jagger, for whom Lennon produced his solo song "Too Many Cooks (Spoil the Soup)," unreleased until thirty years later. Meanwhile, Moon recorded his solo album *Two Sides of the Moon*, which featured Lennon's only anti-Ono song, "Move Over Ms. L."

With Nilsson's gift for gorgeous melodies and his peerless voice, there was speculation that he could be a new McCartney for Lennon; probably Nilsson hoped so himself. But Nilsson got on with McCartney, as well. So McCartney and Linda dropped by the *Pussy Cats* sessions at Burbank Studios the same night Stevie Wonder was there. Wonder was currently in the midst of a streak of chart-topping classics following his 1972 tour with the Rolling Stones.

Everybody was shocked when McCartney entered and one could hear a pin drop—until Lennon said, "Valiant Paul McCartney, I presume?"

McCartney replied, "Sir Jasper Lennon, I presume?" referring to the roles they performed in a 1963 Christmas stage show. They shook hands and soon started jamming.

Lennon sang lead and played guitar, McCartney drummed and sang harmony, Wonder sang and played electric piano, Linda played the organ, Lennon's girlfriend May Pang played the tambourine, Nilsson sang, Jesse Ed Davis played guitar, producer Ed Freeman played bass, and Bobby Keys played sax. They jammed some blues, then covered "Lucille," "Sleep Walk," "Stand by Me," "Cupid," "Chain Gang," and "Take This Hammer."

It should have been a classic moment, but it was past midnight and everyone was coked out of their minds. On the famous bootleg, *A Toot and a Snore*, Lennon says to Wonder, "You wanna snort, Steve? A toot? It's goin' round." A couple tunes later Lennon is looking for some more coke while repeatedly complaining about the technical difficulties he's having with his mike and headphones. On the one hand, it's sad that the last known recording of McCartney and Lennon should be so lackluster. But on the other hand, it's nice to hear that they were friendly again. The "Lucille" cover is almost passable, on par with some of the more coherent *Get Back* outtakes.

With the friendships healing, it was strange timing for Harrison to poison the well. He and Starr had provided a buffer between Lennon and McCartney and made the Beatles a true brotherhood. Harrison had been the one who had pushed hardest for Starr to join. When Starr needed to be replaced on the 1964 tour temporarily due to tonsillitis, Harrison did not want to tour with the temp. When Harrison alienated Starr, the Beatles' crucial third column crumbled for years. Then, when Starr and Harrison put the past behind them and started recording together again in 1980, Lennon was murdered.

Beatlemania had profoundly stressed Harrison out, as had dealing with McCartney's arrogance. As Starr was the glue that seemed to be bringing the group back together, one almost wonders if Harrison's subconscious dark side drove Starr away to sabotage a reunion.

Nineteen seventy-four would see the beginning of a steep decline in record sales for both Harrison and Starr. Starr would never match the tremendous success of his collaborations with Harrison, "It Don't Come Easy" and "Photograph."

WHATEVER GETS YOU THRU THE NIGHT—LENNON

REC. SUMMER 1974, RECORD PLANT EAST, NYC, LENNON (PRODUCER), LENNON (V, G), ELTON JOHN (P, O, V HARMONY), DAVIS (GUITAR), VOORMANN (B), KELTNER (D), KEYS (SAX), JENKINS (PERCUSSION), MOTTAU (ACOUSTIC G), ASCHER (CLAVINET), SINGLE: UK 10/4/74 (36); US 9/23/74 (1), ALSO ON *WALLS AND BRIDGES*, ALTERNATE VERSION: LIVE VERSION WITH ELTON JOHN (BONUS TRACK ON *WALLS AND BRIDGES* REISSUE)

The next installment in the honored line of Lennon songs inspired by TV or advertising came when he was channel surfing in the middle of the night and stumbled across Reverend Ike, an African American televangelist based in New York City (born Frederick J. Eikerenkoetter II). Ike boomed a lot of catchphrases like, "You can't lose with the stuff I use!" and held prosperity seminars. He even appeared on Hank Williams Jr.'s 1986 remake of "Mind Your Own Business."

One night, according to May Pang, Ike said, "Let me tell you, guys, it doesn't matter, it's whatever gets you through the night." Perhaps Ike was echoing Kris Kristofferson's standard, "Help Me Make It through the Night." Kristofferson himself had been inspired by an interview he read in *Esquire* with Frank Sinatra. Asked what he believed in, Sinatra said, "Booze, broads or a Bible . . . whatever helps me make it through the night."

Lennon kept a pad by his bed to write things down so he wouldn't forget them, and dutifully took note. Later he laid down a vague sketch of a demo with an almost country feel. As the song began to take shape in the *Walls and Bridges* sessions, he molded it more in the R&B vein of the current hit "Rock Your Baby" by George McCrae.[5] Lennon had evolved into a formidable producer, with more technique to create a glossier sound than *Mind Games*. And he was listening as funk and soul were coalescing into disco. He included more dance-inflected numbers on the LP, like his first instrumental, the intriguingly named "Beef Jerky," and this song.

Elton John overdubbed piano, organ, and harmony vocals, and the track that emerged is one of Lennon's happiest solo songs, capturing his joie de vivre when he was with friends or in a gang. The lyrics are on the edge of being cleverly trite nonsense, but the effervescent sax and the palpable fun of the two stars singing and jamming carries the party. There's a manic edge that perfectly suited the hedonism of the times. In 1974, Vietnam was over, sex, drugs, and rock had gone mainstream, and it would be another decade before sexual disease and crack would kill the party.

Lennon did a video of himself walking through New York lip-synching the song. Dressed in an all-black cloak and a wide-brimmed black hat with a feather, he looked like a bell-bottomed Dracula Musketeer, walking the tough Lennon strut first seen in *A Hard Day's Night*.

Elton was sure their party on vinyl would hit the top of the charts. But though Lennon had written the bulk of the Beatles' number one hits in the first half of their recording career, he was now pessimistic about his odds of ever getting back in sync with the public. Elton bet him it would hit number one. If Lennon lost, the deal was that he would have to come onstage at one of Elton's concerts and play it with him. Lennon was right about England, where it only reached number thirty-six. But there was a growing schism of taste between the two English-speaking nations, and it shot to number one in the States. Once the leader of the Beatles, he was the last to get an American solo hit under his belt—but he finally did it.

So now it was payback time. At Madison Square Garden on November 28, 1974, Elton gave a concert full of his usual passion and leaps backward from the piano, in silver-sequined suspenders and white sunglasses. Near the end, he invited someone up to the stage whom he was sure "will be no stranger to anybody in the audience." As the crowd roared, Lennon strolled out, chewing gum and making faces. He tuned up with "I Feel Fine" and swallowed, fighting not to get choked up by the ecstatic reaction. The Garden literally bounced as they ripped into "Whatever Gets You thru the Night," "Lucy in the Sky with Diamonds" (Elton's current number one single with Lennon contributing vocals and guitar), and a song Lennon introduced as being "by an old estranged fiancé of mine called Paul," "I Saw Her Standing There." It was his last live appearance.

JUNIOR'S FARM—MCCARTNEY

REC. 1974, SOUND SHOP STUDIOS, NASHVILLE, MIXED AT ABBEY ROAD, MC-CARTNEY (PRODUCER), McCARTNEY (V, B), LINDA McCARTNEY (K, V), LAINE

(G, V), JIMMY MCCULLOCH (G), GEOFF BRITTON (D), SINGLE: UK 10/25/74 (16); 11/4/74 (3)

Prodigy Jimmy McCulloch first gained notoriety as guitarist in the band Thunderclap Newman, who scored with the hippie anthem "Something in the Air" in 1969. In 1974, he was still only twenty-one when he joined Wings as they convened in Nashville to work on McCartney's next single. They also had a new drummer: black-belt karate champ Geoff Britton, who beat out forty-nine others for the position, including Hendrix's old drummer Mitch Mitchell, who resented that he had to audition.

Deep in moonshine country, home base was the 133-acre ranch of Junior "Curley" Putnam, in whose honor the nonalbum single was named. Junior had bought his farm through penning country classics such as "The Green, Green Grass of Home" and "He Stopped Loving Her Today." He took Mc-Cartney's rent money and went on vacation with his wife to Hawaii, leaving his place to the band and Paul and Linda's three daughters.

Opening with great guitar fanfare and galloping like the descendent of "Get Back," "Junior's Farm" was another solid mid-tempo rocker that McCartney produced like clockwork since the days of "Paperback Writer."

Proud of his new wunderkind, at the instrumental break McCartney cried, "Take me down Jimmy!" and the young guy let rip with a cascading solo that no doubt gave the previous Wings member named McCullough pause.

The nonsensical lyrics feature McCartney cheating at poker to win a hand while old guys worry about inflation. Mainly he's just having a blast down on Junior's farm with Eskimos, Oliver Hardy, and sea lions. For the single, the band dressed up in costumes representing the characters in the song.

OH MY MY—STARR

REC. SEPTEMBER 1973, SUNSET SOUND STUDIO, LA, PONCIA/STARKEY (WRITERS), RICHARD PERRY (PRODUCER), STARR (V, D), PRESTON (P, O), VOORMANN (B), KELTNER (D), TOM SCOTT (SAX, ARRANGEMENTS), HORN (ARRANGEMENTS), MARTHA REEVES (BV), MERRY CLAYTON (BV), PONCIA (BV), JIMMY CALVERT (G), SINGLE: US 2/18/74 (5), COVERS: IKE AND TINA TURNER, BETTE MIDLER

"Oh My My" is probably the first song in which disco started to creep into the solo Beatles' music. Written by Starr and his songwriting partner Vini Poncia, it became one of Starr's most successful tunes and perhaps inspired John's own stab at a dance hit with sax solo, "Whatever Gets You thru the Night."

The dance cred of this tune can't be too bad because Ike and Tina Turner covered it on *Soul Train* in 1974. On Starr's version, he's backed by no less than Motown legend Martha Reeves, whose hits with the Vandellas included "Dancing in the Street," from which Keith Richards copped the riff to "Satisfaction." Also singing back-up was Merry Clayton, who stole the show in the Stones' "Gimme Shelter."

The soul divas add gravitas to this complex tale, which begins with Starr being told by his physician to get over to the doctor's office immediately. Starr's scared, but when he arrives he is relieved to discover that the doctor just wants him to boogie and do the slide. The head nurse comes in and starts dancing, too. The doctor assures Starr that said boogying is guaranteed to preserve his longevity.

As Starr and McCartney continue to tour to this day, it would seem that, in truth, boogying has contributed to their longevity. On stage Starr will step out from behind the drums to sing many of his hits in lead singer mode. Although, strangely, he actually only played "Oh My My" for the first time in 2008.

The success of "Oh My My" would provide the template for Starr's disco formula in the second half of the decade, with tunes like "Tango All Night," "Out on the Streets," and "Can She Do It Like She Dances." For connoisseurs of cheese, the songs are fun, but for Starr's career, it wasn't a successful direction.

DARK HORSE—HARRISON

REC. WINTER 1973, AUGUST–SEPTEMBER 1974, AND OCTOBER 1974, FRIAR PARK, HARRISON (PRODUCER), HARRISON (V, G), PRESTON (K), KELTNER (HI-HATS), TOM SCOTT (FLUTE), HORN (FLUTE), CHUCK FINDLEY (FLUTE), WEEKS (B), NEWMARK (D), EMIL RICHARDS (PERCUSSION), ROBBEN FORD (G), LON VAN EATON (BV), DEREK VAN EATON (BV), SINGLE: UK 2/75 (FAILED TO CHART); US 11/18/74 (15), ALSO ON *DARK HORSE*

The year 1974 started out promising for Harrison. He opened his own record label, Dark Horse Records, and signed Ravi Shankar. He then committed to touring with Shankar and five of India's other premiere musicians. The plan was to follow the Concert for Bangladesh model: for the first half Shankar and Co. would play, then Billy Preston would do a set, then Harrison would take over for the second half of the show. Years before Peter Gabriel and others made "World Music" a section at the record store, Harrison was determined to expose the arenas of America to the music that had changed his life. Clapton was originally supposed to join, but when Pattie took off with him that was nixed.

The $4 million expense of the tour meant that Harrison needed to have his next album on hand to promote and in the stores by Christmas to maximize sales. Unfortunately, he did not realistically assess how long it would take him to complete the album before locking in the dates with all the musicians involved with the tour. Thus as the deadline grew closer, he realized with horror that he was out of time, and began to lose his voice to laryngitis.[6] Some have speculated it was psychological; he didn't really want to tour but was doing it because he wanted to help Shankar.

His home demo for "Dark Horse" was terrific enough for him to use as the name of his album and label (though it was too raw to issue as is). But before he could do a proper version, his voice gave out and it was time to fly to the United States in October to begin tour rehearsals. The song was re-recorded practically live in an American studio with the tour band and Preston. By now his voice was unmistakably shot.

Alternate takes of John Lennon's solo songs have been released on the *John Lennon Anthology*, and to some fans they are preferable because you hear his voice before he added studio effects to it, and you can hear the band without echo or layers of synths. The official version of "Dark Horse" sounds like an unpolished version that would be on a *Harrison Anthology*. In this case, that's a shame, because had his voice been in finer form and a little gloss added to the production, it could have been a hit.

Still, while the huskiness of his voice threatens to distract (the critics would dub it "Dark Hoarse"), the strength of the composition, the uplifting chorus, the "Stairway to Heaven"–esque flute by Tom Scott, and the subtly funky keys by Preston nudge it into Harrison's top tier, though just by a nose.

In racing, a dark horse is the one who is not expected to do well and suddenly comes up from behind and wins the race. Harrison, of course, was the dark horse in 1970 when he clobbered the other ex-Beatles with *All Things Must Pass*. Still, though *Living in the Material World* had done well by anyone else's standards, it did not live up to Harrison's first release, and the critics had begun to snipe. Thus Harrison felt the need to beat his chest a bit, singing how people thought they had him figured out and dismissed him, but he surprised them all and won. Anyone who's been a dark horse at some point can relate and share in his triumph.

But weirdly, Harrison later recalled in his memoir, *I Me Mine*, that when he wrote the song he did not know about its racing connotation. He just knew the term from an old joke in which one friend tells another about how a guy in the neighborhood has been sleeping with another man's wife. The second friend expresses surprise that the neighbor was in fact a secret ladies' man:

"He's a bit of a dark horse, isn't he?" So in actuality, Harrison was doing a bit of vampiric gloating with the song.

Perhaps the lines are directed at poor ex-wife Pattie in their games of sexual one-up-manship, as he sings how she thought she was putting one over on him with her supposedly secret affairs, when in actuality he was cheating on her, too. Running on a dark racecourse, indeed.

LET ME ROLL IT—MCCARTNEY

R<small>EC.</small> A<small>UGUST–</small>S<small>EPTEMBER</small> 1973, EMI S<small>TUDIOS</small>, L<small>AGOS</small>, N<small>IGERIA</small>, <small>MIXED AT</small> K<small>INGSWAY</small> S<small>TUDIOS</small>, L<small>ONDON</small>, M<small>C</small>C<small>ARTNEY</small> (<small>PRODUCER</small>), M<small>C</small>C<small>ARTNEY</small> (<small>V, B, G, D</small>), L<small>INDA</small> M<small>C</small>C<small>ARTNEY</small> (<small>K, BV</small>), L<small>AINE</small> (<small>G, BV</small>), A<small>LBUM</small> *B<small>AND ON THE</small> R<small>UN</small>*: UK 11/30/73 (1); US 12/3/73 (1), <small>ALSO</small> B-<small>SIDE OF</small> J<small>ET</small>, G<small>RAMMY</small>: B<small>EST</small> E<small>NGINEERED</small> R<small>ECORDING</small>, N<small>OM. FOR</small> A<small>LBUM OF THE</small> Y<small>EAR</small>

McCartney would later say that he didn't realize he was singing like Lennon in "Let Me Roll It." But the vocals are loaded with reverb, as Lennon was wont to do. The guitar riff epitomizes Lennon's primitivism, like a mellowed out "Cold Turkey" in which the musicians aren't strung out on smack but just rolling up a joint like an olive branch, putting the past behind them. Perhaps it was even more of a rapprochement to Harrison, as the title was lifted directly from the first verse of the first song on *All Things Must Pass*, "I'd Have You Anytime," cowritten by Dylan. (The wheel imagery might have sprung initially from Dylan's "This Wheel's on Fire.") Lennon dug "Let Me Roll It" so much he re-appropriated the riff for his instrumental "Beef Jerky." McCartney played "Let Me Roll It" on just about every tour that followed.

SURPRISE SURPRISE (SWEET BIRD OF PARADOX)—LENNON

R<small>EC. SUMMER</small> 1974, R<small>ECORD</small> P<small>LANT</small> E<small>AST</small>, NYC, L<small>ENNON</small> (<small>PRODUCER</small>), L<small>ENNON</small> (<small>V, ACOUSTIC G</small>), E<small>LTON</small> J<small>OHN</small> (<small>HARMONY V</small>), D<small>AVIS</small> (<small>G</small>), V<small>OORMANN</small> (<small>B</small>), K<small>ELTNER</small> (<small>D</small>), H<small>OPKINS</small> (<small>P</small>), J<small>ENKINS</small> (<small>PERCUSSION</small>), M<small>OTTAU</small> (<small>ACOUSTIC G</small>), A<small>SCHER</small> (<small>CLAVINET</small>), L<small>ITTLE</small> B<small>IG</small> H<small>ORNS</small>: K<small>EYS</small> (<small>SAX</small>), S<small>TEVE</small> M<small>ADAIO</small>, H<small>OWARD</small> J<small>OHNSON</small>, R<small>ON</small> A<small>PREA</small>, F<small>RANK</small> V<small>ICARI</small>, A<small>LBUM</small> *W<small>ALLS AND</small> B<small>RIDGES</small>*: UK 10/4/74 (6); US 9/26/74 (1)

Fung Yee ("May") Pang was born in 1950 to Chinese immigrants with a laundry business and grew up in Spanish Harlem. After being told she was too "ethnic" looking to be a model by the agencies, she worked briefly selling songs to recording artists as a song plugger, then got a job as a receptionist at Allen Klein's ABKCO Records in 1969. She became Lennon and Ono's personal assistant, helping on their films and art exhibitions.

In June 1973, Ono wanted to separate from the toxic Lennon but still wanted to maintain the power to bring him back in the future if she chose. So rather than cut him loose and see him run off with someone outside her sphere of influence, she decided to set him up with Pang and continue to call him multiple times a day.

When Pang came to work one morning, Ono casually informed her that she and Lennon had been fighting for a long time. Ono said Lennon was on the verge of seeing other women, so Pang should become his companion because Ono knew she would treat Lennon well, and Lennon was very attracted to her. Pang was a conventional young lady and said she couldn't do that with a married man who was her boss, but Ono ignored her protestations and said she would let Lennon know they discussed it.

Two weeks later, Lennon suddenly kissed Pang in the elevator on the way to a *Mind Games* session, then tried to come home with her. Pang resisted for two weeks but eventually realized she had feelings for him, too, and let him come over. Upon completion of the album, the couple moved to California and began a year-and-a-half love affair.

The day after they got together, Lennon decided to write a song about Pang in the vein of the Diamonds' 1950s classic "Little Darlin'." He got serious about finishing it in the summer of 1974 for his next album. He celebrates her radiant youth (which no doubt must've been a goad to Ono), their wonderful sex, and how she helps him get through his lonely, pained existence.

Then, in the middle section, he suddenly registers surprise that his feelings for her are deeper than just sex and company for company's sake. He'd been wondering how long the affair could last, but now he admits that she's blown his mind and he thinks that he loves her, so delighted he even spoofs "Drive My Car."

Determined to stay contemporary, he spruced up the tune with R&B horns, then enlisted Elton John to sing harmony and play Hammond organ. (Elton John's two guest appearances on *Walls and Bridges* were some of the few times Lennon sang harmony since leaving the Beatles.) Pang cried when she heard the tune, calling it the nicest present she had ever received.

The opposite of the paranoid, manipulative Ono, Pang was excited by the idea of Lennon working with McCartney again, and encouraged Lennon to reconnect with his long-ignored son Julian. Julian and Cynthia flew out to LA, where they went to Disneyland with Lennon and Pang, and Julian even jammed with Lennon on the "Ya Ya" track of *Walls and Bridges*.

NINETEEN HUNDRED AND EIGHTY-FIVE—MCCARTNEY

Rec. August–September 1973, EMI Studios, Lagos, Nigeria, mixed at Kingsway Studios, London, McCartney (producer), McCartney (v, b, g, d), Linda McCartney (k, bv), Laine (g, bv), Album *Band on the Run*, also B-side to Band on the Run US single

Babbling that other women can't get him because he can't get enough of his lady, this is another McCartney tune in which the lyrics are mainly place-holders to sing and communicate pure excitement while the music builds with cinematic suspense. Why "1985"? Because it was after Orwell's *1984*? Because it rhymed with the previous line while McCartney was stoned at the piano? Why ask why? McCartney degenerates into gibberish as he does a spot-on spoof of Lennon's guttural howls of madness in "Cold Turkey," the song that McCartney once balked at doing, thus prompting Lennon to quit the Beatles. The pianos, Mellotrons, organs, horns, and full orchestra erupt into the pyrotechnic climax of the *Band on the Run* album, then briefly reprise the title song.

SCARED—LENNON

Rec. summer 1974, Record Plant East, NYC, Lennon (producer), Lennon (v, g), Davis (g), Voormann (b), Keltner (d), Hopkins (p), Jenkins (percussion), Mottau (acoustic g), Ken Ascher (electric p), Little Big Horns: Keys (sax), Steve Madaio, Howard Johnson, Ron Aprea, Frank Vicari, Album *Walls and Bridges*

Lennon would refer to his time in Los Angeles as his "Lost Weekend," refer-ring to the novel in which an alcoholic writer goes off on a five-day bender. Lennon knew his alcoholism and drug addictions were spiraling out of con-trol, the government was trying to deport him, his career was in decline, and the love of his life had given him the boot.

"Scared" is a composition as naked as anything on *Plastic Ono Band*, but with slick studio polish and top-notch session men. Like "Mother," it opens with a horror movie sound effect—this time, the chilling howl of a wolf. It evokes Lennon's terror at being lost in the woods, and also the horror of be-ing a werewolf who goes berserk when he drinks his Mr. Hyde potion. The music kicks in with a foreboding shuffle not unlike Cab Calloway's 1931 jazz million seller "Minnie the Moocher."

He panics about growing older in a world of twenty-year-old pop idols and feels alone and homeless, despite May Pang's presence and the fact that millions of people would love to hang out with him. He owns up to the hypocrisy of singing about peace when his heart is filled with jealousy and hate. He rues that those two emotions will be the death of him—as one day they would, though the jealousy and hate would be Mark David Chapman's.

MRS. VANDEBILT—MCCARTNEY

REC. AUGUST–SEPTEMBER 1973, EMI STUDIOS, LAGOS, NIGERIA, MIXED AT KINGSWAY STUDIOS, LONDON, MCCARTNEY (PRODUCER), MCCARTNEY (V, B, G, D), LINDA MCCARTNEY (K, BV), LAINE (GUITAR, BV), HOWIE CASEY (SAX), ALBUM *BAND ON THE RUN*

McCartney went on African safari with roadie Mal Evans in 1966, but whatever he was expecting to find in Lagos, Nigeria, in 1973, it was a lot worse. A corrupt military dictatorship had taken control in a coup. The studio was a disaster with one eight-track recorder. The power would go out and they'd have to rely on backup generators.

When Wings visited the club of local music/political legend Fela Ransome-Kuti, the man berated McCartney for coming to Nigeria to steal African music. In a way, it had naturally been McCartney's goal. When he went to Nashville, he came back with the country song "Sally G"; when he went to New Orleans he came back with a Mardi Gras song. But now he had to play his songs for Ransome-Kuti and prove they had soaked up no Nigerian elements.

On Beatles tours, McCartney was often cautioned to stay in his hotel, but he always snuck out. Now, despite warnings, he went for a walk one night with Linda, and the two were promptly mugged by guys with knives. "Don't kill him, he's a musician!" Linda screamed. The thugs ran off with a bag containing McCartney's demos and notebook of lyrics.

Finally he hit the wall in the studio one day. He was in the midst of singing when he turned corpse white and gasped that he couldn't breathe. They took him outside for fresh air and the insufferable heat made him faint. Linda became hysterical, assuming it was a heart attack. In the end it turned out to be a bronchial spasm caused by too much smoking. No doubt all the stress had accelerated his habit.

At some point, the absurdity reminded him of a catchphrase by English music hall performer Charlie Chester: "Down in the jungle living in a tent, better than a bungalow, no rent." Accepting the situation, he wrote that, really, there was no point in worrying about any of it. In an upbeat variation on "The Continuing Story of Bungalow Bill," he, Laine, and Linda chanted the marching cry, "Ho! Hey Ho!" while saucy bass and sax fell in and crazy monkeys chatter-laughed from the trees.

McCartney didn't release the song as a single in the United States or United Kingdom, so he never played the song live. But it had been released in Europe and Australia, and when he arrived in Kiev in 2008 to do a gig, he was surprised to find that a web poll named it to be the most requested song for him to perform. Apparently the amused acceptance of chaos was a theme Kievians could relate to. McCartney discovered he dug playing "Mrs. Vandebilt" and it became a permanent part of his show, thirty-five years after its release.

NOBODY LOVES YOU (WHEN YOU'RE DOWN AND OUT)—LENNON

REC. SUMMER 1974, RECORD PLANT EAST, NYC, LENNON (PRODUCER), LENNON (V, ACOUSTIC G), DAVIS (G), VOORMANN (B), KELTNER (D), LITTLE BIG HORNS: KEYS (SAX), STEVE MADAIO, HOWARD JOHNSON, RON APREA, FRANK VICARI, ALBUM *WALLS AND BRIDGES*: ALTERNATE VERSIONS: *MENLOVE AVENUE*, *JOHN LENNON ANTHOLOGY*

Of his Lost Weekend compatriots Nilsson, Keith Moon, and saxophonist Bobby Keys, Lennon told *Playboy*, "We couldn't pull ourselves out. We were trying to kill ourselves. I think Harry might still be trying, poor bugger—God bless you, Harry, wherever you are—but, Jesus, you know, I had to get away from that, because somebody was going to die. Well, Keith did. It was like, who's going to die first? Unfortunately, Keith was the one."

When *Playboy* asked why they were so self-destructive, Lennon replied, "For me, it was because of being apart [from Ono]. I couldn't stand it. They had their own reasons, and it was, let's all drown ourselves together. From where I was sitting, it looked like that. Let's kill ourselves but do it like Errol Flynn, you know, the macho, male way."[7]

Moon was haunted by a tragedy from January 4, 1970. One night at an English pub, the other patrons began to attack his Bentley. Someone (maybe Moon, maybe not) floored the car and it ran over Moon's friend/driver/bodyguard Neil Boland, killing him. Boland's daughter conducted an investigation that determined that Moon was not behind the wheel, although other reports say he was. Either way, he never got over the guilt, and girlfriends would recount that he often woke in the night from horrible nightmares. On September 7, 1978, he attended the premiere of *The Buddy Holly Story* with Paul and Linda McCartney, then went home and took thirty-two clomethiazole pills, sedatives to help with alcohol detoxification. He had been told not to take more than three a day, and he died from an overdose.

Lennon got into the press for all the wrong reasons thanks to two debacles that happened at the legendary Troubadour club. Lennon later recounted to *Playboy* that he, May Pang, his favorite session guitarist Davis, and Davis's girlfriend were "drinking, not eating, as usual at those gatherings, and I happened to go take a pee and there was a brand-new fresh Kotex, not Tampax, on the toilet. You know the old trick where you put a penny on your forehead and it sticks? I was a little high and I just picked it up and slapped it on and it stayed, you see. I walked out of the bathroom and I had a Kotex on my head. Big deal. Everybody went 'Ha-ha-ha' and it fell off, but the press blew it up." When a waitress asked him to leave, he demanded, "Do you know who I am?" "Yeah, you're an asshole with a Kotex on his head," she responded. When Annie Peebles came on to sing "I Can't Stand the Rain," Lennon yelled, "Annie! I want to s--- your p----!" and was promptly ejected by the bouncers, while the crowd cheered.

When Pang insisted they call it a night, Lennon tried to strangle her in the car. Back at the house they were staying in (before getting the Malibu place with Starr and Co.), Lennon and Davis started smashing the lights and then proceeded to demolish the place, even pulling the stuffing out of the mattresses. Afterward, they started wrestling, which quickly turned into a fight. Lennon got Davis in a full Nelson and started kissing him on the mouth. When Lennon started jamming his tongue in, Davis bit his tongue, so Lennon grabbed a marble ashtray and hit Davis on the head with it, knocking him unconscious. Davis's girlfriend screamed, so Lennon tried dousing Davis with orange juice. To bandage Davis's head, Lennon wrapped it with a roll of film. When the cops arrived with shotguns, Lennon tried to hide, but they found him and asked him if the Beatles would reunite. Lennon said, "You never know." Davis came to.

When Lennon woke to the carnage the next day, the thing that troubled him was that he had smashed his own guitar. Wrecking somebody else's stuff was one thing, but now he was wrecking his own.[8]

Lennon returned in March with Nilsson to see the Smothers Brothers, the comedy/singing duo who had been taken off the air in the 1960s when their show became too outspokenly liberal. You'd think Lennon would have shown them respect, but instead he and Nilsson kept singing "I Can't Stand the Rain" and heckling them. Eventually they were forced out, but this time Lennon fought back. Unfortunately, his glasses were knocked off and without them he was as blind as a bat. Perhaps for that reason, he ended up hitting a waitress in the melee. He sent her flowers the next day, but the story hit the papers immediately and he looked like a washed-up asshole.

Lennon continues to *Playboy*, "It's embarrassing for me to think about that period because I made a big fool of myself—but maybe it was a good lesson for me. I wrote 'Nobody Loves You (When You're Down and Out)' during that time. That's how I felt. It exactly expresses the whole period. For some reason, I always imagined Sinatra singing that one. I don't know why. It's kind of a Sinatraesque song, really. He would do a perfect job with it. Are you listening, Frank? You need a song that isn't a piece of nothing. Here's the one for you, the horn arrangement and everything's made for you. But don't ask me to produce it."[9]

Lennon got the title from "Nobody Knows You (When You're Down and Out)," a blues song written in 1923 by Jimmy Cox about a millionaire who'd lost it all. It was the only song on *Walls and Bridges* that Lennon wrote in LA; an acoustic demo was recorded in October 1973. An early rehearsal features lonely whistling and stark instrumentation (later released on the outtakes album *Menlove Avenue*). For *Walls and Bridges* he added keyboards, brass, strings, and processed his voice with a ton of reverb like a lady afraid not to wear makeup. An ideal version might have been to start out with the minimalism of the rehearsal versions and then build to Davis's piercing guitar solo backed by full orchestration, but both versions are powerful. The *Lennon Anthology* captures a version in the middle of the two approaches.

Having reached the middle of the decade with few hits and a serious bomb, Lennon felt abandoned by his audience now that he was getting older, ruing that they'd only love him again when he was six feet underground. (Partly true.) After crossing oceans many times to get advice from half-blind witchdoctors (e.g., Maharishi, Janov), whatever peace they seemed to offer always vanished quickly and he was back where he started, exhausted but unable to sleep. Young May Pang asks him if he loves her, and all he can answer is, "It's all showbiz."

PICASSO'S LAST WORDS—MCCARTNEY

Rec. August–September 1973, Ginger Baker's ARC Studios, Lagos, Nigeria, mixed at Kingsway Studios, London, McCartney (producer), McCartney (v, b, g, k), Linda McCartney (bv), Laine (g, v), Ginger Baker (percussion), Album *Band on the Run*

When McCartney and Linda were on vacation in Jamaica, they visited the set of *Papillon*, which was shooting with Dustin Hoffman and Steve McQueen.

Hoffman invited the couple over to dinner and asked McCartney how he wrote songs. When McCartney replied that he just made them up, Hoffman produced the April 23 issue of *Time* with an article about "Pablo Picasso's Last Days and Final Journey" and asked if he could write a song about that. The piece mentioned that Picasso had told his friends, "Drink to me, drink to my health, you know I can't drink anymore," then went to bed and died in his sleep. McCartney started strumming a guitar and singing what would become the chorus. "He's doing it! He's doing it!" Hoffman cried. He later said that the experience was "right under childbirth in terms of great events of my life."

By the time Wings was in Nigeria, McCartney had fleshed out a few more lines. The painter wakes in the middle of the night and sings that he's waiting. Either he's waiting for death or he's already died and waiting for his wife on the other side to join him. Perhaps his near-death experience due to smoking—and the doctors' orders to cut back—helped him relate to Picasso's words.

Cream's drummer Ginger Baker had a studio in a Lagos suburb, Ikeja. He was pushing for McCartney to do the whole album there. McCartney didn't want to but agreed to do one song at Baker's place. Baker and some additional people from the studio filled some cans with gravel and shook them for percussion.

With his technique called cubism, Picasso would paint an object but break it up and show different viewpoints of the object randomly recombined on the same plane, transforming something representational into something abstract. As quoted in Paul Gambaccini's *Paul McCartney: In His Own Words*, McCartney said, "We started off doing it straight. Then we thought, Picasso was kind of far out in his pictures, he'd done all these different kinds of things, fragmented, cubism, and the whole bit. I thought it would be nice to get a track a bit like that, put it through different moods, cut it up, edit it, mess around with it—like he used to do with his pictures. You see the old films of him painting, he paints it once and if he doesn't like it he paints it again, right on top of it, and by about twenty-five times he's got this picture. . . . We were just making it up as we went along. We didn't have any big concept of it in mind at all. I just thought, we'll mess it up, keep messing it up until it sounds good, like Picasso did, with the instinctive knowledge you've got."[10]

The highlight of the tune is the "Sound of Philadelphia"/proto-disco strings arranged by Tony Visconti. In French, a man from a tourist service offers to send free travel guides. Then the tempo changes and Macca, Linda, and Denny sing the "Jet" refrain for a while. A drunken chorus sings, "Drink to me," and then a fade-out to the "Ho Hey Ho" from "Mrs. Vandebilt."

(IT'S ALL DOWN TO) GOODNIGHT VIENNA—STARR

Rec. August 1984, Sunset Sound Recorders Studio, LA, and Producers Workshop, Lennon (writer), Richard Perry (producer), Starr (v, d), Lennon (p, v), Voormann (b), Keltner (d), Preston (clavinet), Lon Van Eaton (g), Davis (g), Carl Fortina (accordion), Horns: Keys, Trevor Lawrence, Steve Madaio, Lon Van Eaton, Backing Vocals: Clydie King, The Blackberries, The Masst Abbots, Single: US 6/2/75 (31), also on *Goodnight Vienna*

The *Ringo* album was a smash, so the idea was—in the time-honored pop tradition—if it ain't broke, don't fix it, make a *Ringo 2*. However, Harrison wasn't around because of the affair with Starr's wife. And McCartney wasn't around because he was taking most of 1974 off. But Lennon and Starr did utilize McCartney's trope of reprising the album's title track at the end of the record (which also, incidentally, filled up space).

Goodnight Vienna's title track is another revelatory Lennon self-portrait, though cloaked in the grotesque gobbledygook of his 1960s books *In His Own Write* and *A Spaniard in the Works*. (Lennon's demo version can be heard on the *Lennon Anthology*.) For some reason, "Goodnight Vienna" was Liverpool slang for "It's all over/time to get out of this place," and the song is about how Lennon was realizing it was time to get out of the Hollywood "Lost Weekend" scene.

The singer can't relax with his girlfriend because she's so pretty, something that had been a problem in the past for the insecure Lennon. He had encouraged first wife, Cynthia, to model herself after Brigitte Bardot, but when Bardot actually invited Lennon over one time in the late '60s, he took so much acid he was reduced to a catatonic, introverted mess and could barely communicate with her. Once during their LA sojourn, Lennon and Pang went to lunch with David Cassidy, and the paranoid Lennon became convinced Pang was flirting with Cassidy. In the song, the singer devolves into a jealous frog who doesn't believe it when his woman tells him she loves him. In Lennon's mind, how could Pang love him when he was no young pretty boy and tried to strangle her when he got wasted? When they were alone, Lennon ripped the glasses off Pang's face and stomped on them, hissing that Ono "had been right about her."[11] He dragged her back to New York on a plane as if they were going to split, then changed his mind a few days later and took her back to LA.

As LA was the capital of the shallow beauties, no doubt his insecurities were running rampant. Throughout Starr's version, Lennon (as backing vocalist) yells to get it up and keep it up. Back in the Beatlemania days he relished performing like a super stud with all the starlets, but ten years on it was getting more difficult for him to care about validating himself. Thus keeping it up was becoming an issue.

So when "the butcher" arrives with his needles, it is tempting for Lennon to go back on smack to deal with his anxieties. Thus Lennon knew it was time to say "Goodnight Vienna" and get out of town.

The lively production made good use of horns and even an accordion, but it only reached number twenty-nine—Starr's last top thirty hit. Earlier singles from the album did well, though: "No No Song" b/w "Snookeroo" made number three in the United States; and "Only You" made number six. But it would be the last album in which Starr was a commercial force to be reckoned with.

For the memorable marketing campaign, Starr re-created a famous scene from the sci-fi flick *The Day the Earth Stood Still*, wearing the space suit of the alien Klaatu. (Thus a Canadian band named Klaatu got some mileage in the beginning of their career with the hoax that they were actually the reformed Beatles with tunes like "Calling Occupants of Interplanetary Craft.") The deliberately cheesy TV commercial for *Goodnight Vienna* had goofy Lennon and Starr banter over images of Starr getting into an Ed Wood–looking Grade Z sci-fi spaceship outside the Capitol Records building and flying around LA.

Lennon would write three other songs for Starr's solo albums: "Cookin' (in the Kitchen of Love)," and two that Starr never recorded: "Nobody Told Me," and with terrible irony, "Life Begins at 40."

COUNTRY DREAMER—MCCARTNEY

REC. OCTOBER 1972, STUDIO UNKNOWN, MCCARTNEY (PRODUCER), MCCARTNEY (V, B), LINDA MCCARTNEY (BV), LAINE (G, BV), HENRY MCCULLOUGH (G), SEIWELL (D), B-SIDE TO HELEN WHEELS: UK 10/26/73 (12); US 12/12/73 (10), ALSO INCLUDED AS BONUS TRACK ON *BAND ON THE RUN*

Another lost gem of a B-side, "Country Dreamer" was an idyllic ode to natural living recorded during the *Red Rose Speedway* sessions in late 1972 but held back for release as the flipside to "Helen Wheels."

McCartney's previous ode to the country, "Heart of the Country," was a bit corny, in the mode of a bouncy Elvis movie tune from the early 1960s. In contrast, this song was mellow and understated. The opening guitar passage sounds almost like Simon and Garfunkel before a second slide guitar twangs. McCartney celebrates having nothing to do but relax outdoors. He praises the simple joys of walking through a field barefoot, wading into a stream, climbing to the top of a hill to dig the view, and maybe doing it in the field. Lennon chided McCartney for not being as radical as him, but actually by living on their ramshackle sheep farm McCartney and Linda were much closer to the dream of many hippies hoping to return to nature in communes.

#9 DREAM—LENNON

REC. SUMMER 1974, RECORD PLANT EAST, NYC, LENNON (PRODUCER), LENNON (V, ACOUSTIC G), DAVIS (G), VOORMANN (B), KELTNER (D), HOPKINS (P), KEYS (SAX), JENKINS (PERCUSSION), MOTTAU (ACOUSTIC G), KEN ASCHER (CLAVINET), THE 44TH STREET FAIRIES (BV) (MAY PANG, LORI BURTON, JOEL DAMBRA), SINGLE: UK 1/24/75 (23); US 12/16/74 (9), ALSO ON *WALLS AND BRIDGES*, COVERS: R.E.M., A-HA

Although they were apart, *Walls and Bridges* features many songs to Ono. "Going Down on Love" and "What You Got" express his regret, while "Bless You" sends his love even though they've moved on to different phases in their lives. The song that best captures his nostalgia for what he and Ono shared is "#9 Dream," in which he looks back at a relationship that once seemed so real but was now just a dream.

When producing Harry Nilsson's album, Lennon created a string arrangement for Nilsson's cover of Jimmy Cliff's reggae song "Many Rivers to Cross" and liked it so much he decided to recycle it and write new words to go with it. Originally the song was called "So Long Ago" (a phrase that remained in the lyrics) and then "Walls and Bridges," which did not end up in the song but became the title of the album. He felt it expressed how he would build both walls and bridges in his relationships with people.

A sumptuous aural phantasmagoria is created with cellos, horns, strings, and that old Beatles standby, backward voices, not to mention an arresting opening very much in the vein of George's post-Beatles slide guitar. (Lennon had instructed Jesse Ed Davis to play like Harrison.)

Wistful, Lennon is haunted by memories of the early days of his and Ono's love, when she fulfilled his dream to have a lover who was a collaborative partner (on "Revolution 9") and also fulfilled his fetish for Asian women. They shared belief in all things magical from the I Ching to reincarnation. Later, he rejected the supernatural while in his existential atheist pose (he was a Libra, embracing then rejecting, trying to find balance), but now he wants to believe again and tap back into the spirit that once suffused the air.

Lennon said, "When real music comes to me—the music of the spheres, the music that surpasses understanding—that has nothing to do with me, 'cause I'm just the channel. The only joy for me is for it to be given to me, and to transcribe it like a medium . . . those moments are what I live for."

The lyrics evoke such a moment, in a much more visual, suggestive way than the didactic "Intuition" on *Mind Games*: Walking past the whispering trees, he hears someone call him as it starts to rain, and the water transforms into a mirror river of sound.

Numerologically, Lennon felt nine was his number since his birthday was October 9 and the Beatles made their debut on *Ed Sullivan* on February 9 (hence "Revolution 9"). May Pang said that the chorus, "Ah! böwakawa poussé, poussé," was from a dream Lennon had and didn't mean anything concrete. Probably what it meant is that Lennon got "pussy" on the airwaves twice in one year, if you count the title to Nilsson's album *Pussy Cats*. He'd gotten a kick out of slipping the "tit tit tit" backing vocals of the Beatles' "Girl" past the censors, as well as the play out groove of *Sgt. Pepper*, which was rumored to be "Fuck you like a superman" backward.

Pang was the woman whispering the backing vocals, but the week "#9 Dream" made it to number nine on the charts, Lennon moved back in with Ono. In the decades to follow, what would Pang feel when she heard herself whispering on the song whenever it happened to drift across the radio?

NOTES

1. Pattie Boyd and Penny Junor, *Wonderful Tonight: George Harrison, Eric Clapton, and Me* (London: Headline Review, 2007), 122.

2. Boyd and Junor, *Wonderful Tonight*, 179–84.

3. Chris O'Dell and Katherine Ketcham, *Miss O'Dell: My Hard Days and Long Nights with The Beatles, The Stones, Bob Dylan, Eric Clapton, and the Women They Loved* (New York: Touchstone, 2009), 262–70.

4. Peter Doggett, *You Never Give Me Your Money* (New York: HarperCollins, 2009), 209.

5. John Blaney, *Lennon and McCartney: Together Alone* (London: Jawbone, 2007), 90.

6. Simon Leng, *The Music of George Harrison: While My Guitar Gently Weeps* (London: Firefly, 2003), 165–69.

7. David Sheff, "January 1981 *Playboy* Interview with John Lennon and Yoko Ono," John-Lennon.com, www.john-lennon.com/playboyinterviewwithjohnlennonand yokoono.htm (October 10, 2011).

8. Albert Goldman, *The Lives of John Lennon* (London: Bantam, 1988), 575–77.

9. Sheff, "January 1981 *Playboy* Interview."

10. Paul Gambaccini, ed. *Paul McCartney: In His Own Words* (New York: Music Sales Corp., 1976).

11. Goldman, *The Lives of John Lennon*, 569–71.

Wings, 1975–1977: (from left) Denny Laine (guitar), Linda McCartney, Paul McCartney, Joe English (drums), and Jimmy McCulloch (guitar). *Captiol Records/ PhotoFest Library*

1976: Pizza and Fairy Tales

Lennon weighs whether to return to McCartney or Ono.

𝒥n the first half of the 1970s, the solo Beatles were all pushing themselves to outdo each other and came up with more than enough material to fill an album a year. By mid-decade, however, their muses started flickering just a bit. So at this juncture, longer breathers between albums becomes necessary to allow enough grade-A material to gather.

At some point in the decade, Lennon sneered at McCartney, "You're all just pizza and fairy tales," even as Lennon's own days on the cultural vanguard were over. But if the post-Fabs' songs were once again just consummately crafted pop rock and nothing more, what was wrong with that? Wasn't that what Beatles songs had been before *Revolver*?

A new Beatles cult appeared among kids who had missed it the first time around. EMI re-released all their singles and they each made the UK top 100, including new singles "Back in the USSR" and "Got to Get You into My Life." Originally, the label planned to capitalize on the TV movie *Helter Skelter* based on the Charles Manson trial by issuing "Helter Skelter" as a new A-side, but more tasteful heads prevailed and it was consigned to the B-side of "Got to Get You into My Life." "Got to Get You into My Life" made it into the top ten and stayed on the charts as long as any Beatles single except "Hey Jude." A two-volume Beatles compilation called *Rock 'n' Roll* also made it to number two in summer 1976.

Back in New York, Lennon and Pang had a new apartment with a room for Julian to stay when he visited, and Lennon had reconnected with pals like Mick Jagger whom Ono had discouraged as "bad influences." In December 1974, when visiting Jagger in the Hamptons, Lennon and Pang saw a cottage by a lighthouse and decided to put an offer on it.

Lennon started asking people whether he should work with McCartney again. Art Garfunkel encouraged him to, and when he mentioned it to Pang, she was ecstatic. In January 1975, McCartney and Linda were in New Orleans recording *Venus and Mars*. On the title track, McCartney sang an ode to the planet of love and the planet of war back in sync. Pang told Roger Freidman of Fox News in 2001 that Lennon "made plans to surprise them down there. He was in a great mood and he really missed Paul."[1]

Between Lennon's plans to buy a house with Pang and reunite with Mc-Cartney, Ono realized she was on the verge of losing Lennon for good. Her own solo work didn't sell without him, and he had given his first wife and son a pretty paltry divorce settlement.

The night before Lennon and Pang were to plan out the New Orleans trip, Ono invited Lennon over to the Dakota for a hypnotherapy technique designed to quit smoking. Pang pleaded with him not to go, but he snapped that she was being ridiculous and he'd be home soon.[2]

When Lennon did not return, Pang called Ono the next day. Ono said Lennon was too wiped out from the hypnotherapy sessions to come to the phone. Pang saw Lennon two days later because they had scheduled dental appointments at the same time, and he was so zombified Pang thought Ono had brainwashed him. Lennon told Pang that he was going back to Ono, but that Ono would still let him see Pang, and their affair continued for another two years.

Biographer Goldman says Lennon described the hypnotherapy process to Pang as: "I was throwin' up all the time. . . . I kept fallin' asleep, and when I woke up, they would do it to me again." But what "it" was has not been elaborated. Goldman maintained that Ono's spiritual advisors were adept at Santeria, as if Ono were a villainous witch who lived, fittingly, in the building where *Rosemary's Baby* had been filmed.[3] Another explanation for his "zombified" state could be that Ono lured him back to smack. Lennon supposedly fell back into addiction for the first couple years of his "househusband" period before kicking it through his own sensory deprivation chamber.

More likely is the fact that (a) he always loved her, and (b) his life was heading toward two commitments to which he had profound ambivalence: moving in with Pang and working with McCartney.

If he teamed again with McCartney, he would have to work his ass off to stay an equal member of the band. If he went with Ono, he could sink into oblivion in the Dakota while she looked after the money.

It's a truism that abusive types like to be dominated; mean bosses visit ball-busting S&M dominatrixes. In Ono, Lennon had found the real-life incarnation of the archetype he wrote about in 1965's "Girl": the spoiled, narcissistic descendent of bankers, classical pianists, and an Emperor of Japan, with an ego big enough to be a bigger bitch than him. She pushed him to cut off contact with childhood friends and fellow musicians, anyone who could threaten her hold on him. Most egregiously she made him choose between her and his own son, like the wicked stepmother in *Hansel and Gretel*. (After Lennon's death it came to light that he had not left Julian much in his will; perhaps because he had given Ono power of attorney and left financial matters to her.)

But she was also funny, idealistic, photogenic, reminded him of his mother, was stern like his maternal aunt, was a force field against a world that crowded him, taught him not to be a chauvinist, gave him a home, and was a prolific fellow artist like his long gone best friend Stu Sutcliffe. The proof in the pudding is that he wrote many longing paeans to Ono. While many Beatles fans wish it were otherwise, Ono truly was the love of his life.

When Pang told Mick Jagger that Lennon had gone back to Ono, Jagger paused for a long time then said, "I guess I've lost a friend."[4]

Ono sealed her hold on Lennon by getting pregnant, once he agreed that she would not be required to be the primary caregiver. As she explained to *Playboy* in 1980,

> I am very clear about my emotions in that area. I don't feel guilty. I am doing it in my own way. It may not be the same as other mothers, but I'm doing it the way I can do it. In general, mothers have a very strong resentment toward their children, even though there's this whole adulation about motherhood and how mothers really think about their children and how they really love them. I mean, they do, but it is not humanly possible to retain emotion that mothers are supposed to have within this society. Women are just too stretched out in different directions to retain that emotion. Too much is required of them. So I say to John—

John confirms, "I am her favorite husband—," and Ono continues,

> "I am carrying the baby nine months and that is enough, so you take care of it afterward." It did sound like a crude remark, but I really believe that children belong to the society. If a mother carries the child and a father raises it, the responsibility is shared.[5]

Lennon's thirty-fifth birthday saw the birth of Sean Ono Lennon and the granting of his green card. With the scandal of Watergate fresh in the public's mind, the Ford administration didn't want any of the FBI's illegal surveillance techniques to be bandied about in the press. It was one of the most joyous days of his life.

Pang said in the years afterward no one believed Lennon wanted to head down to New Orleans to see McCartney. "But then something happened," she told Friedman. "Derek Taylor, the Beatles' publicist, showed me a postcard he'd gotten from John in England. It said, 'Going to New Orleans to see Paul.' And that was it. That was the proof."

While the Beatles reunion was not to be, in 1976 McCartney was finally granted the visa to tour the United States for the first time since 1966 and Wings-mania landed him on the cover of *Time*. Giving the "Wings" hand symbol, the thumbs up, or throwing his fists up in the air amidst bubbles and smoke onstage, McCartney and Linda would never be dangerously cool. But as the six o'clock news covered him at airports shaking hands with the crowd with his wife and little kids in tow, he was perhaps the first family rock and roller, regular pot busts notwithstanding. Amidst the pervasive decadence of the rock scene, it was a unique image. Whereas Starr's and Lennon's kids would publicly state that their fathers left a lot to be desired as parents, no ill reports have surfaced from Family McCartney, so it seems the wholesomeness was real.

Onstage he was one of the most potent showmen of his generation, able to switch from heartrending ballad to shrieking rocker on a dime, jumping up from the piano to dance for joy like Elvis with a bass strapped on. Wings' apogee was captured in the concert film *Rock Show* (released in 1980) and by the number one triple live album *Wings over America* (from which "Maybe I'm Amazed" was finally released as a live single).

Lennon commented, "I kind of admire the way Paul started back from scratch, forming a new band and playing in small dance halls, because that's what he wanted to do with the—he wanted us to go back to the dance halls and experience that again. But I didn't. . . . That was one of the problems, in a way, that he wanted to relive it all or something—I don't know what it was. . . . But I kind of admire the way he got off his pedestal—now he's back on it again, but I mean, he did what he wanted to do. That's fine, but it's just not what I wanted to do."[6]

The year 1975 would turn out to be the last time that Lennon, McCartney, and Harrison would all release new albums in the same year. It was also the year the Apple Records' office at Saville Row was abandoned and all the label's releases except the Beatles' were deleted. Starr's 1976 album *Ringo's Rotogravure* would be the last one on which all Beatles would either play or contribute a song.

In the contest for most consecutive top ten singles in the United States, McCartney won with eight, but surprisingly Starr was number two with seven: "It Don't Come Easy" (number four), "Back Off Boogaloo" (number nine), "Photograph" (number one), "You're Sixteen" (number one), "Oh My My" (number five), "Only You (And You Alone)" (number six), and "Snookeroo/The No No Song" (number three). Unfortunately, "Snookeroo" ended Starr's streak in January 1975.

LET 'EM IN—MCCARTNEY

REC. JANUARY 1976, ABBEY ROAD, MCCARTNEY (PRODUCER), MCCARTNEY (V, B, P), LINDA MCCARTNEY (K, BV), LAINE (G, BV), JIMMY MCCULLOCH (G), JOE ENGLISH (D), STEVE "TEX" HOWARD (TRUMPET), THADDEUS RICHARD (SAX), HOWIE CASEY (SAX), TROY DORSEY (TROMBONE), SINGLE: UK 7/23/76 (2); US 6/28/76 (3), ALSO ON *WINGS AT THE SPEED OF SOUND*, GRAMMY NOM. FOR BEST ARRANGEMENT ACCOMPANYING VOCALISTS

McCartney once referred to writing songs as pulling rabbits out of hats, and in the early days he was surprised at his ability to keep doing it. He wrote "Hello, Goodbye" sitting at the piano with Brian Epstein's assistant Alistair Taylor by asking him to say the opposite of whatever word McCartney threw out. For "Let 'Em In," he just thought about who he'd like to invite to a party and imagined them gradually showing up at his place: Sister Suzy of the Red Stripes (a pseudonym under which Linda had released a solo single), Linda's brother John, Martin Luther (either the leader of the Protestant Reformation or MLK), Phil and Don Everly (at which point in the song McCartney's voice is double tracked in homage to their harmonies), McCartney's brother Michael, his Auntie Gin, and Uncle Ernie (the perverted role Keith Moon played in the movie *Tommy*).

STAND BY ME—LENNON

REC. AUTUMN 1974, RECORD PLANT EAST, NYC, KING/LEIBER/STOLLER (WRITERS), LENNON (PRODUCER), LENNON (V, ACOUSTIC G), DAVIS (G), VOORMANN (B), KELTNER (D), JENKINS (PERCUSSION), MOTTAU (ACOUSTIC G), PETER JAMESON (G), ASCHER (P), FRANK VICARI (SAX), JOSEPH TEMPERLEY (SAX), DENNIS MOROUSE (TENOR SAX), SINGLE: UK 4/18/75 (30); US 3/10/75 (20), ALSO ON *ROCK 'N' ROLL*

Just as Harrison got nabbed for copping "My Sweet Lord," Chuck Berry's publisher Morris Levy sued Lennon for plagiarism. Lennon had slowed down "You Can't Catch Me" into "Come Together" and quoted the first line of the original song. Lennon settled by agreeing to record three songs that Levy owned on his next album, then decided to go all out and make a whole album of 1950s covers.

Lennon teamed up with Spector again to produce, only this time Lennon turned over all control to Spector, as if Lennon was just a '50s teen idol like Fabian who only showed up to sing. The downside of that approach was that Lennon decided to drink while recording, particularly as it was after being dumped by Ono. The October–December 1973 sessions became the biggest party in LA but quickly devolved into chaos. Spector tried to control Lennon's intake of booze but was easily circumvented. Soon, a wasted Lennon was so angered by Spector's time-consuming process that he smashed his headset on the console, starting a fight with Spector. In Spector's house, Lennon freaked out on Spector again, so the producer had his bodyguards tie Lennon face down on the guest bed (shades of *Beyond the Valley of the Dolls*, the Russ Meyer film written by critic Roger Ebert that featured a character based on Spector named Z-Man). During another session, Spector started firing his gun at the ceiling, prompting Lennon to scream that Spector should just kill him next time because if he made Lennon deaf it would end his career. Half of the recordings were train wrecks in which Lennon was obviously wasted, making lewd comments while the thirty-piece orchestra was out of tune. When the entourage poured whiskey into the recording console, they were banned from A&M studios. In the end, four cuts were salvageable, but, sensing he was about to get the boot, Spector disappeared with the tapes.

Lennon gave up on the album, pulled himself together, produced Harry Nilsson's *Pussy Cats* and then *Walls and Bridges*. Levy freaked out that the album didn't have the agreed-upon amount of cover songs, so to stave off a lawsuit, Lennon agreed to quickly record the oldies album again. This time he was the model of professionalism. After spending a few days rehearsing the band at Morris Levy's farm, he recorded the album on October 21–24, 1974.

The most famous Lennon tune to come from the *Rock 'n' Roll* album was his cover of "Stand by Me." Ben E. King originally wrote the song with Jerry Leiber and Mike Stoller ("Hound Dog," "Jailhouse Rock") with the intention that his band, the Drifters, would record it. But the Drifters passed, so he did it solo and it became one of the most enduring hits of modern times, still heard daily on oldies stations, with over 400 covers.

The song is built around the chord progression called "The 50s Progression" or "Stand by Me Changes." The intro sounds like Starr's version of "Only You (And You Alone)," which Lennon had encouraged Starr to cover for his 1974 album *Goodnight Vienna* and on which Lennon played guitar. Lennon's demo for Starr can be heard on the *Lennon Anthology*; it sounds like it could be on *Rock 'n' Roll*.

Though the album is good, "Stand by Me" transcended its setting to become part of Lennon's solo pantheon. Lennon's obvious need for a strong love in his life infused his performance with genuine passion. Like he once did with his cover of "Money," he made the song his own and, for some listeners, surpassed the original.

LISTEN TO WHAT THE MAN SAID—MCCARTNEY

REC. 1975, SEA SAINT STUDIOS, NEW ORLEANS, AND WALLY HEIDER STUDIOS, LA, McCARTNEY (PRODUCER), McCARTNEY (V, B, P), LINDA McCARTNEY (K, BV), LAINE (G, BV), JIMMY McCULLOCH (G), JOE ENGLISH (D), TOM SCOTT (SAX), DAVE MASON (G), SINGLE: UK 5/16/75 (6); US 5/26/75 (1), ALSO ON *VENUS AND MARS*

After only six months, Wings drummer Geoff Britton quit as they were heading to New Orleans in January 1975 to record *Venus and Mars*, the follow-up to *Band on the Run*. As a karate champ, he didn't fit with the other band members' partying ways. He particularly loathed the young Jimmy McCulloch, a drunk who could give Lennon a run for his money in the obnoxious department.

An American drummer named Joe English won the replacement audition, and the new band coalesced around this effervescent single. The melody perfectly expressed McCartney's joyful wonder at the circular trip he had taken over the last five years, falling into the critical wilderness but now back in the pocket again. McCartney took Harrison's Leslie cabinet–treated guitar sound from the bittersweet *Abbey Road* and refashioned it as counterpoint to a euphoric soprano sax and Linda's ebullient vocals.

Saxophonist Tom Scott had played on Starr's "Oh My My," the theme to *Starsky and Hutch*, and with everyone from the Grateful Dead, to Streisand, the Carpenters, Pink Floyd, Steely Dan, Sinatra, and the Blues Brothers. The group was in the studio with Traffic's Dave Mason figuring out what to do with the song when they decided to call Scott in. He turned up in a half hour, listened to the backing track, and improvised his part all in the first take. It was so good no one could believe it, so they kept trying a few more, but nothing matched the first shot out of the box, and so that was that.

The words have a hint of depth with the brief lyric about a soldier boy who kisses a girl and leaves behind a tragic world. In 1975, the last US helicopters flew out of Saigon. Could that be the tragic world left behind? Even though the United States had lost the war, everyone was glad it was over.

Also perplexing is McCartney's use of "the man," which was typically used by the hip community to refer to the cops or the government, generally viewed as an oppressive force to resist. Presumably, McCartney blithely nodding his head back and forth beaming, "Listen to what the man said," didn't help his underground cred. But by then the underground was in ruins, with Patty Hearst and the Symbionese Liberation Army finally captured that September.

SLIPPIN' AND SLIDIN'—LENNON

Rec. autumn 1974, Record Plant East NYC, Penniman/Bocage/Collins/Smith (writers), Lennon (producer), Lennon (v, acoustic g), Davis (g), Voormann (b), Keltner (d), Jenkins (percussion), Mottau (acoustic g), Ascher (p), Frank Vicari (sax), Joseph Temperley (sax), Dennis Morouse (tenor sax), Album *Rock 'n' Roll*: UK 2/21/75 (6); US 2/17/75 (6), Re-entry: UK 1/17/81 (64)

AIN'T THAT A SHAME—LENNON

Rec. autumn 1974, Record Plant East, NYC, Domino/Bartholomew (writers), Lennon (producer), Lennon (v, acoustic g), Davis (g), Voormann (b), Keltner (d), Jenkins (percussion), Mottau (acoustic g), Ascher (piano), Frank Vicari (sax), Joseph Temperley (sax), Dennis Morouse (tenor sax), Album *Rock 'n' Roll*

In September 1974, Pang went to the first Beatlefest convention and met the group's old Hamburg friend Jürgen Vollmer. He was selling some amazing photos from that period and Pang quickly put Lennon in touch with the German. Jürgen had the perfect shot for the cover of Lennon's oldies album, one of Lennon standing in a doorway with McCartney, Harrison, and Sutcliffe walking in front of him in a blur.

In 1956, Little Richard covered an R&B song called "I'm Wise" and changed its name to "Slippin' and Slidin'." Buddy Holly also covered it. Lennon's version features one of his coolest vocals: not sexy, just raw edge, tough strength, and raspy snarling, reedier than it was ten years earlier. The '50s rockers were wild, but even though he was second generation, Lennon's voice sounded meaner, growing up in a war-torn port city, bitter from parental abandonment, playing to whores and sailors. Even when he was having fun, he sounded fierce.

In the 1971 *Rolling Stone* interview, Jann Wenner asked Lennon, "Why do you think [rock and roll] means so much to people?"

> Because it's primitive enough and it has no bullshit, really, the best stuff. And it gets through to you; it's beat, you know. I mean, go to jungle and they have the rhythm and it goes through out the world, and it's as simple as that. You get the rhythm going and everybody gets into it. I think Michael X says he said it, but I read that Eldridge Cleaver or somebody said it, that the blacks gave the middle class whites back their bodies. Put their minds and bodies

together. It's something like that. It gets through. To me it got through, it's the only thing to get through to me out of the things that were happening when I was 15. Rock and roll was real; everything else was unreal.[7]

After "Stand by Me" was released as a single, Lennon planned to release "Ain't That a Shame" backed with "Slippin' and Slidin'." He performed it on his final stage appearance, the ATV special *A Salute to Lew Grade* on April 18, 1975. Grade owned Northern Songs, the company Lennon and McCartney formed to sell their songs on the stock market in the 1960s. Because of their squabbling at the end of the decade, Lennon and McCartney dropped the ball and allowed Lew Grade to snatch up the company, which he owned until Michael Jackson bought it in 1985. Lennon agreed to be on Lew Grade's tribute, but then had all the musicians wear specially designed two-faced masks so that they had a second face coming out of the back of their heads, reflecting his true feelings toward Grade. When Ono became pregnant, however, Lennon decided to retire, and the single was canceled.

SILLY LOVE SONGS—MCCARTNEY

Rec. 1976, Abbey Road, McCartney (producer), McCartney (v, b, p), Linda McCartney (k, bv), Laine (g, bv), Jimmy McCulloch (g), Joe English (d), Steve "Tex" Howard (trumpet), Thaddeus Richard (sax), Howie Casey (sax), Tony Dorsey (trombone), Single: UK 4/30/76 (2); US 4/1/76 (1), also *Wings at the Speed of Sound*, Honors: 31st Greatest Song of All Time by *Billboard* 2008, Cover/Film Appearance: Ewan McGregor in *Moulin Rouge* (2001)

Originally, a lot of the best rock lyrics were gibberish, like "Awopbopaloobop." Then Dylan married the poetry of Allen Ginsberg's "Howl" to the sound of the Animals' "House of the Rising Sun" and changed everything.

In the 1960s, McCartney declared that he vaguely minded anybody knowing anything he didn't know. He was the man about town in London with actress Jane Asher on his arm, seeing all the highbrow plays. He listened to Stockhausen and symphonies, while poets William Burroughs and Richard Brautigan recorded spoken-word albums in his buddy Barry Miles' Indica bookstore.

McCartney watched Lennon pen "Revolution," then wrote his own more subtle and universal ode to Black Power with "Blackbird." Meanwhile, Mick Jagger was also doing his best to keep up with Dylan. *His* actress girlfriend Marianne Faithfull gave him the novel *The Master and the Margarita*, which Jagger transmogrified into "Sympathy for the Devil."

A minority of rock critics like Nik Cohn lamented that Dylan and the Beatles corrupted the nonsensical purity of mindless rock and roll like "Tutti Frutti." He felt the '60s intellectual posers' attempt to be profound was infinitely more annoying.[8] Later critics like Lester Bangs would clamor for more moronic fun and Iggy Stooge and the Ramones would provide it. With stupid lyrics about sniffin' glue or having a "real cool time" and being "loose," they were intelligent people masquerading as idiots to be funny and edgy.

But for the most part, as the '60s became the '70s, the rock intelligentsia was dominated by critics like hyper-intellectual visionary Greil Marcus and Jon Landau, who would become Springsteen's manager and prod him into becoming the successor to John Steinbeck. Their fast-moving brains demanded food for thought in the lyrics.

But by the mid-'70s, McCartney and Linda just wanted to get stoned and chill with the kids on the farm. When he downshifted from "Eleanor Rigby" to odes to comic books like "Magneto and Titanium Man," the critics lambasted him.

So he told the critics to stuff it with the most sublime disco-tinged mini-symphony any supermarket shopper ever heard. Opening with the sound of an automated assembly line like a craftsman clocking in on autopilot, he turned his supple bass into the lead instrument and proved he still had his ear to the ground by serving up the sweetest strings and tastiest horns this side of Philadelphia. Whereas in the '60s the Beatles studied Motown, now McCartney took his cue from the current kings of slick soul, producers Kenneth Gamble and Leon Huff, whose Philadelphia International label featured acts like the O'Jays, Harold Melvin and the Blue Notes (with lead singer Teddy Pendergrass), Lou Rawls, the Three Degrees, and Billy Paul.

"Silly Love Songs" marked the end of an era, just as Lennon's hibernation did. There would be no more visions, just consummately crafted pop rock like there was pre-1966. Only the beat had modernized and now it was Linda, Denny, and Paul chanting, "I love you," instead of John, George, and Paul.

The instrumentation was happy, dammit, because McCartney was happy touring the United States with his family. And just as he had been in sync with his generation when they were desperate for wisdom from his mother's ghost in "Let It Be," he was in sync with them as they just wanted to take quaaludes, live out *Saturday Night Fever*, and forget the My Lai massacre.

Culturally, America had reached an accord. Long hair, denim jackets, and pot were accepted by the mainstream, à la *That '70s Show*. The sexual revolution was even assimilated with '50s nostalgia, when *Happy Days* mom, Marian Cunningham, asked her husband, Howard, if he was feeling frisky.

Still, the critics needling McCartney to "live up to his potential" would periodically get to him. In later decades, he would intermittently team with taskmasters like George Martin, Elvis Costello, or Radiohead's producer Nigel Godrich, or write a symphony, or bare his soul when his partner was murdered or his second wife betrayed him.

Had the critics of 1976 known how much more music McCartney still had in him, they would have understood that you couldn't be heavy *all* the time.

THIS SONG—HARRISON

REC. MAY–SEPTEMBER 1976, FRIAR PARK, HARRISON (PRODUCER), HARRISON (V, G, PERCUSSION), PRESTON (K), WEEKS (B), ALVIN TAYLOR (D), RICHARD TEE (P), TOM SCOTT (SAX), ERIC IDLE (VOICES), SINGLE: UK 11/15/76 (DID NOT CHART); US 11/19/76 (25), ALSO ON *THIRTY THREE & 1/3*

When "My Sweet Lord" dominated the airwaves of 1970–1971, the publishers of the Chiffons' 1963 hit "He's So Fine" accused Harrison of plagiarizing their melody. Unfortunately for Harrison, the Chiffons was one of the girl groups that Phil Spector had *not* worked with, otherwise maybe he could have interceded.

It was long a practice of the Beatles—and everyone else since the beginning of music—to lift melodies and change them just enough to take them out of the plagiarism realm. An example pointed out by the biographer-fans-love-to-hate Albert Goldman was the similarity between Lennon's "I Feel Fine" to Bobby Parker's "Watch Your Step."

Decades after the hip-hop sampling revolution, this practice perhaps seems less egregious. But in the early '70s, the '50s old guard was bitter about being supplanted by a bunch of arrogant girly boys from England and were vehement to squeeze out some payback.

You can hear some significant whiffs of "He's So Fine" in "My Sweet Lord," and on the sheet music the tunes look even more similar, but the case dragged on for years. After the Beatles fired their manager Allen Klein, he bought the publishing for "He's So Fine" so he could torment Harrison by continuing the suit.

The judge finally decided that Harrison had subconsciously plagiarized, added up the sales of "My Sweet Lord," factored in that it contributed to the sales of *All Things Must Pass* and Harrison's greatest hits compilation, and decided George owed $1,599,987 to the song's publisher, Bright Tunes. Then another judge decided that Harrison should just pay Klein $587,000, the exact amount that Klein bought the tune for, so Klein wouldn't profit. Harrison ultimately bought "He's So Fine" himself so he could plagiarize it all he wanted. (Seemingly forgotten in the drawn-out dispute was the fact that Delaney Bramlett had been instrumental in the creation of "My Sweet Lord," both in gospel influence and slide guitar, but if he was compensated by Harrison both sides kept quiet about it.)

Long before the case was resolved, Harrison wrote "This Song," in which he bitched about the whole experience with the same mordant humor he'd used against the taxman a decade earlier, only this time backed with Billy Preston and a super-tight band of predominately black studio musicians. The song defiantly begins by blatantly ripping off the beginning of the Four Tops' "Sugar Pie Honey Bunch" before veering into the most overused rock hook of all time, Chuck Berry's "Little Queenie," most famously recycled in T. Rex's "Bang a Gong" and the Rolling Stones' "It's Only Rock 'n' Roll."

The song transcends its hyperspecific lyrics and clichéd roots to erupt into a joyous boogie that makes you want to dance to Tom Scott's sax break. To today's ears, the sound most resembles the *Saturday Night Live* house band on a particularly rocking night. And actually, Harrison's Monty Python pal Eric Idle directed a video for "This Song" that aired on *Saturday Night Live* on November 20, 1976. It featured Harrison in a courtroom with future Wilbury Jim Keltner as the judge and guest appearances by the likes of the Stones' Ron Wood. Just before the instrumental break, Idle cries out in his wacky falsetto that the riff could be "Sugar Pie Honey Bunch" or "Rescue Me."

SNOOKEROO—STARR

REC. AUGUST 1974, SUNSET SOUND, LA, AND PRODUCERS WORKSHOP, ELTON JOHN/BERNIE TAUPIN (WRITERS), RICHARD PERRY (PRODUCER), STARR (V, D), ELTON JOHN (P), ROBBIE ROBERTSON (G), VOORMANN (B), KELTNER (D), JAMES NEWTON HOWARD (SYNTHESIZER), HORNS: KEYS, TREVOR LAWRENCE, STEVE MADAIO, CHUCK FINDLEY, BACKING VOCALS: CLYDIE KING, LINDA LAWRENCE, JOE GREENE, SINGLE: DOUBLE A-SIDE WITH NO NO SONG: UK 2/21/75 (FAILED TO CHART); US 1/27/75 (3)

One of the 1970s stars who came closest to reaching Beatles heights was Elton John, and he worked with both Lennon and Starr in 1974. For Starr's album *Goodnight Vienna*, Elton John and his lyricist Bernie Taupin contributed "Snookeroo." John kicks things off with "Crocodile Rock"–style piano and Taupin sketches a song based on Starr's upbringing in a working class town in the North of England. It includes the same eye for detail that made John's other working class portrait, "Saturday Night's Alright for Fighting," stand out lyrically as well as musically. The Band's Robbie Robertson delivers on guitar, tasty horns lean in, gospel-sounding ladies back the Ringed One at the mike, and it's an anthem for poor Andy Capps-turned-millionaire-playboys everywhere. It made it to number three in the United States as a double A-side with "The No No Song."

Snooker is a British version of pool with a bigger table and smaller pockets. Basically, Starr sings about being a lazy, no-good guy who hangs out playing pool and refuses to work normal hours while his dad gets drunk and his sister gets a reputation.

He sings that he needs a factory girl who will cook for him and turn him loose at night, which is what he had in Maureen, though she would be the last factory girl with whom he'd bunker down. Technically, she wasn't a factory girl; rather, she left school at fourteen to become a hairdresser trainee. Before Starr knew this drummer thing was going to sustain, his plan had always been to get his own hair salon, so they must've bonded over hair. Maureen was born in 1946 and a regular at the Cavern Club at age fifteen. Starr married her in February 1965 after she became pregnant with the first of their three children.

The lyrics talk about how the family's four-room house is condemned. In 2005, the Liverpool City Council decided they would knock down Starr's birth home at 9 Madryn Street—but after an outcry, it announced the building would be taken apart brick by brick and preserved elsewhere.

GOING DOWN ON LOVE—LENNON

REC. SUMMER 1974, RECORD PLANT EAST, NYC, LENNON (PRODUCER), LENNON (V, G), DAVIS (G), VOORMANN (B), KELTNER (D), HOPKINS (P), JENKINS (PERCUS-SION), MOTTAU (ACOUSTIC G), ASCHER (ELECTRIC PIANO), LITTLE BIG HORNS (KEYS [SAX], STEVE MADAIO, HOWARD JOHNSON, RON APREA, FRANK VICARI), ALBUM *WALLS AND BRIDGES*, ALSO B-SIDE TO JEALOUS GUY (UK 11/18/85)

Lennon opened *Walls and Bridges* with this summary of the disaster his life had become. With an intro of percussion like a slower version of Marvin Gaye's "What's Going On" and "Mercy Mercy Me," Lennon appropriates Kool and the Gang's 1973 "get down, get down" chorus from "Jungle Boogie," still translating R&B into rock like he did since his earliest days of covering Motown. But instead of getting down on the dance floor, he's got to get down on his knees, humbled, beg for the forgiveness of his woman, and pray to God.

Suffocating from the disappearance of his woman's love, he rails that it's unfair and hates her even as he needs her, as if he wasn't the one who drove her away. To distract himself he tries to sow his wild oats but can't perform, so he smashes the lamps and everything else. Waking up surrounded by the destruction of the night before, he gets on his knees, calling out for "Help!" like he did back in 1965. (Perhaps he wrote it after a troubadour night.)

Always one for a dirty pun, the title probably refers to his resolution to be a better lover to his woman if she ever takes him back. As a former chauvinist, he probably didn't go down too often on the groupies who threw themselves at him in the Beatlemania days. (Although maybe that's what "Please Please Me" was about.)

THIS GUITAR (CAN'T KEEP FROM CRYING)—HARRISON

REC. APRIL–JUNE 1975, LOS ANGELES, HARRISON (PRODUCER), HARRISON (V, G, BASS SYNTHESIZER), KELTNER (D), DAVIS (G), GARY WRIGHT (SYNTHESIZER), DAVID FOSTER (P, STRING ARRANGEMENT), UK 2/6/76 (FAILED TO CHART); US 12/8/75 (FAILED TO CHART), ALSO ON *EXTRA TEXTURE-READ ALL ABOUT IT*, ALTERNATE VERSION: *HARRISON AND PLATINUM WEIRD* (REC. 1992, COMPLETED 2006 W/ DAVE STEWART, DHANI HARRISON, STARR, HUDSON)

After the savage reviews for the *Dark Horse* album and tour, Harrison's confidence was at a low. He even wrote "OHNONOTHIMAGEN" on the inner sleeve of the album. "This Guitar (Can't Keep from Crying)" expresses his bitterness at how far he had fallen in the critics' estimation. He criticizes *Rolling Stone* for missing the point of what he was doing, then tells himself it's because of their ignorance. Probably no one bitched more about their critics than the solo Beatles until Public Enemy and Eminem came along.

But Harrison had learned since 1968's "Only a Northern Song," another composition in which he resigned himself to the fact that no one listened to him. That song featured an intriguingly dark soundscape, but the literal lyrics about songwriting were distracting. For "This Guitar" he fashioned his words abstractly enough that the listeners could ignore the theme if they chose to. But no one could miss the desperation in trying to rehash one of his most famous Beatles songs.

It could have been one of the most depressing ex-Beatles tunes ever, but its strange groove compels repeated listening. Gary Wright opens the proceedings with a foreboding synth that wouldn't sound out of place in a '70s horror flick or a *Death Wish* sequel. Drummer Jim Keltner locks into the groove with David Foster on piano, and Foster layers on a fine string arrangement as well.

But despite the group's synergy, the single failed to make the charts on either side of the Atlantic. It was the first release by one of the Fabs to miss completely.

The record label in the middle of the album (*Extra Texture*) featured an eaten away Apple core. It would be Harrison's last top ten LP for twelve years, and the last album from Apple Records until the company was revived for the *Live at the BBC* and *Anthology* releases in the 1990s.

The momentum that carried them out of the sixties into the next decade was sputtering. Crying, indeed.

SALLY G—MCCARTNEY

Rec. 1974, Sound Shop Studios, Nashville, mixed at Abbey Road, McCartney (producer), McCartney (v, b, g), Linda McCartney (bv), Laine (g), Jimmy McCulloch (g), Geoff Britton (d), Buddy Emmons (pedal steel guitar), Vassar Clements (fiddle), Johnny Gimble (fiddle), Single as A-Side: US 12/24/74 (17), also B-Side to Junior's Farm

McCartney validated his choice to record in Nashville by capturing his most authentic country tribute.

While in the country music capital, he and the band went to see Dolly Parton and Porter Wagoner sing their last show together at the Grand Old Opry, visited Johnny Cash and Chet Atkins, and hung out at the drive-in a couple times. "That's about our level," he said at the time. "We're very drive-in-type people."

They also hung in the nightclub district of Printer's Alley. In the famous bar Skull's Rainbow Room, he saw singer Diane Gaffney perform and was inspired to write about a female guitarist singing "A Tangled Mind." From there he made up a traditional country scenario in which the woman makes a fool out of the singer. Now he's learned his lesson and accepts he must move along and forget her lyin' ways.

Shortly after writing the song, McCartney learned Ms. Gaffney was suing a local paper for writing about her without permission. He already had a line about how he didn't know what her last initial G stood for, but he knew it wasn't "good," so he couldn't lose the G. But "Diane G" was changed to "Sally G."

The song went far beyond his earlier country pastiches like "Rocky Raccoon" because he used real Nashville session guys, as Ringo did back in 1970.

The engineer Ernie Winfrey recalls, "Paul was very easygoing, and consequently, all the Nashville players who came in felt at ease. Everybody threw their ideas in."

Winfrey also remembered that McCartney and Linda "were just all over each other. They would come in to listen to a playback, and one would sit in the other's lap. I think Paul's attitude toward Linda showed a lot about him. He was willing to accept any criticism or derision that was handed out over him having her in the band. Based on my observations, he was very patient with her. But she was also a quick learner. He would sing her a harmony part, and she'd jump right on it."[9]

With its bluegrass, pedal steel, two-step feel, it was such a fully realized country song it made number fifty-one on the country chart and number seventeen on *Billboard*'s pop chart on its own, apart from "Junior's Farm." It would be his last single for Apple Records.

BEAUTIFUL GIRL—HARRISON

REC. MAY 24–SEPTEMBER 13, 1976, FRIAR PARK, HARRISON (PRODUCER), HARRISON (V, G), PRESTON (O), WEEKS (B), ALVIN TAYLOR (D), RICHARD TEE (P), ALBUM *THIRTY THREE AND 1/3*: UK 11/19/76 (35); US 11/24/76 (11)

With its jangling twelve-string guitar and vocal harmonies, "Beautiful Girl" sounds, as Harrison scholar Simon Leng says, like it could have come from *Help!* or *Rubber Soul*.[10] Here Harrison's yearning "woos" are put to happier use than they had been on melodramatic older tunes like "Try Some Buy Some," and the chiming electric arpeggios perfectly capture the feeling of seeing a beautiful face for the first time.

It suggests the feeling he may have felt when he first saw Pattie Boyd during the filming of *A Hard Day's Night*. Harrison sings about trembling inside and realizing she's not the kind of girl to pass around. The creepy line hints at the groupies who were part of the permanent background. Although Pattie said in her memoirs that practically the first thing Harrison asked her was to marry him (jokingly), he was nervous enough around her that he asked manager Epstein to accompany them on their first date to help make conversation.[11] Though women across the world wanted him, with this gorgeous-yet-innocent model, Harrison still felt a bit of the dropout electrician's apprentice he had been. The other Beatles' wives of the '60s, Cynthia and Maureen, would emulate Pattie's long straight blond hair with bangs, as would countless followers of swinging London fashion.

Harrison began the song during *All Things Must Pass* but was unable to finish it until he met Olivia Trinidad Arias. Born in 1948 in Mexico City, she was the daughter of a dry cleaner and a seamstress. She went to Hawthorne High in the LA area, and after graduating in 1965 ended up working as a secretary at A&M Records, where Harrison met her in 1974, just before he was about to start the Dark Horse tour. The couple had their son, Dhani, in August 1978 and was married the following month. Years later, she would save him from a knife-wielding psychotic (see "Looking for My Life").

WHAT YOU GOT—LENNON

REC. SUMMER 1974, RECORD PLANT EAST, NYC, LENNON (PRODUCER), LENNON (V, G), DAVIS (G), VOORMANN (B), KELTNER (D), HOPKINS (P), JENKINS (PERCUSSION), MOTTAU (ACOUSTIC G), ASCHER (CLAVINET), LITTLE BIG HORNS (KEYS [SAX], STEVE MADAIO, HOWARD JOHNSON, RON APREA, FRANK VICARI), ALBUM *WALLS AND BRIDGES*, ALSO B-SIDE TO #9 DREAM

When Nilsson and Lennon performed a cover of Jimmy Cliff's "Many Rivers to Cross" for the *Pussy Cats* album, Nilsson tried to scream like Lennon and ruptured his vocal chords. Nilsson didn't tell Lennon because he was afraid Lennon would stop the sessions. It was emblematic of how the Lost Weekend was dragging them all down. When they finished the album, Lennon hightailed it back to New York with Pang and wrote ten songs in a week about his chaotic season in California.

Spurred on by McCartney's *Band on the Run* comeback, Lennon produced one of his finest albums. Also contributing was the pain of Lennon's separation from Ono, in the same way that Dylan's crumbling marriage fueled his mid-seventies masterpiece *Blood on the Tracks*. Lennon's growth as a producer was also apparent between this album and *Mind Games*, with *Walls and Bridges* being his most sophisticated production achievement. *Double Fantasy* was perhaps a tad too slick and soft.

Originally inspired by the O'Jays' "Money Money Money," "What You Got" was Lennon's funkiest rocker, complete with R&B horns. His savage howling was in the vein of "Everybody's Got Something to Hide Except for Me and My Monkey," with a voice six years older and a bit more ragged for wear. One wonders how it would have held up over the years; McCartney's was still strong at seventy, though Dylan's was fried and Jagger's could be marred with distracting affectation.

Singing how he didn't value what he had till after he blew it, he could be referring to Ono, his musical reputation, or the respect of the public. Back when the Beatles were kings of the jungle, he could be an asshole and no one dared say boo. The made-for-VH1 film *My Dinner with Jimi* recounts how he rudely put down the Turtles when they visited London. He was so cruel, one of them quit the music business forever. But as his hits dried up, so did people's patience for him stumbling around hitting waitresses. He concedes he's like the naked clown in "The Emperor's New Clothes," and begs for one more chance.

He did all he could to promote the album, creating an ad campaign called "Listen to This," with buttons, photos, stickers, T-shirts, and posters on the back of two thousand buses. Starr did the voiceover for TV and radio ads just as Lennon narrated ads for Starr's *Goodnight Vienna*. He got another chance, with both Ono and the public.

YOU GAVE ME THE ANSWER—MCCARTNEY

Rec. 1974–1975, Sea Saint Studios, New Orleans, and Wally Heider Studios, LA, McCartney (producer), McCartney (v, p), Linda McCartney (k, bv), Laine (b, bv), Jimmy McCulloch (g), Joe English (d), Album *Venus and Mars*: UK 5/30/75 (1); US 5/27/75 (1), also B-side of Letting Go

McCartney's grandfather played tuba in a brass band. Despite rupturing his eardrum after falling off a wall when he was ten, McCartney's father, Jim, taught himself piano and trumpet. He played ragtime with his first band, the Masked Melody Makers, who wore black masks as a gimmick. Jim eventually led the Jim Mac Jazz Band until he got married and settled down selling cotton. Still, he transmitted his dream to his sons. He encouraged them to play his guitar and piano (which he bought from Brian Epstein's dad's store) and bought them trumpets, though the trumpets didn't stick. He'd take the boys to concerts, play them his old records, and deconstruct the tunes on the radio with them. He hooked up the living room radio with extension cords so they could listen when they were going to sleep. Most crucially, he taught the boys harmony, one of the Beatles' key powers. Jim told Paul to take lessons, but Paul preferred to learn by ear as his father had done. After the group made it big, Jim and Paul's brother would answer his fan mail for him.

McCartney originally wrote "When I'm Sixty-Four" on the living room piano before teaming with Lennon. He revived it as a birthday present for his dad at the end of 1966 and decided to include it on *Sgt. Pepper*. From then on, his homages to the music hall style of his father's day would become a regular feature of Beatles albums, with tunes including "Your Mother Should Know," "Martha My Dear," and "Honey Pie." Maybe one of his best was "You Gave Me the Answer." In the 1920s, Rudy Vallee and Al Jolson had to sing through megaphones because the recording equipment got such bad reception, so McCartney applied a filter to his vocals to imitate that sound. He loved the dancing of Fred Astaire and envisioned the song as something Astaire could sing to a starlet as they glided across the ballroom. He sings to his beloved that he loves her even though they'll never be crowned by the aristocracy, but decades later, Jim Mac's son would be knighted and become Sir Paul McCartney.

NOTES

1. Roger Friedman, "Beatles: Lennon Planned to Visit McCartney in 1974," *Fox News* September 25, 2001, www.foxnews.com/story/0,2933,35067,00.html (October 10, 2011).

2. Peter Doggett, *You Never Give Me Your Money* (New York: HarperCollins, 2009), 234.

3. Albert Goldman, *The Lives of John Lennon* (London: Bantam, 1988), 652.

4. Doggett, *You Never Give Me Your Money*, 233–35, 248.

5. David Sheff, "January 1981 *Playboy* Interview with John Lennon and Yoko Ono," John-Lennon.com, www.john-lennon.com/playboyinterviewwithjohnlennon andyokoono.htm (October 10, 2011).

6. Sheff, "January 1981 *Playboy* Interview."

7. Jann S. Wenner, "January 1971 *Rolling Stone* Interview with John Lennon and Yoko Ono," JannSWenner.com, www.jannswenner.com/Archives/John_Lennon_Part1.aspx (October 10, 2011).

8. Nik Cohn, *Awopbopaloobop Alopbamboom: The Golden Age of Rock* (St. Albans: Paladin Press, 1970), 145–46.

9. Bill DeMain, "When We Was Fab: Nashvillians Remember Paul McCartney and Wings' Working Vacation Here in 1974," *Nashville Scene*, 2002, http://alt .nntp2http.com/tv/ilovelucy/2010/04/bfc220f9a7dfd679f6b6b1a5d2e6fc26.html (October 11, 2011).

10. Simon Leng, *The Music of George Harrison: While My Guitar Gently Weeps* (London: Firefly, 2003), 192.

11. Pattie Boyd and Penny Junor, *Wonderful Tonight: George Harrison, Eric Clapton, and Me* (London: Headline Review, 2007), 61.

John Lennon circa 1980. *PhotoFest*

• 7 •

1980: Other Plans

Lennon and McCartney debate whether they should reunite for Saturday Night Live.

$\mathcal{I}$n 1976, promoter Bill Sargent offered the Beatles $50 million for one reunion show. Then Sid Bernstein, the promoter of the Beatles' Shea Stadium concerts, asked them to reunite for a benefit concert for Cambodian refugees, which he estimated would raise $230 million.

On April 24, 1976, *Saturday Night Live* producer Lorne Michaels appeared on the live show to offer the Beatles $3,000 to reunite. "Divide [the money] up any way you want," he said. "If you want to give less to Ringo, that's up to you."

Lennon told *Playboy*, "Paul and I were together watching that show. He was visiting us at our place in the Dakota. We were watching it and almost went down to the studio, just as a gag. . . . He and Linda walked in, and he and I were just sitting there, watching the show, and we went, 'Ha-ha, wouldn't it be funny if we went down?'"

McCartney later recalled, "[John] said, 'We should go down there. We should go down now and just do it.' It was one of those moments where we said, 'Let's not and say we did.'"[1] Lennon said, "We nearly got into a cab, but we were actually too tired."

The *SNL* night was the last time Lennon saw McCartney. "That was a period when Paul just kept turning up at our door with a guitar. I would let him in, but finally I said to him, 'Please call before you come over. It's not 1956 and turning up at the door isn't the same anymore. You know, just give me a ring.' He was upset by that, but I didn't mean it badly. I just meant that I was taking care of a baby all day and some guy turns up at the door."[2]

In 2000, VH1 made a good movie about the *SNL* evening called *The Two of Us*, written by long-time fan Mark Stanfield. The movie is primarily one long conversation between Lennon and McCartney over the course of the day as they hang out at the Dakota then wander around New York and return in time for the show. (Linda and Ono are not present.)

It was directed by Michael Lindsay-Hogg, who had done the Beatles film *Let It Be*. As he actually knew Lennon, he helped Jared Harris deliver the most convincing portrait of the prickly Lennon yet to appear on film. Aidan Quinn did well as Paul McCartney, and McCartney later told him that he liked the film. (A 2000 British TV movie called *In His Life: The John Lennon Story* starring Philip McQuillen also did a good job of showing all facets of his personality.)

Though they no longer hung out in person, the ex-partners still spoke on the phone about cats and babies, though their relations could be rocky. After one heated conversation, McCartney thought Lennon was affecting a "tough American" pose, so Macca snapped, "Fuck off, Kojak!" and slammed down the receiver.

One Beatle did make it to *SNL* in 1976, however—George Harrison, who sang beautiful duets of "Here Comes the Sun" and "Homeward Bound" with Paul Simon.

In the continued absence of a reunion, more nostalgia vehicles surfaced. The stage musical *Beatlemania* began in 1977, notable for giving singer-songwriter Marshall Crenshaw his first break. The year 1978 saw the release of three Beatles-related movies. Singularly disastrous was the feature *Sgt. Pepper's Lonely Hearts Club Band*, in which the Bee Gees and Peter Frampton played the titular group and covered Beatles songs while trying to save their town Heartland from evildoers.

The two other films, however, remain enduring classics. *I Wanna Hold Your Hand* was a warm-hearted farce following the antics of a bunch of teenagers during the week the Beatles first played *Ed Sullivan*, helmed by future *Forrest Gump* director Robert Zemeckis. Harrison himself helped produce the mockumentary *The Rutles: All You Need Is Cash*. Monty Python's Eric Idle teamed up with the Bonzo Dog Doo-Dah Band's Neil Innes for this hilarious precursor to *Spinal Tap*, which also resulted in a hauntingly catchy soundtrack album. The year 1979 would see the airing of Dick Clark's so-so made-for-TV movie *The Birth of the Beatles*.

With such tunes as "Can She Do It Like She Dances," Starr's albums could also be quite amusing, though not always intentionally. *Ringo's Rotogravure* (1976) continued his "Star-Studded Guest Star" format and alternated oldie covers with country and even a mariachi number. But it barely made the top thirty in the United States and didn't chart in the United Kingdom, so for

Ringo the 4th (1977) Starr focused on slick disco-tinged tunes for the Studio 54 crowd, only cornier, with a little more synth, and mixed with a healthy dose of schmaltz. For those who dig '70s cheese, it's the kind of stuff the lounge singer on *The Love Boat* or *The Towering Inferno* might have sung. Some of it was actually pretty tight in a campy way, like "Out on the Street," in which Starr, to a disco beat, outruns the cops, picks up a chick, and gets in a knife fight. He also did a serious take of Gamble and Huff's R&B "Drowning in the Sea of Love." But it barely made it to number 162. The follow up, 1978's *Bad Boy*, dropped the disco and moved back to rock but still only hit number 129, even with the help of a prime time TV special.

Meanwhile, McCartney and Harrison both entered a soft period. As easy listening music was rebranded adult contemporary, the biggest sellers of the day (Lionel Richie, Christopher Cross, Air Supply) sported tepid synths and drums perfect for aging baby boomers in offices whose ears hurt after years of loud concerts. To an extent, the ex-Fabs had to target that niche because they would often do at least ten spots better on it. For instance, Harrison's "Blow Away" made it to number two on the US adult contemporary chart but only number sixteen on the Hot 100. In a few years, the "gated" big drum sound would add some toughness back to mainstream pop. But whereas the Rolling Stones rose to the challenge of punk with *Some Girls*, McCartney and Harrison were content with their growing families as they recorded on yachts and vast estates.

McCartney was still pushing the envelope, however, with his 1980 album *McCartney II*, in which he experimented with synthesizers. The hit single "Coming Up" would be one of the songs that stirred Lennon from his five-year hiatus. He jokingly complained about not being able to get it out of his head. Lennon began working on a new solo album without the old regulars like Jim Keltner and Jesse Ed Davis because he feared he would start partying with them. Also, he felt he was too friendly with them to be bossy enough to get things how he really wanted. Instead, he brought on *Ram* veteran guitarist Hugh McCracken and David Bowie's axe man Earl Slick.

Eventually Lennon decided to give half of the album's space to Ono as a way to hold on to her in the face of her intensifying affair with art dealer Samuel Green and relapse into heroin. He also noticed that the B-52s' "Rock Lobster" sounded like Ono's "cartoon alien-meets-Shonen Knife banshee" music of the early 1970s. New Wave bands increasingly cited her as an influence.

In "Beautiful Boy," his ode to his son Sean, Lennon sang, "Life is what happens while you're busy making other plans." He did not originate the aphorism, though it has often been attributed to him. Sadly, fate had other plans, and the idyll the solo Fabs enjoyed would come to an abrupt end.

(JUST LIKE) STARTING OVER—LENNON

REC. AUGUST 4, 1980–LATE SEPTEMBER 1980, HIT FACTORY, MIXED AT RE-
CORD PLANT EAST, NYC, LENNON/ONO/JACK DOUGLAS (PRODUCERS), LEN-
NON (V, G), MCCRACKEN (G), SLICK (G), LEVIN (B), NEWMARK (D), SMALL (K),
JENKINS (PERCUSSION), BACKING VOCALS: MICHELLE SIMPSON, CASSANDRA
WOOTEN, CHERYL MASON JACKS, ERIC TROYER, SINGLE: UK 10/24/80 (1);
US 10/20/80 (1), ALSO ON *DOUBLE FANTASY*, HONORS: NO. 53 *BILLBOARD* ALL
TIME TOP SONGS, GRAMMY NOM. FOR 1981 RECORD OF THE YEAR

"(Just Like) Starting Over" was originally titled "My Life," inspired in part by
the Beach Boys' "Don't Worry Baby." Other influences were Buddy Holly's
"Raining in My Heart," as the song morphed into "I Watch Your Face" and
then "Don't Be Crazy," which became the basis for the verse. Another composition called "The Worst Is Over" ended up being the chorus. In Bermuda,
he combined the pieces. When he recorded it at the Hit Factory in New York
a few weeks later, he added "(Just Like)" when he realized Tammy Wynette
had already used the title "Starting Over."

To open what would be the first track on his comeback album, Lennon recorded a Japanese wishing bell to contrast with the bells of doom that
opened his first solo album. Then, as if picking up where he had just left off
with *Rock 'n' Roll*, Lennon sang this fifties-styled song in his "Elvis Orbison"
voice. The lyrics celebrate how much he and Ono have grown, yet because
of the day-to-day hustle of life they have not had any alone time to make love
together, so he suggests flying off for a vacation to rekindle their spark; it'll be
like falling in love again and starting over. For the music video, Lennon and
Ono, ever the exhibitionists, pretended to make love. The B-side "Kiss Kiss"
had Ono faking an orgasm.

Lennon picked "(Just Like) Starting Over" to be his comeback single
because he felt it fit thematically with his return. The single made it to number
three in the United States, but the response was not the unanimous outcry
of joy that Lennon had hoped for. One British headline even barked, "Get
down, Lazarus!"

In morbid irony, Lennon's murder sent "(Just Like) Starting Over" to
the top of the charts on both sides of the Atlantic. (See chapter 8, "1985:
Borrowed Time," regarding his death.) It would be his biggest solo American
hit, staying at number one for five weeks. Inscribed in the playout wax of the
single was, "One world, one people."

GIRLS' SCHOOL—MCCARTNEY

REC. 1977, ABBEY ROAD, McCARTNEY (PRODUCER), McCARTNEY (V, B), LINDA McCARTNEY (K, BV), LAINE (G, BV), JIMMY McCULLOCH (G), JOE ENGLISH (D), DOUBLE A-SIDE TO MULL OF KINTYRE: UK 11/11/77 (1); US 11/14/77 (33)

CAFÉ ON THE LEFT BANK—MCCARTNEY

REC. 1977, MOBILE STUDIO ON *FAIR CAROL* YACHT, McCARTNEY (PRODUCER), McCARTNEY (V, B, K), LINDA McCARTNEY (K, BV), LAINE (G, BV), JIMMY Mc-CULLOCH (G, BV), JOE ENGLISH (D), ALBUM *LONDON TOWN*: UK 3/31/78 (4); US 3/27/78 (2)

These solid rockers counter the notion that McCartney went flaccid during this period.

Denny Laine lived on a houseboat, so he suggested making the next album (which would end up being called *London Town*) on the water. So in May 1978, the group set up shop on the yacht *Fair Carol* in the Virgin Islands, on the border between the Caribbean and the Atlantic, east of Cuba, Jamaica, Haiti, and Puerto Rico. The band established a routine of a three- or four-hour session in the morning, followed by water skiing, swimming, and eating lunch cooked by the captain/chef. When they played, dolphins would swim around the boat digging the sound.[3]

As was McCartney's wont, he held prime cut "Girls' School" off the album to serve as the rocking B-side to the softer A-side (in this case, "Mull of Kintyre"), a tradition going back to "Another Day"/"Oh Woman Oh Why." Like that earlier B-side, this one sports a riff that seems strangely reminiscent of a tune on *Led Zeppelin III*, in this case, a simplified "Celebration Day."

The song came about when McCartney was in Hawaii reading the back of the newspaper where they had the ads for the porno flicks. McCartney wrote down the titles—*School Mistress, Curly Haired, Kid Sister, The Woman Trainer*—and made up a song based on them.[4] It was another creation in the Beatles tradition of "found art," like when Lennon lifted all the words for "Being for the Benefit of Mr. Kite" from a vintage poster.

Guitarist McCulloch loved rocking out in concert and was generally frustrated by the low-key songs of the album that would become *London Town*, but here he had a perfect vehicle to let it rip with Laine.

In the United Kingdom, the A-side "Mull" became the biggest noncharity single of all time, yet it flopped mysteriously in the United States. "Girls' School" did better in the States, reaching number thirty-three. It would've been a great video to see them on the yacht rocking this one out to the dolphins.

"Café on the Left Bank" is another propulsive mid-tempo rocker from the *London Town* sessions. The lyrics and McCulloch's guitar work carry some of the cosmopolitan glamour of Duran Duran's "Rio" and "Hungry Like the Wolf" four years early. It's a travelogue sketch of hanging amidst Parisian crowds, dancing in the nightclubs, staggering back to your car and eating breakfast in the bars.

McCartney wanted to see what it would be like to record while the yacht was actually moving, which would have been a very Duran Duran moment, but unfortunately the motion flung Joe English into his drums and the concept was quickly abandoned.

BLOW AWAY—HARRISON

REC. MARCH–OCTOBER 1978, FRIAR PARK, HARRISON/RUSS TITELMAN (PRODUCERS), HARRISON (V, G), WEEKS (B), STEVE WINWOOD (HARMONIUM, SYNTHESIZER), NEWMARK (D), NEIL LARSEN (ELECTRIC P), COOPER (CONGA, COW BELL), SINGLE: UK 2/16/79 (51); US 2/14/79 (16), ALSO ON *GEORGE HARRISON*

Due to endless rain, Harrison's estate leaks and rots, and it's bringing him down. But suddenly he realizes that all he has to do in life is to love his new wife and son and be happy, and he lets the bad feelings blow out of his mind. The wind blows the clouds away, a rainbow appears, and the warm breeze fills his head with light.

Harrison again uses the weather as a metaphor for emotion, in the tradition of "Here Comes the Sun" and "All Things Must Pass." The song may be completely literal, and it may also represent dark periods of his life (like when he was addicted to "blow") that can now be forgotten thanks to his new domestic bliss.

Harrison's state of mind also improved thanks to finding interests outside the music business and religion, specifically Formula One racing and movie producing, starting with Monty Python's *Life of Brian*.

As was his tradition, the video for "Blow Away" was pretty wacky, with Harrison doing kooky smirks like Lennon, singing beside giant wind-up ducks, and doing a few dance moves. Listeners of AOL Radio chose "Blow Away" as the second favorite Harrison solo song in 2010, behind "My Sweet Lord."

WOMAN—LENNON

Rec. August 4, 1980–late September 1980, Hit Factory, mixed at Record Plant East, NYC, Lennon/Ono/Jack Douglas (producers), Lennon (v, k), McCracken (g), Slick (g), Levin (b), Newmark (d), Small (k), Jenkins (percussion), Backing vocals: Michelle Simpson, Cassandra Wooten, Cheryl Mason Jacks, Eric Troyer, Single: UK 1/16/81 (1)/ US 1/12/81 (2), also on *Double Fantasy*, Covers: The Shadows, Ozzy Osbourne

Lennon wrote "Woman" to be the grown-up version of the *Rubber Soul* song "Girl" he wrote when he was twenty-five. At that time, since he could have practically any woman, he fantasized about a girl who was indifferent to him, put him down, and made him feel like a fool. In his fantasy, he regretted his love for this dream girl because it was an S&M relationship and she believed pain was pleasure. Of course, Lennon was the one who was so preoccupied with pain that it might as well have been his middle name.

In Ono, he found a woman with an ego big enough to handle him, but he was actually the one who caused the majority of pain in the relationship. Thus fifteen years later, his update is another apology song. It's also a successor to early Beatles tunes like "Thank You Girl," in that it's tailored to fit all his female fans. Lennon's sentimental idealism is as strong as it was in 1963 as he reminds Ono they were destined for each other, astrologically and otherwise, and says she holds the fate of his inner child in her hands. It's a pop psychology, New Age greeting card for every man who at some point needs to apologize for his thoughtlessness.

With a glistening modern sheen, he pulled out all the stops for his comeback by laying on heart-tugging strings and Beatles harmonies (by three female backing singers and one male). But for all its slick commerciality, the song never fails to lift the spirits when the crowd gathers in Central Park on his birthday to sing his songs.

After Lennon's death, the single made it to number one in England but was kept at number two in the States by Blondie's "Rapture."

I'M LOSING YOU—LENNON

Rec. August 4, 1980–late September 1980, Hit Factory, Lennon/Ono/ Jack Douglas (producers), Rick Nielsen (g), Bun E. Carlos (d), Levin (b), Album: *John Lennon Anthology*: UK 11/2/98 (62); US 11/3/98 (99), Alternate Version: *Double Fantasy*

When Lennon tried to call Ono from Bermuda but couldn't get through, he got mad and wrote this bluesy rocker. He rues how Ono's saying she's not getting enough but still won't do it with him because she can't forget all the bad things he did in the past. Lennon concedes he hurt her but counters that it was long ago. Exasperated, he cries for her to get down off the cross and let go of yesterday's hang-ups—universal marital strife, amplified by the fact that Lennon transgressed more than most husbands.

Double Fantasy producer Jack Douglas started out engineering the landmark *Who's Next* and *Imagine* albums. He worked with Patti Smith, Blue Oyster Cult, and the New York Dolls and produced three mid-seventies Aerosmith albums, including the seminal *Toys in the Attic* with "Sweet Emotion," "Walk This Way," and the overlooked "No More No More." As one of the midwives to some of the heaviest rock of the '70s, he was perhaps slightly restless with Lennon's current sedate incarnation and suggested Lennon try cutting "I'm Losing You" with another up-and-coming band he had produced, Cheap Trick.

When the power pop group made its debut in 1977, Cheap Trick was quickly tagged as the bridge between Beatles melodicism and punk energy with hits like "Surrender" and "I Want You to Want Me." Guitarist Rick Neilson garnered further attention by always wearing his trademark flipped-up ball cap and hamming it up onstage like one of the Bowery Boys. None other than George Martin was producing their latest album, so Lennon said bring them in. Neilson's wife had just given birth, but she gave him permission to go with drummer Bun E. Carlos.[5]

On the track, Lennon counts it off tough like a dick, and the guitar matches his attitude, the most primitive and edgy slab on a Lennon track since the *Plastic Ono* days. (Though today the song sounds more contemporary than the soft rock the Fabs drifted into at the close of the '70s.) Afterward, Lennon told the drummer he wished guitarist Neilson was around when he did "Cold Turkey," as Lennon felt Clapton "choked" on that one.

But Lennon didn't bring them back for any other songs, and their version didn't end up on the album. The regular session guys listened to the Cheap Trick version in their headphones and laid down a less gritty version. Some speculate it was because the cut would have sounded out of place amidst the rest of the glossy album. Some say Ono didn't like Neilson and Carlos. Some say Lennon thought it sounded too much like "Cold Turkey." Some say Cheap Trick's manager asked for too much money. Some say Lennon was mad that somebody leaked news about the sessions to *Rolling Stone* when he was trying to keep everything secret because he was nervous he might not "have it" any more.

The track saw the light of day eighteen years later when it was released on the *John Lennon Anthology*. Cheap Trick later covered "Cold Turkey,"

"Day Tripper," and "Magical Mystery Tour" and was the house band for the *Sgt. Pepper* fortieth anniversary concert at the Hollywood Bowl.

COMING UP—MCCARTNEY

REC. JULY 1979, HOME STUDIO IN SUSSEX OR SCOTLAND, MCCARTNEY (PRO-DUCER), MCCARTNEY (V, G, B, D, K), SINGLE: UK 4/11/80 (2); US 4/14/80 (1), ALSO ON *MCCARTNEY II*, ALTERNATE VERSION: COMING UP (LIVE AT GLASGOW) B-SIDE, GRAMMY NOM. FOR 1980 BEST ROCK VOCAL PERFORMANCE FOR LIVE AT GLASGOW VERSION

Unstable Jimmy McCulloch came to blows with McCartney and left the band (and soon after ODed), followed quickly by drummer Joe English, who felt like touring with the McCartneys was too much like a circus. Denny Laine brought some friends in to replace them, and the next Wings album *Back to the Egg* (produced by Sex Pistols' producer Chris Thomas) was competent but yielded no grade-A classics. Tiring of the band thing, McCartney holed up in his Scottish farm with a new synthesizer and a sixteen-track recorder. Kraftwerk and Brian Eno were innovating techno, but to the mainstream white rock scene, synthesizers could still be as suspect as disco. McCartney just decided to improvise stuff for himself to see what the machine could do, laying synth riffs under nonsequitors like, "I just want a temporary secretary" (like maybe he just wanted disposable session musicians).

When Wings started out for the next tour, McCartney was busted for pot in Japan (see "Wanderlust"). McCartney later mused he had a subconscious desire to sabotage the Wings pattern, which had become a rut for him. He canceled the tour and released the proto-techno solo stuff as *McCartney II*, a futuristic bookend to his first solo album done ten years earlier in between bands. The album's opening track, "Coming Up," was a big hit, but the rest of the album left people nonplussed or unimpressed. Its stock would rise twenty years later after the trance and electronica scenes discovered it.

With Macca playing all the instruments himself, "Coming Up" was minimalist bubblegum funk that was, per Keith Cameron of *Mojo*, "built upon a groove that melds Stevie Wonder's 'Superstition' with the Afrodelica of Talking Heads, ecstatically drug-suggestive in mood."[6] Sprinkled throughout were random electronic sounds that McCartney originally figured he would eventually clean up but in the end left as it. He occasionally sped up his voice by using a tool called vari-speed, while a high-pitched Linda sang harmony in the background. The lyrics could be another sexual pun, but they also assure the listener that he's a friend and lover one can always rely on. The song then expands to an "Imagine"-like message of peace and understanding, with everyone sharing everything for free.

Debuting in May 1980 on *Saturday Night Live*, the video was an impressively amusing promo in which every member of the twelve-piece band was actually played by McCartney, except for two backing vocalists played by Linda, one with mustache. McCartney, the lead singer, was defiant in his cheesy relish, while the shifty-eyed keyboardist was a mix of Ron Mael of Sparks and Hitler, spasmodically repressing his left hand from rising to a full heil. The bassist was the deliriously cheerful McCartney of Beatlemania days, and other impersonations included Neil Young, Frank Zappa, Roxy Music saxophonist Andy McKay, and a guitarist who could have been Hank Marvin from the Shadows or Buddy Holly himself. OutKast would lift the concept for their successful 2003 "Hey Ya" video, setting it in a Beatlemania-era TV studio. McCartney's "band" was dubbed the Plastic Macs, and Lennon soon exclaimed that the song was driving him "crackers" in a good way.

Before its official release, a live version was captured in Glasgow, Scotland, on December 17, 1979, on the last night of Wings' UK tour. McCartney said he knew he had a hit when he saw how some young guys started jumping around euphorically to the rapid-fire riff. The live version was put on the B-side of the single along with a *Venus and Mars*–era instrumental outtake. While the studio version made it to number two in Britain, in the United States and Canada, the more techno-phobic DJs flipped the single over and made the live version a number one hit. With *McCartney II* being either too indulgent or too ahead of its time, the label quickly inserted an extra one-sided single of the live version to spruce up sales.

ATTENTION—STARR

REC. JULY 11–21, 1980, SUPER BEAR STUDIOS IN BEAR-LES-ALPES, FRANCE, MCCARTNEY (WRITER/PRODUCER), STARR (V, D), MCCARTNEY (B, P, PERCUSSION, BV), LINDA MCCARTNEY (BV), LAURENCE JUBER (G), HOWIE CASEY (SAX), LLOYD GREEN (PEDAL STEEL G), ALBUM *STOP AND SMELL THE ROSES*: UK 11/20/81 (DID NOT CHART); US 11/20/81 (98)

Starr wrapped the goofy feature *Caveman* in early 1980, then called McCartney to ask for some help in the studio. They met in France in July and recorded two McCartney songs, "Attention" and "Private Property," along with a cover of the old Cavern standard "Sure to Fall" (sung on the Beatles' *Live at the BBC* collection by McCartney).

"Attention" is a peppy showtune in the vein of something Sammy Davis Jr. or Frank Sinatra might have sung in a Technicolor movie like *Come Blow Your Horn*. Starr asks for his love's attention for a while, as that's all anybody really wants, and exhorts her to "give it all she's got" because we only get it if we try, etc. Then the bridge kicks up a wistful notch as producer McCartney plays his masterful bass against bounding piano, he and Linda "oooooooh," and Star feels happy that his woman has time to give him. He looks around and sees love in the children, who know how to just live in the present. It's a swinging throwback to the cartoon Ringo might have sung while the Yellow Submarine followed him around, an up-tempo "Goodnight" by the warm-hearted everyman who made the Beatles more accessible than Pete Best ever could.

Unfortunately, despite songs by Ron Wood, Harry Nilsson, and Stephen Stills, no one gave attention to the album *Stop and Smell the Roses*, and Starr's label dropped him. The 1980s would be a long decade for him.

WITH A LITTLE LUCK—MCCARTNEY

REC. 1977, MOBILE STUDIO ON *FAIR CAROL* YACHT, MCCARTNEY (PRODUCER), MCCARTNEY (V, B, K), LINDA MCCARTNEY (K, BV), LAINE (G, BV), JIMMY MC-CULLOCH (G, BV), JOE ENGLISH (D), SINGLE: UK 3/23/78 (5); US 3/20/78 (1), ALSO ON *LONDON TOWN*, FILM APPEARANCE: *SUNBURN* (1979)

With its startlingly wimpy synth and drums and self-help affirmations to ignore bad weather like the willow tree does, this is quite possibly the whitest song ever. It's a blindly optimistic "We Can Work It Out" without the frustration, angst, or organic instrumentation.

The promotional film came out two months after the Sex Pistols played their last gig and was McCartney's most un-rock-and-roll video yet. Mc-Cartney, Linda, and Laine play the song while dorky mellow adults from the local insurance office and their kids dance around in a mind-set somewhere between boredom, happiness, and Stepford soma. For anyone who wants to make fun of white people dancing, this is exhibit number one, as wide-collared adults bounce up and down like middle school kids in Wichita. The producers got some black people to smile and dance and do the best they could, but it's beyond a lost cause.

Thirteen years earlier, the Beatles had mocked the whole promo film process by being too cool to actually bother to lip-synch, glaring at the camera—whatever they felt like doing in their stoned arrogance. Without Lennon's surly edge, McCartney has completely forgotten he was once the antidote to corn. But that makes it more entertaining if you enjoy period cheese. "With a Little Luck" can't help but be nostalgic though for those who grew up in the '70s, as it was played at every bank and drugstore, and he still slipped, "With a little fuck," past the censors with the first line.

"With a Little Luck" marks the rise of the soft era of the solo Beatles more than "Silly Love Songs" because that earlier tune still had some R&B disco-fied heft to the beat. Still, beyond any critics' snarky comments, it must've been a fine life, hanging on a couple yachts in the Virgin Islands with your family, just singing this ditty in the afternoon sun with the wind from the waves blowing back your hair. McCartney wrote this song when Linda was expecting James, just as Stella McCartney's birth had inspired the name Wings.

DEAR YOKO—LENNON

Rec. August 4, 1980–late September 1980, Hit Factory, mixed at Record Plant East, NYC, Lennon/Ono/Jack Douglas (producers), Lennon (v, k), McCracken (g), Slick (g), Levin (b), Newmark (d), Small (k), Jenkins (percussion), Backing vocals: Michelle Simpson, Cassandra Wooten, Cheryl Mason Jacks, Eric Troyer, Album *Double Fantasy*: UK 11/17/80 (1); US 11/17/80 (1), Grammy win for Album of the Year 1980

One key to the Beatles' overwhelming success was that they seamlessly fused black R&B girl group music with '50s rock and roll. "Dear Yoko" saw Lennon continuing the formula, only now the girl group inspiration was Shirley and Company's disco hit "Shame Shame Shame" (1975).[7] Recorded on August 14 in six takes, the drummer rode the backbeat while Hugh McCracken's funky guitar sliced like Morse code coming out of an early Jackson 5 record. McCracken also added slide guitar and four different kinds of harmonica.

Meanwhile, Lennon did his most spot-on Buddy Holly impersonation since the BBC days, much truer to Holly's quirky, hiccupping, high-pitched mannerisms than covers done on his *Rock 'n' Roll* album. As the last song on the last album released while Lennon was alive, "Dear Yoko" brought him full circle back to the namesake of his old band (a spoof on Buddy Holly's Crickets) and the guy who made him want to write songs in the first place—Holly proved you could be a star even if you didn't look like Elvis; all you needed to do was write and sing brilliant rock and roll.

"Dear Yoko" also follows the *Imagine* tradition by making his last song on the album a musically euphoric tune that is kept from being a classic only by Lennon name-checking his wife, as was the case with "Oh Yoko!" nine years earlier. A hymn to his codependency, he misses her even if she's gone for just an hour, but he knows that wherever he is, her spirit is watching over him, and he thanks the goddess for smiling on their love. In the fade-out, he nags Ono to hang out with him more instead of spending her time selling her $250,000 prized dairy cows, her latest business coup at the time the song was recorded.

LONDON TOWN—MCCARTNEY

REC. 1977–1978, ABBEY ROAD, MCCARTNEY (PRODUCER), MCCARTNEY (V, B, K), LINDA MCCARTNEY (K, BV), LAINE (G, BV), JIMMY MCCULLOCH (G, BV), JOE ENGLISH (D) SINGLE: UK 8/11/78 (60); US 8/14/78 (39), ALSO ON *LONDON TOWN*

Ironically, McCartney wrote this ode to London in Australia with Laine during the Wings over the World tour, then recorded it in the Caribbean. Like "Eleanor Rigby," it's about urban loneliness, only in the first person and mellower, with gentle keyboards by McCartney and Linda instead of piercing strings.

In the song, McCartney walks the dirty London sidewalk, feeling unable to interact with the ordinary people he passes, only able to retell the same old stories to his wife. A few moments of whimsy—passing someone playing the flute, someone wearing pink balloons on their shoes—do little to lift his melancholy. It's a Wings version of Morrissey's "Every Day Is Like Sunday," with an instrumental break by McCulloch that briefly recalls Harrison's slide guitar.

It would be one of McCulloch's last hurrahs with the band. Perhaps the loneliness of the tune hinted at how Wings continually crumbled back to just the core of McCartney, Linda, and Laine. After the first Wings musicians quit right before *Band on the Run*, McCartney had gone to great lengths to give all the band members their own solo songs on Wings albums, but in the end they still left anyway.

BEAUTIFUL BOY—LENNON

REC. AUGUST 4, 1980–LATE SEPTEMBER 1980, HIT FACTORY, LENNON/ONO/ JACK DOUGLAS (PRODUCERS), LENNON (V, G), McCRACKEN (G), SLICK (G), LEVIN (B), NEWMARK (D), SMALL (K), JENKINS (PERCUSSION), ROBERT GREEN-RIDGE (STEEL DRUM), ALBUM *DOUBLE FANTASY*

Lennon resented the fact that Cynthia got pregnant right as Beatlemania was exploding, but he appreciated how she had always been there for him, so he married her (though he ran away to Spain with manager Brian Epstein the week Julian was born). He spent a few years with Cyn and Julian when he wasn't on tour and wrote Julian the lullaby "Good Night." But soon it became more fun to save the world than be a good parent.

In "Beautiful Boy," he assures his second son that the monster is gone, replaced by a good father. Reflecting Sean's half-Asian heritage, Lennon hired a Jamaican steel drummer to play an archetypal Asian melody. The steel drum also spoke of Bermuda, where Lennon had written the song, as do the sound effects of waves that open the track along with a Tibetan wishing bell.

As Lennon tucks Sean in bed, he reminds him to say a little prayer that every day is getting better. He'd come a long way from 1967, when he sneered in McCartney's "Getting Better" that it couldn't get any worse. (Still, even that year his son inspired his art, as Julian's drawing provided the inspiration for "Lucy in the Sky with Diamonds.")

The journey between the two "getting betters" is the cornerstone of the Lennon myth, in which the antihero artist triumphed over his demons to become the healthy father he never had.

In philosopher Joseph Campbell's theory of myth, the hero journeys into the darkness and brings back a new discovery to benefit society. Elvis reminded repressed white people of the healing power of sexual ecstasy. Brando acted like a realistic slob, thus casting a spotlight on the phony theatricality of the movies and leading the way to greater realism in all the arts.

But while famous artists are given the keys to the culture, many still can't find the light. Elvis died on the toilet. Brando seemed lost in his girth and his own family's psychodramas.

Like McCartney and Dylan, Lennon found the Grail to be the basic thing humans have been trying to do since time immemorial: being a good husband and father, and in so doing remaking their own painful childhood into their child's carefree youth.

McCartney later counted "Beautiful Boy" as one of his favorite songs by Lennon.

MULL OF KINTYRE—MCCARTNEY

Rec. August 1977, RAK Mobile Studio at Spirit of Ranachan Studio/ McCartney's Scottish farm, AIR Studios, London, Abbey Road, McCartney/Laine (writers), McCartney (producer), McCartney (v, g), Linda McCartney (bv), Laine (g, bv), Joe English (d), The Campbeltown Pipe Band (pipes), Single: UK 11/11/77 (1); US 11/14/77 (33), Cover: Glen Campbell

Kintyre is a peninsula in southwest Scotland. Mull is an old Gaelic word meaning a tip of the land that has a sharp drop into the sea, without any trees. McCartney had owned High Park Farm there since 1966, with his mobile studio in the barn.

One day McCartney realized he dug bagpipes, but there were no modern bagpipes songs. So he started writing one on an evening in August 1974. Gradually it morphed into a tune that celebrated his beloved farm, where the mist rolled in from the sea. After McCulloch and English left the band, McCartney finished it with Laine and Tony Wilson, the Pipe Major with the Campbeltown Pipe Band.

The video revealed to the rest of the world the land's beauty and why McCartney loved it so much. It opened on him strumming the song sitting on a fence, and but for the fashion of his clothes, it could've been a 100 years ago. The camera panned a vast meadow that overlooked the water and peered down onto a beach with marching bagpipers. The promotional film climaxed in a happy nighttime sing-along with the local villagers around a campfire.

An acoustic waltz with bagpipes was the ultimate counterprogramming in November 1977, when the Clash was singing "No Elvis, Beatles, or Rolling Stones in 1977" in proto-rock even more raw than when Iggy and the Stooges were singing "1969" and "1970." On the other end of the spectrum, within a month the Bee Gees released "Stayin' Alive." For the mainstream masses weary of Johnny Rotten and Steve Jones cursing on national TV, and alarmed that the economy was falling apart, "Mull of Kintyre" seemed to embody the values the natural folk cherished since time immemorial, like a forgotten song from Brigadoon. In the United Kingdom, soccer fans made it a staple of games. It became the biggest selling single in the United Kingdom ever, replacing "She Loves You," which had held the record for fourteen years (indicating that Beatlemania peaked early, though of course sustained). It would hold the record until 1984 when Bob Geldof and Band Aid did "Do They Know It's Christmas" for the starving masses in Ethiopia, the successor to the Concert for Bangladesh. McCartney was on that song as well, so he could console himself that he was still part of the top British single ever. "Mull of Kintyre" still holds the top spot for biggest noncharity single in the United Kingdom. It was released just two months after the birth of his son, so that must've been one of McCartney's finest Christmases.

In the United States, however, Capitol Records totally dropped the ball and it barely registered, which convinced McCartney to drop the label for Columbia in the States for five years. Thus in the United States he assumes no one knows it and never plays it live, though he's been known to break it out in Canada.

WATCHING THE WHEELS—LENNON

Rec. August 4, 1980–late September 1980, Hit Factory, mixed at Record Plant East, NYC, Lennon/Ono/Jack Douglas (producers), Lennon (v, k), McCracken (g), Slick (g), Levin (b), Newmark (d), Small (k), Jenkins (percussion), Matthew Cunningham (hammer dulcimer), Backing vocals: Michelle Simpson, Cassandra Wooten, Cheryl Mason Jacks, Eric Troyer, Single: UK 3/27/81 (30); 3/13/81 (10), also on *Double Fantasy*, Film Appearance: *Funny People* (2009) (acoustic demo from *John Lennon Anthology*)

"Watching the Wheels" was Lennon's summary of where he'd been during the five years since he last recorded, which was in his room watching shadows on the wall—"I'm Only Sleeping" on the five-year plan. And good for him, he earned his rest.

In the song, the same people who nagged him to get up back on that 1966 track now treat him like a lazy dreamer heading for ruin because he's no longer trying to make it in the rat race. But for his own peace of mind, he had to get off of the "merry-go-round" and stop chasing "success" with all its ups and downs. Now he is happy just to watch the endless cycle from a detached distance, with no more goals, needs, or demons driving him. Gradually, the people judging him realize they're the ones who aren't happy and start asking him for the answer.

The song echoes "The Fool on a Hill," a Beatles song that McCartney wrote and Lennon proclaimed to be a good one. The regular people put down the fool, but he's the one who's happy, just watching as the world turns.

Originally Lennon had planned to write an ode to Tennessee Williams. It was an interesting subject because many of Williams's plays mirrored the Epstein-Lennon relationship of the early '60s, with the sexually magnetic brute giving the fragile femme nervous breakdowns. Gradually the song turned into "Memories" and at some point emerged as "Watching the Wheels." The demo on the *John Lennon Anthology* shows its original acoustic guitar hook to be very close to Dylan's "Mama You've Been on My Mind." For the final version, Lennon slowed it down and soldered off the Dylan-esque riff. He then added a hammer dulcimer, lots of echo, and gorgeous production sheen to the piano, giving a bittersweet grandeur to a song about finally arriving at the place of inner peace Lennon and Harrison had been striving for since "Help!"

NOTES

1. "And in the End . . ." Vh1.com, 2000, www.vh1.com/artists/news/1436073/20000201/beatles.jhtml (October 10, 2011).

2. David Sheff, "January 1981 *Playboy* Interview with John Lennon and Yoko Ono," John-Lennon.com, www.john-lennon.com/playboyinterviewwithjohnlennonandyokoono.htm (October 10, 2011).

3. Geoffrey Giuliano, *Blackbird: The Life and Times of Paul McCartney* (Toronto: Da Capo, 1991), 212.

4. John Blaney, *Lennon and McCartney: Together Alone* (London: Jawbone, 2007), 122.

5. Robert Rodriguez, *Fab Four FAQ 2.0: The Beatles' Solo Years, 1970–1980* (Milwaukee: Backbeat Books, 2010), 88–91.

6. Keith Cameron, "Coming Up's Invitation to the Dance," *Mojo*, no. 213 (August 2011), 87.

7. "Dear Yoko," The Beatles Bible.com, www.beatlesbible.com/people/john-lennon/songs/dear-yoko/ (October 10, 2011).

The wedding of Ringo Starr and actress Barbara Bach in London, April 27, 1981: (from left) George and Olivia Harrison, Starr and Bach, Paul McCartney, Bach's son Gianni (in front), Linda and James McCartney. *Getty Images*

· 8 ·

1985: Borrowed Time

Lennon pays the price for speaking his mind.

When *Double Fantasy* was released on November 17, 1980, it didn't break the top ten on either side of the Atlantic. *Melody Maker* slammed it as "indulgent sterility . . . a god-awful yawn." Still, Lennon and Ono plowed forward, doing lots of publicity and working on the follow-up album.

Meanwhile, a suicidal born-again Christian named Mark David Chapman was obsessing on Lennon's "blasphemous" comments and "phony" lifestyle. Chapman was enraged by Lennon's thirteen-year-old "more popular than Jesus" statement and by the instructions in "Imagine" to envision a reality without heaven.

Chapman later commented: "I would listen to this music and I would get angry at him for saying that he didn't believe in God . . . and that he didn't believe in the Beatles. This was another thing that angered me, even though this record ["God" (1970)] had been done at least ten years previously. I just wanted to scream out loud, 'Who does he think he is, saying these things about God and heaven and the Beatles?' Saying that he doesn't believe in Jesus and things like that. At that point, my mind was going through a total blackness of anger and rage."[1]

A recent article in *Esquire* had detailed Lennon's six apartments in the Dakota and Ono's Egyptian antiques, fur coats, dairy farm, and other shrewd real estate investments. Chapman believed it all made Lennon a hypocrite after he'd sung about imagining no possessions. Chapman's favorite novel was J. D. Salinger's *Catcher in the Rye*, in which a friendless teenager wanders New York alone, railing against phonies while gradually having a nervous breakdown. Chapman read it over and over in the weeks leading up to Monday, December 8. Chapman sang, "Imagine John Lennon dead," and voices began telling him to shoot the ex-Beatle. Also, Chapman said, "I thought by killing him I would acquire his fame."

On Monday, Chapman loitered around the Dakota with the plan to shoot Lennon. But when Lennon emerged at 5 p.m., Chapman changed his mind. Instead, he just asked Lennon to sign a copy of *Double Fantasy* for him. (The very album would later go on sale in 2003 for $525,000.) Then Lennon headed to the studio.

After Lennon and Ono were done working they debated whether to get a bite, but Lennon wanted to go home to say goodnight to Sean. Every evening at 11 p.m. the Dakota locked its guard gate. Had Lennon arrived just ten minutes later, Chapman would have been kept out. But Lennon's limo pulled up at 10:54 p.m., and Mark David Chapman was standing in the courtyard.

Chapman shot Lennon in the back four times. The police got Lennon to the emergency room by 11:07 p.m., but he was dead on arrival. Howard Cossell announced it during NBC Monday Night Football, and soon fans began gathering at the Dakota to cry, sing, and hold a candlelit vigil.

Two hours after Lennon had been shot, Starr called Lennon's first wife, Cynthia. She later recalled, "The memory of Ringo's words, the sound of his tearful voice crackling over the transatlantic line, is crystal clear: 'Cynthia, I'm so sorry, John's dead.' I had only one clear thought. My son, our son [Julian], was at home in bed, I had to get back to Ruthin so that I could tell him about his father's death."[2]

Starr and girlfriend Barbara Bach flew to New York to be there for Ono. Ono said she could only handle seeing Starr, but he replied that he was "RingoAndBarbara" now, like she had once been "JohnAndYoko."

When McCartney woke to the news, he first attempted to go to the studio to channel his emotions through music. With George Martin and Denny Laine, he worked on the appropriately bleak "Rain Clouds." But finally he and Martin decided it was better to just take some time off.

When McCartney left the studio, the press swarmed him, sticking microphones in his face. Numb, he chewed gum and said he'd been in the studio because he didn't want to sit at home.

"Why?" a reporter asked.

McCartney's head tilted back, his eyebrows widened, and he said, "Look, I didn't feel like it."

"What time did you hear the news?"

"This morning sometime."

"Very early?"

"Yeah."

For a beat, everyone stood around. Wanting to escape the tone-deaf reporter who kept asking inane questions, McCartney said expressionlessly,

"Drag, isn't it? Okay, cheers." Then went home to watch the news with his children and cry through the night.

Harrison had been recording songs for his next album with Al Kooper, the organist from Dylan's "Like a Rolling Stone" who went on to be a founding member of Blood, Sweat, and Tears. Kooper went over to Friar Park to keep Harrison company. Harrison and Lennon had not spoken for years after a falling out (see "All Those Years Ago") and Harrison was beside himself with rage. His manager pushed him to issue a statement, which read, "After all we went through together, I had and still have great love and respect for John. I am shocked and stunned. To rob life is the ultimate robbery in life. This perpetual encroachment on other people's space is taken to the limit with the use of a gun. It is an outrage that people can take other people's lives when they obviously haven't got their own lives in order."

Ono informed the press that there would be no funeral for John. "John loved and prayed for the human race. Please pray the same for him." He was cremated and his ashes were scattered in Central Park. Ono couldn't sleep with the crowd singing below her windows, so she requested people disperse then gather in Central Park on Sunday for ten minutes of silent prayer. That Sunday, 30,000 people assembled in Liverpool and more than 225,000 people filled Central Park.

Lennon once sang that everybody loves you when you're six feet underground, and by January 6, 1981, the British top five held three Lennon songs, a record unmatched before or since ("Imagine" at number one, "Happy Xmas" at number three, "(Just Like) Starting Over" at number four). Later in the month, "Woman" would join the top ten and "Give Peace a Chance" would make it back up to number thirty-three. *Double Fantasy* went to number one on both sides of the Atlantic and won the Grammy for Album of the Year.

Chapman pleaded guilty and received twenty years to life for second-degree murder. He has been denied parole six times to date. The Strawberry Fields memorial was later established in the park across the street from the Dakota, and large crowds continue to gather there every year on his birthday to sing his songs.

McCartney's next album, *Tug of War* (1982), included two odes to Lennon, "Here Today" and the title track. After Lennon's death, McCartney became concerned with making big statements and collaborating with heavyweights again, such as Stevie Wonder, Michael Jackson, Carl Perkins, and 10cc's Eric Stewart. He would return to the big canvas of "Let It Be" with songs like "Ebony and Ivory," "Pipes of Peace," "Tug of War," and "The Pound Is Sinking."

Ten years earlier, McCartney got his do-it-yourself craving out of his system with *McCartney*, then followed it up with the heavily orchestrated *Ram*. At the onset of the new decade, he repeated the pattern, releasing the homemade

McCartney II and then reuniting with Beatles producer George Martin to create one of his most musically ambitious albums, his best since *Band on the Run*.

The producer of all the Beatles' albums except *Let It Be*, Martin was classically trained and thus the essential middleman who was able to translate the Beatles' ideas into arrangements that could be realized by other musicians. The true fifth Beatle, it was he who realized that the group did not have to have Lennon *or* McCartney as a front man but could instead have both.

McCartney had a huge stack of songs for *Tug of War*, but Martin told him straight out that many of them weren't up to snuff and if their revived partnership was going to work, McCartney would have to listen to some truths he might not want to hear. Martin encouraged McCartney to drop Wings and just hire the session musicians who fit the song. If he wanted the drumming to sound like a certain player, he should get that player, as opposed to asking the Wings drummer to imitate another musician.

McCartney wanted to issue a double album, but Martin talked him out of it. This time, unlike with *The White Album*, McCartney listened. The second-tier songs were held off for 1983's *Pipes of Peace*. *Tug of War* was number one all over the world and nominated for the Album of the Year Grammy.

Laine played on half of *Tug of War* and was anxious to return to performing, but McCartney was worried he would be killed next and did not want to tour, so on April 27, 1981, Laine and McCartney announced that Wings had ended.

Harrison's label told him that one-third of the tracks on 1981's *Somewhere in England* were not pop enough and forced him to come up with new songs. Afterward, he decided it was time to take an extended sabbatical from the industry he'd come to resent. He had one album left on his contract, so he banged out *Gone Troppo* (1982) as efficiently as possible and did zero promotion for it. Even his brother, one of the gardeners on his estate, didn't know he'd put it out.[3] Thus it didn't make the top 100, although those who actually listened to it found it to be a solid effort.

He spent most of the middle of the decade producing some of the best British indie films of the period (*The Long Good Friday*, *Mona Lisa*, *Withnail and I*). Unfortunately, he also produced the Madonna and Sean Penn bomb, *Shanghai Surprise*, for which he stirred from hibernation enough to record the theme song with a Madonna sound-alike and also some Cab Calloway–styled instrumental tracks. Mainly, he gardened, raced cars, and, according to some reports, got back into cocaine while growing distant from his religious community.

Starr's *Old Wave* (1983) contained some great tunes, but no label was interested in putting the record out in the United States or United Kingdom. Starr forged ahead and got RCA to release it in Canada, Australia, New Zealand, Germany, Holland, Mexico, Brazil, and Japan, but it flopped. It would be his last album for nine years.

As Lennon had decided to give up half the space on his comeback album to Ono, that meant he still had half an album waiting in the vaults. It would be a few years before Ono could face the task of revisiting the material, but in 1984 the sequel to *Double Fantasy* emerged. *Milk and Honey* again consisted of half Lennon, half Ono songs. Many of the Lennon songs were superior to those that had ended up on *Double Fantasy*; they had just been passed over because they did not fit the theme of a "heart talk" between husband and wife. Thus they poignantly served as unknowing final statements.

In 1982, the first full-length feature Beatles documentary was released, *The Compleat Beatles*, directed by Patrick Montgomery. Moodily evocative, it remains as fine a recap as is possible in the span of two hours.

Also in 1982, the release of *Thriller* catapulted Michael Jackson into the stratosphere. To date, Jackson-mania remains the last time a performer came close to matching the universal popularity of the Beatles, Elvis, or Sinatra. Other performers like Madonna, Springsteen, Prince, and U2 would be huge, but the media had grown too diverse, with too many channels and too many demographics for one band to encapsulate the spirit of the times the way the Beatles did when they arrived to a nation with just three TV networks. It was the end of an era in many ways.

BORROWED TIME—LENNON

REC. 8/6/80, HIT FACTORY, LENNON/ONO (PRODUCERS), LENNON (V, G), MC-CRACKEN (G), SLICK (G), LEVIN (B), NEWMARK (D), SMALL (K), JENKINS (PERCUSSION), SINGLE: UK 3/9/84 (32); US 5/14/84 (108), ALSO ON *MILK AND HONEY*

In June 1980, Lennon planned to sail from Rhode Island to Bermuda. Ono checked the routes with the ancient Japanese practice of katatagae, which seeks to avoid unlucky directions in travel, and Lennon embarked on the *Megan Jaye*, a forty-three-foot Hinckley centerboard sloop.

Apparently the katatagae wasn't working, because the yacht sailed right into a massive storm. The rest of the crew was wiped out by seasickness. But to Lennon's surprise and pride, he realized all his time spent in the junkie trenches had made him immune to seasickness. He ended up taking the wheel by himself throughout the night, howling old sea shanties into the wind and spray as he imagined his sailor father and father's father had done.

Staring into the abyss of the blackest ocean in the throes of a storm was a mental jolt as heavy as the drugs he'd hit when he was younger, and in the calm aftermath he found himself feeling more alive than he had in years. After holing up in his apartment watching TV for half a decade, he had stared down the sea and felt like a man again. He felt like he had it in him to get back into the game. Maybe the katatagae was right after all.

When they docked in Bermuda, Bob Marley's 1973 tune "Hallelujah Time" wafted out to him, in which Marley sang that we had to keep living on borrowed time. Lennon took the line as a title for his own reggae tune, not suspecting his own time would be up in less than half a year (and Marley's soon thereafter). Lennon recorded two demos of the song, accompanying himself on his acoustic guitar.

When the *Double Fantasy* sessions started back in New York on August 6, it was the second song he laid down. He told the band to think of the Isley Brothers' "Twist and Shout" and "Spanish Twist."

A bright, slightly phased guitar slices in one channel while a laid-back bass percolates in the other. As a strumming acoustic guitar grows louder, Lennon starts calling out about when he was younger, the same phrase from "Help!" and "She Said She Said." In those songs he contrasted how happy he was when he was young compared to how angst-ridden he was in his twenties, living in confusion and despair. As the percussion and keyboards kick in to complete the calypso feel, Lennon celebrates how much happier he is now that he's older, like an updated "My Back Pages."

No longer the blowhard big mouth, he admits that the more he sees the less he knows. Having come full circle on a vast Odysseus journey, he proclaims he wouldn't change any of it but is glad to be living in a less complicated time of his life. He laughs how he used to worry about acne and what to wear and if his current lover really loved him. Now that he knows his woman loves him; he just needs to worry about standing up.

Lennon planned to overdub horns onto the tune, but he ended up setting the song aside, a bit frustrated, as once again his band could not quite play reggae right. The Beatles were hip enough to try ska way back in 1964 with "I Call Your Name," but in truth no one listening to that song would know that's what it was supposed to be. And as stated before, McCartney's frustrated perfectionism with "Ob-La-Di Ob-La-Da" was the first serious rupture in the band. But whether or not "Borrowed Time" missed the mark as reggae, the tune showed that, for brief moments anyway, Lennon had arrived at his destination.

TAKE IT AWAY—MCCARTNEY

Rec. October 1980–March 1981, AIR Studios, London, Martin (producer), McCartney (v, g, b, p), Starr (d), Martin (electric piano), Linda

MCCARTNEY (BV), STEVE GADD (D), ERIC STEWART (BV), SINGLE: UK 6/21/82
(15); US 6/21/82 (10), ALSO ON *TUG OF WAR*

"Take It Away" could be another Beatles-esque pun. On the one hand,
it's the old showbiz verb meaning to begin a performance. McCartney also
wanted to take away the pain of the loss of his friend by distracting himself
through his work as an entertainer. When both Epstein and Lennon died,
McCartney's instinct was to head to the studio. In the song, music helps lift
the spirits of the "soul survivor."

Musically, "Take It Away" is one of McCartney's most sophisticated singles. Starr drummed alongside session stalwart Steve Gadd. Originally George
Martin intended his piano as a guide track only, to be removed from the final
mix, but McCartney decided to keep it.[4] They layered the uplifting brass with
harmonies molded by 10cc's Eric Stewart, who would become McCartney's
frequent collaborator over the next decade. And McCartney's bass was out
front like one of the lead instruments.

Despite the infectious mood, some lyrics hint at the ambivalence that
would lead him to abandon touring for the decade: driving alone for hours and
miles, then hanging in bars after the show with flowers fading.

The video was one of the first to go into heavy rotation on MTV. It follows the rise of a band made up of McCartney, Starr, Martin, Gadd, Stewart,
and Linda as they start out playing in McCartney's home, get discovered, and
hit the big time. It's nice to see a giddy Martin banging his rousing piano as if
he was a regular member of the band, which he always was anyway.

ALL THOSE YEARS AGO—HARRISON

REC. MARCH–OCTOBER 1980 AND NOVEMBER1980–FEBRUARY 1981, FRIAR
PARK, HARRISON/MARTIN (PRODUCERS), HARRISON (V, G), STARR (D), MC-
CARTNEY (BV), LINDA MCCARTNEY (BV), LAINE (BV), AL KOOPER (K), HERBIE
FLOWERS (B), COOPER (SYNTHESIZER, PERCUSSION), SINGLE: UK 5/15/81 (13);
US 5/11/81 (2), ALSO ON *SOMEWHERE IN ENGLAND*

Starr went to Harrison's Friar Park in November 1980 to record two songs
Harrison wrote for him, "All Those Years Ago" and "Wrack My Brain,"
along with a cover of '50s ballad "You Belong to Me." "Wrack My Brain"
was Harrison's cry of angst at being forced to write contemporary pop songs
by his label. Like Lennon, Harrison gave Starr compositions that he would
have felt too naked singing himself. It ended up on Starr's next album, *Stop*

and Smell the Roses, along with the cover, but Starr passed on "All Those Years Ago." It was in a key that was too high for him to sing, and he wasn't crazy about the words.

Next Starr hit New York City, where Lennon gave him the demos for "Nobody Told Me" and "Life Begins at Forty." They set a date for Lennon to produce some sessions for Starr on January 14. But, of course, Mark David Chapman intervened.

Harrison and Lennon hadn't been close for many years. Harrison refused to let Ono play at the Concert for Bangladesh, so Lennon didn't. In 1974, Harrison came to New York to play Madison Square Garden and started yelling at Lennon for all the times he'd let him down, ripping Lennon's glasses off his face. Lennon didn't retaliate, apparently because he felt guilty, and agreed to play a few songs at Harrison's Garden gig. A few days later, all the Beatles were supposed to meet to sign the paperwork to dissolve their company formally, but Lennon didn't show. Rather, he just had a balloon messengered to the meeting with the note, "Listen to this balloon." Harrison yelled at Pang over the phone that he didn't need Lennon onstage. Lennon later finally signed, but he and Harrison didn't reconcile.

In 1980, Harrison published his autobiography, *I Me Mine,* available for the reasonable price of 148 British pounds. In the book, he barely acknowledged Lennon, which peeved him since, as Lennon would grumble in *Double Fantasy* interviews, Harrison had been like a "disciple" of his when they were younger. When Harrison read that Lennon had been hurt, he called him, but Lennon didn't return the call before he was killed.

For "All Those Years Ago," Harrison decided to remove Starr's vocals and replace them with his own, refashioning the lyrics as a tribute to his fallen friend. He sang that, regardless of the rough patches in their relationship, he always looked up to Lennon because he spoke the truth in songs like "All You Need Is Love" and "Imagine." He celebrated how Lennon could make people both laugh and cry, and disparaged the closed-minded ones that persecuted him, especially "the devil's best friend" Chapman. But Harrison was comforted because he knew that Lennon's spirit was now free, and he sent out a prayer to him.

Starr's drumming was already on the recording. Harrison invited McCartney, Linda, and Denny Laine to Friar Park to add backing vocals. Thus it was the first tune since "I'm the Greatest" to feature three Beatles. It was also the first song Harrison, McCartney, and Starr had worked on together since "I Me Mine," which ended up being the group's last song, after they had done much of *Abbey Road* as a trio without Lennon. They would not work together again until *The Beatles Anthology.* Martin provided the string arrangements, and longtime Beatles engineer Geoff Emerick worked on the track as well.

Warner Brothers executive Mo Astin had instructed Harrison to speed up the beat of his new songs to appeal to younger audiences. Since Harrison was pasting new lyrics and vocals over a track that had been finished before the murder, the tone is weirdly upbeat, but it still reached number two as a US single, though the album was Harrison's first not to go gold.

The "All Those Years Ago" video was a montage of clips and photos from all eras of Lennon's life and did a sensitive job encapsulating his remarkable odyssey. Harrison overrode his earlier animosity and gave equal time to Ono's image.

IN MY CAR—STARR

Rec. April–July 1982, Startling Studios, Ascot, Joe Walsh's Santa Barbara studio, Joe Walsh, Richard Starkey, Mo Foster, Kim Goody (writers), Joe Walsh (producer), Starr (v, d, percussion), Joe Walsh (g, bv), Mo Foster (b), Gary Brooker (k), Chris Stainton (k), Backing vocals: Steve Hess, Mark Easterling, Patrick Maroshek, Album *Old Wave*: not released in UK or US; released June 1983 elsewhere

Starr didn't feel safe in the United States after Lennon's murder, so he returned to Tittenhurst Park, the English estate he bought from Lennon in 1973. Lennon had recorded *Imagine* there, and Starr decided to create his next album there in the spring of 1982. All Starr's albums bear the stamp of their producer, and this time around it was none other than Joe Walsh.

After coming to national prominence with his band Barnstorm's "Rocky Mountain Way" in 1973, Walsh was invited to join one of the groups that came closest to capturing the Beatles' level of success in the 1970s, the Eagles. During the "Hotel California" era, Walsh also had solo hits like "Life's Been Good" and "In the City." Starr and Walsh met in LA in the mid-seventies and got on well, not surprising as both shared a happy-go-lucky party guy outlook; "Life's Been Good" could've been about Starr's life as much as Walsh's. By the time Starr was gearing up for his sequel to *Stop and Smell the Roses*, the Eagles had disbanded. Thus Walsh had time to help with Starr's next installment, wryly titled *Old Wave* during the New Wave era, in which the second British invasion exploded on MTV.

To kick *Old Wave* off right, the album snaps to attention with a very '80s sounding keyboard played by Gary Brooker, who had been in Procol Harum. Walsh kicks in with a propulsive riff that perfectly captures the joy of the open road. The piano joins in and crystallizes the thrill of leaving your troubles behind you down the highway, while the guitar shimmers with just a hint of Byrds-like jangle. Walsh was well suited to the song, as he had been one of the cowriters of "Life in the Fast Lane," though "In My Car" is a much less decadent affair. Unlike that well-sketched Eagles classic, the words here just exist to give Starr an excuse to croon in his unpop baritone. For the fade-out, Walsh calls out the title filtered with echo like "In the City," a perfect ending for a team-up unique in the solo Beatle's canon.

Ironically, when he first started going out with Barbara Bach, he flipped his car into lampposts and was flung out of the vehicle. Somehow, both he and Barbara emerged almost unscathed, at which point he proposed, and had the totaled Mercedes turned into a coffee table. Nevertheless, his enthusiasm for cruising was undimmed.

Since *Old Wave* was not released in the United States, and the hook was so catchy, Walsh did his own version of "In My Car" on his 1987 album *Got Any Gum?* He downplayed the synth and toughened up the guitar, adding a touch of "Sweet Child O' Mine" at the end. He promoted it with a typically goofy video in which he cavorted around California golfing out of his sunroof and abducting women in gas stations. Twenty-one years later Walsh married Barbara Bach's sister Marjorie and became Starr's brother-in-law.

NO MORE LONELY NIGHTS—MCCARTNEY

Rec. 1983, AIR Studios, London, Abbey Road, CTS Studios, London, Martin (producer), McCartney (v, p), Linda McCartney (bv), David Gilmour (g), Herbie Flowers (b), Stuart Elliot (d), Anne Dudley (synthesizer), Eric Stewart (bv), Single: UK 9/24/84 (2); US 10/8/84 (6), Film Appearance: *Give My Regards to Broad Street*, nom. for Best Original Song BAFTA and Golden Globe

Unlike *Magical Mystery Tour*, *A Hard Day's Night*, *Help!*, or *Live or Let Die*, *Give My Regards to Broad Street* was a movie title that did not suggest a great song since "Give My Regards to Broadway" already existed.[5] So McCartney quit worrying about coming up with a title theme and just concentrated on writing a song that would be good to sing on a rooftop at sunset. When the "No More Lonely Nights" scene arrived in the film, it was like he was back on the *Ed Sullivan Show* singing "Till There Was You." Just as he did twenty years ago, he still cocked his head to the side, bird-like, with big boyish Disney eyes cast skyward. Now that he was older, he also added a world-weary squint to his repertoire of singing expressions. Then he hit the chorus backed by cellos as fireworks exploded behind him.

"No More Lonely Nights" is actually a very sophisticated single, in contrast to the movie it was written to support. Sonically it's a classy ballad in the vein of "My Love." Thematically it celebrates Linda as his rock of stability as did "Maybe I'm Amazed."

But unlike those other songs, there are hints of trouble behind closed doors. He's waiting a day to call her after having spent a lonely night away from her. Why are they separated? He sings that he will wait until she can laugh again and not cry, even if it takes a couple of years. What could he have done that was so bad?

Loose lips sank no ships at Fort McCartney, and we'll probably never know. Then again, his life could have been completely blissful with Linda, and he could have been drawing on earlier romantic angst from Jane Asher, or just making the damn thing up. Linda herself sings very nice, breathy "la-la-las" on it.

Either way, the song is also notable (for those keeping score) for being another "Right" song, as McCartney asserts once again that he will do what he feels to be right.

The soundtrack to *Give My Regards to Broad Street* consisted of harmless remakes of both Beatles and solo McCartney songs, along with two new pop rockers, "Not Such a Bad Boy" and "No Values." He first heard the latter song in a dream and woke up assuming it was a Rolling Stones song. When he realized they didn't have a song called "No Values," he wrote it for himself.

The requisite ballad "No More Lonely Nights" was the last tune recorded for the project. Often the big hits of albums are the last ones recorded because the artist has a chance to see how the rest of the album is shaping up and can more clearly determine what elements are still missing (e.g., Springsteen's "Dancing in the Dark" and Eminem's "The Way I Am").

McCartney came up with the outline for the song while jamming at Martin's studio. Then Dave Gilmour came by, as Pink Floyd was on the verge of falling apart. In three hours Gilmour and the rest of the band learned the tune, then McCartney played piano and sang live while Gilmour laid down his glistening solo.

I'M STEPPING OUT—LENNON

Rec. 8/6/80, Hit Factory, Lennon/Ono (producers), Lennon (v, g), McCracken (g), Slick (g), Levin (b), Newmark (d), Small (k), Jenkins (percussion), Single: UK 7/15/84 (88); US 3/18/84 (55), also on *Milk and Honey*, Alternate version: *John Lennon Anthology* has additional verse

In June 1980 in Bermuda, Lennon went out to a disco with his assistant Fred Seaman. He woke up the next day hung over but realized he'd had a good time and was inspired to write "I'm Stepping Out."

In the song, he wakes up with the blues, but now that he's older he no longer bothers to wonder why, he just accepts that he needs to get out and get on with it. He paints a portrait of his househusband days, watching *Sesame Street* until Sean's asleep. Since there are only summer reruns on, he needs to put on his best outfit and get out into the city, though he promises the wife he'll be back before one.

The fact that Ono was drifting away from him gives "I'm Stepping Out" its bittersweet undercurrent; there's both fear and excitement in realizing that if she does leave him, he will still get by on his own. The guitars capture the mix of emotions well: a vague loneliness in the tentative verse and the chugging excitement of the chorus as he hopes the nightlife might cheer him up, complemented by subtle, sparkling piano.

The middle section expresses the state of mind he'd been in for the last five years, telling himself he doesn't have to do anything he doesn't feel like just to please other people. It was lifted from a 1979 demo of his called "Real Life." But the chorus may also represent his desire to step back into the music world once again, after being the most famous shut-in since Greta Garbo. Suitably, the song was the first tune the band recorded when the *Double Fantasy* sessions started on August 6, 1980.

THE POUND IS SINKING—MCCARTNEY

REC. OCTOBER 1980–MARCH 1981, AIR STUDIOS, LONDON, MARTIN (PRODUCER), MCCARTNEY (V, G, SYNTHESIZERS), LINDA MCCARTNEY (BV), LAINE (G), ERIC STEWART (BV), STANLEY CLARKE (B), ALBUM *TUG OF WAR*: UK 4/26/82 (1); US 4/26/82 (1) GRAMMY NOM. FOR ALBUM OF THE YEAR

For this track's complex backing vocal arrangement, 10cc's Eric Stewart joins Linda and Laine, which is appropriate as the song covers similar territory to 10cc's 1974 hit "The Wall Street Shuffle." It's an example of the Beatles moving into thematic areas more commonly associated with middle age, in this case the stock market. The song is sadly as relevant today as it was in 1984, focusing on a stock market crash in which only the strong survive. All the currencies plunge: the pound, the peso, the lira, the mark, the franc, and the drachma. Naturally, the only ones doing well are the two countries from which McCartney is somewhat alienated, Japan and the Soviet Union.

McCartney had been working on "The Pound Is Sinking" since 1977. In the summer of 1980, he fused it with another fragment, "Hear Me Lover." Passages from the latter do not seem to have anything to do with the main theme, probably because McCartney just cobbled the scraps together and made a glorious production of it, although they could relate in very subtle ways.

In the first section, McCartney assumes a "stiff upper lip," a very proper English voice to berate a woman for not having the skills of her extraordinary father. It may be pure surrealism, unless McCartney had a financial advisor he liked who retired and whose daughter took over.

Or, the haughty affront to the woman in question could be the singer's first line of attack in attempting to push her away for reasons that (perhaps) become clearer in the "Hear Me Lover" section.

In this bit, McCartney pleads mysteriously with his lover that he can't be held responsible for doing something that she knows didn't happen because he only knew her for a minute. Then, when he repeats that it didn't happen, he says it didn't happen *only for a minute*—and anyway, his lover's heart wasn't in it anymore.

The confusing cry of angst brings to mind Cynthia Lennon's statement in her memoir that when the Beatles hit it big, "It appeared from the evidence on the solicitor's desk at this time that Paul had been a bit of a town bull in Liverpool. Claims for paternity suits rolled in. He found himself in great demand in more ways than one. Whether the claims were true is anybody's guess."[6]

No doubt when those claims came in—true or not—McCartney felt his gut plunge like the market on a very bad day.

I DON'T WANNA FACE IT—LENNON

Rec. August 1980, Hit Factory, Lennon/Ono (producers), Lennon (v, g), McCracken (g), Slick (g), Levin (b), Newmark (d), Small (k), Jenkins (percussion), Album *Milk and Honey*: UK 1/23/84 (3); US 1/23/84 (11)

Originally demoed in 1977 on acoustic guitar, Lennon did a new demo on his 1980 trip to Bermuda, then it was one of the first he recorded for the *Double Fantasy* sessions. Interestingly, most of the tunes that got passed over for that album were ones he recorded at the beginning of the session.

Lennon thought about giving it to Starr for his next album, but as was the case with the other songs Lennon offered him, Starr couldn't handle performing them after Lennon's death, although the raw emotion might have saved Starr's album from obscurity. Lennon's assistant Fred Seaman gave Lennon's son Julian a copy and Julian considered doing a cover, but Ono stopped him, in another manifestation of the wicked stepmother syndrome. Why the world couldn't handle two versions of "I Don't Wanna Face It" only Ono knows.

As on the rest of *Milk and Honey*, the band rocks harder here than on the tunes selected for *Double Fantasy*. Lyrically, it falls into the honored Lennon tradition of self-loathing going back to "I'm a Loser" and "Nowhere Man," but with a more humorous edge that comes from the detachment of age. He lays out all his contradictions: he wants to go where no one knows him but wants to be in the hall of fame; he wants to save humanity but can't stand people; he sings for his supper but can't cook; he demands the world to give him some truth but looks the other way when it comes to him. U2's Bono would emulate Lennon's self-deflating approach in many of his post–*Joshua Tree* albums to take the piss out of his own messianic pose, starting with the Lennon homage "God: Part 2."

The raucous version released on the *John Lennon Anthology* ends with Lennon remarking (like Starr at the end of "Helter Skelter"), "My [guitar] pick got half the size."

WANDERLUST—MCCARTNEY

Rec. October 1980–March 1981, AIR Studios, London, Martin (producer), McCartney (v, g, b, p), Linda McCartney (bv), Laine (g, b, g synthesizer), Eric Stewart (bv), Adrian Sheppard (d, percussion), The Philip Jones Brass Ensemble (horns), Album *Tug of War*

The stately piano and Philip Jones Brass Ensemble give "Wanderlust" perhaps the finest sense of grandeur of any McCartney composition, which is why it was one of the newer songs he performed in *Give My Regards to Broad Street*. The mournful weariness in his vocals seems to carry the tragedy of his estranged partner's murder.

So it is first disappointing to learn that lyrically it recounts the story of his near bust for pot during the recording of *London Town* on the yachts in the Virgin Islands. US Customs raided them and gave them a stern warning about the consequences of holding weed. The captain of the yacht then told McCartney he was not going to stand for drugs on his boats and a bad argument ensued. Seriously irritated, McCartney wanted to find another boat, and some other people in the dock said he could use their catamaran, called *Wanderlust*. The name became associated with freedom in McCartney's mind.[7]

A much worse experience occurred in January 1980. When Wings landed in Tokyo, security quickly discovered a 219-gram (7.7-ounce) bag of pot in McCartney's luggage. They immediately escorted him to jail and canceled the sold-out shows. There has been some dispute over the years whether it was he or Linda who packed it so blatantly, either because they were stoned or because they assumed they were untouchable. The bust carried a mandatory sentence of five years, and it was a scary week for Macca in prison as Japanese politicians called for his trial. He was living the opening section of "Band on the Run" for real. After nine days, Japan wanted to avoid an international incident and allowed him to return to Scotland.

As McCartney laments being harassed for a petty crime, one can feel the toll his cumulative pot busts have taken on him. In the big picture, the counterculture's dependence on drugs became their Achilles heel. From *The News of the World* colluding with Scotland Yard to imprison the Stones for drugs in 1967, to the Beatles' busts, to Abbie Hoffman hiding underground for years after a coke bust, governments used drugs as an excuse to jail anyone who didn't get with their program.

The Beatles once planned to escape the Blue Meanies by buying their own Greek island, one of the fantasies of the Summer of Love that never came to fruition. But you can hear the same yearning to escape in McCartney's sad "Wanderlust" refrain. Ten years later the "band on the run" is still running because he wanted to smoke instead of drink.

CLEANUP TIME—LENNON

Rec. 8/13/80, 9/5/80, 9/17/80, Hit Factory, Lennon/Ono/Jack Douglas (producers), Lennon (v, g), McCracken (g), Slick (g), Levin (b), Newmark (d), Small (k), Jenkins (percussion), Horns: Howard Johnson, Grant Hunderford, John Parran, Seldon Powell, George "Young" Opalisky, Roger Rosenberg, David Tofani, Ronald Tooley, Album *Double Fantasy*

When the other kids teased Lennon because his dad had disappeared and his mom was "living in sin" with another guy on the other side of town, he learned to be a tough fighter with a razor-sharp wit to scare anyone from making fun of him. He was also a thug to hide his bisexual side. He was known

to enjoy circle jerks as a teen (yelling "Winston Churchill!" when he came
to distract the other guys), had a liaison with his gay manager, enjoyed more
than his share of coed orgies, and shared an affinity with glam rock stars like
Elton John and Bowie. Ono would opine that he was in the closet and dug
her because she looked like a man (as he says himself on "Polythene Pam").
It was this combination of toughness and sexual ambiguity that allowed him
to sell "effeminate" hair to the world, and he continued to be a lightning rod
for changing sexual mores in his role as househusband.

Before Lennon returned to the public eye in 1980 with the "househusband" PR campaign, John Irving's 1978 novel *The World According to
Garp* became a best-seller by encapsulating the effects of feminism and gay
liberation on the United States. It told the story of an eccentric family in
which the title character stayed home with the kids while his wife worked,
his mom became an icon to the radical feminist movement, and his best
friend was a transsexual former linebacker. The John Hughes–penned feature *Mr. Mom* (1983) starring Michael Keaton also reflected the changing
times as women broke the glass ceiling.

Along with "(Just Like) Starting Over," "Cleanup Time" was the last
tune Lennon wrote in Bermuda in June 1980, inspired by a conversation
with producer Jack Douglas about getting off drugs and alcohol. Back in New
York, on August 13 in the studio, Tony Levin came up with a distinctive bass
riff and they laid down the music. On September 5 horns were overdubbed,
and on September 17 Lennon did his vocals. The backing vocals singing,
"cleanup," were actually a vocoder, a device that captured the sound of the
horns and then turned them into vocals, a trick also used on Queen's "Bohemian Rhapsody."

Once Lennon had painted idealistic vignettes of young love. Now he
presented the portrait of a nuclear family protected from "rats" disturbing
their harmony through their isolation from the outside world. In the gender
reversal, Ono is in charge of managing the money while Lennon makes bread.
(He kept boasting in interviews how he made bread as if he had invented
penicillin.)

He uses the same image of the king and queen that he used twelve years
earlier in "Cry Baby Cry." But that eerie song was an account of the stulti-
fying ennui of his domestic life with Cynthia and Julian in the stockbroker
belt outside London. Paradoxically, twelve years later amidst the world's most
hectic city, Lennon settled down.

For all the radicalism of his youth, in the end he asserts that home with
wife and son represents the fulfillment of his life. Having succeeded beyond
his wildest expectations and sowed his oats, he could now enjoy healthy domesticity. Though, in keeping with his offbeat family history, it's domesticity

with an *Addams Family* tint. The "Cleanup Time" chorus reminds him and Ono to stay off the heroin and speaks of casting the perfect spell in harmony with the gods, angels, and oracles.

If the overarching story of Lennon's work was of a troubled, violent young man searching for answers who eventually found peace by growing to be a good father and husband, this and "Woman" are the happy ending fade-out of a bohemian *It's a Wonderful Life.*

I DON'T WANT TO DO IT—HARRISON

REC. NOVEMBER 1984, LOS ANGELES, DYLAN (WRITER), DAVE EDMUNDS (PRODUCER), HARRISON (G, V), CHUCK LEAVELL (K), MICHAEL SHRIEVE (D), KENNY AARONSON (B), JIMMY VAUGHAN (G), RELEASED MAY 1985 AS A SINGLE (DID NOT CHART), ALSO ON *PORKY'S REVENGE* SOUNDTRACK AND *LET IT ROLL: SONGS BY GEORGE HARRISON*

This lost gem was written by Bob Dylan circa 1970 but never recorded by him. Harrison laid down an acoustic demo during the *All Things Must Pass* sessions. Structurally, the song was pretty much in place then, but Harrison dropped it for fourteen years.

Out of nowhere, "I Don't Want to Do It" was revived through the prodding of Dave Edmunds. Edmunds was a Welsh rocker who had solo hits, formed Rockpile with Nick Lowe, and produced the likes of the Flaming Groovies, Stray Cats, and Fabulous Thunderbirds. Edmunds was commissioned to put together the soundtrack of the ignominious *Porky's Revenge* (1985), sequel to *Porky's* (1982), which, along with *Animal House* (1978), instigated the '80s wave of raunchy teen sex comedies. Edmunds did his own songs for the movie and also got others to contribute. Somehow it was decided to revive Dylan's understated, melancholy composition for the occasion.

"I Don't Want to Do It" has a unique place in Harrison's oeuvre, with a sound different from any other period. It's a little more rich, deep, and organic than *Gone Troppo* and without the pop sheen of 1987's *Cloud Nine.* The piano matches the poignancy of the lyrics, accompanied by an organ, perhaps in honor of Dylan's mid-sixties classics. Michael Schrieve's drums give the song a faster-paced momentum than the song would have possessed had it been on *All Things Must Pass,* as it was recorded after the changes brought about by a younger generation of coked-up New Wavers with drum machines. As usual, Harrison does his own back-up vocal harmonies. It's too bad this very appealing sound with Edmunds was a one-off.

Dylan's lyrics are unusually generic and seem to be not quite finished, which could be why he never released it. It opens with the singer wishing he could have another day of youth, because back then he knew what was true and all he had to do was play in the yard. Then the singer takes his woman into his arms, swearing he doesn't want to make her cry. Perhaps it was written by Dylan when he was contemplating leaving his wife and children to go back on tour. Ultimately he realizes he doesn't want to leave his home and family—and he didn't for another half decade. Harrison could certainly relate, as this was the only song he released in the five years between 1982's *Gone Troppo* and 1987's *Cloud Nine*, except for a few songs for the movie *Shanghai Surprise* (1986). The man didn't want to do it.

Around this period Harrison also recorded a version of Dylan's *Desire* outtake "Abandoned Love," which ended up on Dylan's career retrospective *Biograph*. One of Dylan's best, it's exciting to hear Harrison perform such a deep-cut Dylan tune, though Harrison's modern pop approach can't match the rustic, fiddle-haunted soul of Dylan's original.

GROW OLD WITH ME—LENNON

REC. JULY OR NOVEMBER 1980, THE DAKOTA, LENNON/ONO (PRODUCERS), LENNON (V, P), ALBUM *MILK AND HONEY*: UK 1/23/84 (3); US 1/23/84 (11), ALTERNATE VERSION: *JOHN LENNON ANTHOLOGY* WITH GEORGE MARTIN ORCHESTRATION, COVERS: MARY CHAPIN CARPENTER, THE POSTAL SERVICE, GLEN CAMPBELL

Robert and Elizabeth Browning were Victorians who wrote famous love poems to each other, such as Elizabeth's *Sonnets from the Portuguese* (1850), with the famous opening, "How do I love thee? Let me count the ways." Taking "Let Me Count the Ways" as a title, Ono wrote a touching song on the piano, then called Lennon while he was in Bermuda to play it to him over the phone. He was deeply moved, and she suggested he write a Robert Browning song back to her, as if they were the reincarnation of the poets. They began to see *Double Fantasy* as a concept album in which each song would respond to the previous track, as if husband and wife were talking to each other.

That afternoon Lennon was watching a movie on TV about a baseball player whose girlfriend sent him a poem by Robert Browning called "Rabbi Ben Ezra" that began with, "Grow old along with me! The best is yet to be." Starting with those lines but writing new lyrics beyond, he called Ono back and played his new song over the phone. As he polished it, he and Ono planned it to be a standard that people would play in church when couples got married, with full symphonic backing.

Back at the Dakota, Lennon recorded it in November in their bedroom with piano and drum machine. They meant for it and "Let Me Count the Ways" to be included on *Double Fantasy* but wanted to get the album out for Christmas sales and ran out of time. Thus they ended up on *Milk and Honey*.

In the 1990s, "Grow Old with Me" was one of four demos that Ono gave to McCartney so he and the two surviving Beatles could turn it into a Beatles reunion song for the *Beatles Anthology*. But the group decided it was too much work to bring it up to sound quality standards and focused on other songs. In 1998, Ono asked George Martin to arrange an orchestral backing so the song could be completed how she and Lennon originally envisioned it. The accompaniment was recorded at Abbey Road, with Martin's son Giles playing bass, and this version was included on the *John Lennon Anthology*. (It is interesting that Martin said his hearing was too far gone to work on the Beatles' *Anthology* but he was able to do this song three years later.)

To these ears, the unadorned demo is the more moving recording, with its beautiful bridge defined even without the embellishment of the other instruments. At the time of *Milk and Honey*'s release, this was the only version of the song Ono could locate. Even though Lennon had done other demos, apparently the cassettes had been stolen. In 2009, some of the other demo versions with Lennon on acoustic guitar and piano surfaced among bootleggers.

The lyrics express Lennon's driving desire for union, to meld together like two branches of one tree, a craving that drove him ever since being denied unity with his mother as a child. His childhood best friend Pete Shotton had referred to he and Lennon as "Siamese twins."[8] But while Lennon had Shotton for friendship, McCartney for artistic partnership, and women for sex, it wasn't until Ono that Lennon found all aspects he craved in one package, including someone who could act as a mother to him as well.

In a fragile voice, he looks forward to spending the rest of his life with Ono. No longer alienated from God, Lennon asks Him to bless their love, and gently assures his wife that the best is yet to come. Whatever fate decrees, they will see it through because—despite all the ups and downs—their love is true.

The song was Lennon's last recording.

HERE TODAY—MCCARTNEY

REC. 1981, AIR STUDIOS, LONDON, MARTIN (PRODUCER), MCCARTNEY (V, G), JACK ROTHSTEIN (VIOLIN), BERNARD PARTRIDGE (VIOLIN), IAN JEWEL (VIOLA), KEITH HARVEY (CELLO), ALBUM *TUG OF WAR*

The last time McCartney talked to Lennon on the phone was just before *Double Fantasy* came out. Lennon was looking forward to getting back into the game after five years, laughing, "This housewife wants a career!"

McCartney later recalled, "That is a nice thing, a consoling factor for me, because I do feel it was sad that we never actually sat down and straightened out our differences out. But fortunately for me, the last phone conversation I ever had with him was really great, and we didn't have any kind of blow-up."[9]

After McCartney told a reporter, shell-shocked, that Lennon's death was a "drag," he was attacked for seeming flippant. The accepted wisdom began to form that Lennon had been the wild visionary martyr who gave the Beatles soul while McCartney was the sappy popster who churned out hits for grandmas. The mythification began in earnest with Philip Norman's epic group biography/social history, *Shout! The Beatles in Their Generation*. Published in 1981, Norman's account was superbly written and brought a new level of gravitas to the Beatles' story, but he viewed Lennon warmly at the expense of McCartney, who was portrayed as an uptight, cheap guy who wrote uncool tunes that Lennon finally couldn't stand anymore (like "Hello, Goodbye" and "Ob-La-Di, Ob-La-Da"). McCartney would spend much of the ensuing decades attempting to correct the misconceptions and remind people that he had been a visionary, too, coming up with the soundscape of "Tomorrow Never Knows," for instance.

As for the "drag" comment, McCartney had just spent the last seven years hoping to work again with Lennon. Lennon's death was one of the worst things that could have happened to him, and some judgmental reporter was implying it was inappropriate that he didn't stay at home grieving. In such a situation, on punch-drunk autopilot, anyone would want to get away as soon as possible.

Still, McCartney would play the moment over in his mind and ruminate over how close he and Lennon really were. In the song "Here Today," McCartney sings that he knows Lennon would scoff at him were McCartney to be presumptuous enough to think he really knew him. But McCartney remembers they were brothers once. He begins the first verse with just himself on acoustic guitar, but soon Martin's string quartet joins in, in the tradition of "Yesterday."

Scholars suggest McCartney subconsciously wrote "Yesterday" about the loss of his mother when he was fourteen. That was another death in which he "said something wrong." Upon learning his mother had passed, he wondered aloud, "What are we going to do without her money?" and afterward felt ashamed.

McCartney then recalls the day his school friend Ivan Vaughn brought him to see Lennon's band play for the first time. After the gig, McCartney played Eddie Cochran's "Twenty Flight Rock" for the band and Lennon was secretly impressed, as McCartney had been by Lennon. But both played it cool. Lennon waited a while to ask Vaughn to invite McCartney into the band. When Vaughn conveyed the message, McCartney was secretly pleased but kept a poker face before finally nodding, "Well, okay," and riding off on his bike. After the break-up they became guarded with each other again. After Lennon's death, McCartney said, "I would not have been as typically human and standoffish as I was if I knew John was going to die. I would have made more of an effort to try and get behind his 'mask' and have a better relationship with him."[10]

McCartney consoles himself in the song by remembering the night he and Lennon cried together. He explained,

> We were in Key West in 1964. We were due to fly into Jacksonville, in Florida, and do a concert there, but we'd been diverted because of a hurricane. We stayed there for a couple of days, not knowing what to do except, like, drink. I remember drinking way too much, and having one of those talking-to-the-toilet bowl evenings. It was during that night, when we'd all stayed up way too late, and we got so pissed that we ended up crying— about, you know, how wonderful we were, and how much we loved each other, even though we'd never said anything. It was a good one: you never say anything like that. Especially if you're a Northern Man[11]

> And we talked a lot and we got way too deep and got into each other's characters. We never had enough time to do that with the Beatles, so this was probably a good thing. And we ended up crying. I'm just reminding myself that we got that intimate. That's why we loved each other so much in the Beatles.[12]

McCartney sings that they never really understood each other, but for most of the group's history, Lennon was always there smiling. The warmest aspects of the clips from Beatlemania is how the guys were always trying to make each other laugh during interviews. Lennon would even flick McCartney in the back of the head while McCartney would be trying to talk intelligently to a reporter. Often when they were giving a performance on TV they'd look over and beam at each other, which of course was encouraged by manager Epstein, but in the end if it wasn't real, there probably wouldn't be two thousand books on them.

McCartney was also probably buoyed by the fact that Lennon had said a few days before his murder, "Throughout my career, I've selected to work with . . . only two people: Paul McCartney and Yoko Ono. . . . That ain't bad picking."[13]

Twenty-five years after recording "Here Today," McCartney could still get choked up playing it, as he did during a secret show at LA's Amoeba Records in in 2007. The audience cheered him on as he tried to not get too teary-eyed.

NOBODY TOLD ME—LENNON

REC. 8/7/80, HIT FACTORY, LENNON/ONO (PRODUCERS), LENNON (V, G), MCCRACKEN (G), SLICK (G), LEVIN (B), NEWMARK (D), SMALL (K), JENKINS (PERCUSSION), SINGLE: UK 1/9/84 (6); US 1/9/84 (5), ALSO *MILK AND HONEY*, COVERS: FLAMING LIPS, BIG & RICH

Lennon began this song in 1976 with the title "Everybody's Talkin', Nobody's Talkin'," a nod to his friend Harry Nilsson, who had covered Fred Neil's "Everybody's Talkin'" to indelible effect in *Midnight Cowboy*.

Lennon figured he would give it to Starr for his next album. As he had always done for his friend, Lennon did a guide version in the studio. During the *Double Fantasy* sessions, Lennon did ten takes, with live vocals each time.

The sardonic lyrics reflect a '60s fighter resigned to the apathy of the disco era, where everyone's making a lot of noise but not really saying or doing anything. People smoke but don't get high, and Nazis lurk under the stairs, as Lennon sensed the rightward turn his two countries were about the take under Reagan and Thatcher. Their conservatism would make Nixon seem like a liberal centrist by comparison.

One of the Beatles' favorite girl groups, the Shirelles, had a hit called "Mama Said (There'd Be Days Like This)," but Lennon didn't really have a mother, so nobody told him. But it doesn't bother him because he's hip to the statues of Katmandu—that is, he's incorporated a detached Buddhist perspective. (The lyric is a quote from the poem "The Green Eye of the Yellow God" by J. Milton Hayes.)

Lyrics aside, it's one of his happiest *sounding* songs, more so for being laid back as opposed to the "we're gonna be happy if it kills us" euphoria of "Whatever Gets You thru the Night." He sounds refreshed and eager to be back in the studio with open-minded wonder, still musing over a UFO he might've seen with May Pang back in 1974. (He wrote in the *Walls and Bridges* liner notes, "On the 23rd August 1974 at 9 o'clock I saw a UFO.—J. L." The night it actually happened, he thought about calling the police but knew what kind of response he'd get if he said, "I'm John Lennon and I just saw a UFO.")

Lennon was also going to give Starr another slogan song he'd written for the baby boomers, a country tune called "Life Begins at Forty," as both he and Starr hit that milestone in 1980. (Lennon's demo can be heard on *The John Lennon Anthology*.) But after the murder by Chapman, the irony of the songs was too depressing for Starr. So a few years later, Ono polished Lennon's best take of "Nobody Told Me," with jaunty bass to the fore and rippling arpeggios recalling the fade-out of "A Hard Day's Night."

When the song came across the airwaves in 1984, it was as if Lennon's ghost had risen up from the sidewalk where he'd been shot, cracking, "Nobody told me there'd be days like this." The band captured the bustle of the city he loved as he turned in his surprise final anthem for all the hippies-turned-yuppies, looking around both amused and alarmed by all the changes that kept coming. And like the best of his work, it spoke for everyone else as well, from kids to senior citizens—a last good-bye as buoyant as his first hello.

NOTES

1. Jack Jones, *Let Me Take You Down: Inside the Mind of Mark David Chapman, the Man Who Killed John Lennon* (New York: Villard Books, 1992), 179.

2. Cynthia Lennon, *John* (New York: Three Rivers Press, 2005), 7.

3. Chris Ingham, *The Rough Guide to the Beatles* (London: Rough Guides Limited, 2009), 138.

4. John Blaney, *Lennon and McCartney: Together Alone* (London: Jawbone, 2007), 153.

5. Blaney, *Lennon and McCartney*, 167.

6. Peter Brown and Stephen Gaines, *The Love You Make: An Insider's Story of the Beatles* (New York: McGraw-Hill, 1983), 134.

7. Blaney, *Lennon and McCartney*, 155.

8. Philip Norman, *Shout! The Beatles in Their Generation* (London: Elm Tree, 1981), 23.

9. Joan Goodman, "December 1984 *Playboy* Interview with Paul and Linda McCartney," The Ultimate Experience Beatle Interview Database, http://www.beatlesinterviews.org/db1984.pmpb.beatles.html (October 10, 2011).

10. Bill Harry, *The Paul McCartney Encyclopedia* (London: Virgin Books, 2002).

11. John Harris, "I'm Still Standing," *Guardian*, June 10, 2004.

12. "Paul McCartney on Poetry and Lennon," ABC Good Morning America, April 30, 2001, *ABC News*, http://abcnews.go.com/GMA/story?id=127011&page=1 (October 10, 2011).

13. Jonathan Cott, "The Lost Lennon Tapes," *Rolling Stone* (December 2010).

The Traveling Wilburys, 1988: (from left) Roy Orbison, Jeff Lynne, Bob Dylan, Tom Petty, George Harrison. *PhotoFest*

· 9 ·

1989: When We Was Fab

Harrison and McCartney reach second-act highs with a little help from their friends.

$\mathcal{M}$cCartney's brief alliance with Michael Jackson gave him a number two hit with "The Girl Is Mine" (1982) and a number one hit with "Say Say Say" (1983), but their relationship soured after Jackson bought the Lennon-McCartney song library in 1985 for $47.5 million. McCartney had been given the option to buy the songs but passed when Ono would not split the costs with him.

As he no longer felt safe touring, McCartney wrote and starred in the feature film *Give My Regards to Broad Street* (1984). The film was gorgeously shot and filled with fine music but put everyone to sleep with its weak plot concerning the disappearance of the master tapes for McCartney's next album ("Worth millions!"). Mainly, the film showed McCartney driving around London to old hits like "Band on the Run" until discovering that his assistant accidentally locked himself in a subway shed with the tapes.

After critics lambasted the film, he took a year off and then returned to the studio with producer Hugh Padgham, architect of the progressive '80s sound on albums by the Police, Phil Collins, Peter Gabriel, and XTC. Despite being an interesting departure, for the first time McCartney's new album (*Press to Play*) didn't have a hit single and quickly disappeared.

Just as McCartney's career was hitting a rough patch, Harrison was reinvigorated. He had been glad to get out of the business after *Gone Troppo* in 1982. But in 1985, Dave Edmunds enlisted Harrison, Clapton, Starr, and Rosanne Cash to support Carl Perkins for Perkins' 1985 TV special. The pre-Wilburys-like experience reminded Harrison of how fun musical camaraderie could be, and he entered a second golden age. There had been the one-two punch opener of *All Things Must Pass* and the Concert for Bangladesh. Then, in the late 1980s, the dark horse returned with a new double feature—*Cloud Nine* and the Traveling Wilburys—denim jacket and beard replaced by big shoulder pads, earrings, and spiky mullet.

In both eras he partnered with iconoclastic producers Phil Spector and Jeff Lynne—two of the top five record producers of all time, as declared by *The Washington Times* in 2008. (The other three were George Martin, of course, Quincy Jones, and the duo of Brian Eno and Daniel Lanois.)[1] As Chris Ingham wrote in *The Rough Guide to the Beatles*, "It seems that Lynne was probably what George needed all along—a trusted musical pal who could record his voice properly, tidy things up at the back and encourage him to enjoy being an ex-Beatle."[2]

Along with George Martin, Phil Spector, Jim Keltner, Klaus Voormann, and Billy Preston, Lynne (born December 30, 1947) would be the closest thing to a fifth Beatle in the solo era, going on to produce the rest of Harrison's solo albums, *The Beatles Anthology* reunion, numerous Starr tracks, and McCartney's *Flaming Pie* album—which was apropos, as he once said that his band Electric Light Orchestra had attempted to pick up where "I Am the Walrus" left off.

Jeff Lynne's first band, the psychedelic Idle Race, released two singles that can be heard on the *Nuggets II* garage rock compilation: "Imposters of Life's Magazine" and "Days of the Broken Arrows." The latter in particular is an early example of Lynne's way with a hauntingly catchy melody. The Fabs dug the Idle Race and invited them down to Abbey Road during the making of *The White Album* sessions. Lynne was only twenty at the time, and the experience was so surreal for him that he couldn't sleep for days.

The Idle Race made little progress despite critical acclaim, so Lynne joined the Move, a psychedelic band who copped the Who's "auto-destruction" shtick by smashing TVs with axes. The group was big in England but never caught on in the States, and gradually morphed into Electric Light Orchestra.

ELO's plan was to continue to explore the highly orchestrated phase of the Fabs' career but do it on stage, for which Lennon later dubbed them "sons of the Beatles." Incorporating elements of classical music, hooky pop melodies with dense harmonies, and studio orchestration, Lynne composed, sang, arranged, and produced such ELO hits as "Evil Woman," "Do Ya," "Livin' Thing," "Sweet Talkin' Woman," "All over the World," "Don't Bring Me Down," and "Xanadu" (with Olivia Newton-John). He also played guitar, bass, keyboards, drums, and cello.

But by the mid-eighties ELO was ending as a unit, so when Harrison approached him to produce and play bass on his next album, Lynne leapt at the chance. He loved Harrison's slide guitar and was the perfect midwife to help Harrison embrace the current pop sound of the era.

They began recording *Cloud Nine* in Harrison's home studio on January 5, 1987, with regulars Jim Keltner and Gary Wright on hand, and Starr, Clapton, and Elton John joining the sessions occasionally. The album made the top ten on both sides of the Atlantic and birthed the number one single "Got My Mind Set on You," a song Harrison had originally wanted to record with the Beatles.

In January 1988, the Beatles were inducted into the Rock and Roll Hall of Fame, but the occasion was marred by sour grapes on McCartney's part. The afternoon of the event, McCartney sent the Hall the message saying, "I was keen to go and pick up my award, but after twenty years, the Beatles still have some business differences, which I hoped would be settled by now. Unfortunately, they haven't been, so I would feel like a complete hypocrite waving and smiling with them at a fake reunion."[3]

Thus McCartney missed out on Mick Jagger's hilarious introduction speech in which he thanked the Fabs for breaking down the doors for all British acts to follow. Then Starr, Harrison, Ono, Julian, and Sean came up. Starr cracked everyone up with his tipsy "life of the party" persona. Sean thanked people for letting him be up there "for doing nothing." Ono couldn't resist a little dig at McCartney: "John would certainly have been here."

Harrison said, "I don't have to say much, because I'm the quiet Beatle. It's unfortunate Paul's not here, because he was the one with the speech in his pocket. We all know why John can't be here. I'm sure he would be. It's hard, really, to stand here supposedly representing the Beatles. But it's what's left, I'm afraid. But we all loved him so much, and we all love Paul very much."[4]

That summer, Harrison needed a B-side for a single, so he enlisted Lynne and pals Bob Dylan, Tom Petty, and Roy Orbison to help create "Handle with Care." When Harrison submitted it, the label realized it wasn't a throwaway B-side and asked for the super group to come up with an entire album.

Dylan was about to go on tour, so the five musicians banged out the basic tracks over nine days in May at Dave Stewart's home studio. When an equipment malfunction resulted in some audible glitches, Harrison told Lynne, "We'll bury 'em in the mix." They kept using the phrase whenever someone messed up, inspiring Harrison to come up with the group name the Trembling Wilburys. Lynne tweaked it to "Traveling" and the others agreed. It hinted at that old Western vibe Dylan had been pursuing since *The Basement Tapes*. The album, *Volume 1*, went triple platinum, was nominated for Grammy Album of the Year, and won a Grammy for Best Rock Performance by a Duo or Group.

Lynne was fashioning one of the most recognizable sounds of the late '80s/early '90s on *Cloud Nine*, the Traveling Wilburys albums, Roy Orbison's hit "You Got It," and Tom Petty hits like "Runnin' Down a Dream" and "Learning to Fly." Wikipedia described it as possessing "minimal, acoustic instrumentation and a sparse, 'organic' quality that generally favours light room ambience," a "jangling compressed acoustic guitar sound pioneered by Roger McGuinn and a heavily gated snare drum sound."[5] He would also mix the bass drums and bass high and add delay and reverb to the guitar. The epitome of the sound was probably Petty's "Free Fallin'."

Meanwhile, McCartney knew an overhaul was in order and reached out to Elvis Costello (born Declan MacManus). Though he originally rose to fame as a member of the late '70s punk/New Wave movement due to his angry intellectual persona, the sophistication of his snarky wordplay and torch song melodies made him a genre all to himself. He also had a Liverpudlian mother, a musician father like McCartney, and had joined the Beatles fan club at eleven.

As Lynne did with Harrison, Costello cajoled McCartney into getting back in touch with the Beatles' qualities he had previously suppressed to prove he could make it alone. First, Costello persuaded McCartney to get his 1962 Hofner violin bass out of mothballs. McCartney did so, deciding the past was now far enough away. From then on, he played it regularly.

McCartney relished working with Costello, whose cynical persona was reminiscent of Lennon's. However, when Costello started answering back in song to McCartney's lyrics, as Lennon did in "Getting Better," McCartney initially balked. He feared they were setting themselves up for too close a comparison, but he eventually relaxed. Thus Costello joined the ranks of singing partners who compete for McCartney's girl. Lennon did so in "You're Gonna Lose That Girl," Michael Jackson in "The Girl Is Mine," and Costello in "You Want Her Too."

In 1987 and 1988, McCartney and Costello recorded an album's worth of acoustic demos. Twelve were eventually re-recorded for various albums or B-sides, but the demos are actually superior to the overproduced official versions. The up-tempo "My Brave Face" demo features the duo's high-pitched harmonies accompanied solely by acoustic guitar and has the strength and purity of the Fabs in 1963. "Don't Be Careless Love" is also fantastic in the demo (as can be heard on YouTube), but for *Flowers in the Dirt*, McCartney dropped Costello's voice in the mix and glopped it up with '80s production gauze. At the concert for Linda's memorial in 1999, Costello knocked their fourth *Flowers* composition, "That Day Is Done," out of the park, accompanied just with piano. Hopefully, Macca and Costello will officially release the original demos one day soon.

Probably their finest collaboration was "Veronica," which appeared on Costello's 1989 album *Spike*. A shimmering up-tempo number, paradoxically it was about Costello's grandmother, who suffered from Alzheimer's. It was Costello's biggest hit in the United States, making it to number nineteen in *Billboard*'s Hot 100 and number one on the modern rock chart.

Of the twelve McCartney-Costello songs that have so far seen official release, the only ones on which the two sing together are "My Brave Face," "You Want Her Too," and "Veronica." The others include "Back on My Feet," the B-side to McCartney's "Once upon a Long Ago" (on bonus reissues of *Flowers in the Dirt*), "Don't Be Careless Love" and "That Day Is Done" on *Flowers in the Dirt*, "Mistress and Maid" and "The Lovers That Never Were" on McCartney's *Off the Ground* (1993), "Pads, Paws, and Claws" on Costello's *Spike* (1989), "So Like Candy" and "Playboy to a Man" on Costello's *Mighty Like a Rose* (1991), and "Shallow Grave" on Costello's *All This Useless Beauty* (1996).

After 1983's *Old Wave*, for the rest of the decade Starr only appeared on McCartney's *Give My Regards to Broad Street* album, Artists United Against Apartheid's "Sun City" (with son Zak Starkey), and a Grammy-nominated cover of "Act Naturally" with Buck Owens.

Giving up on finding a new label, in 1984 Starr took a gig narrating the TV show *Thomas the Tank Engine and Friends*. Based on a series of children's books, the show became a success in the United Kingdom and then around the world. Starr narrated two seasons, and when it spun off an American PBS series, *Shining Time Station*, he played Mr. Conductor, for which he was nominated for a Daytime Emmy in 1989. "John had the intellectuals; Paul had the teenies and George the mystics; I always got the mothers and babies," he quipped.[6] It was nice timing, as he was the first Beatle to become a grandfather, when Zak had a daughter named Tatia Jayne Starkey in 1985.

He also appeared in Sun Country Classic Wine Cooler commercials and a Pizza Hut commercial in which he walks around musing that the time is right "to bring the lads back together." But in the end it's the Monkees who show up. "Wrong lads," he says.

GOT MY MIND SET ON YOU—HARRISON

Rec. January–August 1987, Friar Park, Rudy Clark (writer), Harrison/Lynne (producers), Harrison (v, g), Lynne (b, k), Keltner (d), Horn (sax), Cooper (percussion), Single: UK 10/12/87 (2); US 10/3/87 (1), also on *Cloud Nine*, Covers: "Weird Al" Yankovic "(This Song's Just) Six Words Long"

In the early '60s, James Ray's first single had flopped and he was broke and living on a rooftop when he was discovered by songwriter Rudy Clark, the same guy who would later write "The Shoop Shoop Song (It's in His Kiss)" and the Rascals' immortal "Good Lovin'." Clark got Ray a deal and gave him the songs "If You Gotta Make a Fool of Somebody" and "I've Got My Mind Set on You (Parts 1 & 2)."

The Beatles always dug hip, obscure R&B, the secret classics that never made it onto oldies stations, and they would often play "If You Gotta Make a Fool of Somebody" live. So when Harrison visited his sister in St. Louis in 1963, he bought James Ray's album. Right around that time, Ray died of a drug overdose, barely into his twenties, which is our loss, as his strong, clear voice on "Got My Mind Set on You" attests. Matched with imposing horns, groovy strings, a trilling gospel choir, and even a banjo, the song rises to a dynamic crescendo.

Harrison wanted to give the Beatles treatment to "Got My Mind Set on You" back in the early days, but it never happened. That was all right, because in 1987, after Harrison had taken five years off to recharge, gotten over his resentment of the game, and grown hungry to stage one final comeback, he couldn't have found a better statement of intent—a proclamation that anything can be accomplished if you put your mind to it.

Harrison ditched the original verses about bad luck following the singer, stacked on more than ten saxophones, lifted the drums from the intro of "My Sharona," and processed them into the ultimate '80s big drum sound. Warner Brothers grinned: Harrison had finally gotten with the program. The label shelled out for a slick video with a purple-jacketed Harrison doing backflips in his study while his furniture comes to life, and rammed through the last number one US single by any solo Beatle.

The song crossed over from the baby boomers to the high school kids, the last time the solo Beatles were commercially potent with the youth. It also made Harrison the Beatle with the second-most number one solo singles in the United States: Harrison had three, McCartney had nine, and Lennon and Ringo were tied for two. Sometimes you just need to take a five-year power nap so you can dig the fight again.

MOVE OVER BUSKER—MCCARTNEY

Rec. March–May 1985, October–December 1985, Hog Hill Mill Studios, Sussex, McCartney/Stewart (writers), McCartney/Hugh Padgham (producers), McCartney (v, b, p), Stewart (g, bv), Carlos

ALOMAR (G), JERRY MAROTTA (D), RUBY JAMES (BV), KATE ROBINS (BV), ALBUM *PRESS TO PLAY*: UK 9/1/86 (8); US 8/25/86 (30)

Movies still preoccupied McCartney. *Press to Play*'s cover featured him and Linda in the black and white mold of an old studio publicity photo. McCartney further worked through the feelings of his failed assault on the movie industry in this pub rocker refitted with a modern sound.

As in a surreal Bob Dylan tune, McCartney meets a famous actor in each of the three verses. The first is Nell Gwynne, an actress and mistress of King Charles II in the 1600s. She started out selling oranges in the theater as cover for the fact that her real job was to be a liaison between the male patrons and the actresses backstage, who were also prostitutes. Hence, McCartney sings to her that he'll have one of her oranges, but she tells him to "Move Over Busker," as if, after his movie's flop, he's been demoted to playing for change in the streets.

In the next verse he sees Mae West. Quoting her famous catchphrase, McCartney tells her he'll come up and see her sometime, but she tells him to "Move Over Busker." Perhaps being rejected by two famous actresses was the way his subconscious expressed being shot down at the box office.

In the middle eight he beats his chest and asserts that no one can hold him back and his time will come again. We see both the desperation and steely drive that kept him working for the chart hits. He sings that he wants to stay with the action, knowing if he doesn't grab it now, his "great illusion" will vanish, before busting out with a Little Richard howl.

In the third verse, he's nursing his injured pride when he sees a satisfied Errol Flynn being called into his trailer by a lusty lady. Flynn's getting the love now, but McCartney tells him to move over, busker, because Flynn's day is done and McCartney's is on the way. In the tradition of his '70s albums, the refrain "good times coming" echoes the second song on *Press to Play*, "Good Times Coming/Feel the Sun."

HANDLE WITH CARE—THE TRAVELING WILBURYS

REC. 4/5/88, LUCKY STUDIOS, MALIBU, HARRISON/LYNNE/DYLAN/PETTY/ ORBISON (WRITERS), LYNNE/HARRISON (PRODUCERS), HARRISON (V, G), LYNNE (V, G, K), TOM PETTY (B, G, V), BOB DYLAN (V, ACOUSTIC G, HARMONICA), ROY ORBISON (V, ACOUSTIC G), KELTNER (D), IAN WALLACE (TOM TOMS), SINGLE: UK 10/24/88 (21); US 11/28/88 (45), ALSO ON *TRAVELING WILBURYS VOL. 1*,

COVERS: JENNY LEWIS AND THE WATSON TWINS, FEATURING BEN GIBBARD (OF DEATH CAB FOR CUTIE), CONOR OBERST (OF BRIGHT EYES), AND M. WARD

In spring 1988, Jeff Lynne was in LA working on both Roy Orbison's comeback album *Mystery Girl* and Tom Petty's *Full Moon Fever*. When Harrison came to town, he had dinner with Lynne and Orbison and told them that the next day he needed to do a B-side for the European twelve-inch single of "This Is Love." They said they would help.

Since they needed a studio fast, Harrison called Bob Dylan, who had one in his place in Malibu. Dylan's guitar was at Petty's house, so Harrison said he'd pick it up. Petty had toured with Dylan in 1986 and 1987 and the two had written Petty's "Jammin' Me" single together. When Harrison got the guitar from Petty, he invited him to come by the session.

The next day, all five of them were hanging in Dylan's garden, trying to come up with a song. Harrison saw a beat-up, battered box in Dylan's garage marked "handle with care." A folk-rock composition quickly took shape, with everybody contributing lyrics and singing different sections. With Jim Keltner drumming, they recorded it in a couple hours.

A warm-hearted Harrison sings the praises of his woman and asks her to treat him gently, as he's been sent up, shot down, fobbed off, fooled, robbed, ridiculed, terrorized, overexposed, commercialized, sent to meetings, and generally made uptight by the roller coaster of his life.

Then he passes the baton to Orbison, with his one-of-a-kind vibrato in full "Only the Lonely" effect. Next up are Dylan and Petty, singing together. Petty's reedy voice could sound like a stronger, more normal version of Dylan's, and the contrast makes Dylan's voice sound fleshed-out, rough-hewn, and nasal, audibly grinning at the camaraderie as everyone joins in. Ten years earlier or later, Dylan might not have been such an unassuming team player. But in the mid-eighties he was in a slump, writing theme songs for failed TV pilots such as *Band of the Hand* (1986). Harrison and Petty were the guys with the hits at the moment, and he was happy to be part of the gang.

Orbison and Lynne take their shot at the bridge, then Harrison's slide guitar duets with Dylan's inimitable harmonica, wailing like it did twenty-seven years earlier during Dylan's first professional gig, as a session man on Harry Belafonte's "Midnight Special."

BACK ON MY FEET—MCCARTNEY

REC. AUGUST 1986, POWER STATION, NYC, 1987, ABBEY ROAD, MCCARTNEY/
MCMANUS (WRITERS), PHIL RAMONE (PRODUCER), MCCARTNEY (V, B), TIM

RENWICK (G), NICK GLENNIE-SMITH (K), CHARLIE MORGAN (D), LOUIS JARDIM (PERCUSSION), SINGLE B-SIDE TO ONCE UPON A LONG AGO: UK 11/16/87 (10)

Listeners either praised or hated McCartney's *Press to Play*, with its experimental techno sound. It failed to even go gold and was his worst-selling album. The commercial drop-off that hit Starr and then Harrison had finally caught up to McCartney. As workaholic as ever, he immediately started the next record with Billy Joel's band and producer Phil Ramone, who had produced all Joel's albums from 1976 to 1986. They created an early version of "Back on My Feet."

Ramone was dead center in the mainstream, but to spruce up the lyrics McCartney turned to Costello. In their first meeting, they both brought unfinished songs for the other to help fill in, like McCartney did with Lennon in the old days. Costello immediately helped bring "Back on My Feet" into sharp focus with concrete, vivid details.

In the first two verses, the protagonist is an old man railing at the thunderstorm pouring down on him, vowing to bounce back in the face of bruising setbacks. The defiance turns into cheerful optimism in the final verse, as a resilient young girl becomes the new protagonist, yelling that she'll be back on her feet to the passing traffic. The characters ask us for a hand but warn us not to pity them, as they've seen things we'll never see.

McCartney was still in movie mode and tells us that the song is "in CinemaScope." Each verse begins with cinematic terminology: "Reveal a," "Cut to the," "Focus in on," "Cut back again to a . . ." At the end, McCartney sings that the song fades out as he pulls down the shade. Both the imagery and the resolve to overcome failure make it a close cousin to "Move Over Busker."

The amazing thing about McCartney is the number of times he's rebounded from setbacks that would have discouraged someone with less fortitude: *Magical Mystery Tour*, *Wild Life*, Heather Mills. Perhaps the cost of producing so many successes was the inevitable dud, but the guy was a machine that never stopped.

The B-side "Back on My Feet" marked a moment of resurgence. The nonalbum A-side "Once upon a Long Ago" featured an impressive orchestral lushness but also sappy lyrics about puppy dog tails, blowing balloons, and children searching for treasure, not to mention a Kenny G–like sax solo perfect for the corporate luncheon crowd. Costello had arrived just in time to remind McCartney how not to be corny.

To *Musician*, Costello said, "There's no denying that [McCartney] has a way of sort of defending himself by being charming and smiling and thumbs-up and all the bit. I said once that I thought he should try and step from behind that, at least insofar as the music was concerned."[7]

Re-energized and refocused, with his next album and subsequent world tour McCartney would indeed be back on his feet.

END OF THE LINE—THE TRAVELING WILBURYS

REC. MAY 7–16, 1988, DAVE STEWART STUDIOS, LA, SUMMER 1988, FRIAR PARK, HARRISON/LYNNE/DYLAN/PETTY/ORBISON (WRITERS), LYNNE/HARRISON (PRODUCERS), HARRISON (V, G), LYNNE (V, G, K), TOM PETTY (B, G, V), BOB DYLAN (V, ACOUSTIC G, HARMONICA), ROY ORBISON (V, ACOUSTIC G), KELTNER (D), SINGLE: UK 2/20/89 (52); US 2/25/89 (63), ALSO ON *TRAVELING WILBURYS VOL. 1*, FILM APPEARANCES: GEORGE HARRISON-PRODUCED *CHECKING OUT* (1989), *KNOCKED UP* (2007)

Beatlemania ignited in March 1963 during the group's second British package tour. The headliners were Americans Chris Montez and Tommy Roe, enjoying hits with "Let's Dance" and "Sheila," respectively. The Beatles were clearly surpassing them, but the poor sports refused to give up the final spot of the show, saying they'd quit instead.

But in May and June, when the Beatles toured with one of their idols, Roy Orbison, he was cool with switching the order. Orbison was a founding father of rock from the Sun Records label, home to Elvis, Johnny Cash, Jerry Lee Lewis, and Carl Perkins. The boys loved him for his operatic voice and because he wrote his own stuff, like fellow pioneers Buddy Holly and Chuck Berry. The previous September, Lennon had penned their first British number one, "Please Please Me," as homage to Orbison.

Twenty-five years later, the friendship led to Orbison's membership in the Traveling Wilburys. That same year, Orbison released his Jeff Lynne–produced comeback album *Mystery Girl* and returned to the record charts with "You Got It," his final hit before he died of a heart attack on December 6, 1988.

When it came time to make the video for the Wilburys' second single from *Volume 1*, "End of the Line," Orbison had already passed away, so the group plays the song on a train with a rocking chair reserved for him, empty save for his guitar. When his quavering, ghostly vocals come up, the lights flicker and the video cuts to his picture in a frame. The rest of the group listens meditatively, two icons from the '60s and two worthy successors from the '70s honoring a '50s master who blazed the trail for them all.

Harrison's intro for the song recalls the extended intro of "I'm Looking through You" on the American edition of *Rubber Soul*, and the video itself recalls the scene on the train in *A Hard Day's Night* when the boys played "I Should Have Known Better" to Pattie Boyd and her friends.

The laid-back but persistent drums mirror the rhythm of a train that never stops even as one era's innovations turn to the next era's golden brown retro revival. The sepia tinge of the video underscores the passage of time and evokes the Western mythos that inspired the band's name.

Perhaps even more than "Handle with Care," "End of the Line" captures the friendship that infused the Wilburys project. Petty sings the verses and the others take turns on the chorus, except for Dylan. It's a treat to see Dylan relaxed, happy to take the backseat, and let his batteries recharge before his mid-nineties career-reviving third act, just smiling at George like John and Paul did in their TV performances back in 1964–1965.

MY BRAVE FACE—MCCARTNEY

REC. 1989, OLYMPIC SOUND STUDIOS, LONDON, McCARTNEY/McMANUS (WRITERS), McCARTNEY/MITCHELL FROOM/NEIL DORFSMAN (PRODUCERS), McCARTNEY (V, G, B, TAMBOURINE), LINDA McCARTNEY (BV), HAMISH STUART (G), ROBBIE McINTOSH (G), DAVID RHODES (EBOW G), CHRIS WHITTEN (D), MITCHELL FROOM (K), CHRIS DAVIS (SAX), CHRIS WHITE (SAX), DAVE BISHOP (SAX), SINGLE: UK 5/8/89 (18); US 5/8/89 (25), ALSO ON *FLOWERS IN THE DIRT*

As writer John Blaney pointed out, many of the musical aspects of "My Brave Face" that people assumed were McCartney's Beatles-esque contributions—the bridge, the descending harmonies, the melodic bass—were actually Costello pushing McCartney to sound like his old self again. The twelve-string Rickenbacker was also, of course, a Fab staple.[8]

Lyrically, Costello's influence is clear through the song's multisyllabic, tumbling cascade of finely detailed imagery conveying a guy's agony over his woman leaving him: He leaves TV dinners uneaten on a table laid out for two and breaks the dishes instead of washing them.

Initially, McCartney considered asking Costello to coproduce his next album, but in the end Costello was too lo-fi indie for McCartney's sensibility at the time. When they first recorded "My Brave Face" in early 1988, Costello wanted to double-track the backing vocals, then drop them down a couple levels of quality, like how Keith Richards created the raw power of "Street Fighting Man" by recording through a cheap tape recorder. McCartney probably would've been more receptive to such an approach twenty years later, after his avant-garde albums as the Fireman (see "Nothing Too Much Just out of Sight").

"My Brave Face" was the last US top forty hit for any of the solo Beatles. Like the plot of *Broad Street*, the "My Brave Face" video reflected McCartney's paranoia about being ripped off, with a Japanese McCartney fanatic stealing all his memorabilia before getting caught and thrown in jail. After his Tokyo pot bust, no doubt McCartney enjoyed putting a Japanese in prison.

WHEN WE WAS FAB—HARRISON

Rec. January–August 1987, Friar Park, Harrison/Lynne (writers), Harrison/Lynne (producers), Harrison (v, g), Starr (d), Lynne (b, g, k), Cooper (tambourine), Bobby Kok (cello), Single: UK 1/25/88 (25); US 1/30/88 (23), also on *Cloud Nine*

Michael Jackson wore a *Sgt. Pepper*-style jacket when he collected an honor at the White House from President Reagan in 1984 for his efforts against drunk driving. The following year, Jackson's archrival Prince tried to emulate the psychedelic vibe of *Sgt. Pepper* with *Around the World in a Day* and the "Raspberry Beret" video. XTC released *Pepper*-esque records under the pseudonym the Dukes of Stratosphear. In LA, the Paisley Underground bands revived the '60s sound, with the Bangles eventually rising to mainstream success. The Beatles' spirit still pervaded the mid-1980s, so as Harrison emerged from his five-year hiatus, he decided to see if he could score another Beatles nostalgia hit in the vein of "All Those Years Ago." (Whether he was truly nostalgic or needed the money is open for debate; probably both.)

Harrison later told *Creem* that the "Yer Blues" drum intro came first: "Before I wrote the song, or when I sat down to write it, I thought, 'This one's gonna start with Ringo going, "One, two, DUHtabumb, DUHtabumb."' That was the intro in my head; that was the tempo it was always going to be."[9]

Since Lynne's goal for ELO had been to take up where "I Am the Walrus" left off, he did so here with a vengeance, piling on the cellos, timpani, "oooooohs," backward tape loops, and "All You Need Is Love" horns. Eight years later, for "Free as a Bird," he would again try to cram in as many Beatles touchtones as possible.

Legend has it that the term "Fab Four" was originated by Brian Epstein's press officer, Tony Barrow, in an early press release. Throughout the song the backing vocals chant, "Fab!" as well as, "Gear," old Liverpool slang for "cool."

Harrison sings about arriving like strangers in the night, evoking the Sinatra ode to one-night stands that topped the chart in 1966, as well as Robert A. Heinlein's sci-fi novel *Stranger in a Strange Land*, about a psychic human raised on Mars who returns to Earth as a messiah figure preaching free love and spirituality. To the Bible Belt, the Beatles were like the mutants from the

1963 sci-fi flick *Children of the Damned*, in which pied pipers come to lead their kids to rebellion with long hair and mind-altering drugs.

Now a happily married man, Harrison looks back at wild nights of doing everything imaginable and waking in the dawn to women caressing him—women doomed to be "casualties" as the group pressed on to the next city. Next Harrison remembers the group's nemeses: taxes and cops and ultimately, "the bus" (death) that took Lennon away. In the middle eight, Harrison pauses to wistfully remember his lost friendship that didn't have the time to be healed. Then the "Walrus" march resumes as Harrison asserts that intense media attention amplified the conflicts between the Beatles, but life goes on—and they still send each other pullovers. On the way to the fade-out, he sings snatches of two of the Beatles' biggest influences, Dylan and Smokey Robinson ("it's all over now, baby blue" and "you really got a hold on me").

In the video, Harrison stands in front of a brick wall strumming his guitar and singing. A van marked "Fab Gear" pulls up and Starr gets out to give Harrison a cello. A third hand comes out of Harrison's jacket to play it and for a moment he flashes into his *Sgt. Pepper* suit (which he had recently reacquired). Soon the Walrus from *Magical Mystery Tour* is playing bass while Starr plays drums. (McCartney was asked to appear but was unavailable.) Harrison bounces an apple (their record label's symbol) off Starr's timpani. Lynne has a cameo playing a violin. In the end, Harrison levitates and sprouts eight arms waving like a Hindu god. At one point, a passerby carries the *Imagine* album to represent Lennon. Other walk-ons include Elton John, Paul Simon, Derek Taylor, Jeff Lynne, Gary Wright, Ray Cooper, and Neil Aspinall.

The song was released as a single in January 1988 with a cover updating Harrison's image from Voormann's *Revolver* cover. It was Harrison's last top forty hit in the United States.

YVONNE'S THE ONE—MCCARTNEY

Rec. March–May 1985, McCartney's Sussex studio, McCartney/ Eric Stewart (writers), McCartney (v, g), other musicians unknown, unreleased

Eric Stewart, born near Manchester, England, in 1945, was in Wayne Fontana and the Mindbenders when they had the hit "The Game of Love" in 1965. In 1972 he cofounded 10cc, whose songs would include "I'm Not in Love."

Stewart knew McCartney from the Mindbender days and hung out with him and Linda in the '70s. As Denny Laine faded from McCartney's orbit, McCartney asked Stewart to collaborate with him. Stewart sang backing vocals on *Tug of War, Pipes of Peace*, the "Spies Like Us" single, and *Give My Regards to Broad Street*. He cowrote seven of the tunes that ended up on *Press to Play*. He also sang backing vocals and played guitar and sometimes keyboards on almost all its tunes. McCartney said working with Stewart reminded him of how he and Lennon would sit facing each other with guitars, like a mirror.

"Yvonne's the One" was a song they attempted in February 1985 for *Press to Play*. Musically it's in the vein of *The White Album*'s "I Will," but with a much more bittersweet, honest lyric. The first time the singer sees Yvonne he falls head over heels, but she tells him flat out there are others besides him. He can't get over his jealousy, so he has to put her out of his life.

In 1995, 10cc would attempt a synthy, reggae version for their *Mirror Mirror* album, with McCartney on rhythm guitar, but it's too weirdly upbeat and loses the pathos of McCartney's quavering vocals. McCartney's version remains unreleased but can be heard on YouTube.

DEVIL'S RADIO—HARRISON

Rec. January–August 1987, Friar Park, Harrison/Lynne (producers), Harrison (v, g), Starr (d), Lynne (b, k), Cooper (percussion), Clapton (g solos), Elton John (p), Album *Cloud Nine*: UK 11/2/87 (10); US 11/2/87 (8), Single: US promo only (4) on Mainstream Rock charts

Harrison would pass a little church when he would take Dhani to school, and one day their billboard read, "Gossip: The Devil's Radio . . . Don't Be a Broadcaster."[10] Thus inspired, Harrison corralled a very cool band to lay down some solid rock and roll: Starr, Eric Clapton, Elton John, and Jeff Lynne. Lyrically, Harrison rails at the gossip-obsessed media much like Don Henley's 1982 top three hit "Dirty Laundry," reviling them as salacious vultures polluting the airwaves.

Harrison and Henley had been tarred by exposés in the past, and it would get worse in the 1990s. After the court case of Hollywood madam Heidi Fleiss, four of her call girls wrote a memoir called *You'll Never Make Love in This Town Again* (published 1996) about their sexual experiences with celebrities. In one vignette, one of the call girls said she was at a party when Harrison strolled up, strumming his ukulele, and casually asked, "How about a blow job, love?" She knew she should be annoyed by his monumental callousness, but decided she would probably never again have the opportunity to fellate a Beatle. Harrison kept singing and playing his ukulele while she serviced him, then zipped up and wandered back into the party singing and playing without so much as a thank-you.

While the anecdote must have been distressing to Olivia, it was nothing compared to the way Albert Goldman attempted to annihilate Lennon and Ono in his notorious 1988 biography, *The Lives of John Lennon*. Ono was so devastated she considered suicide after reading it. Basically, Goldman dredged up every half-rumor possible, often with barely one nebulous source to back it up. He also repeatedly asserted that Lennon was lazy, when the man was one of the most prolific multimedia artists of the twentieth century. Goldman also painted Harry Nilsson as a sycophantic hustler, deaf to the brilliant songs that captivated both Lennon and McCartney.

McCartney urged people not to read it, and U2 attacked Goldman in the song "God Part 2," warning that Bono was going to get Goldman if instant karma didn't get him first. Still, for all of the flaws of Goldman's book, he did unearth a trove of information about Lennon, particularly his post-Beatles years, with fascinating and hilarious memories from figures such as Jesse Ed Davis. Though traumatic, it was a corrective against the whitewashed, saintly image of Lennon that threatened to take hold after his assassination. The same year, 1988, saw the release of Ono's sanctioned *Imagine: John Lennon* feature documentary, with most of Lennon's rough edges glossed over. In later years, historians could enjoy Goldman's valuable anecdotes while ignoring his more egregious and unfounded accusations.

Lennon's death coincided with the arrival of a new era that saw a more complex assessment of icons, where it became necessary to distinguish the hero's contributions to society from his personal flaws. Another figure caught in the crosshairs of this change was Bill Clinton, who believed he could philander with the impunity enjoyed by his idol John Kennedy but discovered otherwise. Lennon, like Martin Luther King and Kennedy, would be dead before most of his scandals became widely known.

PICTURE SHOW LIFE—STARR

Rec. April–July 1982, Startling Studios, Ascot, Joe Walsh's Santa Barbara studio, John Reid/John Slate (writers), Joe Walsh (producer), Starr

(V), WADDY WACHTEL (LEAD G), FREEBO (B, TUBA), SHERWOOD BALL (G), KAL
DAVID (G), PETER BUNETTA (D), BRUCE MACPHERSON (O), SAM CLAYTON (PER-
CUSSION), JOE LALA (PERCUSSION), JOCKO MARCELLINO (PERCUSSION), GARRETT
ADKINS (TROMBONE), LEE THORNBURG (TRUMPET), DAVID WOOFORD (SAX), AL-
BUM *OLD WAVE*: NOT RELEASED IN UK OR US/RELEASED JUNE 1983 ELSEWHERE

Initially, this jaunty tune captures the feel of LA's Sunset Strip: cars cruise,
warm arid breeze blows back the palm fronds. Girls model their mini-skirts
while boys try to entice them with drinks and drugs. Everyone's trying to
con someone to survive another Hollywood night. Guys like Starr have been
hustling in showbiz so long, there's nothing else he knows how to do.

Then the upbeat music turns eerie, as if Starr is having a premonition that
Old Wave will be his last album for almost a decade and he'll spend the time
lost in oblivion, narrating a kids' show.

But he picks himself back up and gets pumped again. Hollywood is rocking, and the people in the picture show business may win or lose, but they're
being who they want to be.

The guitars by Joe Walsh and Waddy Wachtel are just right, not too
'70s or too '80s. Wachtel was one of the top session men of the laid-back
Southern California sound, playing on records by Stevie Nicks, Linda Ron-
stadt, James Taylor, and Warren Zevon. Later, Keith Richards would tap
him for the X-pensive Winos. The song's just a great groove with piano,
organ, and solid drum snare.

THAT'S WHAT IT TAKES—HARRISON

REC. JANUARY–AUGUST 1987, FRIAR PARK, HARRISON/LYNNE/WRIGHT
(WRITERS), HARRISON/LYNNE (PRODUCERS), HARRISON (V, G, FIRST G SOLO),
LYNNE (B, G, K), KELTNER (D), CLAPTON (SECOND G SOLO), COOPER (PERCUS-
SION), ALBUM *CLOUD NINE*, ALSO B-SIDE OF CHEER DOWN US

"That's What It Takes" was the second of three songs Lynne and Harrison
wrote together for *Cloud Nine*. Lynne had the chorus and Harrison worked
on the verses with him.

The song ascends through the verse and bridge so gradually one almost
gets restless, but the gospel-tinged chorus arrives just in time, doubly satisfying
due to the wait. It's nonreligious inspirational pop, employing lots of uplifting words like "shine," "dawn," "smile" and some chestnuts like "not fading
away." It's just a guy asserting that he's got to be strong and unafraid to take

chances, which is always a good message whether you're driving to work or going on a jog or dealing with real problems.

Just as Young Turk Elvis Costello would pull McCartney's suppressed Beatleness out of him, here Lynne gets Harrison to return to translucent twelve-string guitar arpeggios like it was 1965. Clapton plays one of the solos.

FIGURE OF EIGHT—MCCARTNEY

Rec. September 1987–February 1989, recording location unknown, McCartney/Steve Lipson/Trevor Horn (producers), McCartney (v, g, b, celeste, percussion, handclaps), Steve Lipson (g, computer programming), Trevor Horn (k, handclaps), Chris Whitten (d, handclaps), Linda McCartney (Minimoog, handclaps), Album *Flowers in the Dirt*: UK 6/5/89 (1); US 6/6/89 (21), Alternate version: Single, UK 11/13/89 (42); US 11/14/89 (92)

"Figure of Eight" is another McCartney anthem for couples learning to get along harmoniously. He's been trying to learn since "What You're Doing" and "We Can Work It Out," and maybe he's getting a little wiser.

The subtle groove sneaks up on you until, after a couple of listens, you realize it may be one of his catchiest jams. He's exasperated that he and his woman seem to go around in circles, like an infinite figure of eight, instead of progressing in a reliable straight line. He debates whether he should just throw in the towel and head out into the night alone. But in the end he knows it's better to stay together and take care of each other instead of splitting up and falling back into the singles scene, which would no doubt be an even worse figure of eight.

For the album version, he recorded the bass, vocals, and drums live before Trevor Horn added keyboards and handclaps. He remade it for release as a single with his touring band playing live in the studio.

THIS IS LOVE—HARRISON

Rec. January–August 1987, Friar Park, Harrison/Lynne (writers/producers), Harrison (v, g), Lynne (b, g, k), Keltner (d), Cooper (tambourine), Single: UK 6/13/88 (55); US 7/25/88 (did not chart), also on *Cloud Nine*

"This Is Love" may be the birth moment of the signature element in Lynne's formula: an intro featuring a chugging rhythm guitar pierced by a bottleneck slide, recycled to great effect in "I Won't Back Down," "Into the Great Wide Open" and Harrison's "Cheer Down."

The chorus' autopilot happiness was reflected in a buoyant video of Harrison singing on a rocky Hawaiian shore amid crashing waves. But in the second verse, the backing vocals take on a bittersweet hue as Harrison sings about little things in life that come from out of nowhere to change you forever. The lyric's vagueness allows the listener to insert whatever profound experience snuck up on them, whether in a sad way—as hinted by the backing vocals—or an empowering one, expressed by a persistent, ascending guitar. When Harrison later sings that we can triumph over the crises in our lives because we created them ourselves, the song takes on a depth that its pop sheen initially belied. It's the sound of grown men reaching back to the melodies of their youth to be re-inspired while coloring the sound with the soulful wisdom of accumulated experience, running at full gallop, back in sync with the times.

PUT IT THERE—MCCARTNEY

Rec. September 1987–February 1989, Hog Hill Mill Studios, Sussex, McCartney (producer), McCartney (v, g, percussion), Hamish Stuart (b, percussion), Chris Whitten (hi-hat, percussion), Peter Henderson (computer programming), Single: UK 1/29/90 (32); US 5/1/90 (failed to chart), also on *Flowers in the Dirt*

Both Lennon's and McCartney's mothers passed away when the boys were teens, but McCartney's had been stable and loving, while Lennon's had been a party girl who couldn't deal with motherhood. And while Lennon never had a father, McCartney had a strong one who taught his boys to always lift their caps to the ladies. Thus the Beatles had both an angry rebel and a happy showman.

"Put it there if it weighs a ton" was an old Liverpool expression that McCartney's dad, Jim, often repeated. Here McCartney turns in one of his finest acoustic ballads, up there with "Yesterday" and "Blackbird." It's a tribute to his father, who also sees McCartney assuming the mantle with his own son, James. It speaks of a father's desire to help his son through whatever problems he's facing.

In the aftermath of a fight with James, McCartney draws on the memory of his own dad's warmth and strength to reach out to his son and smooth things over. James was born in 1977, which would have made him twenty-two when the song was recorded.

McCartney's quavering, high-pitched voice brings to mind "Dear Friend," in which he sought to heal his relationship with Lennon. It now suggests the fragility of the father-son relationship. Many strands of bittersweet emotions run through the song, from the sadness of having lost a parent to the anxiety of fighting with one's child. In the end, the death of a parent underscores how quickly life goes by, making it even more imperative to work out problems with one's children before it's too late.

The song's popularity during his concerts convinced him to release it as the fourth single from *Flowers in the Dirt*, which he paired with his unreleased 1972 tribute to his daughters, "Mama's Little Girl."

NOTES

1. "Top 5: Knob-twiddlers," *Washington Times*, October 6, 2010.

2. Chris Ingham, *The Rough Guide to the Beatles* (London: Rough Guides Limited, 2009), 138.

3. Peter Doggett, *You Never Give Me Your Money* (New York: HarperCollins, 2009), 293.

4. "Beatles Accept Award Rock and Roll Hall of Fame Inductions 1988," Rock and Roll Hall of Fame + Museum Rockhall's Channel, www.youtube.com/watch?v=NO-HK_csGwk (October 10, 2011).

5. "Jeff Lynne," Wikipedia, http://en.wikipedia.org/wiki/Jeff_Lynne (October 10, 2011).

6. "Ringo Starr," *TV Guide* (March 11–17, 1989).

7. John Blaney, *Lennon and McCartney: Together Alone* (London: Jawbone, 2007), 187.

8. John Blaney, *Lennon and McCartney*, 187–88.

9. J. Kordosh, "December 1987 *Creem* Interview with George Harrison," Beatles number9.com, http://beatlesnumber9.com/creem.html (October 10, 2011).

10. Kordosh, "December 1987 *Creem* Interview."

The Beatles, March 30, 1995. *Getty Images*

• *10* •

1997: The Song We Were Singing

Twenty-four years after the break-up, the Beatles reunite.

The Fabs were relatively quiet for the first half of the '90s. After sitting out the '80s on *Thomas the Tank Engine* and booze, Starr went to rehab and formed the All-Starr band, a rotating team of two- or three-hit wonders from various decades that accompanied him on live tours. He also enjoyed a terrific reboot with producer Don Was; 1992's *Time Takes Time* tied with *Ringo* for his finest solo album. Also, when *Thomas the Tank Engine* was sold to the United States and was spun off as *Shining Time Station*, Starr got 8 percent of the deal, which was a huge amount of money. Between that, touring, and recording, he was safe.

In 1989–1990, McCartney played to 2,843,297 people in thirteen countries, offering up as many Beatles hits as non-Beatles songs. All his concerts in America sold out. On April 21, 1990, he played for the most people in a stadium ever: 184,000 at Maracanã Stadium in Rio de Janeiro, Brazil. In 1990, he also picked up the Grammy Lifetime Achievement Award.

Briefly, McCartney let himself go gray, but he stopped that in time for one of his only three rock CDs of the decade, *Off the Ground* (1993). He was now the world's top concert draw, but album-wise he was incidental in the alternative and hip-hop era. Other forms interested him, anyway. He released a series of classical albums, as well as electronica albums with the Fireman, his side project with producer Martin "Youth" Glover.

After George Martin added a string quartet to "Yesterday" in 1965, McCartney's interest in classical had grown consistently. Thus he accepted when the Royal Liverpool Philharmonic Orchestra commissioned him to write a piece to celebrate their 150th anniversary in 1991. As McCartney couldn't read or write music, he enlisted conductor Carl Davis to help, and prepared by attending operas and classical concerts. The 97-minute *Liverpool Oratorio* was performed by a 90-piece orchestra, 160 choristers from the Royal Liverpool Philharmonic Choir, 40 choristers from the Liverpool Cathedral, and 4 top classical singers.

McCartney was commissioned to write a second symphony by the president of EMI's classical division, which debuted in 1997 as *Standing Stone*. This time McCartney played the music he wanted into a computer and it would transcribe it into sheet music. McCartney indulged his love of avant-garde chance when the computer occasionally made mistakes and came up with atonal, discordant notes. Some McCartney corrected, but some he kept.[1]

At one point McCartney and his associates were working on the piece at Abbey Road. The band Oasis was next door playing too loud, and the supposed Beatles disciples ignored requests to turn it down. When McCartney's people persisted in telling them to be quiet, the band stormed out of the studio enraged. Guitarist Noel Gallagher later confused MTV when he kvetched in an interview, "Sitting around with a bunch of lesbians writing doesn't sound classical to me."[2] So much for respect for your elders. This despite the fact that Oasis' biggest hit was named after Harrison's 1968 soundtrack *Wonderwall*.

Harrison, meanwhile, had a much more subdued presence on the second Wilburys album (impishly dubbed *Vol. 3*). He did a twelve-day tour of Japan with Clapton in 1991, then, having restocked his bank account, returned to Friar Park.

In 1989, the Associated Press ran a story that Harrison had rejected McCartney's suggestion that the three remaining Beatles get back together. "As far as I'm concerned, there won't be a Beatles reunion as long as John Lennon remains dead," Harrison said.[3] But then his financial health took a turn for the worse.

After splitting with Allen Klein in the 1970s, Harrison brought Denis O'Brien on as his personal manager and for years they enjoyed a good relationship. But O'Brien ran Harrison's money through a maze of other countries to dodge taxes (as might have been expected from the composer of "Taxman"). O'Brien then mixed all Harrison's personal finances with Harrison's production company, Handmade Films, which O'Brien cofounded and benefited from significantly. When the Madonna/Sean Penn bomb *Shanghai Surprise* (1986) grievously wounded the company, Harrison was on the verge of bankruptcy. He sued O'Brien for 25 million pounds for mismanagement, of which he eventually collected 11 million. Still, he remained in financial straits, and finally had to bite the bullet and agree to a Threetles reunion. So you can thank Madonna for "Free as a Bird."

In January 1992, the *Anthology* project began to be assembled, spearheaded by Apple Corporation chief executive Neil Aspinall (1941–2008).

Aspinall met McCartney and Harrison at the Liverpool Institute when he was twelve years old. Later, he drove the Beatles' van, fathered a child with Pete Best's mom in 1962, was portrayed by Norman Rossington in *A Hard Day's Night*, became an executive at the Beatles' label, Apple, and led numerous lawsuits against Apple Computers from 1978 to 2006 for infringing on the Beatles' company name.

As the Beatles disintegrated in 1969, Aspinall began assembling their vast archive of footage into a documentary with the working title *The Long and Winding Road*. It had been shelved for decades but was now resumed as a massive multimedia endeavor that included a three-part TV documentary, huge coffee table book, and three double-albums of rarities, alternate versions, and live performances.

Harrison and Aspinall asked Ono if she had any unreleased Lennon demos so that the other Beatles could use them as the basis for possible new Beatles songs. When McCartney came to New York to induct Lennon into the Rock and Roll Hall of Fame in 1994, Ono gave him two cassette tapes that featured "Free as a Bird," "Real Love," "Now and Then," and "Grow Old with Me."

Ono commented, "I did not break up the Beatles, but I was there at the time, you know? Now I'm in a position where I could bring them back together and I would not want to hinder that. It was kind of a situation given to me by fate."[4]

Ono told McCartney three of the four songs were already well known to Lennon fans, which surprised him. "Grow Old with Me" had been on *Milk and Honey*; a version of "Real Love" appeared in the *John Lennon: Imagine* 1988 documentary and on its soundtrack; and "Free as a Bird" had been broadcast in the radio series *The Lost Lennon Tapes*.

The obvious choice to produce the record was Martin, but he declined, having suffered significant hearing loss. So Harrison insisted on Jeff Lynne.

McCartney initially balked. "He's such a pal of George's. They'd done the Wilburys, and I was expecting him to lead it that way. To tell you the truth, I thought that he and George might create a wedge, saying, 'We're doing it this way,' and I'd be pushed out. As I said to him, 'A lot of people are very wary of your sound.' I said, 'You've got a sound.' He said, 'Oh, have I?'"[5]

Lynne did have a sound, and it could threaten to become a cookie cutter. His comeback album for rock forefather Del Shannon—1991's *Rock On!*—inserted Shannon into the same ELO backdrop as Orbison and Harrison. But it was also one of the best-selling sounds of the era.

Harrison said he wouldn't record if Lynne wasn't on board, and Starr, who had worked with Lynne on some tracks for *Time Takes Time*, supported

Lynne as well. McCartney acquiesced. Despite his fears, he ended up impressed enough to ask Lynne to produce his next album, 1997's *Flaming Pie*.

The *Anthology* was unveiled in November 1995 to strong sales and reviews. McCartney was rejuvenated by the experience, and *Flaming Pie* was one of his strongest albums. It hit the charts at number two on both sides of the Atlantic, his best showing since *Flowers in the Dirt* and *Tug of War*. The same year, he was knighted by the Queen and became Sir Paul McCartney.

FREE AS A BIRD—THE BEATLES

Rec. 1977, February–March 1994, New York and McCartney's home studio, Sussex, Lynne (producer), Lennon (v, p), McCartney (v, bv, acoustic g, p, electric and upright b), Harrison (v, bv, lead g, acoustic g, slide g, ukulele), Starr (d, percussion), Single: UK 12/4/95 (2); US 12/12/95 (6), also on *Anthology 1*, Grammy win for 1997 Best Pop Performance by a Duo or Group with Vocal

The group decided to record "Free as a Bird" first because it was more unfinished than "Real Love," and thus gave the other Beatles more opportunity for input—but was more fully sketched than "Now and Then," which Harrison didn't care for. They did not gravitate toward "Grow Old with Me," perhaps because it was strongly linked to Ono and had already been prominently released on *Milk and Honey*.

Lennon recorded the 1977 demo of "Free as a Bird" with a portable tape recorder's small mic on top of his piano, so the vocal and the piano couldn't be isolated from each other. But Lynne said that was good in a way because it meant Lennon played piano on the song.

Lennon played some basic doo-wop chords like a somnambulist, the mood reflecting his ambivalence in the first half of his five-year sabbatical. He was glad to be taking the extended time off. But having been addicted to attention since the 1950s, he also got panic attacks when it felt like he no longer existed to the outside world. Thus he is happy to be free and to have found a home but often looks back at the life he once knew. Lyrically, that was as far as he got. He mumbled the rest, so McCartney and Harrison fleshed out the words from there.

Lennon was notorious for not always keeping the same tempo, so Lynne had to edit the demo so that it kept consistent time by isolating Lennon's voice as much as possible and laying it over a click track. McCartney's original idea was to go for a '40s Gershwin-like sound, but that was rejected for a more basic approach. Lynne and some session musicians played a demo backing track to show the Beatles what the song might sound like, and the Beatles played on the final version.

Starr said, "At the beginning it was very hard, knowing that we were going in there to do this track with him [John]. It was pretty emotional. He wasn't there. I loved John."[6]

McCartney said, "I invented a little scenario; he's gone away on holiday and he's just rung us up and he says, 'Just finish this track for us, will you? I'm sending the cassette—I trust you.' That was the key thing, 'I trust you, just do your stuff on it.' I told this to the other guys and Ringo was particularly pleased, and he said, 'Ahh, that's great!' It was very nice and it was very irreverent toward John. The scenario allowed us to be not too, 'Ahh, the great sacred fallen hero.' He would never have gone for that. John would have been the first one to debunk that—'A fucking hero? A fallen hero? Fuck off, we're making a record.' Once we agreed to take that attitude it gave us a lot of freedom."[7]

McCartney and Harrison added their distinctive backing vocals. On the second half of the demo, Lennon had just sung wordlessly to sketch it out, leaving three sections where McCartney and Harrison could sing verses, similar to a Traveling Wilburys song. That makes "Free as a Bird" the only Beatles song on which all three sing lead, except for some rarities on the *Anthology* ("Christmas Time [Is Here Again]" and the live "Shout"). McCartney marveled, "It was like he [John] was in the next room. Fuck, I'm singing harmony with John! It's like an impossible dream."[8]

Then McCartney got uptight about Harrison's guitar solo, the age-old tug-of-war that ruptured the band up before. "I told Jeff Lynne that I was slightly worried about this because I thought it might get to sound a little bit like 'My Sweet Lord' or one of George's signature things. I felt that the song shouldn't be pulled in any way, it should stay very Beatles, it shouldn't get to sound like me solo or George solo, or Ringo for that matter. It should sound like a Beatles song. So the suggestion was made that George might play a very simple bluesy lick rather than get too melodic. And he did: what he played was almost like a Muddy Waters riff. And that really sealed the project. I thought—I still think—that George played an absolute blinder, because it's difficult to play something very simple, you're so exposed."[9]

The first notes of Harrison's solo are almost jarringly intense for an otherwise sedate song, expressing Harrison's continued sense of loss over Lennon.

For the fade-out, McCartney did his "woo," and it faded, then came back with the rising orchestra sound of "A Day in the Life" and Harrison playing ukulele like old-time British musician George Formby. Lennon's mother had also played the ukulele. To cap it off, they ran Lennon's voice backward saying the Formby catchphrase, "Turned out nice again," which strangely sounded like him saying, "John Lennon."

The song premiered as part of the *Anthology* mini-series in November 1995. It was a fitting time of year, as the group had always released albums in time for Christmas. The song garnered mixed reviews; some carped it was second-tier Lennon processed into '90s Lynne, whereas others felt it coalesced and were thrilled to hear the Beatles back in the top forty again.

In the video, a bird flies past 80 to 100 Beatles references: Penny Lane, the Liverpool docks, Martha the sheepdog, a sitar, Abbey Road. We see a bird's-eye view, but never the bird itself, because typically, the band members couldn't agree on what the bird should look like. (Perhaps McCartney wanted a blackbird and Harrison a blue jay?) Harrison wanted to be the ukulele player seen only from behind at the end, but the video director didn't want any live Beatles to appear and said no—then felt bad about it when Harrison died six years later.

AFTER ALL THESE YEARS—STARR

Rec. February–September 1991, February 1992, California, Starkey/ Johnny Warman (writer), Lynne (producer), Starr (v, d, percussion), Lynne (g, b, p, k, bv), Album *Time Takes Time*: 5/22/92 (failed to chart in UK or US), also B-side of Weight of the World Single UK 5/4/92 (74)

Whatever issues Lennon and Harrison had, Starr and McCartney loved being Beatles, which was why the group was huge, balanced between two happy dudes and two angst-ridden dudes. The two happy dudes are still out on the road and it's a pity they don't tour together. But at least we have this joyful ode to Beatlemania. Jeff Lynne continues his stint as the seventh Beatle as he and Starr play everything on the track themselves.

Johnny Warman, an English guy known for his 1981 album *Walking into Mirrors* and the single "Screaming Jets," wrote the song. Warman had been friends with Starr since 1977, when he was on Starr's own short-lived record label, Ring O' Records. When Starr started work on his first album since the ill-fated *Old Wave*, he and Warman headed out to Starr's place in Monaco to bang out some tunes and came up with a crop of winners: "Don't Go Where the Road Don't Go," "After All These Years," and the religiously optimistic "Everyone Wins" (which eventually surfaced on 2010's *Y Not*).

They also wrote the curio "Runaways." The production evokes a very '80s apocalyptic LA underworld (with part of a riff swiped from "Hungry Like the Wolf"), while Starr tried on the Goth pose of Peter Murphy, Billy Idol, Bowie, or Iggy Pop. It's conceptually interesting in a cheesy way, but Starr can't be bothered to sing in tune on the chorus.

"After All These Years," however, is a great track, recycling Chuck Berry's deathless "Little Queenie" riff ("Bang a Gong," "It's Only Rock 'n' Roll") to paint a picture of the British Invasion circa 1964 as they toured the world, set boys and girls dancing everywhere, and inspired the American folk rock response. It evokes great concert footage like the night the group played DC after the *Sullivan Show*, when they were still tight because they could still hear themselves play. No time to think about anything but the next gig and the romance that waited in the new city.

Starr quotes a tune they covered back then called "Bad Boys" and boasts how they caused fear in the heartland, and for a moment one scoffs— c'mon, the lovable mop-tops? But then you remember how, to a large number of older conservatives, the arrival of long hair and drugs marked the decline of Western civilization, with Alice Cooper and Marilyn Manson mere dwindling encores. But, Starr croons, they never meant to hurt anyone (maybe Lennon did).

In the end, Starr asserts that circling the globe with his band is in his DNA. He started playing live in his teens in the 1950s, and was at the Hollywood Bowl in 2010 doing jumping jacks and dancing on stage half the time, drumming the other half. He looked amazing for a seventy-year-old guy, especially one who as a young boy was in the hospital with tuberculosis and appendicitis.

HOPE OF DELIVERANCE—McCARTNEY

REC. 1992, HOG HILL MILL STUDIOS, SUSSEX, McCARTNEY/JULIAN MENDELSOHN (PRODUCERS), McCARTNEY (V, G, B), LINDA McCARTNEY (AUTOHARP, BV), HAMISH STUART (BV), ROBBIE McINTOSH (G), BLAIR CUNNINGHAM (PERCUSSION, BV), PAUL "WIX" WICKENS (P, LINNDRUM, DRUM PROGRAMMING, PERCUSSION, BV), DAVID GIOVANNINI (PERCUSSION), DAVE PATTMAN (PERCUSSION), MAURIZIO RAVALICO (PERCUSSION), SINGLE UK 12/28/92 (18); US 1/12/93 (83), ALSO ON *OFF THE GROUND*

"Hope of Deliverance" is another McCartney anthem to optimism, but with no cheese, just classy grace. The lyrics recall the stiff upper lip of World War II–era Britain. They're married to bossa-nova percussion, an accordion, and a twelve-string acoustic guitar vaguely reminiscent of Trini Lopez's "If I Had a Hammer" or a relaxed take on the 1940s Latin hit "Besame Mucho," an old standby of the Beatles in their Cavern days.

The storyline of McCartney's classical piece *Liverpool Oratorio* followed his own life, beginning with his childhood in Liverpool. When he returned to Liverpool to write it, he was flooded with memories from the 1940s. Perhaps the same memories informed this song as well.

Maybe the 1987 feature *Hope and Glory* also inspired him. The film was based on director John Boorman's experience as a little kid in London during the Nazi bombings and how his family tried to hold together during the chaotic times. The film's title came from the patriotic British song "Land of Hope and Glory." McCartney's song expresses the same unsinkable determination not to give into despair despite the encroaching darkness.

As it sprang from English history, the song resonated more in the United Kingdom, making it to number fifteen there but only number eighty-three in the United States. (It did reach number nine on the US adult contemporary chart.) Despite the possible World War II connotations, it became the most played record on German radio ever. It was one of McCartney's biggest-selling singles in Europe, with sales of over 4 million, helped by a colorful dance remix video in which it looks like the crowd is all on really good ecstasy.

DON'T GO WHERE THE ROAD DON'T GO—STARR

Rec. February–September 1991, February 1992, California, Starkey/ Johnny Warman/Gary Grainger (writers), Lynne (producer), Starr (v, d, percussion), Lynne (g, p, b, k, chorus), Horn (sax), Suzie Katayama (cello), Album *Time Takes Time*

By the late 1980s, Starr was blacking out often and getting violent. He later said, "I came to one Friday afternoon, and was told by the staff that I had trashed the house so badly they thought there had been burglars, and I'd trashed Barbara so badly they thought she was dead."[10]

In October 1988, Starr and Bach entered a detox clinic in Tucson, Arizona, for a six-week alcohol and cocaine treatment program, trying to ignore the press constantly flying overhead.

He realized he needed something besides Tommy the Tank Engine to focus on and, with producer David Fischof, came up with the concept for his All-Starr Band. The idea was to assemble a team of musicians who were concert draws in their own right. Starr would sing some Beatles songs and some solo songs, and then he would take a backseat on the drums while the other artists sang their hits.

The first incarnation of the All-Starr Band featured regulars Jim Keltner, Billy Preston, and Joe Walsh, along with Dr. John, Levon Helm and Rick Danko of the Band, and E Street Band members Clarence Clemons and Nils Lofgren. They made their debut in Dallas on July 23, 1989, to ten thousand people and toured North America through the summer. New incarnations would follow every one to three years. By 2010, there had been eleven All-Starr bands featuring the likes of Sheila E., Jack Bruce, Edgar Winter, Zak Starkey (his son), Todd Rundgren, Billy Squier, Richard Marx, Randy Bachman, Peter Frampton, John Waite, John Entwistle, Howard Jones, Greg Lake, Felix Cavaliere (The Rascals), Eric Carmen, and many more. Starr released live albums like baseball programs, ten to date, which are five more live albums than McCartney has issued.[11] The structure helped him get back on his feet.

In 1990, Starr recorded a cover of the Beatles' "I Call Your Name" for a TV special marking Lennon's birth and death anniversaries. Featuring Jeff Lynne, Tom Petty, Walsh, and Keltner, the track was produced by Lynne, who went on to produce two of the best songs on Starr's first album in nine years, *Time Takes Time*, including this one.

Lynne gives Starr a tougher drum sound and plays a louder, fiercer guitar than had been heard heretofore on a Ringo tune, like "In My Car" on steroids. Lynne layers in some Petty-esque acoustic rhythm guitars, then Suzie Katayama on cello where the lead guitar would typically be. Ringo jumps in, angry, bitter, recounting how he woke up from a nightmare, beaten up and alone in rehab with the walls closing in, and one's first reaction is, "Holy shit, this is a Ringo tune that truly rocks."

As with much of the album, the lyrics are heavier than those on Starr's previous work. He sings of once being at the epicenter of the world, but from what he can barely remember of the past, he blew it. Friends who used him when times were good have all disappeared. Still, he's back with a vengeance and warning us to learn from him: don't drive/live drunk, or you'll end up driving where the road don't go and end up nearly killing yourself. With this song he fashioned an anthem for anyone who has driven their life off a cliff but has rebuilt themselves and hit the road with reborn determination.

GET OUT OF MY WAY—MCCARTNEY

Rec. 1992, Hog Hill Mill Studios, Sussex, McCartney/Julian Mendelsohn (producers), McCartney (v, b), Linda McCartney (harmonium, train whistle, percussion), Stuart (g), McIntosh (g), Cunningham (d), Wickens (p), Frank Mead (alto sax), Nick Payne (baritone sax), Andy Hamilton (tenor sax), Nick Pentelow (tenor sax), Martin Drover (trumpet), Album *Off the Ground*: UK 2/2/93 (5); US 2/9/93 (17)

Here McCartney incorporates the live rocking sound his band perfected while touring the globe in 1989 and 1990. After sitting out the 1980s, spooked that he'd be shot next, by the end of the decade, McCartney was eager to play live again. This old-school barnburner conveys the thrill of rocking out onstage where he belongs, shaking his head in ecstasy, with moves as distinct and recognizable as Elvis's and James Brown's.

Rested up in fall 1991, McCartney decided to do the next album, *Off the Ground*, with his touring band. Inspired by leading a road-tested group for the first time since 1979, McCartney tried a simpler approach than the complicated productions of the 1980s. By late 1991, he had recorded several demos on a Sony Walkman cassette machine. In the past, he figured out the entire arrangement and performed it on the demo, then instructed the musicians to re-create it. This time he let the band flesh it in.

After two weeks of rehearsals, he adopted the recording schedule the Beatles observed back in the early days: noon to 8 p.m., five days a week, playing and singing live for each take. In the last decade he would've spliced together the best version of a song from many takes, but now he went for the take with the best overall performance.[12]

They recorded "Get Out of My Way" live in the studio, then later added three saxes, a trumpet, and Linda on the harmonium train whistle. It's in the same vein as *Press to Play*'s "Move Over Busker," but that earlier song sounds mid-tempo compared to this freight train barreling through. McCartney snarls at all the other cars to get out of his lane as he floors it back home to his real fine woman, sort of a bullet train redo of John's "When I Get Home" from *A Hard Day's Night*.

HEADING FOR THE LIGHT—TRAVELING WILBURYS

Rec. April–May 1988, LA and Friar Park, Harrison/Lynne (producers), Harrison (g, v), Lynne (b, g, bv), Orbison (bv), Petty (g, bv), Dylan (g,

BV), HORN (HORNS), KELTNER (D), COOPER (TAMBOURINE), ALBUM *TRAVELING WILBURYS VOL. 1*: UK 10/18/88 (16); US 10/18/88 (3), GRAMMY NOM. FOR ALBUM OF THE YEAR, WON BEST ROCK PERFORMANCE BY A DUO OR GROUP; SINGLE: US PROMO ONLY (7) ON MAINSTREAM ROCK CHART

Slicing guitars and relentless drums propel a tune melodically reminiscent of "All Those Years Ago" retrofitted as another anthem to turning one's life around. It would have sounded right at home on *Cloud Nine*, but since it is on *Traveling Wilburys: Vol. 1*, it features Lynne, Keltner, Petty, and Dylan on guitars, and all of them plus Roy Orbison on backing vocals.

To a beat like an unstoppable train, Harrison barely escapes numerous close calls: hanging by his fingernails over the edge, tumbling through the thorns, drowning in the rain. But in the end, nothing can keep him from heading down the road toward the light in his worn-out shoes. Harrison could be alluding to the substance abuse that periodically bedeviled him, but the lyrics' images are metaphors to serve anyone's experience. Whatever the conflict, the important thing is the singer is back on track.

WEIGHT OF THE WORLD—STARR

REC. FEBRUARY–SEPTEMBER 1991, FEBRUARY 1992, CALIFORNIA, BRIAN O'DOHERTY/FRED VELEZ (WRITERS), DON WAS (PRODUCER), STARR (V, D, PERCUSSION), MARK GOLDENBERG (G), JAMES "HUTCH" HUTCHINSON (B), BENMONT TENCH (K), BACKING VOCALS: ROGER MANNING, ANDREW STURMER, SINGLE: UK 5/4/92 (74), ALSO ON *TIME TAKES TIME*

The chiming chords that open the song—and the album *Time Takes Time*— could be off the Byrds' 1967 *Younger Than Yesterday*. One of Starr's finest singles, "Weight of the World" also saw the birth of the formula that would carry him through the next two decades: mid-sixties jangle pop with a nineties gloss set to lyrics reflecting the maturity that comes with age.

Starr croons with empathy to his lover that he knows her father let her down, never held her like he was supposed to, and abandoned her mother. Starr admits that he hasn't always been there for her either, but he says he can't handle the heavy burden of guilt she's laying on him. In *Abbey Road* he sang with the others about "carrying that weight," but here he says the weight of her resentments are dragging her down and she needs to let the past go. Everybody's had rough lives, he maintains. If you stay hung up on the past, you deny yourself a happy future.

Don Was produced half the album, and it was Starr's best reviewed since *Ringo*. The single was his first to make the UK charts (at number seventy-four) since 1976's "Only You (and You Alone)." But the album failed to chart, so soon Starr was looking for a new label again. For some reason he never worked with Don Was again, which is a pity, though his next producer, Mark Hudson, would continue the marriage of thoughtful lyrics and '60s folk-rock guitar.

FISH ON THE SAND—HARRISON

Rec. January–August 1987, Friar Park, Harrison/Lynne (producers), Harrison (v, g), Lynne (b, k), Starr (d), Album *Cloud Nine*

With Harrison cracking out the twelve-string Rickenbacker, Starr on drums, and Lennon/McCartney student Lynne on bass, keyboards, and backing vocals, this song is as about as Beatles-esque as you can get while missing two Beatles (except for the occasional whiff of synth[13]).

To the casual listener, it's another Harrison song that could be an ode to his woman, without whose love Harrison is like the fish of the title dying on the sand. But since the object of Harrison's love is in the sun, moon, daylight, and wind, it's no doubt God, though Harrison's learned to be ambiguous enough in his lyrics so as not to drive off the mainstream fans. As Harrison implores God to give him a sign that He's there, it's clear that, seventeen years after "My Sweet Lord," spiritual connection was still taking a long time.

YOUNG BOY—MCCARTNEY

Rec. 1995–1997, Steve Miller's Idaho studio, McCartney (producer), McCartney (v, g, b, d, Hammond organ), Steve Miller (g, bv), Single: UK 4/28/97 (19), also *Flaming Pie*

Back in 1969, an argument over Allen Klein caused a Beatles recording session to be canceled. The others stormed off, but McCartney loitered around the studio. Steve Miller wandered in and asked if he could use the space. McCartney said sure, and ended up bashing the drums and adding the bass to a Miller tune appropriately entitled "My Dark Hour." Miller would go on to recycle the riff for his 1977 hit "Fly Like an Eagle."

Years later, McCartney's son James found the 1969 Steve Miller album in his dad's collection. Remembering the old session, McCartney called Miller up and asked if he wanted to do some new tunes. Miller had a studio in Idaho, so there the duo laid down a bunch of tracks that ended up on *Flaming Pie*.[14]

Acoustic and electric guitars rise to a fine crescendo as McCartney looks on fondly bemused as his son struggles to find love. McCartney knows all he can offer is sympathy and a galvanizing song to inspire James (and young boys everywhere) not to give up searching until he finds the woman who's right for him. He knows his son needs independence, so McCartney keeps his advice to himself, except to suggest that if his son does what he loves, he'll be happy, which will make him attractive. Then love will find him.

He also counsels his boy to avoid confrontation and meditate. Ironically, even though McCartney was the second to bail out of the Maharishi's camp in 1968, in his later years he would frequently sing meditation's praises.

POOR LITTLE GIRL—HARRISON

Rec. July 1989, Friar Park, Harrison/Lynne (producers), Harrison (v, g, banjo), Lynne (b, k), Ian Paice (d), Horn (sax), Richard Tandy (p), Single: US 10/89 promo only (21) on Mainstream Rock chart, B-side of Cheer Down, also on *Best of Dark Horse 1976–1989*

After the Traveling Wilburys' first album was recorded in spring 1988, Harrison recorded three songs at his Friar Park estate with Jeff Lynne and most of the crew from *Cloud Nine*: "Poor Little Girl," "Cockamamie Business," and "Cheer Down." They were all solid rockers that stuck close to the successful Beatles-meets-Lynne formula.

On "Poor Little Girl," Harrison's vocals alternate with Jim Horn's juicy "Savoy Truffle"–style sax. Then, like "That's What It Takes," it ascends to an even better hook: an uplifting chorus layered with rich keyboards, piano, and soaring harmonies, all punctuated by a timpani sound reminiscent of the Beatles' "What You're Doing" and Phil Spector.

The lyrics address the market forces of the music biz in a more accommodating way than the bitter "Blood from a Clone" off *Somewhere in England*. The record label told Harrison that their polls said hit records were songs "of love gained or lost directed at fourteen-to-twenty-year-olds," and here he comes up with a lyric that fits the bill but to which he can also relate.[15]

The saucy horns match the single-mindedness of a horny boy pursuing a snooty girl with a hole in her heart, both of them isolated by their predetermined roles in the endless game. But the chorus suggests that inside they both have the yearning for a deeper level of happiness even though they're too young to understand their feelings. When we get out of the mind-sets of sex and materialism, we're all bursting with a love and joy that is connected to everyone, with a feeling that's almost too intense to be understood or expressed. Hopefully as we get a little older we can start to figure it out.

THE SONG WE WERE SINGING—MCCARTNEY

REC. 1995–1997, HOG HILL MILL STUDIOS, SUSSEX, LYNNE/MCCARTNEY (PRODUCERS), MCCARTNEY (V, G, B, DOUBLE B, D, HARMONIUM), LYNNE (G, K, BV), ALBUM *FLAMING PIE*: UK 5/5/97 (1); US 5/27/97 (2); GRAMMY NOM. FOR ALBUM OF THE YEAR

In 1997, two years after the *Anthology* documentary was released, McCartney released an autobiography covering his youth and the Beatles era called *Many Years from Now*, cowritten with longtime friend Barry Miles. No doubt the *Anthology* process produced surplus memories that couldn't fit in the group version of the story. Some critics of the memoir complained McCartney was obsessed with correcting the image that Lennon was the avant-garde Beatle by portraying himself as the group's original radical artist who created the tape loops in "Tomorrow Never Knows," among other experiments. Regardless, the book is a terrific account of what it was like to live such a charmed life. Some of the most compelling passages come when he describes his life in mid-sixties Swinging London. On a day off, he'd make a bunch of wild tape loops, then go over to a friend's place, light a joint, have a glass of wine, listen to all the fantastic music everyone was discovering, old and new, and talk into the night.

McCartney released *Flaming Pie* the same year as his memoir, and its opening track, "The Song We Were Singing," is the aural equivalent of such reminiscences. McCartney and disciple Jeff Lynne play all the instruments, including—for that "We Can Work It Out" touch—a harmonium, capturing the intimacy of *Rubber Soul* songs like "Norwegian Wood." McCartney and friends talk about composers, the cosmos, and how to fix the world, but they always come back to playing the guitar and singing more songs. It captures those heady nights when anything seemed possible and the hip young actually changed the trajectory of the world.

One almost craves more lyrics, but looking back over the classic early (and even the late) Beatles songs, they're often made up of only a few lines (see "I'll Follow the Sun"). Thus in its structure the song further fits its subject matter.

CHEER DOWN—HARRISON

Tom Petty, Rec. July 1989, Friar Park, Harrison/Lynne (producers), Harrison (v, g), Lynne (b, g, k, bv), Ian Paice (d), Richard Tandy (p), Cooper (percussion), Single: UK 11/27/89; US 3/24/89 (failed to chart), on *Let It Roll: Songs by George Harrison*, Film Appearance: *Lethal Weapon 2*

Harrison's slide guitar slow-fires like a laser beam across Lynne's favorite backdrop of chugging rhythm guitar, gradually building with the addition of Lynne's fine piano. Cowritten with Tom Petty, the song suggests how the Beatles might have sounded thirty years later: backing harmonies like days of yore but modernized by punched-up beat and bass. Harrison's bottleneck solo is another fine example of his synthesis of Indian technique and Pete Drake–style country rock.

The title was a phrase of Olivia's. When Harrison would get too worked up, she'd chide him, "Okay, cheer down, big fella." The song alludes to the ways her stabilizing influence helped him keep perspective in the face of aging and money troubles. Like Cat Stevens's "Moonshadow," it suggests he can live without teeth, hair, and cash, as long as he has her.

The song was produced in 1989 as a nonalbum single to promote the Mel Gibson action feature *Lethal Weapon 2*.

BEAUTIFUL NIGHT—MCCARTNEY

Rec. 1995–1997, Hog Hill Mill Studios, Sussex, Abbey Road, Lynne/McCartney (producers), McCartney (v, g, b, p, Wurlitzer electric piano, Hammond organ, percussion), Starr (d, bv, percussion), Linda McCartney (bv), Lynne (g, bv), George Martin (orchestration), 3 trumpets, 2 trombones, 3 horns, 16 violins, 5 violas, 4 cellos, 2 double bass, 1 flute, 1 oboe, Single: UK 12/15/97 (25), also on *Flaming Pie*

McCartney originally attempted "Beautiful Night" with producer Phil Ramone in 1986. Musically it is reminiscent of their big song together, "Once
Upon a Long Ago," and lyrically it has the same fairy-tale feel with visions of
castles in the sky and missions to Lorelei. But while McCartney liked the song,
he felt it hadn't really come off.

A decade later, dark clouds gathered on the horizon. Linda was diagnosed
with breast cancer in 1995 and it spread to her liver. When Starr's first wife,
Maureen, died of leukemia, McCartney recorded the gentle elegy "Little Willow" for her kids. Perhaps he was having a premonition of the rough times
ahead for his own family. After writing "Little Willow" in February 1996, he
took a break from the *Flaming Pie* project.

He had almost completed the album by February 1997 but wanted to
work with Starr again after the *Anthology* project. Thus Starr finally appeared
on a McCartney solo album, even though McCartney had appeared on Starr's
many times. Before bringing Starr into the studio, he went back to "Beautiful
Night" and revised the lyrics.

Starr accompanies McCartney on drums as McCartney sings at the piano.
With the knowledge that he might not have much time left with Linda,
McCartney sings that nothing feels as good as being with her, even being
knighted. He feels helpless in the face of Linda's worsening condition and
can't understand why such horrible things happen. But he resolves to make
their last nights together beautiful and just celebrate being with her, and not
think about the whys.

The song takes a tense turn as he confronts the fact that things can go
wrong in life—but, he quickly adds, things can go right (the cancer could go
into remission). In the middle of the night death looms, but McCartney vows
to always be at her side for all the time they have left.

Then Starr and the band kick up the tempo, determined to make it the
best night possible, with Starr taking a turn singing, "Beautiful night!" as
George Martin leads a thirty-eight-piece orchestra of strings, flutes, trumpets,
and horns, ringing the halls of Abbey Road like 1967.

The song was released as the third single from the album in December
1997, accompanied by a classy video directed by Julian Temple featuring Starr
and Linda in her last video appearance.

REAL LOVE—LENNON

REC. 1977, 1980, NEW YORK, FEBRUARY 1995, HOG HILL MILL STUDIOS,
SUSSEX, LENNON (DOUBLE-TRACKED V, P), McCARTNEY (BV, P, B, ACOUSTIC G,

HARPSICHORD), HARRISON (BV, LEAD AND ACOUSTIC G, HARMONIUM), STARR (D, TAMBOURINE), SINGLE: UK 3/4/96 (4); US 3/4/96 (11), ALSO ON *ANTHOLOGY 2*, ALTERNATE VERSION: *JOHN LENNON ANTHOLOGY*, COVERS: REGINA SPEKTOR, ADAM SANDLER IN FILM *FUNNY PEOPLE* (2009)

Beatles biographer John T. Marck said "Real Love" originated in 1977 as a song for a stage play Lennon was writing called *The Ballad of John and Yoko*. The play never materialized, but there was a short memoir of the same name included in his posthumous 1986 collection, *Skywriting by Word of Mouth*.

It is strange that Lennon overlooked this beautiful song when he was recording *Double Fantasy*. Captured on the *Lennon Anthology*, it features one of his gentlest, most heartfelt lyrics and melodies. Watching Sean playing with his little toys, he sees how Sean, like John once was, is just looking for love from his parents. Lennon reflects how when he was younger he had thought he was in love but hadn't actually found what he needed (which must've saddened Cynthia Lennon to hear). Now, however, he's at last found fulfillment with his wife and son, and all the demons that once drove him have faded at last.

The slow and deliberate piano descends to a pleasing gospel underpinning for the "waiting for love" passage before ascending to the chorus and circling back again. Lennon's playing is raw and not intended for release, but the clarity of his vision makes the song complete.

However, he felt compelled to keep tinkering with it. First, he merged it with another song called "Baby Make Love to You," then in 1979 attempted to fuse it with another song he'd been working on called "Real Life." The sixth take from his 1980 demo was used to open the 1988 feature documentary *Imagine: John Lennon* and released on its soundtrack.

The Beatles went back to the 1977 version for their next reunion single. Strangely, its sound quality on 1998's *Lennon Anthology* is pretty acceptable, whereas the version used in 1995's *Beatles Anthology* sounds like they had a tape of a tape, forcing them to process Lennon's voice as if he's singing through a tube. Did Ono give them a copy of a copy and then find the original later?

Lynne and Beatles engineer Geoff Emerick sped up the original by 12 percent, changing it from D minor to E flat. Perhaps they did it to make Lennon's voice sound more young and pop to the teen record buyers, but in doing so they lost the gravitas of the piece. Starr's drums come on a bit heavy, like every other Lynne tune. Harrison's *Abbey Road*–esque guitar embellishments are fine, but Lynne overdoes it. He piles on guitars, including the one Harrison played in *Magical Mystery Tour*, a Fender jazz bass guitar, a double bass once owned by Elvis' bassist Bill Black, a Baldwin combo harpsichord used by Lennon on "Because," and a harmonium reminiscent of the one on "We Can

Work It Out." The clutter renders a potential classic two dimensional with no space to breathe. It's better than "Free as a Bird," but in the end, Lennon's demo carries the true emotion.

The song made its debut on the second installment of the *Beatles Anthology* TV special on November 20, 1995, then was released as a single in March 1996. It debuted in the United Kingdom at number four but was impeded when the biggest station in Britain, BBC Radio 1, didn't include it with the sixty songs on regular rotation because it wasn't "contemporary," resulting in protests from fans and politicians.

Unlike "Free as a Bird," "Real Love" was more or less complete as a demo, so the other three functioned primarily as Lennon's sidemen. McCartney was keen to tackle the most unknown of all the Lennon demos, "Now and Then," next, but Harrison didn't like that one. When he and McCartney tried to write a song together called "All for Love" in the spring of 1995, the session ended in fierce argument. "It's just like being back in the Beatles," Harrison said dourly.[16] "Real Love" was the end of the Beatles' road.

NOTES

1. John Blaney, *Lennon and McCartney: Together Alone* (London: Jawbone, 2007), 228.

2. "Oasis' Gallagher Brothers Go Off on Rock's Old Guard," MTV.com, October 29, 1997, www.mtv.com/news/articles/1425552/oasis-gallagher-brothers-go-off-on-rocks-old-guard.jhtml (October 10, 2011).

3. Associated Press, "No 3-Beatle Reunion, George Harrison Says," *New York Times*, December 1, 1989.

4. "Free as a Bird," The Beatles Bible.com, www.beatlesbible.com/songs/free-as-a-bird (October 10, 2011).

5. "The Beatles Reunion Recording Sessions: The Unofficial Story of the Reunion Sessions," Reunion Sessions, http://reunionsessions.tripod.com/al/faabsessions/1994a.html (October 10, 2011).

6. "The Beatles Reunion Recording Sessions."

7. "The Beatles Reunion Recording Sessions."

8. Peter Doggett, *You Never Give Me Your Money* (New York: HarperCollins, 2009), 313.

9. "The Beatles Reunion Recording Sessions."

10. "Ringo," *Independent*, October 28, 1995.

11. Chris Ingham, *The Rough Guide to the Beatles* (London: Rough Guides Limited, 2009), 144.

12. Blaney, *Lennon and McCartney*, 212–14.

13. Simon Leng, *The Music of George Harrison: While My Guitar Gently Weeps* (London: Firefly, 2003), 248-49.

14. Blaney, *Lennon and McCartney*, 223.

15. J. Kordosh, "December 1987 *Creem* Interview with George Harrison," Beatles number9.com, http://beatlesnumber9.com/creem.html (October 10, 2011).

16. Doggett, *You Never Give Me Your Money*, 315.

George Harrison, January 1987. *Getty Images*

2005: Never without You

The solo Beatles face down death and life thereafter.

$\mathcal{I}$n 1998, Linda died of breast cancer. The following year, McCartney went into the studio with a band that included Pink Floyd's Dave Gilmour and howled an album of rock-and-roll classics from his youth, *Run Devil Run* (1999), a chilling and invigorating portrait of catharsis.

Starr, meanwhile, teamed up with producer Mark Hudson (born 1951) and his band the Roundheads. *Vertical Man* (1998) became Starr's biggest hit since *Ringo's Rotogravure* (1976), so they continued the formula with *Ringo Rama* (2003) and *Choose Love* (2005). Starr's continued pursuit of a jangle pop sound dovetailed with Hudson's first break in showbiz as part of a trio of brothers who had a Saturday morning kids show called *The Hudson Brothers' Razzle Dazzle Show*, sort of a budget Sid and Marty Croft meets the Monkees/Bay City Rollers program. Ironically, Hudson went on to work with Ozzy Osbourne, the Scorpions, and Aerosmith, cowriting the latter's Grammy winner "Livin' on the Edge" (1993). He also worked with Hanson, appropriately, and Harry Nilsson. On their trilogy of Ringo albums, anthems to peace and love filled with Beatles references abounded, as did celebrity guest appearances from the regular crew (McCartney, Harrison, Clapton, Preston, Walsh, Petty, David Gilmour, Brian Wilson) and some surprises. Hudson brought in friends like Osbourne and Steven Tyler, young Turks like Scott Weiland, Alanis Morissette, and Shawn Colvin, and icons like Willie Nelson and Chrissie Hynde.

In November 2000, on the thirtieth anniversary of the break-up, the Beatles compilation *1* was released featuring every number one single the band released in the United States and United Kingdom. It stunned everyone by selling over 31 million copies, becoming the seventh best-selling album since

1991, and the best-selling album in the United States of the 2000s. It continues to be the fastest selling album in history.

When the compilation sold 18 million copies in thirty-six days, a shocked Harrison told the German News agency DPA, "I thought it would do well, but not that well. It is like a new Beatlemania. I suddenly noticed that everyone had the album, even the six- and seven-year-olds. They act as if I belong to a boy band."

He also told DPA that he had stockpiled enough songs for three albums, but denied that Jeff Lynne would produce his follow up to *Cloud Nine*. "I have stopped working with Jeff because I did not want him to make ELO albums out of my songs," he said—impishly, because he was, in fact, working with Lynne again. He also vowed to use no computers or drum machines.[1]

Harrison worked on the songs for the album whenever the mood struck him over the decade plus since *Cloud Nine*. He had been sidetracked by the *Anthology* project, and then a bout with cancer. Harrison started smoking in 1957 and quit in 1992, but in 1997 he developed a lump on his neck and in his lung. But after undergoing two operations for cancer and radiotherapy, he was doing well. By mid-1999, he had completed most of the demos, with his son, Dhani, often playing with him.

Then a horrible assault contributed to the cancer's return. In 1999, thirty-six-year-old Michael Abram kicked his heroin addiction, but ironically that made his schizophrenia worse. His mother tried to get him back on medication, but the bureaucracy of England's National Board of Health kept putting her off. Abram went through an obsession with Oasis, then switched his focus to the Beatles. As he later told his lawyer, he became convinced they were "witches," with Harrison in particular being "a witch on a broomstick, who talked in the Devil's tongue—an alien from Hell."[2] Perhaps the song he was referring to was "My Sweet Lord," in which Harrison midway switches from singing "Hallelujah" to singing Hare Krishna chants. Abram believed that Harrison was possessing him, and that it was Abram's mission from God to kill him.

On December 30, a young female stalker broke into Harrison's home in Maui and was arrested. The same night in England, Abram went to Harrison's Friar Park.

The main gates had security cameras, but on other parts of the estate the fence was falling down. At 3:30 a.m., the sound of breaking glass woke Harrison and Olivia. From downstairs, Abram yelled for Harrison. Harrison went to investigate in his pajama bottoms while Olivia called the police. In a scene reminiscent of that year's box office hit *The Sixth Sense*, Harrison came face to face with Abram holding a long kitchen knife. Trying to calm Abram and himself, Harrison chanted the Hare Krishna Mantra—probably the words that made Abram believe he was a witch in the first place. Abram attacked.

Harrison later recounted, "I thought I was dying. I vividly remember a deliberate thrust of a knife and I could feel the blood entering my mouth and hear my breath exhaling from the wound."[3]

Rolling Stones drummer Charlie Watts told the *Observer*, "I spoke to Ringo about a month after it happened and he told me exactly what went on, and it was horrific. George was stabbed about forty times. It happened outside his bedroom on the landing. He would have been dead if he'd been lying in bed, he wouldn't have been able to fight. The papers did say that one wound punctured his lung, but a lot of the others were just as horrific. The man was slashing him everywhere. George's wife hit him again and again on the head with this brass lamp, but he just wouldn't stop. There was blood everywhere."[4]

First Olivia hit him with a fireplace poker, then smashed the antique lamp on the head. Olivia later told Katie Couric, "George was coaching me, I have to say. And George was very brave and people don't know that. Because he had already been injured and he had to jump up and bring him down to stop him from attacking me. You know, he saved my life too."

Katie Couric: "You saved each other's lives."

Olivia Harrison: "Yes, we did. And that was an interesting experience. Because, you know, not a lot of people get tested like that, thank God."[5]

The lamp knocked Abram out, ending the fifteen-minute assault. The police carried him away. Harrison's condition was critical for a day, then he was back home. Harrison said to the press, "He wasn't a burglar and he certainly wasn't auditioning for the Traveling Wilburys."

Tom Petty faxed him, "Aren't you glad you married a Mexican girl?"

Abram was acquitted of attempted murder due to insanity. He was treated then released after nineteen months in 2002.

Harrison got aggressive about finishing the album, and began giving Dhani detailed notes on how he wanted the sound and the artwork. For a while he said he planned to call it *The World Is Doomed*. Abram had punctured Harrison's lung, and the cancer returned there. In May 2001, he had an operation at the Mayo Clinic, but it was discovered the cancer had spread to his brain. Harrison went to Switzerland for treatment, continuing to work on the album at a studio there. By November 2001 he was bone thin and hallucinating from medication. He flew to Staten Island's University Hospital in a last-ditch attempt to see if experimental radiation treatment would help.

McCartney visited him there ten days before he died. "The years just stripped back. It was good, it was like we were dreaming. . . . He was my little baby brother, almost, because I'd known him that long. . . . We were laughing and joking, just like nothing was going on. I was impressed by his strength."

When Lennon was killed, no one expected it, but here the former blood brothers had a chance to cry and laugh together one last time. On *Larry King Live* with Starr, McCartney said, "It was just the best, because we just sat like this—if you don't mind—." He took Starr's hand to demonstrate, in a strange echo of the first smash hit that introduced them to American shores forty years earlier. "We sat just stroking hands like this, and this was a guy I'd known since he was a little kid, and you don't stroke hands with guys like that, you know, it was just beautiful."

"Not unless you're secure," said Starr.

King and McCartney chuckled, then McCartney continued, "And we just spent a couple hours and it was really lovely, it was like, a favorite memory of mine."[6]

Harrison died on November 29 from lung cancer in a Hollywood Hills mansion that McCartney once leased and Courtney Love once owned. Cremated at the Hollywood Forever Cemetery, his ashes were scattered in India in the Ganges River in a private ceremony of Hindu custom.

A few months after his death, a reissued "My Sweet Lord" made it to number one in the United Kingdom again. In January 2002, Dhani, Lynne, and Olivia returned to the detailed notes Harrison had left on how to finish the album. They added the instruments Harrison wanted, using sessions Harrison had booked himself.

Brainwashed was released a year after his death in November 2002 to reviews calling it one of his greatest albums. It was nominated for Grammies for Best Pop Vocal Album, Best Male Pop Vocal Performance (for the track "Any Road"), and won Best Pop Instrumental Performance for "Marwa Blues" (B-side of "Any Road").

ANY ROAD—HARRISON

Rec. 1988–2002, Harrison/Lynne/Dhani Harrison (producers), Harrison (v, g, banjulele), Lynne (b, p, bv), Keltner (d), Dhani (electric g, bv), Single: UK 5/12/03 (37), also on *Brainwashed*, Grammy Nom. for 2004 Best Male Pop Vocal Performance

The early 1970s was prime time for folk mystics in similar mold to Harrison: Donovan, Cat Stevens, and Nick Drake. They all sang about traveling the road to wisdom in songs like Stevens's "On the Road to Find Out" and Nick

Drake's "Road." Harrison was a late-comer with "Heading for the Light" and this gem, written in 1988 during the making of his video for "Cloud Nine." He performed "Any Road" nine years later during an interview on VH1, but it would not be released on album until 2002.

Harrison sings of speeding in planes, trains, and race cars, and a mood of jubilant propulsion is established with the banjulele, a ukulele-banjo combination. Back on record for the first time in more than a decade, his voice is reedier, embodying the calm wisdom Harrison only sang of in his younger days.

The Beatles had long looked to Lewis Carroll for inspiration, and the refrain of "Any Road" was inspired by the scene in *Alice's Adventures in Wonderland* in which the Cheshire Cat asks the heroine where she is going.

> "I don't much care where—" said Alice, "—so long as I get SOMEWHERE," Alice added as an explanation.
>
> "Oh, you're sure to do that," said the Cat, "if you only walk long enough."

Harrison sings that if you don't know where you're going, any road can get you there. The first half of the song is an upbeat variation on "Heading for the Light." It almost sounds like a montage from *The Lord of the Rings*, as Harrison journeys through grottoes, caves, wind, ice, and snow. But gradually he expands the metaphor to mean different periods of one's life, musing on how at various times you can be cool and at others lame. As always, he reminds us to look outside the worries of the moment and remember the cosmic "now" beyond time. He signs off reminding us to bow to God and call him Sir, and then rides off into the sunset with some Monty Python–esque, high-pitched, "Arriba!"

"Any Road" was the opener on Harrison's last album and his final single. Though it lost the 2004 Grammy Awards for Best Male Pop Vocal Performance to Justin Timberlake's "Cry Me a River," the single's B-side ("Marwa Blues") won the Grammy for Best Pop Instrumental Performance.

PARTY—MCCARTNEY

Rec. March 1999, Abbey Road, Jessie Mae Robinson (writer), Chris Thomas/McCartney (producers), McCartney (v, b), Dave Gilmour (g), Mick Green (g), Ian Paice (d), Pete Wingfield (p), Album *Run Devil Run*: UK 10/4/99 (12); US 10/5/99 (27)

When McCartney's mother died from breast cancer in 1956, he buried himself in the distraction of rock and roll. When Linda passed away from the same disease in 1998, he returned to the music of the '50s. He got the album title *Run Devil Run* from a brand of bath salts used to ward off evil he saw being sold at an herbal medicine shop on 87 Broad Street in Atlanta. Rock and roll was always his balm.

"Party" was a deep cut from the 1957 Elvis movie *Lovin' You*. Wanda Jackson later covered it and her version can be heard in the 1989 film classic *Dead Poets Society*. The tune was also included in the 2010 Broadway show *Million Dollar Quartet*, based on the day Elvis, Johnny Cash, Carl Perkins, and Jerry Lee Lewis all recorded together at Sun Studios. McCartney used the song as his tool to correct some infuriating revisionism that had been going around about him.

Backbeat is a very good 1994 film about the Beatles' early days. (That is to say, it's good for Beatles fans; it's hard to say if nonfans would be bored or not.) Like Dick Clark's 1979 telefilm *The Birth of the Beatles*, it spotlighted their stint in Hamburg, the Vegas of Europe, in their raw early days when they all wore Gene Vincent leather suits. Forced to play for six to eight hours a day to drunken sailors and whores, they were turned on to over-the-counter speed to keep going and it welded them into an incendiary tight unit. (The Beatles' first drummer, Pete Best, didn't do speed, though, one of the things that kept him at a distance from the others.) The movie tells the story through the eyes of Stuart Sutcliffe, Lennon's painter best friend whom Lennon drafted to play bass, even though he couldn't play. His musical ineptitude led to serious tension between Stu and perfectionist Mc-Cartney, who could play better. It was a precursor to the John–Yoko–Paul triangle, but luckily for Western civilization, Stu hooked up with German artist Astrid Kirchherr and graciously stepped aside.

While the audiences back in Hamburg experienced the Beatles' music as intense hard rock, the creators of the film believed that kids in the mid-'90s would not since they were accustomed to the likes of Nirvana and Metallica. So the producers enlisted hot rockers of the era to reinterpret the music for modern kids, and the actors lip-synched to it. Dave Pirner of Soul Asylum and Greg Dulli of the Afghan Whigs did the vocals, Sonic Youth's Thurston Moore played guitar with Gumball's Don Fleming, Mike Mills of R.E.M. took bass, and Dave Grohl (Nirvana/Foo Fighters) played drums. A very hip band, but neither vocalist sounded anything like Lennon or McCartney.

The film also fell prey to the same fallacy that almost all Beatles movies do: that Lennon was primarily a vulnerable, mixed-up softy and, as often as not, a prickly asshole. The movie also portrays Harrison as an innocent little boy afraid of the groupies, when by all accounts he was as big a player as any of them.

And it showed McCartney as preppy, aloof, and snobby. McCartney complained, "One of my annoyances about the film *Backbeat* is that they've actually taken my rock 'n' rollness off me. They give John the song 'Long Tall Sally' to sing and he never sang it in his life. But now it's set in cement. It's like *The Buddy Holly* and *Glenn Miller* stories. *The Buddy Holly Story* does not even mention Norman Petty, and *The Glenn Miller Story* is a sugarcoated version of his life. Now *Backbeat* has done the same thing to the story of the Beatles."[7]

Ironically, the same year *Backbeat* was released, the fantastic missing link *Live at the BBC* was issued. It was a two-CD set that consisted of live in-studio performances by the Beatles over the course of their fifty-two appearances on the BBC between 1962 and 1965. Here with perfect clarity you can hear how tight they were, and the amazing revelation was what a fiend Ringo was on the drums back then, when they were touring and performing almost every day.

It's true their early guitar sound predated the use of hard rock distortion (which the Beatles had inaugurated with "I Feel Fine," along with the Kinks), so to kids who thought Soundgarden defined rock, the Beatles would sound soft. Thus *Backbeat* is what it is, and it does a good job of capturing a milieu that was important to their evolution.

The interesting thing is, in his return to roots on *Run Devil Run*, McCartney does not sound like the Beatles from the BBC (which was presumably, what they sounded like in Hamburg), but he sounds like the band in *Backbeat*. Showing up with his own gang including Pink Floyd's Gilmour and Deep Purple's drummer Ian Paice, he scorches with the clear goal of wiping the *Backbeat* band and everybody else off the map. With the hellhounds of Linda's death on his trail, he does.

LOOKING FOR MY LIFE—HARRISON

Rec. July 1999–October 2001, Friar Park, Swiss Army Studios, Switzerland, and on the road, Harrison/Lynne/Dhani Harrison (producers), Harrison (v, g), Lynne (acoustic and 12-string g, b, p, bv), Dhani (electric and acoustic g, bv), (d) uncredited (probably Keltner), Album Brainwashed: UK 11/18/02 (29); US 11/18/02 (18), Grammy nom. for Best Pop Vocal Album, Best Male Pop Vocal Performance (for Any Road), won Best Pop Instrumental Performance for Marwa Blues

Having enjoyed an idyllic existence in his garden for years, Harrison rues that he never anticipated life could explode at any moment. When he sighs that we've no idea what he's been through, it's as if Lennon has survived his shooting and is singing about it. When Harrison asks the Lord to listen to him and help him find his faith again, you know he truly does have something to plead about, like Job.

Featuring just Harrison with his son, Dhani, and Lynne, Lynne steps back and lets the guitars speak for themselves, with just a few deft touches, like giving the chorus' drums a timpani-like depth for an epic feel.

Ironically, the song was written before the knife attack, perhaps in response to his cancer diagnosis or earlier eras of substance abuse. Still, as he strums intensely with his son, it's hard to think of anything but that night at the end of 1999 that saw him on the floor soaked in blood next to the knocked-out body of Abram, Olivia sobbing beside him.

NO OTHER BABY—MCCARTNEY

Rec. March 1999, Abbey Road, Dickie Bishop/Bob Watson (writers), Chris Thomas/McCartney (producers), McCartney (v, b), Dave Gilmour (g, bv), Mick Green (g), Ian Paice (d), Pete Wingfield (Hammond o), Single: 11/25/99 (42); US 11/23/99 (failed to chart), also on *Run Devil Run*

Linda had been conflicted about taking cancer medication, knowing that it had been tested on animals. When she died on the family ranch in Tucson, Arizona, on April 17, 1998, McCartney's final words to her were, "You're up on your beautiful Appaloosa stallion. It's a fine spring day. We're riding through the woods. The bluebells are all out, and the sky is clear-blue."[8]

She was cremated in Arizona and her ashes were taken back to the family farm in Sussex to be scattered there. McCartney encouraged fans to donate to breast cancer research charities that did not test on animals, "or the best tribute—go veggie." He resolved to continue her vegetarian food company and keep it free of any genetic modifications.

Harrison, Starr, and Dave Gilmour attended the memorial service in London, and another was held in Manhattan. In April 1999, a year after her death, the Concert for Linda was held at the Royal Albert Hall featuring McCartney, Elvis Costello, the Pretenders, George Michael, and Tom Jones.

Of all the songs on *Run Devil Run*, the one that most clearly expressed McCartney's grief was "No Other Baby."[9] Dickie Bishop wrote it in 1957 with Bob Watson and performed it with his band, the Sidekicks. It was one of the first quasi-rock tunes written by a Brit to be covered by an American

(Bobby Helms). At that point, Brit rock was considered a weak imitation of the original.

The version that made an impression on McCartney was The Vipers' 1958 skiffle version, produced by no less than George Martin. It actually sounds a bit like a peppy number on *Live at the BBC* called "Lonesome Tears in My Eyes." McCartney recorded "No Other Baby" for his first album of covers, the 1988 *Russian Album/Back in the USSR*, originally recorded in an epic two-day session, for sale in the Soviet Union only. On *Run Devil Run*, he recasts the song as a slow and grieving epic, highlighted by Gilmour's piercing guitar.

The video perfectly captures McCartney's desolation after Linda's death. Gorgeously shot in black and white, it features him stranded in the middle of the ocean in a lifeboat. Rowing through ice floes and through storms in the blackest night, he wakes in the morning with sharks circling the boat. Some bloggers commented that the sharks were eerily prescient of Heather Mills.

In 2000, a TV movie, *The Linda McCartney Story* aired starring Elizabeth Mitchell and Gary Bakewell. Whatever slings and arrows she suffered in the early days had long since faded in the face of their solid marriage, their stable children, and the idealism of their vegetarianism and defense of animals.

SHAKE A HAND—MCCARTNEY

Rec. March 1999, Abbey Road, Joe Morris (writer), Chris Thomas/McCartney (producers), McCartney (v, g, b), Dave Gilmour (g), Mick Green (g), Ian Paice (d), Pete Wingfield (p, Hammond o), Album *Run Devil Run*

In the 1950s artists generated hits quickly. When the Orioles went to number one on the R&B chart with "Crying in the Chapel" in 1953, Joe Morris wrote "Shake a Hand" in clear emulation of the phrasing and inflection of "Chapel," and Faye Adams recorded it fast enough to knock the Orioles out of the number one spot.

In 1958, Little Richard did his version of "Shake a Hand." Of course, McCartney was Little Richard's number one disciple, save perhaps for Prince, one of the few people who can match McCartney in his prolific output and ability to do entire albums by himself. (Check out *Live at the BBC* to hear McCartney doing more Little Richard impersonations like "Lucille" and "Ooh! My Soul!") Macca recalled, "I have this image of being in Hamburg, there was one bar that had a pool table and a great jukebox. And that was the only place I ever heard

"Shake a Hand." Every time we went there, I put it on. I never had the record, but I knew I wanted to do it. It always takes me back to that bar."[10]

Along with Gilmour, McCartney brought in guitarist Mick Green, who had been in Billy J. Kramer and the Dakotas, which Brian Epstein managed. On "Shake a Hand" both Gilmour and Green take their turns doing distinct solos. Green called his "rough and ready," while Gilmour's was "smooth and tasteful."[11]

It's interesting to compare McCartney's Little Richard voice in 1999 with his take on "Long Tall Sally" in 1964. It's deeper but amazingly intact and strong compared to the voices of Dylan and Jagger—the former a croak of its former self, the other overly mannered.

I DON'T BELIEVE YOU—STARR

Rec. February–September 1991, February 1992, California, Andy Sturmer/Roger Manning (writers), Don Was (producer), Starr (v, d, percussion), Michael Landau (g), David Grissom (acoustic g), James "Hutch" Hutchinson (b), Benmont Tench (p, Hammond B-3), backing vocals: Andrew Sturmer, Roger Manning, Album *Time Takes Time*

A jewel that could have come off *Rubber Soul*, "I Don't Believe You" was written by Andy Sturmer and Roger Manning, who also added backing vocals and acoustic guitars. They were members of the band Beatnik Beach, which eventually morphed into the San Francisco power pop band Jellyfish. Also playing on Jellyfish's debut album was Jason Falkner, who had been a member of the '80s band the Three O'Clock. That band had been part of a short-lived movement called the Paisley Underground, made up of bands in the 1980s who were trying to sound folk-rock-garage in opposition to the synthesizers and drum machines dominating the pop charts. The Bangles were the biggest group to make it out of this scene, epitomizing the movement with their 1985 single "Going Down to Liverpool."

The Ringed One speak-sings his lines as the backing singers answer him in harmony. The song is a perfect homage by third-generation musicians emulating bands like the Knickerbockers ("Lies"), Monkees ("Sunny Girlfriend"), and Rutles ("Ouch!"), who themselves were emulating the Beatles circa "You're Gonna Lose That Girl" and "Run for Your Life."

Many mid-sixties garage nuggets (such as Syndicate of Sound's "Little Girl") featured an agitated singer berating a girl who has done him wrong and warning her that he's at the end of his rope. Here Starr expresses his exasperation that his woman has lied to him and used his credit cards to buy fancy clothes and "powder for her nose." Now he's going to put her in her place and kiss her good-bye, just in time for the rollicking instrumental in which he cries, "Ole! Ole!"

In the early '60s, McCartney wrote quite a number of these tunes, too, including one for Starr called "If You've Got Troubles" that went unreleased until being included on volume one of the *Anthology*. Oasis had already pilfered the riff (via bootleg) for 1994's "Up in the Sky."

JENNY WREN—MCCARTNEY

REC. 2003–2005, OCEAN WAY RECORDING, LA, NIGEL GODRICH (PRODUCER), MCCARTNEY (V, ACOUSTIC G, FLOOR TOM), PEDRO EUSTACHE (DUDUK), SINGLE: UK 11/21/05 (22), ALSO ON *CHAOS AND CREATION IN THE BACKYARD*, GRAMMY NOM. FOR 2007 BEST MALE POP VOCAL PERFORMANCE

McCartney composed this song in the canyons of Los Angeles in the fingerpicking style he had used on *The White Album*'s "Blackbird" and "Mother Nature's Son" and *Flaming Pie*'s "Calico Skies." Along with its guitar technique, it shares with "Blackbird" the use of a bird as a metaphor for a woman rising above her oppressive background—though with the guitar tuned to "D," the mood is darker and lonelier.

For possibly the first time in Western pop, the solo was played on the duduk, a woodwind instrument from Armenia, by Pedro Eustache of Venezuela.

Jenny Wren was a character from *Our Mutual Friend*, a novel by Charles Dickens, who often focused on urchins struggling to survive the poverty of industrial England. Part of Heather Mills's (born January 12, 1968) appeal to McCartney was probably her own waif-like tragic past, which inspired in him a desire to protect her.

In the song, Jenny Wren's home is broken up by poverty and darkened by a "wounded warrior." Mills's father was a paratrooper, and her grandfather was a colonel. The colonel did not want Mills's parents to marry, and when they did he never saw them again. Mills's father was reportedly abusive, and her mother left him and her children when Mills was nine, eventually taking up with an actor on the British soap *Crossroads*. Mills claimed that her father threw her brother against a window for dirtying the carpet with crayons, necessitating a trip to the hospital. Meanwhile, the lack of necessities forced Mills and her siblings to shoplift.

Mills would also write in her memoirs that when she was eight a swimming pool attendant kidnapped and sexually assaulted her.

Eventually, Mills left with her sister to live with her mother and mother's boyfriend. Like Jenny Wren taking wings, Mills wrote in her memoir that at fifteen she ran away with the fair and lived in a box at Waterloo Station. Her father would later claim that she greatly exaggerated and just left on the weekends with a guy who worked at the fair. Regardless, her childhood saw much hardship to overcome.

Mills was a model until August 8, 1993, when a police motorcycle hit her while responding to an emergency call. Her lower left leg had to be amputated six inches below the knee. She became a charity activist, focusing on a campaign to get rid of landmines.

FROM A LOVER TO A FRIEND—MCCARTNEY

Rec. 2/27/01, Henson Recording Studios, LA, Kahne/McCartney (producer), McCartney (v, b, p), Anderson (12-string electric guitar with a capo on the first fret), Laboriel Jr. (d), Gabe Dixon (b), Single A-side: UK 10/29/01 (45); Re-issued November 2001 as B-side of Freedom (did not chart), also on *Driving Rain*

At the Pride of Britain Awards in April 1999, Mills presented an award on behalf of the Heather Mills Health Trust the same night that McCartney presented an award dedicated to Linda, a year after her death. They didn't talk then, but McCartney was impressed with Mills's speech and contacted her about her charity, later donating £150,000.

In November 1999, Mills and her sister stayed overnight at McCartney's Peasmarsh, Sussex, estate while he added backing vocals to a song the sisters had written to raise money for Mills's foundation. Mills invited McCartney to her thirty-second birthday in January 2000. His presence there set the tabloids chattering.

Many widowed fathers feel guilt over seeing someone new. McCartney not only had his children watching him, he had the public. He asked his children for their blessing and they told him as long as he was happy it was okay with them, but McCartney still kept things secret for a while. But in March 2000, the couple revealed their relationship to the world.

In the haunting piano ballad "From a Lover to a Friend," McCartney struggles with guilt as he asks Linda's spirit to let him love again. It was recorded live with session musicians, then edited from different takes. His vocals strain perhaps more than they used to, but it suits the vulnerability of his confusion. He hated being alone and always had a girlfriend, from Jane Asher to Frannie Schwartz to Linda with little down time in between. He wants to move on from grieving and embrace his new love for Mills, but is unsure if it's the right thing to do after thirty years with Linda.

While singing to Linda, he is also singing to Mills, asking her to let him love her now that he's realized she's someone he can trust.

He sings of feeling duty bound to tell the truth, perhaps to both his children and the press. But in interviews, he stated that he wasn't sure what the song meant and didn't think too much about it.[12] Either he trusted his subconscious and let it do its job unsupervised or he wanted to evade the issue, having already said an uncomfortable amount in the song.

The Guardian called it a masterpiece, "so delicate and honest." It was released as the A-side of a single on October 29, 2001, but on November 5 it became the B-side to his September 11 anthem "Freedom," with proceeds going to the families of the firemen and police officers who perished in the World Trade Center attack.

BETWEEN THE DEVIL AND THE DEEP BLUE SEA—HARRISON

REC. 1991, HAROLD ARLEN/TED KOEHLER (WRITERS), HARRISON (V, UKULELE), JOOLS HOLLAND (P), MARK FLANAGAN (ACOUSTIC LEAD G), JOE BROWN (ACOUSTIC RHYTHM G), HERBIE FLOWERS (B, TUBA), COOPER (D), ALBUM *BRAINWASHED*

Harrison's love for pre-rock jazz and blues was evident as early as *Let It Be*'s "For You Blue," and as he grew older his favorite music became old-time artists like Hoagy Carmichael, Cab Calloway, and Django Reinhardt. His son, Dhani, said that he would always play their music on his ukulele around the house.

Pianist Jools Holland was a founder of the band Squeeze and in 1991 had his own TV special called *Mr. Roadrunner*. Harrison appeared in a segment performing the pop standard "Between the Devil and the Deep Blue Sea" on his ukulele, accompanied by Holland's band. The performance was included on *Brainwashed* with such a clean mix one wouldn't know it was recorded eleven years before the album was released.

The song was originally popularized by Cabell "Cab" Calloway III (1907–1994), whose career bridged the golden eras of jazz. He took over as bandleader at the famed Cotton Club from Duke Ellington, and later, bebop innovator Dizzy Gillespie would get his start in Calloway's band. The songwriting team

Arlen/Koehler also wrote "Stormy Weather" together. The man who wrote the music, Harold Arlen, also did the music for *The Wizard of Oz* and wrote "Blues in the Night" and "That Old Black Magic" with Johnny Mercer. In classic old-school fashion, the bouncy music belies the angst of the singer. He just wants to forget the lady who does him wrong and brings chaos into his life, but he loves her too much to give her the boot like he knows he should. Or maybe he secretly loves being tormented.

YOUR WAY—MCCARTNEY

REC. 2001, HENSON RECORDING STUDIOS, LA, KAHNE/MCCARTNEY (PRO-DUCERS), MCCARTNEY (V, G, D, KNEE SLAPS), ANDERSON (B, PEDAL STEEL, BV), LABORIEL JR. (D, ELECTRONIC D, BV), GABE DIXON (O, BV), ALBUM *DRIVING RAIN*: UK 11/12/01 (46); US 11/13/01 (26)

Written in Jamaica, this was another fine addition to McCartney's collection of low-key country tunes like "County Dreamer," with nice Pete Drake–style pedal guitar and a pleasing, unobtrusive almost non-hook.

Mills's love has sent McCartney onto a mellow trip into the stratosphere. In many earlier songs McCartney maintained he was right, but here he sings that *her* way is strong and right, both the way she lives her own life and the way she gives him love.

It seemed there was much that was admirable about Mills. During the Croatian War in 1990, she established a refugee crisis center in London, which aided over twenty people fleeing the war. She drove to Croatia by herself to deliver donated supplies, funding the effort through Austrian modeling assignments. The police officer who hit her with his motorcycle was cleared, but the police awarded her £200,000. She used that money, and the profits from selling her story to *The News of the World*, to set up the Heather Mills Health Trust to provide children with prosthetic limbs after being injured by landmines. Nothing if not resilient, she was known for taking off her leg on TV to make a point, doing so once on *Larry King Live*. She fought to stop the clubbing of seals and the eradication of landmines. With the help of a ghost-writer, she published her memoir, *Out on a Limb*, in 1995 (renamed *A Single Step*) and donated the proceeds to Adopt-A-Minefield.

McCartney proposed to Mills on July 23, 2001, giving her a £15,000 diamond and sapphire ring from Jaipur, India (hence the song "Riding to Jaipur" on the *Driving Rain* album).

"Your Way" hints at Heather Mills's firm will, something that initially attracted him though would later cause considerable consternation. Friends must have been shocked when she got McCartney to give up weed, saying she wouldn't marry him unless he did so. She maintained she'd never taken any drugs, while he smoked ganja as frequently as others drank tea. Her way must have been strong indeed to induce McCartney to swear off the crutch that he once secretly wrote "Got to Get You into My Life" about.

ANYWAY—MCCARTNEY

Rec. 2003–2005, Ocean Way Recording Studio, LA, strings at AIR Studios, London, Nigel Godrich (producer), McCartney (v, g, Hofner b, d, Steinway and Bosendorfer Grand Pianos, Moog synth, harmonium), Millennia Ensemble (strings), Album *Chaos and Creation in the Backyard*: UK 9/12/05 (10); US 9/13/05 (6), Grammy Nom. for 2006 Album of the Year, Best Pop Vocal Album, and Producer of the Year

McCartney wrote some of his most beautiful love songs for Linda, but since their marriage was so stable they were mainly odes to domestic tranquility. The 1990s examples like "I Owe It All to You" and "Wine Dark Open Sea" from *Off the Ground* are peaceful and evocative but never quite reach the top tier of McCartney's canon because they were written out of the need to write ballads, as opposed to being written because he needed to exorcise pain out of his system. Although Heather Mills would play havoc with his emotions, she was a dark muse that brought an infusion of intense love songs into the third act of his career.

"Anyway" finds him at his piano jonesing for her to call him. Now that he was older and no longer the baby-faced beauty, he was more vulnerable to the whims of the younger woman he pinned his heart to. The '60s songs that expressed his dissatisfaction in his relationship with Jane Asher always held the defiant hint of an ultimatum—"If you blow it with me, baby, I got a million more out there"—but the McCartney of the Mills years was more humble. He just wanted secure love and did not want to play games. Once the most eligible bachelor on earth and now a clingy older guy yearning for a younger chick, McCartney took us on his journey through life every step of the way.

He wonders, if she really loves him like she says she does, why doesn't she call? He's back to the worrying that normal mortals experience and tries to remember when it was exactly that he fell in love with her. He encourages her to make her new home with him and gently pleads for her to get in touch so they can heal each other's sorrow.

From the earliest days McCartney would imagine himself to be the artists he loved when writing a new song, like when he pretended to be Ray Charles while composing "She's a Woman" on the way to Abbey Road Studios. As he finished the arrangement for "Anyway," he pretended he was a Southern Randy Newman, with a little Curtis Mayfield thrown in.[13]

McCartney may have also borrowed the moment of drama from a piano passage in Lennon's composition "Now and Then," the song the Threetles didn't remake for the *Anthology* because Harrison felt it was too unfinished. McCartney was always anxious to tackle the song and loved harmonizing with Lennon on it.[14] To date McCartney has not attempted a remake (though he should), but Lennon's original can be heard on YouTube. At approximately 4:30 Lennon does a haunting little piano passage that seems oddly reminiscent of "Anyway" at approximately 1:40.

Radiohead producer Nigel Godrich stripped away any corny edges and gave McCartney a pure, classy piano sound, then upped the emotion even further at the bridge with the addition of the Millennia Ensemble strings, a Moog synth, and harmonium mixed just right.

PISCES FISH—HARRISON

REC. JULY 1999–OCTOBER 2001, FRIAR PARK, SWISS ARMY STUDIOS, SWITZERLAND, AND ON THE ROAD, HARRISON/LYNNE/DHANI HARRISON (PRODUCERS), HARRISON (V, G, B, UKULELE), LYNNE (ELECTRIC G, K, PERCUSSION), KELTNER (D), DHANI HARRISON (ELECTRIC G), MIKE MORAN (K), MARC MANN (K), ALBUM *BRAINWASHED*

"Pisces Fish" is one of Harrison's most cinematic songs, even more so than "Ballad of Sir Frankie Crisp." As Harrison strolls around a favorite lake, the stately tempo, vocals, and attitude imbue him with the gravitas of a wise man—then he undercuts the solemnity by noting all the dogs and geese crapping everywhere.

In his mind, the local brewery and the Catholic bell tower blend together, both churning out opium for the masses. He turns again to the Eastern ideal of calming the mind through meditation to transcend the pain of the temporal world, something more urgent than ever with his body wracked from suffering.

As he sings of being a Pisces fish with the river running through his soul, his mantra-like "mmmms" gently descend an octave. Harrison scholar Leng points out that it mirrors the way a river travels down from the mountains to the sea.[15] Harrison's weary but strong voice conveys a depth that has seen the abyss and now faces death with serenity. He vows to continue swimming until he finds the ocean of bliss that flows through all of us if we're disciplined enough to tap into it.

But his reverie is interrupted by rowers whose blades cut into the water, like blades once cut into him. All the locals suffering from petty annoyances further mar his stroll. A bike rider's chain gets caught just as the monk in the bell tower gets tangled in his rope. A farmer rues that he has to put his mad cows to sleep, reminding Harrison of his own mortality.

Harrison reminds himself to enjoy the beauty of the moment before it's too late. Like Lennon in "Nobody Told Me," he calms himself by thinking of his favorite temple on an island and the Gods who can only be found in silence. He looks ahead to escaping the constant cycle of birth and death and finally ascending to peace.

In an interview he once said, "When people see me they see a Beatle. But for me it was all such a long time ago. Sometimes I ask myself if I was really there or whether it was all a dream."[16] He sings how his life seems like a made-up novel, and how he himself reflects all the contradictions of life, a decadent rockstar spiritual seeker.

Despite Harrison's issues with the Catholic Church, his stoicism brings to mind another Pisces, Jesus, facing death with unmovable calm. The song also recalls the ending of Hermann Hesse's *Siddhartha*, a novel that focused on the spiritual odyssey of an Indian man who lived during the same time as the Buddha. The title character's name is a combination of two Sanskrit words that translate as "achieve" and "meaning."

In the climax, Siddhartha's disciple peers into his guru's smiling face and perceives the endless death and rebirth of countless souls. He realizes Siddhartha's calm expression is the same as the Buddha's, and bows and cries, filled with love.

NEVER WITHOUT YOU—STARR

Rec. September 2003, Rocca Bella Studio, UK, Whatinthewhatinthe? Studio, US, Starkey/Hudson/Gary Nicholson (writers), Hudson/

STARR (PRODUCERS), STARR (V, D?), ERIC CLAPTON (GUITAR SOLO), HUDSON (G, BV), STEVE DUDAS (G), GARY BURR (G, BV), SINGLE: 10/25/03 (FAILED TO CHART), ALSO ON *RINGO RAMA*

Gary Nicholson's songs have been sung by Willie Nelson, Garth Brooks, Robert Plant, B. B. King, and the Blues Brothers. In the 2010 feature *Crazy Heart*, Jeff Bridges sings Nicholson's "Fallin' and Flyin'." Producer Hudson brought Nicholson's "Never without You" to Starr in 2003 when Harrison was very much on Starr's mind. They decided they could turn the lyrics into an ode to Starr's fallen brother, and enlisted Eric Clapton to play tribute to Harrison's guitar style. Starr sings to Harrison that his songs will continue and he won't be forgotten, referencing various Harrison titles while Clapton quotes musically from "What Is Life" and "All Things Must Pass."

In its lyrical ultra simplicity, the song is actually one of the most succinct summations of why millions continue to live vicariously through the Beatles. Starr remembers when they were in headlines across the world, riding in limousines to premieres with bright spotlights, brothers having a blast together through the phenomenal days and nights. Unlike Harrison and Lennon, for Starr it was almost always fun, and he savored it for all of us.

On the first anniversary of Harrison's death, November 29, 2002, Clapton and Lynne organized the Concert for George at the Royal Albert Hall featuring Starr, McCartney, Preston, Shankar, Lynne, Petty, and Keltner. Dhani played acoustic guitar throughout the show. McCartney cracked, "Olivia said that with Dhani up on stage, it looks like George stayed young and we all got old."

HEATHER—MCCARTNEY

REC. 2001, HENSON RECORDING STUDIOS, LA, KAHNE/MCCARTNEY (PRODUCERS), MCCARTNEY (V, B, G, P), ANDERSON (BV), LABORIEL JR. (D), GABE DIXON (BV), KAHNE (SAMPLED STRINGS), RALPH MORRISON (VIOLIN), ALBUM *DRIVING RAIN*

One morning after breakfast with Mills, McCartney sat down at the piano and a wordless melody flooded out expressing how she revitalized him. The keys were tinged by the grief he still carried for Linda, only two and a half years gone, and the guilt he felt now that part of him was letting her go. The music spoke of driving into the rain of emotions stirred by bringing a new stepmother into his family. It spoke of how the dark nights of loss made the euphoria of new love even more intense.

Mills asked him what Beatles album the song was on, and he said he'd just made it up.[17] He felt so alive he considered making his next album, *Driving Rain*, a dance record, though in the end stuck to the rock he knew best.

BRAINWASHED—HARRISON

Rec. July 1999–October 2001, Friar Park, Swiss Army Studios, Switzerland, and on the road, Harrison/Lynne/Dhani Harrison (producers), Harrison (v, g, b), Lynne (electric & 12-string g, k, p), Keltner (d), Dhani Harrison (acoustic g, bv), Jon Lord (p), Sam Brown (bv), Jane Lister (harp), Bikram Ghosh (tabla), Isabella Borzymowska (spoken word), Album *Brainwashed*

In November 2001, Harrison underwent radiotherapy at New York's Staten Island University Hospital. It was there that a radiation oncologist named Dr. Gilbert Lederman became the final embodiment of all the toxic aspects of Beatlemania. He discussed Harrison's private health issues with TV crews, and brought his son into Harrison's hospital room to play guitar. Harrison was having trouble breathing and just wanted peace. "Please stop talking," Harrison said, but Lederman ignored him and asked him to autograph the guitar. Harrison said, "I do not even know if I know how to sign my name any more." So the doctor grabbed Harrison's hand and tried to lead him into spelling it out. Later, a lawsuit was filed against him and settled out of court on the condition that the guitar be destroyed.

With angry fanfare, Harrison, Dhani, Lynne, Keltner, and Jon Lord crash in for Harrison's final fiery sermon. It was as relevant as ever, released as the United States headed toward war in Iraq on the pretext of weapons of mass destruction. The song rails against all the forces that conspire to brainwash us, like a nightmarish Dr. Seuss book co-authored by Bob Dylan and Lennon circa "Working Class Hero." From the time we're born, the military, media, press, computers, mobile phones, and satellites all brainwash us to want money and status instead of the bliss of eternity. Harrison rues that they've brainwashed everyone he knows, like *Invasion of the Body Snatchers*, but he won't quit fighting. "God! God! God!" he shouts, imploring Him to show the masses the light.

Harrison then shifts tactics and tries to brainwash us himself with cleansing chants. A tranquil lady reads from yoga sutras from 150 B.C. over musicians recorded during Ravi Shankar's *Chants of India* album in 1996. At the end of the song, Harrison and Dhani chant the prayer "Namah Parvati" together.

In their 2002 obituary for Harrison, *Entertainment Weekly* gave their top five list for areas in which Harrison pioneered: staging the first large-scale charity rock concert, funding Monty Python, writing the original "Wonderwall," releasing the first triple album, and inspiring "Layla."

They missed the biggest one: More than the Beatles and the movie *Lost Horizon*, Harrison was the foremost midwife in introducing the West to the wisdom of the East. When Abram took his Hare Krishna chants to be satanic, he would almost be killed for it. Certainly Harrison indulged in far more hedonism than he did in altruistic activity, but technically the definition of a martyr is "a person who is put to death or endures great suffering on behalf of any belief, principle, or cause." Like the older Beatle he used to follow around and emulate, he was outspoken on the philosophical and religious issues that still grip us today and was grievously injured by people who perceived him to be a spiritual threat.

Meanwhile, the two Beatles who just loved performing and kept it light are still with us today, underscoring the wisdom of the old saw about not discussing politics and religion.

But Harrison stayed true to the message he'd laid out as early as 1965: Don't listen to their lies about the good life; open your eyes and think for yourself.

NOTES

1. "Beatles George's Pension Plan, DPA, 8 January 2001," Beatle City.com, www.beatlecity.com/bnews_harrison.htm (October 10, 2011).

2. Peter Doggett, *You Never Give Me Your Money* (New York: HarperCollins, 2009), 327–29.

3. "Harrison Attacker Ruled Insane," ABC News.com, November 15, 2000, http://abcnews.go.com/Entertainment/story?id=113210&page=1 (October 10, 2011).

4. Barbara Ellen, "Proper Charlie," *Observer*, July 8, 2000.

5. Katie Couric, "Interview with Olivia Harrison," November 26, 2002, transcript: http://willybrauch.de/In_Their_Own_Words/oliviaharrison.htms (October 10, 2011).

6. Larry King, "Interview with Paul McCartney and Ringo Starr," June 26, 2007, transcript: http://transcripts.cnn.com/TRANSCRIPTS/0706/26/lkl.01.html (October 10, 2011).

7. "Backbeat," Wikipedia, http://en.wikipedia.org/wiki/Backbeat_%28film%29 (October 10, 2011).

8. Chrissie Hynde, "Tears and Laughter," *USA Weekend*, October 30, 1998.

9. Peter Ames Carlin, *Paul McCartney: A Life* (New York: Touchstone, 2009), 313.

10. *Run Devil Run* album liner notes (1998).

11. John Blaney, *Lennon and McCartney: Together Alone* (London: Jawbone, 2007), 243.

12. Blaney, *Lennon and McCartney*, 252.

13. Blaney, *Lennon and McCartney*, 273.

14. Peter Doggett, *You Never Give Me Your Money* (New York: HarperCollins, 2009), 313.

15. Simon Leng, *The Music of George Harrison: While My Guitar Gently Weeps* (London: Firefly, 2003), 296.

16. "Beatles George's Pension Plan, DPA, 8 January 2001," Beatle City.com, www.beatlecity.com/bnews_harrison.htm (October 10, 2011).

17. Blaney, *Lennon and McCartney*, 257.

Paul McCartney and Ringo Starr rehearse for the David Lynch Foundation Change Begins Within Concert at New York City's Radio City Music Hall on April 4, 2009. *Getty Images*

• *12* •

2011: Ever Present Past

McCartney's dark muse inspires a third act revival, while Starr pens his memoirs through song.

As Starr turned in richly detailed reminiscences of Liverpool, McCartney dealt with his relationship with Heather Mills head on. From the euphoria of early love to the aftermath of his marriage's implosion, he wrote and performed with a startling new level of honesty and vulnerability.

The couple separated in 2006 and in 2008 the divorce was front-page news, as was the fact that McCartney had declined to get a prenuptial agreement. Mills wanted £125 million and McCartney countered with £15.8 million. She tried to prove he had over £750 million ($1.2 billion), while he maintained he had only £450 million.

To scare him into settling, Mills leaked documents that bummed out Beatles fans across the globe. Smearing him as frequently drunk and high, the worse allegations were that he stabbed her in the forearm with a broken wine glass, pushed her over a table, and pushed her in a bathtub when she was pregnant with their daughter.[1] The British papers and Mills's exes rushed to McCartney's defense, pointing out the numerous lies and embellishments in Mills's memoir and interviews.

Mills's father had been sent to prison for eighteen months for fraud. Her sister said that he could never come up with enough money and would tell them they had to find their own food and clothes themselves, so they turned to shoplifting rather than get a beating. Mills became adept at stealing food from the supermarket by the time she was ten. She was put on probation when she stole gold chains to fund a moped.

In 1986, she found her first sugar daddy in Alfie Karmal, ten years her senior, who bought her clothes, Cartier jewelry, and a breast reduction from

34E to 34C. She then told him she was going to Paris on a modeling contract, but she was really there as the mistress of a Lebanese millionaire, doing soft-core photo shoots for sex-ed manuals among other full frontal assignments. Later, she returned to England and asked Karmal to marry her, which he agreed to only on the condition that she would see a psychiatrist for eight weeks for her compulsive lying.

News of the World later maintained she worked as a call girl, with clients including the Saudi billionaire weapons dealer Adnan Khashoggi. The paper supported its allegations with an affidavit from call girl Denise Hewitt, whom they paid £50,000 for the story.[2] Hewitt said she had worked together with Mills, who often had lesbian sex as part of her job for clients. Hewitt said Mills claimed to make up to £10,000 in a single night. Khashoggi's personal secretary confirmed he had been Mills's client and said Khashoggi appreciated that she was very athletic in bed. *The Daily Mail* also found other call girls who said they worked with Mills many times. The real question is, when did McCartney learn about her past?

After Mills's attempt to smear McCartney with her leak, her PR advisor quit. The papers ranked her as one of the most hated celebrities, and at last someone supplanted Ono as the woman Beatles fans most loved to despise. Mills announced her plans to sue *The Daily Mail*, *The Sun*, and *The Evening Standard*. In response, *The Sun* listed six words with a blank box next to each one: "Hooker, Liar, Porn Star, Fantasist, Trouble Maker, Shoplifter," and noted, "It is not clear what exactly she plans to sue us about."[3]

Trying to get more money, Mills threatened to release tapes of McCartney in therapy talking about problems with Linda. The High Court put a gag order on her, threatening her with imprisonment. The judge decided McCartney's net worth was £450 million and awarded Mills £24.3 million ($35 million) on March 17, 2008, plus £35,000 a year for their daughter Beatrice's nanny and school.

The judge said Mills was "kindly" but much of her evidence was "not just inconsistent and inaccurate but also less than candid," and that she was a "less than impressive witness." On May 12, 2008, they were divorced.

Mills would go on to lose on *Dancing with the Stars*, while McCartney would find new love in Nancy Shevell. In the 1980s, McCartney and Linda had befriended Shevell (born 1960) and her husband in the Hamptons, and both Linda and Shevell faced breast cancer around the same time. After McCartney separated from Mills, Shevell divorced her husband and began seeing Macca in November 2007. In 2011, he proposed with a $650,000 1925 Cartier solitaire diamond engagement ring (as compared to the $25,500 ring he gave Mills). Again, he asked for no prenup, but Shevell was the daughter of Mike Shevell, a shipping and transportation mogul worth half a billion dollars. She was a vice president in his company and sat on the board of the Metropolitan Transportation Authority. The couple prepared a one-page document in which Shevell agreed to leave his children's trust funds alone should they split. "I just like being in love," McCartney said.

He continued to be a stunning fountain of music, prompting Dylan to say to *Rolling Stone*, "I'm in awe of McCartney. He's about the only one that I am in awe of. He can do it all. And he's never let up. . . . He's just so damn effortless."[4] Along with more classical albums (*Working Classical* [1999], *A Garland for Linda* [2000], and *Ecce Cor Meum* [2006]) and experimental records (*Liverpool Sound Collage* [2000], the Fireman's *Electric Arguments* [2008]), he released two of his best rock albums: *Chaos and Creation in the Backyard* (2005) and *Memory Almost Full* (2007), the latter of which became one of the year's top-selling albums in the United Kingdom.

Starr meanwhile had a couple of minor publicity dust-ups. He released the song and album *Liverpool 8*, then outraged his hometown when he said he didn't miss it. He also posted a bizarre video on his website on October 10, 2008.

"Peace and love, peace and love, please," he said, flashing the peace symbol he now flashed everywhere, the phrase having become his own mantra. His cartoon hippie bonhomie belied his cranky message: "Do not send fan mail to any address you have. Nothing will be signed after the 20th of October. If that has the date, it's gonna be tossed. I'm warning you with peace and love." He shoved the peace symbol aggressively into the lens. "*Peace and love. I have too much to do* so no more fan mail. Thank you, thanks and no objects to be signed. *Nothing!* Anyway, peace and love, peace and love."

He later explained on Sir Terry Wogan's *BBC Radio 2* morning show that he was irked that signing fan mail was such a time-consuming task when people were just using it to make money. "I was signing and then they were on eBay the next day. So anyway I just decided, I think I've done my share. That's it." Starr defended himself that he had already "done millions" of autographs and hadn't anticipated the negative reaction his video generated. "I honestly didn't think it was going to be world news."

It was news because forty years after breaking up, the Beatles were still the biggest sellers worldwide. In 2009 alone, they sold the third-highest number of albums of any act in the United States, according to Nielsen SoundScan, with 3.3 million copies sold. In November 2010, they sold 2 million individual songs and more than 450,000 albums in their first week of release on Apple's iTunes, and were one of the year's top ten selling artists.

A new generation discovered the Beatles through the 2006 musical *Across the Universe* and the *Rock Band* video game. Cirque du Soleil's Beatles musical, *Love*, debuted in Vegas in 2006 and was a perennial hit. More indie films came out as well, such as 2009's *Nowhere Boy* focusing on Lennon's teenage years in Liverpool.

Liverpool Hope University announced in 2009 that it was offering a major in the Beatles, and many other colleges and universities, such as New York University, offered courses on the group's music and effect on society.

Even the Vatican forgave them. In 2008, its newspaper, *L'Osservatore Romano*, issued a statement regarding Lennon's "more popular than Jesus" comment. "The remark by John Lennon, which triggered deep indignation, mainly in the United States, after many years sounds only like a 'boast' by a young working class Englishman faced with unexpected success, after growing up in the legend of Elvis and rock and roll. The fact remains that thirty-eight years after breaking up, the songs of the Lennon-McCartney brand have shown an extraordinary resistance to the passage of time, becoming a source of inspiration for more than one generation of pop musicians."

FINE LINE—MCCARTNEY

Rec. 2003–2005, RAK Studios, London, AIR Studios, London, Ocean Way Recording, LA, Nigel Godrich (producer), McCartney (v, g, b, d, p, spinet, percussion), Millennia Ensemble (strings), Single: UK 8/29/05 (20); US 8/29/05 (failed to chart), also on *Chaos and Creation in the Backyard*, Grammy nom. for 2006 Best Male Pop Vocal Performance (Fine Line), Album of the Year, Best Pop Vocal Album, Producer of the Year (Godrich)

With this song McCartney improves upon the barrelhouse piano of "Flaming Pie" with a more universal lyric, abetted by Radiohead producer Godrich's glittering sheen and uplifting strings. The album takes its title from the lyrics musing on the slim line between bravery and foolhardy mistakes, which could be referring to the artistic process or his recent marriage. But in the end, his marriage was both chaos and creation: Mills took 3–6 percent of his net worth but reinvigorated his music and gave him three albums of passion and angst. Perhaps after decades of stability, his subconscious craved drama. Above all, of course, she gave him his daughter, Beatrice.

When McCartney played the song to Godrich, he played the wrong bass note, but Godrich had him keep it in, as it fit the theme.

FADING IN AND OUT—STARR

Rec. mid 2004–early 2005, RoccaBella Studio, UK, Whatinthewhatinthe? Studio, US, Village Recorder, LA, Starkey/Hudson/Gary Burr (writers), Hudson/Starr (producers), Starr (v, d, percussion), Hudson (b, acoustic g, electric g, bv), Gary Burr (acoustic g, electric g, b, bv), Robert Randolph (lead g), Mark Mirando (electric g), Dan Higgins (horns), Gary Grant (horns), Jim Cox (horn arrangement), Single: release information not available, Album *Choose Love*: UK 7/25/05 (failed to chart); US 6/7/05 (failed to chart)

Starr always liked to work with country artists, and songwriter Gary Burr had been around since writing Juice Newton's "Love's Been a Little Bit Hard on Me" in 1982. Later he wrote for Kelly Clarkson, Ricky Martin, Christina Aguilera, and Faith Hill.

As the music looks back to his halcyon days, a jaunty Starr stares down his own mortality and resolves to make the most of the time he's got left. He muses on how ephemeral life is: one moment you're the hottest act on the planet, the next a faded footnote. Lennon once sighed, cynical and world-weary, that it was all "just showbiz." But Starr refutes that and maintains that no matter where you are in life, "the Light" never leaves you—his own subtle allusion to the faith he found after getting sober. Despite fading in and out numerous times throughout his career, losing record deals and losing friends to excessive lifestyles, he kept soldiering on. Now he's trying to figure out what it's all for, praying he's done his share of good, and encouraging people not to give up no matter how old they are.

THIS NEVER HAPPENED BEFORE—MCCARTNEY

Rec. 2003–2005, RAK Studios, London, Nigel Godrich (producer), McCartney (v, electric g, b, d, p), The Los Angeles Music Players (strings), Single: US 2005 promo to *Adult Contemporary*, also on *Chaos and Creation in the Backyard*, Film Appearance: *The Lake House* (2007)

A happier companion piece to "From a Lover to a Friend," this song puts any reservations about starting a new era with Mills behind him. Inspired by Burt Bacharach[5] and a great tune for piano bars in expensive hotels, it showed McCartney could still produce an "And I Love Her" or "My Love" all these years later.

It emphasizes the guiding theme of his life and that people shouldn't go it alone. Certainly McCartney didn't want to. After having been married thirty years, a stereotypical rockstar widower might have dated around a little longer, but only three years after Linda's death he married Mills on June 11, 2002, in Ireland.

Soon Mills was cooking meat-free Christmas dinners for the large McCartney brood. He helped her get over chocolate while she tried to get him off the weed. He donated a million to her Adopt-A-Minefield campaign against landmines and promoted it on his world tour. Their first year married, Mills suffered a miscarriage, but on October 28, 2003, they gave birth to Beatrice Milly McCartney, named after Mills's mom and McCartney's aunt.

FREE DRINKS—STARR

Rec. mid 2004–early 2005, RoccaBella Studio, UK, Whatinthewhatinthe? Studio, US, Village Recorder, LA, Starkey/Hudson/Burr/Dudas/Grakai (writers), Hudson/Starr (producers), Starr (v, d, loop), Hudson (b, acoustic g, electric g, harmonica, bv), Gary Burr (acoustic g, electric g, bv), Steve Dudas (acoustic g, electric g, bv), Dean Grakai (bv), Album *Choose Love*

A dark climax for the *Choose Love* album, "Free Drinks" glamorized Starr's playboy/*Arthur*-like lifestyle even as the sinister music hinted at madness and disaster lurking just around the corner.

Starr's usual self-empowerment reminders were nice, and the modern retro sound was cool, but one wishes Starr would offer more glimpses into his real existence like this one. Boasting about his life of sunbathing by day, blackjack and roulette by night, it shared the specificity of rappers' lyrics, of whom Courtney Love once famously compared to Bret Easton Ellis's *American Psycho* for their slavish devotion to listing all brand names. While Starr doesn't go that far, his snapshot of Chagalls on the wall of his hotel suite with a dress on the floor says it all. With his next album, *Liverpool 8*, he would get even more specific, publicly stating he was choosing to release his memoirs through songs rather than pen an autobiography.

In "Free Drinks," Starr's voice calls out through a processor like a consciousness once removed through a steady imbibement of any and all intoxicants. Musically, it's surf rock meets Ennio Morricone's spaghetti western soundtracks. The reverb, delay, and tremolo also recall the *Pulp Fiction* soundtrack or a sped-up "Wicked Game" by Chris Isaac, while the persistent beat pounds like a guy on a rager with no end in sight. Laughing, Starr sounds unhinged on absinthe or cracking up in an old black-and-white film like *The Lost Weekend* or *Reefer Madness.*

Starr jets to Spain, hooks up in a disco, then loses the woman, but it doesn't matter because there's more everywhere. He shops in Juan Les Pins, Cannes, and Saint-Tropez, and invites girls to stay at his suite in Saint Paul's Colombe D'or. In the final verse, he wakes up flying in first class, unsure where he is, but who cares? Though part of him whispers he may be heading for a fall.

TOO MUCH RAIN—MCCARTNEY

REC. 2003–2005, AIR STUDIOS, LONDON, NIGEL GODRICH (PRODUCER), MC-CARTNEY (V, G, B, D, P, AUTO HARP, MARACAS), ALBUM *CHAOS AND CREATION IN THE BACKYARD*

At the end of *Modern Times* (1936), the Tramp Charlie Chaplin sits beside homeless orphan Paulette Goddard on the side of the road in the dawn. She starts crying that there's no use in trying. "Buck up," he exhorts her. "Never say die. We'll get along!" Re-inspired, she vows to keep fighting and stands. "Smile," he reminds her. Hand in hand, they head off down the highway in one of the most iconic shots of the Great Depression.

Chaplin wrote a song for the film called "Smile," and McCartney was inspired to pen his own take on the theme for his wife Mills, who had lived through many rough periods. But while Chaplin's "Smile" has a gentle middle section that speaks of a day growing brighter, the stirring sadness of "Too Much Rain" offers no hope of a happier mood.

McCartney and Linda shared a harmonious rapport, but in Mills he found someone with a deeper well of sorrow. He tries to talk her out of her unhappiness by convincing her that she doesn't need to focus on it. Ostensibly McCartney is trying to cheer her up, but the song reflects his growing frustration in being married to a troubled woman when he just wants a cheerful life without drama. When McCartney tells her she's got to learn to laugh and vow to be happy again, it almost sounds like an ultimatum. The timeless piano, strumming acoustic guitar, and prominent bass create a true sense of drama for a moment fraught with decision.

When Mills's relationship with McCartney was new, the goal of landing him as a husband perhaps medicated bipolar tendencies with the thrill of the hunt. She boasted that men always proposed to her within ten days. Earlier whirlwind courtships had resulted in proposals in sixteen and twelve days, respectively—though at least one of the men backed out when they realized she had a compulsive lying problem. A former call girl and friend of Mills said that Mills told her she planned to tell McCartney he had to marry her or she'd leave him.

But once she'd landed him, she started complaining he was boring, with no social life. She did not like living at his isolated home in Peasmarsh, and complained that they never had parties or did anything fun; the most he ever did was sometimes go to the bar with his roadie. But McCartney was in his sixties and had already enjoyed more parties than most. He'd been a homebody for thirty years, while Mills craved distractions, perhaps from a naturally depressive state.

Originally, McCartney felt deep empathy for the damaged little girl he saw in Mills ("Jenny Wren"), but now he was drowning in her rain. McCartney and Mills separated on May 17, 2006.

RIDING TO VANITY FAIR—MCCARTNEY

Rec. 2003–2005, Ocean Way Recording, LA, Nigel Godrich (producer), McCartney (v, g, b, p, toy glockenspiel, Wurlitzer electric p), James Gadson (d), The Los Angeles Music Players (strings), album *Chaos and Creation in the Backyard*

With this song, McCartney could be continuing the "Jenny Wren" trend of referencing English lit, this time with Thackeray's *Vanity Fair*, about a social climber who marries a rich man to make it to the top. But Mills actually did give an interview to the US magazine *Vanity Fair* in 2002. It was just a few weeks before their June 11 wedding, around the same time as an incident on June 2 when McCartney yelled that he didn't want to marry her and threw her $25,500 engagement ring out a hotel window. (It was later found with a metal detector.)

McCartney recorded the song fourteen months before the couple decided to split. Godrich slowed the tempo and added foreboding studio trickery and strings. McCartney returns to the vulnerability of "Dear Friend," only now he's singing to his fiancée/wife instead of to Lennon. Realizing that Mills is a much more unpredictably volatile person than he originally perceived, he speak-sings how he chose his words carefully, strove to be gentle, and tried to laugh off her put downs, but he's finally decided he's had enough.

When he sings that he realizes she doesn't need his help anymore, he may be stating that she treated him well before they were married, but now that they tied the knot without a prenup, she's guaranteed a big chunk of money, and so she doesn't need to be nice to him anymore. Regardless, he tells her to do what she has to do (file for divorce?), but he's not going to waste time thinking about her anymore. But of course he continues to obsess. He says he wanted to have a true friendship with her, but she is not truly open to it. He sings that she doesn't fool anyone, but of course she had fooled him, and he's regretting the fact that he didn't heed the red flags during that day at *Vanity Fair* shortly before they wed.

Most of the love songs McCartney wrote when he was with Linda were happy, and of the ones that reflected periods of conflict, the woman was always mad at the singer. The blame was never on Linda, whether it was in "Lonely Pigeon," in which a husband gets kicked out of the bedroom, or in "Six O'Clock" (given to Starr), in which the husband realizes he's not working hard enough in the relationship. After thirty years with Linda, his guard was down.

Critics were surprised at how honestly the "sappy one" dealt with his crumbling relationship with Mills. The full story was as starkly chronicled as Springsteen's *Tunnel of Love*.

THE OTHER SIDE OF LIVERPOOL—STARR

REC. 2009, ROCCABELLA, UK, ROCCABELLA, LA, STARKEY/DAVE STEWART (WRITERS), STARR/BRUCE SUGAR (PRODUCERS), STARR (V, D, PERCUSSION), DAVE STEWART (ELECTRIC G), BILLY SQUIRE (G), KEITH ALLISON (G), BENMONT TENCH (O), MICHAEL BRADFORD (B), BRUCE SUGAR (K), ANNE MARIE CALHOUN (V), CINDY GOMEZ (BV), ALBUM *Y NOT*: UK 1/12/10 (FAILED TO CHART); US 1/12/10 (58)

Starr returns to the poor side of Liverpool he sang about in 1974's "Snookeroo." But that song was upbeat; this one is gritty, opening with his barmaid mother being abandoned by his father when Starr was three. He sings how he got by with help from his friends, in this case two boyhood best friends with whom he'd play in the bomb sites of World War II, pretending they were musketeers, detectives, or cowboys.

In the neighborhood of the Dingle, Starr had to join a Teddy boy gang or be beaten up. Then he'd have to go with the gang to other towns to have fights. Toughs would fight with hammers and stick razor blades behind their lapels.[6] Starr would wear a heavy belt with a sharp buckle to defend himself. He was small but could run; something that would save him from a different kind of horde in the Beatlemania years.

An escape from the gang violence was rock, which was just starting to roll. To avoid being drafted, Starr became an apprentice engineer working on the shop floor, where he met two other friends celebrated in "The Other Side of Liverpool." They'd listen to Alan Freed, hang out at the Cavern, and formed a skiffle band. Starr had learned to drum when he'd been confined to a sanatorium for two years with tuberculosis. They brought in percussion instruments for the boys to play in their beds to let off steam. Starr and his mates began playing for the factory guys at lunchtime, and moved up to clubs and weddings. He'd found his one ticket out of the factory life.

Starr sings his thank you to his friends with a new assurance; after all these decades he was pushing himself to be a better singer. Only the slightly corny female backing vocals mar the strong instrumentation featuring no less than Billy Squire alongside Dave Stewart, the highlight being the evocative organ. The album, *Y Not*, gave Starr his highest US chart appearance since 1976, at fifty-eight.

MR. BELLAMY—MCCARTNEY

Rec. October 2003–February 2007, AIR Studios, London, Hog Hill Studios, Sussex, Kahne (producer), McCartney (v, p, b, d, o, electric g), Kahne (programming), Horns/orchestra (unknown), Album *Memory Almost Full*: UK 6/4/07 (5); US 6/5/07 (3)

Mills rode McCartney to quit weed. While he was undoubtedly addicted to it, it didn't seem to hinder him from amassing between 400 and 800 million pounds, partly through owning more than 25,000 songs and movie copyrights like *Brokeback Mountain* and *Good Night and Good Luck*. In 2003, he was making 40 million pounds a year, a higher yearly income than anyone else in the United Kingdom.

When the couple separated in May 2006, there was no longer anyone around to tell Macca not to smoke—or insist he be social. Perhaps he hit the pipe with a vengeance and wrote this song about a man getting high and vowing to never come down again, now that she's no longer around to spoil his view.

But in the tradition of Beatles double meanings, McCartney also seems to be on the ledge of a skyscraper debating whether to jump. Police officers cautiously approach to talk him down, moving slow so as not to frighten him. While being free from Mills let him do what he wanted to again, it also left him distraught enough to envision jumping to his death, at least for as long it took him to write the song.

Weary horns open the cinematic tour de force of suspenseful piano and classical flourishes. McCartney asked Radiohead's Thom Yorke to play the piano, but he demurred, thinking he couldn't do the piece justice, and McCartney played it to fine effect.[7]

The press noted that the title was an anagram for "Mills Betray Me," while the album title *Memory Almost Full* was an anagram for "For My Soul Mate LLM" (Linda Louise McCartney). The "Glass Onion"/"Paul Is Dead" tea leaf readers were still out in full force—or maybe McCartney leaked the idea himself, like the old days in which he would write his album liner notes under the pseudonym Clint Harrington.

NOTHING TOO MUCH JUST OUT OF SIGHT—THE FIREMAN

Rec. 2007–2008 (in one day), Hog Hill Mill Studios, Sussex, McCartney/Youth (writers/producers), Album *Electric Arguments*: UK 11/24/08 (79); US 11/24/08 (67)

McCartney roars like a raw B. B. King or Screamin' Jay Hawkins amidst psychedelic swamp rock akin to Jimi Hendrix's "Voodoo Child (Slight Return)," alternating between trying to coax his woman to lay down beside him and raging that she's betrayed him. He could also be trying to give Joe Cocker a run for his money. McCartney loved John Belushi's *Saturday Night Live* spoof of Cocker so much that he paid the comedian to come to McCartney's birthday party and do it in person.

Macca's first experiments with techno, 1980's *McCartney II*, received mediocre response at the time, so he explored '90s ambient electronica under the pseudonym the Fireman with scant publicity for their first two albums, 1993's *Strawberries Oceans Ships Forest* and 1998's *Rushes*. His partner in the endeavor was Martin "Youth" Glover, a white guy born in Africa in 1960. An original member of the UK band Killing Joke, Youth went on to produce or remix the Verve, Primal Scream, U2, INXS, Depeche Mode, and founded Dragonfly Records, the first psychedelic trance label.

Youth also joined McCartney and the Super Furry Animals for McCartney's ambient *Liverpool Sound Collage* in 2000, which used fragments of Beatles' studio conversations set to various beats and dissonant grooves. On *The White Album* McCartney hated Lennon and Ono's "Revolution 9," but in

"Plastic Beetle" he set a similar avant-garde soundscape to sampled drums and synth loops, presumably for hipsters coming down from acid in an industrial loft at 5:30 a.m.

The Fireman's 2008 album, *Electric Arguments,* was the first to have vocals and more conventionally structured songs. As with the other albums, McCartney and Youth would do a song a day, and McCartney would improvise on the spot, sometimes with an idea of the melody and lyrics, sometimes not. McCartney was often just the vocalist, putting down his contribution, then letting Youth mix the rest, which Macca enjoyed. The album's title came from the poem "Kansas City to St. Louis" by Allen Ginsberg. McCartney dug how Ginsberg and fellow Beatles maestro William Burroughs would look at "the beauty of word combinations rather than their meaning," and how Burroughs liked to cut up passages of text and tape them back together randomly to create surreal and abstract poetry.

SOME PEOPLE—STARR

REC. MID 2004–EARLY 2005, ROCCABELLA STUDIO, UK, WHATINTHEWHATINTHE? STUDIO, US, VILLAGE RECORDER, LA, STARKEY/HUDSON/BURR/DUDAS/DEAN GRAKAL (WRITERS), HUDSON/STARR (PRODUCERS), STARR (V, O, D, AND PERCUSSION), HUDSON (B, ACOUSTIC G, BV), GARY BURR (ACOUSTIC G, BV), STEVE DUDAS (ELECTRIC G), ALBUM *CHOOSE LOVE*

"Some People" revisits the folk rock of "Weight of the World," but this time both Starr and the loved one he's singing to have learned to let go of the past. Starr's vocals could threaten to veer into an autopilot drone, and his lyrics could border on self-help triteness—reminding people to keep trying even though it's rough, etc. But the overall message bears repeating: forget the memories that are hanging you up. After a brief nod to Weezer's "Buddy Holly," the Round Heads launch into a fine instrumental break that embodies the equanimity Starr recommends, taking its time like something on side two of a Beatles or Byrds LP from 1965.

EVER PRESENT PAST—MCCARTNEY

REC. 2003, 2006–FEBRUARY 2007, HOG HILL MILL STUDIOS, SUSSEX, KAHNE (PRODUCER), MCCARTNEY (ELECTRIC G W/ TONE PEDAL VOX AC30, HOFNER B, ELECTRIC HARPSICHORD, FLUGELHORN, ACOUSTIC G, POSSIBLY CLAVIOLINE),

SINGLE: UK 11/5/07 (85); US 5/15/07 (DIDN'T CHART), ALSO ON *MEMORY ALMOST FULL*

In early 2008, as his divorce reached a crescendo, McCartney underwent a heart angioplasty. But he quickly bounced back, like the unstoppable android suggested by the fast-paced computerized music of "Ever Present Past."

Many people experience time speeding up as they get older. Some philosophers have speculated that it could be because with every passing year, a year in our life becomes a smaller fraction of the time we've experienced being alive. When we're five, every year is one-fifth of our existence. When we're sixty-five, every year is just one-sixty-fifth.

In a plaintive quaver, McCartney rues that the wild ride of his life has gone by in an instant. Now a senior citizen (!), he is still ravenous to discover new things and rushes to accomplish all he still wants to do before the hour grows too late, even at the expense of being a good lover. His nose ever to the grindstone, he reflects on the secret to his longevity and efficiency. He hung out and observed the scene, but didn't get caught up in the excesses of his fellow rockstars who went off the rails.

The video was a slick update of Robert Palmer's promo for "Addicted to Love" with McCartney and a bevy of suited beauties doing some low-key, deft dance moves in a museum.

LIVERPOOL 8—STARR

REC. 2006–2007, ROCABELLA, UK, WHATINTHEWHATINTHE? STUDIO, LA, DAVE STEWART/STARR (WRITERS/PRODUCERS), STARR (V, D, PERCUSSION), DAVID STEWART (ACOUSTIC G, ELECTRIC G), SEAN HURLEY (B), BACKING VOCALS/CLAPS: STARR, GARY BURR, STEVE DUDAS, BRENT CARPENTER, HUDSON, BRUCE SUGAR, KEITH ALLISON, ORCHESTRATION ARRANGED BY DAVID STEWART, CONDUCTED BY SUZIE KATAYAMA, SINGLE: UK 12/4/07 (99); US 1/7/08 (FAILED TO CHART), ALSO ON *LIVERPOOL 8*

Every year the European Union spotlights a city as a Capital of Culture to foster the city's renewal and raise visibility through cultural events. Liverpool was designated a Capital of Culture for 2008, and Starr headlined the opening ceremony. Two days before his *Liverpool 8* album was released, Starr sang the title track to a crowd of 20,000 atop a 100-foot platform.

Liverpool 8 was the postal zone of the Toxteth neighborhood where Starr was born. He sings about the sailors and the factories, and how he got out playing Butlin's holiday camp with Rory Storm, then onto the red lights of Hamburg, all the way to Shea Stadium. Starr got some flak for the Dr. Seuss simplicity of the rhyme scheme, but for fans the strings tug the heart as he croons like Sinatra in the evening's last spotlight. He sings that he left his hometown but always carried it with him in his soul—and certainly few icons have done as much to mythologize the city of their birth or make it such an integral part of their image. The orchestra swells and Starr leads a "Hey Jude"–esque bridge to the song's climax of crowds chanting, "Liverpool!"—custom-made for the fire works that erupted at St. George's Hall the night of the opening ceremony.

A week later he appeared on BBC's *Friday Night with Jonathan Ross* and the talk show host asked him, "Are there any things you miss about Liverpool?"

"Ahh, no." The audience laughed and Starr beamed. "No, I love Liverpool. I was a child. I grew up in Liverpool. My family members are in Liverpool. But you know. . . . "

Ross laughed, "I love your honesty."

Starr didn't expect the Liverpudlian outcry that erupted. Eventually, he commented, "I apologize to those people [who were offended], as long as they live in Liverpool, not outside. . . . No real Scouser took offense—only, I believe, people from the outside. . . . It's silly that whoever took offense took offense."

Increasing recurrence of faux pas not withstanding, perhaps the finest summary of Starr's contribution came from Beatles biographer Bob Spitz when an interviewer asked him which Beatle he liked best. "By the time I finished working on the book eight and half years later, I realized the true hero of the Beatles' story was Ringo Starr. He was a lovely guy, the other Beatles loved him unconditionally, he never had a bad word to say about anybody, he loved being a Beatle, he was a fantastic drummer, and he only ever wanted what was best for the group. And so Ringo, I think, is the true hero of this book and for me he came out at the end as really the character I could identify with the most. And, funnily enough, I found out that when the Beatles first came to the United States, they were selling those buttons, 'I love John,' 'I love Paul.' The 'I love Ringo' buttons out sold the others five to one. So maybe Ringo has all the magic of the story, maybe he isn't just the luckiest man alive."[8]

THAT WAS ME—MCCARTNEY

Rec. 2003, 2006–February 2007, Abbey Road, Hog Hill Mill Studios, Sussex, Kahne (producer), McCartney (v), Wickens (k), Anderson (lead

G), LABORIEL JR. (D), RAY (RHYTHM G, B), ALBUM *MEMORY ALMOST FULL*: UK 6/4/07 (5); US 6/5/07 (3), GRAMMY: LIVE VERSION ON *AMOEBA'S SECRET* NOM. FOR 2009 BEST MALE POP VOCAL PERFORMANCE; ALSO FROM *AMOEBA'S SECRET*, I SAW HER STANDING THERE NOM. FOR BEST SOLO ROCK VOCAL PERFORMANCE

McCartney's touring band backs him for this strong retro rocker in the vein of "Crazy Little Thing Called Love" or the first song he played when he met Lennon, "Twenty Flight Rock." McCartney looks back in amazement over his life, with memories both universal (scout camp, school plays, the beach, the altar) and specific to him (the Cavern Club, on TV with the band), crying out, "That was me!" with justifiable pride.

VINTAGE CLOTHES—MCCARTNEY

REC. 2003, 2006–FEBRUARY 2007, ABBEY ROAD, HOG HILL MILL STUDIOS, SUSSEX, KAHNE (PRODUCER), MCCARTNEY (V, MELLOTRON), WICKENS (K), ANDERSON (LEAD G), LABORIEL JR. (D), RAY (RHYTHM G, B), ALBUM *MEMORY ALMOST FULL*

As "Vintage Clothes" opens with a ringing, unfettered piano that sounds like it could be from 1970, McCartney exhorts us not to live in the past, then celebrates wearing vintage clothes, the conundrum of his life as he plowed ever forward.

He sums up the Beatles' appeal in the early days: running and leaping with irrepressible joie de vivre, uncaring that they "looked like girls," inspiring millions to crack the conformity of squares. And he's still joyful as the Beatles perennially come back into fashion and their music continues to break sales records on iTunes.

Even as their albums became more preoccupied with memories, both Mc-Cartney and Starr made some of their best music yet. They were determined to maximize their time left, living in the past and the present simultaneously.

NOTES

1. Jon Clements, "Can We Believe Heather This Time?" *Daily Mirror*, October 19, 2006.

2. Matt Born, "Heather Was a High-Class Hooker Paid Thousands," *Daily Mail*, June 12, 2006.

3. Tara Conlan, "*Sun* Turns Up the Heat on Mills McCartney," *Guardian*, July 25, 2011.

4. Jann Wenner, "Bob Dylan Hits the Big Themes, from Religion to the Atomic Age," *Rolling Stone*, May 2007.

5. John Blaney, *Lennon and McCartney: Together Alone* (London: Jawbone, 2007), 273.

6. The Beatles, *The Beatles Anthology* (San Francisco: Chronicle Books, 2000), 37.

7. Spin.com, "Thom Yorke Declines Duet with Paul McCartney," *Spin*, November 13, 2007.

8. "The Beatles Biographer Bob Spitz Interview (part 1) with Face Culture," YouTube, www.youtube.com/watch?v=8BdxR81W34g (accessed October 10, 2011).

Epilogue: Further Listening

**** *Songs that would have made the top tier had space allowed.*
*** *Solid hits or strong deep cuts.*
** *For hardcore fans only.*
* *Historical curiosities or guilty pleasures.*

1970

Coochy Coochy/*Beaucoups of Blues* ★★
$15 Draw/*Beaucoups of Blues* (Starr) ★★★½
If Not for You/*All Things Must Pass* (Harrison) ★★★
The Art of Dying/*All Things Must Pass* ★★½
Let It Down/*All Things Must Pass* ★★½
Beware of Darkness/*All Things Must Pass* ★★½
I'd Have You Anytime/*All Things Must Pass* ★★½
I Live for You/*All Things Must Pass 30th Anniversary* ★★★
Look at Me/*John Lennon/Plastic Ono Band* ★★★½
Love/*John Lennon/Plastic Ono Band* ★★★
Well Well Well/*John Lennon/Plastic Ono Band* ★★

1971

Eat at Home/*Ram* ★★★
Long Haired Lady/*Ram* (McCartney) ★★★
Smile Away/*Ram* ★★
Heart of the Country/*Ram* ★★
3 Legs/*Ram* ★½
Get on the Right Thing/Recorded during *Ram*, released on *Red Rose Speed-way* ★★½
Little Lamb Dragonfly/Recorded during Ram, released on *Red Rose Speed-way* ★★
A Love for You/Recorded during Ram, released on the *In Laws* soundtrack 2003 ★★
How Do You Sleep/*Imagine* (Lennon) ★★½
I Don't Want to Be a Solider/*Imagine* ★★½
Some People Never Know/*Wild Life* (McCartney) ★★★
Wild Life/*Wild Life* ★★
Bangladesh (Live)/*The Concert for Bangladesh* (Harrison) ★★

1972

Give Ireland Back to the Irish/Single (McCartney) ★½
Mary Had a Little Lamb/Single (McCartney) ★★
Little Woman Love/B-side of Mary Had a Little Lamb ★★★
Attica State/Some Time in New York City (Lennon) ★★½
Seaside Woman/Single by Suzy and the Red Stripes (McCartney) ★★★

1973

Single Pigeon/*Red Rose Speedway* ★★★½
Big Barn Bed/*Red Rose Speedway* ★★½
One More Kiss/*Red Rose Speedway* ★★
The Mess/B-side of My Love (McCartney) ★★★½
I Lie Around (Denny Laine lead vocal)/B-side of Live and Let Die ★★★
Sue Me Sue You Blues/*Living in the Material World* (Harrison) ★★★½
The Day the World Gets 'Round/*Living in the Material World* ★★★
The Light That Lighted the World/*Living in the Material World* ★★★
Try Some Buy Some/*Living in the Material World* ★★

Miss O'Dell/B-side of Give Me Love (Give Me Peace on Earth) (Harrison) ★★★
Six O'Clock/*Ringo* ★★★½
I Know (I Know)/*Mind Games* (Lennon) ★★★
Meat City/*Mind Games* ★★★
Tight A$/*Mind Games* ★★★
Aisumasen/*Mind Games* ★★½
You Are Here/*Mind Games* ★★
No Words/*Band on the Run* ★★★½
Mamunia/*Band on the Run* ★★★
Since My Baby Left Me/produced 1973, released on *Menlove Ave.* (1986) ★★★
Be My Baby/produced 1973, released on *John Lennon Anthology* (1998) ★★

1974

Lucille/A Toot and a Snore in '74/recorded March 28, 1974/Bootleg; see
    YouTube (Lennon and McCartney) ★★
Old Dirt Road/*Walls and Bridges* (Lennon) ★★★½
Steel and Glass/*Walls and Bridges* ★★★
Bless You/*Walls and Bridges* ★★★
Only You (And You Alone)/*Goodnight Vienna* (Starr) ★★
The No No Song/*Goodnight Vienna* ★★
I Saw Her Standing There/Lennon & Elton John Live 11/28/74, released on
    Lennon boxed set 1990 ★★
Simply Shady/*Dark Horse* (Harrison) ★★★½
Hari on Tour/*Dark Horse* ★★½
Ding Dong/*Dark Horse* ★

1975

Rip It Up/Ready Teddy/*Rock 'n' Roll* (Lennon) ★★★
Bony Maronie/*Rock 'n' Roll* ★★★
Bring It on Home to Me/*Rock 'n' Roll* ★★★
Peggy Sue/*Rock 'n' Roll* ★★½
Be Bop a Lula/*Rock 'n' Roll* ★★½
Move Over, Ms. L/B-side of Stand by Me ★★★
Magneto and Titanium Man/*Venus and Mars* ★★★
Venus and Mars-Rock Show/*Venus and Mars* (McCartney) ★★½
Letting Go/*Venus and Mars* ★★
Fame/David Bowie Single (Lennon) ★★★½
You/*Extra Texture* (Harrison) ★★★

1976

San Ferry Anne/*Wings at the Speed of Sound* (McCartney) ★★★
Beware My Love/*Wings at the Speed of Sound* ★★
A Dose of Rock 'n' Roll/*Ringo's Rotogravure* ★★½
Hey Baby/*Ringo's Rotogravure* ★★½
Cookin'/*Ringo's Rotogravure* ★★½
Las Brisas/*Ringo's Rotogravure* ★★
Woman Don't You Cry for Me/*Thirty Three & 1/3* (Harrison) ★★★
Crackerbox Palace/*Thirty Three & 1/3* ★★★
True Love/*Thirty Three & 1/3* ★★
Here Comes the Sun/*Saturday Night Live* (Harrison & Paul Simon) ★★★

1977

Out on the Streets/*Ringo the 4th* ★★½
Drowning in the Sea of Love/*Ringo the 4th* ★★
Tango All Night/*Ringo the 4th* ★½
Can She Do It Like She Dances/*Ringo the 4th* ★

1978

Girlfriend/*London Town* (McCartney) ★★½

1979

Soft-Hearted Hannah/*George Harrison* ★★★
Love Comes to Everyone/*George Harrison* ★★
Not Guilty/*George Harrison* ★★
Faster/*George Harrison* ★★
Goodnight Tonight/Single (McCartney) ★★
Daytime Nighttime Suffering/B-side of Goodnight Tonight ★★★
Arrow through Me/*Back to the Egg* (McCartney) ★½
Rockestra Theme/*Back to the Egg* ★½
Wonderful Christmastime/Single ★★

1980

Waterfalls/*McCartney II* ★★
Coming Up (Live)/*McCartney II* ★★
On the Way/*McCartney II* ★★
Check My Machine/*McCartney II* ★½

1981

Lay His Head/recorded for *Somewhere in England*, released as B-side to Got
    My Mind Set on You ★★
Teardrops/*Somewhere in England* (Harrison) ★★
Wrack My Brain/*Stop and Smell the Roses* (Starr) ★★

1982

Ballroom Dancing/*Tug of War* (McCartney) ★★★½
Ebony and Ivory/*Tug of War* ★★★
Tug of War/*Tug of War* ★★★
The Girl Is Mine/*Tug of War* ★★½
Rainclouds/B-side of Ebony and Ivory ★★★
That's the Way It Goes/*Gone Troppo* (Harrison) ★★★

1983

The Man/*Pipes of Peace* (McCartney) ★★★½
Say Say Say/*Pipes of Peace* ★★★
Pipes of Peace/*Pipes of Peace* ★★½
So Bad/*Pipes of Peace* ★★

1984

Not Such a Bad Boy/*Give My Regards to Broad Street* (McCartney) ★★
We All Stand Together/Single (McCartney) ★★
Abandoned Love/Bootleg; see YouTube (Harrison) ★★★

1985

Spies Like Us/Single (McCartney) ★½

1986

Pretty Little Head/*Press to Play* (McCartney) ★★★
Write Away/*Press to Play* ★★½
Press/*Press to Play* ★★
Only Love Remains/*Press to Play* ★★

1987

Wreck of the Hesperus/*Cloud Nine* ★★★
Cloud Nine/*Cloud Nine* (Harrison) ★★½
Once Upon a Long Ago/Single (McCartney) ★★★

1989

My Brave Face/Bootleg acoustic version; see YouTube (McCartney/
  Costello) ★★★½
Don't Be Careless Love/Bootleg acoustic version; see YouTube (McCartney/
  Costello) ★★★½
You Want Her Too/Bootleg acoustic version; see YouTube (McCartney/
  Costello) ★★★½
This One/*Flowers in the Dirt* (McCartney) ★★★
Distractions/*Flowers in the Dirt* ★★★
OuEst Le Soleil/*Flowers in the Dirt* ★★★
That Day Is Done/*Flowers in the Dirt* ★★
Flying to My Home/B-side of My Brave Face (McCartney) ★★★½

1990

New Blue Moon/*Traveling Wilburys Vol. 3* ★★★
Inside Out/*Traveling Wilburys Vol. 3* ★★★

1991

Singin' the Blues/*Unplugged* (McCartney) ★★★½

1992

What Goes Around/*Time Takes Time* (Starr) ★★★
Golden Blunders/*Time Takes Time* ★★★
Don't Know a Thing (About Love)/*Time Takes Time* ★★½

1993

Off the Ground/*Off the Ground* (Paul McCartney) ★★★
I Owe It All to You/*Off the Ground* ★★½
Winedark Open Sea/*Off the Ground* ★★½
Absolutely Sweet Marie (Live)/*Bob Dylan 30th Anniversary Celebration* (Harrison) ★★★

1997

Flaming Pie/*Flaming Pie* ★★★
Calico Skies/*Flaming Pie* ★★½
If You Wanna/*Flaming Pie* ★★½
Great Day/*Flaming Pie* ★★

1998

One/*Vertical Man* (Starr) ★★½

2001

Driving Rain/*Driving Rain* (McCartney) ★★★
I Do/*Driving Rain* ★★
Lonely Road/*Driving Rain* ★★
Back in the Sunshine/*Driving Rain* ★★
Freedom/Single (McCartney) ★½
A Horse to the Water/*Jools Holland's Small World, Big Band* (Harrison) ★★½

2002

Rising Sun/*Brainwashed* (Harrison) ★★★★
Marwa Blues/*Brainwashed* ★★★
Rocking Chair in Hawaii/*Brainwashed* ★★½
Stuck Inside a Cloud/*Brainwashed* ★★

2005

English Tea/*Chaos and Creation in the Backyard* (McCartney) ★★★
Friends to Go ★★
A Certain Softness/*Chaos and Creation in the Backyard* ★★

2007

Dance Tonight/*Memory Almost Full* (McCartney) ★★½
Only Mama Knows/*Memory Almost Full* ★★½

2008

Sing the Changes/*Electric Arguments* (McCartney) ★★½
Sun Is Shining/*Electric Arguments* ★★★

2010

Everyone Wins/*Y Not* (Starr) ★★
Walk with You/*Y Not* ★★

2011

Best Love/*Rare Bird Alert* (Paul McCartney guest spot on Steve Martin blue-
    grass album) ★★★½

Appendix A: Solo Beatles No. 1 Singles

In 2000, the Beatles released the album *1*, which gathered every single by the band that had topped the charts in either the United States or the United Kingdom. The collection itself went on to top the charts across the globe and became the best-selling CD of the twenty-first century, to date having sold over thirty-one million copies. It is the seventh best-selling album since 1991, the year Billboard revised its chart system.

In 2002, Elvis's estate followed suit with *Elvis 30 #1 Hits*, noting on the liner notes, "Before anyone did anything, Elvis did everything!" Indeed, Elvis had thirty number ones, whereas the Beatles had twenty-seven.

The solo Beatles had twenty number ones on either the U.S. or U.K. charts, bookended by Harrison's "My Sweet Lord," which topped the charts in 1970 and then returned to the number-one position after his death in 2002.

McCartney had eleven number ones, Lennon four, Harrison three, and Starr two. Of Lennon's four, only "Whatever Gets You thru the Night" was number one in his lifetime. "Imagine" topped the charts ten years after its initial release in 1971.

Technically, McCartney is tied with Starr for only two number-one singles in his own name ("Coming Up" and "Pipes of Peace") because his others were either credited to Paul and Linda McCartney ("Uncle Albert/Admiral Halsey"), Paul McCartney and Wings ("My Love," "Band on the Run"), Wings ("Listen to What the Man Said," "Silly Love Songs," "With a Little Luck," "Mull of Kintyre"), Paul McCartney and Stevie Wonder ("Ebony and Ivory") or Paul McCartney and Michael Jackson ("Say, Say, Say").

Three of the hits in this compilation ("Ebony and Ivory," "Say Say Say," and "Pipes of Peace") I did not profile in the book because they epitomize the McCartney stereotype I have tried to provide a corrective to:

281

soft, slick, synth tinged, and borderline saccharine. But on their own, the songs themselves are fine—affecting even, if you're in the right mood. Two of them reflect his attempt to veer away from "Silly Love Songs" and get back to "Let It Be" statements in the aftermath of Lennon's murder. They represent the last time he was on top of the singles charts (and thus truly a part of the young generation's zeitgeist).

Solo Beatles No. 1 Singles

1. My Sweet Lord
2. Uncle Albert/Admiral Halsey
3. Imagine
4. My Love
5. Give Me Love (Give Me Peace on Earth)
6. Photograph
7. You're Sixteen
8. Band on the Run
9. Whatever Gets You thru the Night
10. Listen to What the Man Said
11. Silly Love Songs
12. Mull of Kintyre
13. With a Little Luck
14. Coming Up (Live)
15. (Just Like) Starting Over
16. Woman
17. Ebony and Ivory
18. Say Say Say
19. Pipes of Peace
20. Got My Mind Set on You

Appendix B: 1970–2011 Anthology (The Yellow, Green, and Indigo Albums)

*I*n 1973, the Beatles authorized Allen Klein to compile a retrospective of their career in order to compete with a successful bootleg named *Alpha-Omega*. The resulting collection was released as two double-albums, *1962–1966* and *1967–1970*, commonly referred to as *The Red Album* and *The Blue Album*, with fifty-four songs total. *1962–1966* topped the charts in the United Kingdom and *1967–1970* in the United States (before being supplanted by McCartney's *Red Rose Speedway*).

This anthology of the solo Beatles era was compiled in the same tradition. The solo Beatles had fifty-six top-ten hits, and a four-record anthology could have been compiled with just those songs, but there were some classics that didn't make it that high on the chart ("Mind Games" and "Stand by Me," for example), so the overview was expanded to three volumes.

Three top ten hits were omitted because they would be of interest to completists only: "Bangla Desh," "Mary Had a Little Lamb," and the deathless "Spies Like Us."

Sixteen of the songs below were hits but not profiled in the book because in this author's opinion they were not quite the artists' best. These include "Only You," "Venus and Mars/Rock Show," "You," "Crackerbox Palace," "Maybe I'm Amazed (Live)," "Wonderful Christmastime," "Goodnight Tonight," "Rockestra," "Waterfalls," "Ebony and Ivory," "The Girl Is Mine," "Say Say Say," "Pipes of Peace," "We All Stand Together," "Once Upon a Long Ago," and "This One."

1969–1974 (The Yellow Album)

Side One
1. Give Peace a Chance
2. Instant Karma
3. Maybe I'm Amazed
4. My Sweet Lord
5. What Is Life
6. Another Day
7. Power to the People

Side Two
1. It Don't Come Easy
2. Imagine
3. Uncle Albert/Admiral Halsey
4. Hi Hi Hi
5. Back Off Boogaloo
6. My Love
7. Happy Xmas (War Is Over)

Side Three
1. Give Me Love (Give Me Peace on Earth)
2. Live and Let Die
3. Mind Games
4. Helen Wheels
5. You're Sixteen
6. Jet
7. Photograph

Side Four
1. Band on the Run
2. Whatever Gets You thru the Night
3. Oh My My
4. Junior's Farm
5. Dark Horse
6. Only You *Starr*
7. #9 Dream

1975–1983 (The Green Album)

Side One
1. Listen to What the Man Said
2. The No No Song

3. Venus and Mars/Rock Show *McCartney*
4. Stand by Me
5. Silly Love Songs
6. You *Harrison*
7. Let 'Em In

Side Two
1. Maybe I'm Amazed (Live) *McCartney*
2. Crackerbox Palace *Harrison*
3. Mull of Kintyre
4. With a Little Luck
5. Blow Away
6. Wonderful Christmastime *McCartney*
7. Rockestra *McCartney*

Side Three
1. Goodnight Tonight *McCartney*
2. Coming Up
3. (Just Like) Starting Over
4. Waterfalls *McCartney*
5. Woman
6. Watching the Wheels

Side Four
1. All Those Years Ago
2. Take It Away
3. Ebony and Ivory *McCartney*
4. The Girl Is Mine *McCartney*
5. Say Say Say *McCartney*
6. Pipes of Peace *McCartney*

1984–2005 (The Indigo Album)

Side One
1. Nobody Told Me
2. No More Lonely Nights
3. Borrowed Time
4. We All Stand Together *McCartney*
5. I'm Stepping Out
6. Once Upon a Long Ago *McCartney*

Side Two
1. Got My Mind Set on You
2. My Brave Face
3. When We Was Fab
4. This One *McCartney*
5. Handle with Care
6. Put It There
7. End of the Line

Side Three
1. Weight of the World
2. Hope of Deliverance
3. Free as a Bird
4. Real Love
5. Young Boy
6. Beautiful Night
7. Flaming Pie

Side Four
1. No Other Baby
2. From a Lover To a Friend
3. Any Road
4. Never without You
5. Jenny Wren
6. Fine Line
7. Liverpool 8

Album Discography

$\mathscr{O}$f the songs included in this book (listed below in bold):

- Ten came from *All Things Must Pass*.
- Eight from *Imagine* and *Band on the Run*.
- Seven from *Plastic Ono Band*, *Ram*, and *Walls and Bridges*.
- Six from *Double Fantasy*, *Cloud Nine*, and *Chaos and Creation in the Backyard*.
- Five from *Milk and Honey* and *Brainwashed*.
- Four from *McCartney*, *Mind Games*, *Ringo*, *Tug of War*, *Time Takes Time*, and *Memory Almost Full*.
- Three from *Wild Life*, *Some Time in New York City*, *Rock 'n' Roll*, *London Town*, *Traveling Wilburys Vol. 1*, *Flowers in the Dirt*, *Flaming Pie*, *Run Devil Run*, *Driving Rain*, and *Choose Love*.
- Two from *Living in the Material World*, *Goodnight Vienna*, *Venus and Mars*, *Wings at the Speed of Sound*, *Thirty Three and 1/3*, *Old Wave*, and *Off the Ground*.
- One from *Beaucoups of Blues*, *The Concert for Bangladesh*, *Red Rose Speedway*, *Dark Horse*, *George Harrison*, *Somewhere in England*, *McCartney II*, *Stop and Smell the Roses*, *Give My Regards to Broad Street*, *Press to Play*, *Anthology 1*, *Anthology 2*, *John Lennon Anthology*, *Ringo Rama*, *Liverpool 8*, *Electric Arguments*, and *Y Not*.

The remaining tracks came from thirteen nonalbum A-sides, eight nonalbum B-sides, and one bootleg (see Singles Discography). Most are available on various "best of" compilations.

287

Key: L = Lennon; M = McCartney; H = Harrison; S = Starr; 0 = did not chart

1970

Sentimental Journey (S) UK 3/27/70 (7); US (22)

McCartney UK 4/7/70 (2); US 4/20/70 (1): **Maybe I'm Amazed, Man We Was Lonely, Junk, Every Night**

Beaucoups of Blues (S) UK 9/25/70 (did not chart); US 10/5/70 (65): **Beaucoups of Blues**

All Things Must Pass (H) UK 11/27/70 (1); US 11/27/70 (1), Grammy nom. for Album of the Year: **My Sweet Lord, What Is Life, All Things Must Pass, Apple Scruffs, Isn't It a Pity, Awaiting on You All, Hear Me Lord, Run of the Mill, Behind That Locked Door, Ballad of Sir Frankie Crisp (Let It Roll)**

John Lennon/Plastic Ono Band UK 12/11/70 (8); US 12/11/70 (6): **Mother, God, Working Class Hero, I Found Out, Remember, Isolation, Hold On**

1971

Ram (Paul & Linda McCartney) UK 5/21/71 (1); US 5/17/71 (2): **Uncle Albert/Admiral Halsey, Another Day, The Back Seat of My Car, Monkberry Moon Delight, Too Many People, Dear Boy, Ram On**

Imagine (L) UK 10/7/71 (1); US 9/9/71 (1): **Imagine, Jealous Guy, It's So Hard, Oh Yoko!, Gimme Some Truth, Crippled Inside, How?, Oh My Love**

Wild Life (Wings) UK 11/15/71 (8); 12/6/71 (10): **Love Is Strange, Dear Friend, Tomorrow**

The Concert for Bangladesh (H): UK 1/10/72 (1); US 12/20/71 (2), Grammy win Album of the Year: **Wah-Wah**

1972

Some Time in New York City (Lennon with Yoko Ono) UK 9/15/72 (11); US 6/12/72 (48): **New York City, Woman Is the Nigger of the World, Angela**

1973

Red Rose Speedway (Paul McCartney & Wings) UK 5/3/73 (4); US 4/30/73
(1): **My Love**

Living in the Material World (H) UK 5/30/73 (2); US 5/30/73 (1): **Give Me
Love (Give Me Peace on Earth), Don't Let Me Wait Too Long**

Ringo (S) UK 11/23/73 (7); US 11/2/73 (2): **I'm the Greatest, You're
Sixteen, Photograph, Oh My My**

Mind Games (L) UK 11/16/73 (13); US 11/2/73: **Mind Games, Bring On
the Lucie (Freeda Peeple), Only People, Out the Blue**

Band on the Run (Paul McCartney & Wings) UK 11/30/73 (1); US 12/3/73
(1), Grammy win for Best Engineering, nom. for Album of the Year:
**Helen Wheels, Jet, Band on the Run, Let Me Roll It, Nineteen
Hundred and Eighty Five, Mrs. Vandebilt, Picasso's Last Words,
Country Dreamer**

1974

Walls and Bridges (L) UK 10/4/74 (6); US 9/26/74 (1): **Whatever Gets You
Thru the Night, Surprise Surprise (Sweet Bird of Paradox), Scared,
Nobody Loves You (When You're Down and Out), #9 Dream,
Going Down On Love, What You Got**

Goodnight Vienna (S) UK 11/15/74 (30); US 11/15/74 (8): **Snookeroo, (It's
All Down To) Goodnight Vienna**

Dark Horse (Harrison) UK 12/20/74 (did not chart); US 12/9/74 (4): **Dark
Horse**

1975

Rock 'n' Roll (L) UK 2/21/75 (6); US 2/17/75 (6); Re-entry: UK 1/17/81
(64): **Stand by Me, Slippin' and Slidin', Ain't That a Shame**

Venus and Mars (Wings) UK 5/30/75 (1); US 5/27/75 (1): **Listen to What
the Man Says, You Gave Me the Answer**

Extra Texture (Read All About It) (H) UK 10/3/75 (16); US 9/22/75 (8): **This
Guitar (Can't Keep from Crying)**

1976–1979

Wings at the Speed of Sound UK 3/26/76 (2); US 3/22/76 (1): **Let 'Em In, Silly Love Songs**

Ringo's Rotogravure UK 9/17/76 (did not chart); US 9/17/76 (28)

Thirty Three and 1/3 (H) UK 11/19/76 (35); US 11/24/76 (11): **This Song, Beautiful Girl**

Wings over America (live) UK 12/10/76 (8); US 12/10/76 (1)

Ram (instrumental version) (Percy "Thrills" Thrillington/M) UK 4/29/77 (did not chart); US 5/16/77 (did not chart)

Ringo the 4th UK 9/30/77 (did not chart); 9/30/77 (162)

London Town (Wings) UK 3/31/78 (4); US 3/27/78 (2): **Café on the Left Bank, With a Little Luck, London Town**

Bad Boy (S) UK 4/21/78 (did not chart); US 6/16/78 (129)

George Harrison UK 2/23/79 (39); US 2/23/79 (14): **Blow Away**

Back to the Egg (Wings) 6/8/79 (4); 6/11/79 (8)

1980–1985

McCartney II UK 5/16/80 (1); US 5/26/80 (3): **Coming Up**

Double Fantasy (Lennon with Yoko Ono) UK 11/17/80 (1); US 11/17/80 (1), Grammy win Album of the Year: **(Just Like) Starting Over, Woman, Dear Yoko, Beautiful Boy, Watching the Wheels, Cleanup Time**

Somewhere in England (H) UK 6/5/81 (13); US 6/5/81 (11): **All Those Years Ago**

Stop and Smell the Roses (S) UK 11/20/81 (did not chart); US 11/20/81 (98): **Attention**

Tug of War (M) UK 4/26/82 (1); US 4/26/82 (1), Grammy nom. for Album of the Year: **Take It Away, The Pound Is Sinking, Wanderlust, Here Today**

Gone Troppo (H) UK 11/5/82 (did not chart); 11/5/82 (108)

Old Wave (S) June 1983; unreleased in UK or US: **In My Car, Picture Show Life**

Pipes of Peace (M) UK 10/31/83 (4); US 10/31/83 (15)

Milk and Honey (Lennon with Yoko Ono) UK 1/23/84 (3); US 1/23/84 (11): **Borrowed Time, I'm Stepping Out, I Don't Wanna Face It, Grow Old with Me, Nobody Told Me**

Give My Regards to Broad Street (M) UK 10/22/84 (1); 10/22/84 (21): **No More Lonely Nights**

1986–1989

Press to Play (M) UK 9/1/86 (8); US 8/25/86 (30): **Move Over Busker**
Cloud Nine (Harrison) UK 11/2/87 (10); US 11/2/87 (8): **Got My Mind Set on You, When We Was Fab, Devil's Radio, That's What It Takes, This Is Love, Fish On the Sand**
Traveling Wilburys Vol. 1 UK 10/18/88 (16); US 10/18/88 (3), Grammy nom. for Album of the Year, won Best Rock Performance by a Duo or Group: **Handle with Care, End of the Line, Heading for the Light**
CHOBa B CCCP (M) released USSR 10/31/88; UK 9/30/91 (63); US 10/29/91 (did not chart)
Flowers in the Dirt (M) UK 6/5/89 (1); US 6/6/89 (21): **My Brave Face, Figure of Eight, Put It There**

1990–1999

Traveling Wilburys Vol. 3 UK 10/29/90 (14); US 10/29/90 (11)
Unplugged (The Official Bootleg) (M) UK 5/13/91 (7); US 6/4/91 (14)
Paul McCartney's Liverpool Oratorio (with Carl Davis/classical) UK 11/7/91 (36); US 10/22/91 (177)
Live in Japan (Harrison) UK 7/13/92 (did not chart); US 7/13/92 (126)
Time Takes Time (S) 5/22/92 (did not chart UK or US): **After All These Years, Don't Go Where the Road Don't Go, Weight of the World, I Don't Believe You**
Off the Ground (M) UK 2/2/93 (5); US 2/9/93 (17): **Hope of Deliverance, Get Out of My Way**
Strawberries Oceans Ships Forest (The Fireman/M/experimental) UK 11/15/93 (did not chart); US 2/22/94 (did not chart)
Anthology 1 (The Beatles) UK 11/20/95 (2); US 11/20/95 (1): **Free as a Bird**
Anthology 2 (The Beatles) UK 3/18/96 (1); US 3/18/96 (2): **Real Love**
Flaming Pie (M) UK 5/5/97 (1); US 5/27/97 (2): **Young Boy, The Song We Were Singing, Beautiful Night**, Grammy nom. for Album of the Year
Standing Stone (M/classical) UK 10/6/97 (classical 1); US 9/23/97 (classical 1)
Vertical Man (S) UK 6/15/98 (85); US 6/15/98 (61)
Rushes (The Fireman/M/experimental) UK 9/21/98 (did not chart); US 10/20/98 (did not chart)
John Lennon Anthology UK 11/2/98 (62); US 11/3/98 (99): **I'm Losing You**
Run Devil Run (M) UK 10/4/99 (12); US 10/5/99 (27): **Party, No Other Baby, Shake a Hand**
Working Classical (M/classical) UK 10/18/99 (classical 2); US 10/19/99 (1)

2000–2011

Liverpool Sound Collage (M/experimental) UK 8/21/00 (did not chart); US 9/26/00 (did not chart)

Driving Rain (M) UK 11/12/01 (46); US 11/13/01 (26): **From a Lover to a Friend, Your Way, Heather**

Brainwashed (H) UK 11/18/02 (29); US 11/18/02 (18), Grammy nom. for Best Pop Vocal Album: **Any Road, Looking for My Life, Between the Devil and the Deep Blue Sea, Pisces Fish, Brainwashed**

Ringo Rama UK 3/24/03 (did not chart); US 3/24/03 (113)

Choose Love (S) UK 7/25/05 (did not chart); US 6/7/05 (did not chart): **Fading In and Out, Free Drinks, Some People**

Twin Freaks (M/Freelance Hellraiser/experimental) UK only 6/13/05 (did not chart)

Chaos and Creation in the Backyard (M) UK 9/12/05 (10), US 9/13/05 (6), Grammy nom. for Album of the Year, Best Pop Vocal Album, Producer of the Year (Godrich): **Jenny Wren, Anyway, Fine Line, This Never Happened Before, Too Much Rain, Riding to Vanity Fair**

Ecce Cor Meum (M/classical) UK 9/25/06 (classical 2); US 9/25/06 (classical 2)

Memory Almost Full (M) UK 6/4/07 (5); US 6/5/07 (3): **Mr. Bellamy, Ever Present Past, That Was Me, Vintage Clothes**

Liverpool 8 (S) UK 1/14/08 (91); US 1/14/08 (94): **Liverpool 8**

Electric Arguments (The Fireman/M/experimental) UK 11/24/08 (79); US 11/24/08 (67): **Nothing Too Much Just out of Sight**

Y Not (S) 1/12/10 (did not chart); US 1/12/10 (58): **The Other Side of Liverpool**

Ocean's Kingdom (M/classical) UK 10/3/11; US 10/4/11

Singles Discography

$\mathcal{O}$f the nonalbum singles included in this book:

- Lennon had five A-sides (*Give Peace a Chance, Cold Turkey, Instant Karma, Power to the People,* and *Happy Xmas* [*War Is Over*]).
- McCartney had four A-sides (*Hi Hi Hi, Live and Let Die, Junior's Farm, Mull of Kintyre*), six B-sides (*Oh Woman, Oh Why, C Moon, Mama's Little Girl, Sally G, Girls' School, Back on My Feet*), and one bootleg track (*Yvonne's the One*).
- Harrison had two A-sides (*I Don't Want to Do It, Cheer Down*) and one B-side (*Poor Little Girl*).
- Starr had two A-sides (*It Don't Come Easy, Back off Boogaloo*) and one B-side (*Early 1970*).

These tracks are available on various "best of" compilations, except for McCartney's B-sides and bootleg. Hopefully he will rectify this with a compilation soon; until then, there is YouTube, Amazon, and eBay.

Songs featured in this book are in bold. Key: L = Lennon; M = McCartney; H = Harrison; S = Starr; ★ = Yoko Ono track; 0 = did not chart

1969

Give Peace a Chance b/w Remember Love★ (L) UK 7/4/69 (2); US 7/21/69 (14)

Cold Turkey b/w Don't Worry Kyoko★ (L) UK 10/24/69 (14); US 10/20/69 (30)

1970

Instant Karma b/w Who Has Seen the Wind★ (L) UK 2/6/70 (5); US
2/20/70 (3)

Beaucoups of Blues b/w Coochy Coochy (S) US only 9/5/70 (87)

Mother b/w Why★ (L) US only 12/28/70 (43)

My Sweet Lord b/w **What Is Life** (UK)/**Isn't It a Pity** (US) (H) UK
1/15/71 (1); US 11/23/70 (1)

1971

What Is Life Single b/w **Apple Scruffs** (H) US only 2/15/71 (10)

Another Day b/w **Oh Woman Oh Why** (M) UK 2/19/71 (2); US
2/22/71 (5)

Power to the People b/w Open Your Box★ (L) UK 3/12/71 (7); US
3/22/71 (11)

It Don't Come Easy b/w **Early 1970** (S) UK 4/9/71 (4); US 4/9/71 (4)

Bangla Desh b/w Deep Blue (H) UK 7/30/71 (10); US 7/30/71 (23)

Back Seat of My Car b/w Heart of the Country (M) UK only 8/13/71 (39)

Uncle Albert/Admiral Halsey b/w **Too Many People** (M) US only
8/2/71 (1), Grammy win for Best Arrangement Accompanying Vocalists

Imagine b/w **It's So Hard** (L) US only 10/11/71 (3)

Happy Xmas (War Is Over) b/w Listen the Snow Is Falling★ (L) US
12/1/71 (0); UK 11/24/72 (4)

1972

Give Ireland Back to the Irish b/w Instr. version (M) UK 2/25/72 (16); US
2/28/72 (21)

Back Off Boogaloo b/w Blindman (S) UK 4/1/72 (2); US 3/17/72 (9)

Woman Is the Nigger of the World b/w Sisters O Sisters★ (L) US only
4/24/72 (57)

Mary Had a Little Lamb b/w Little Woman Love (M) UK 5/29/72 (9); US
5/5/72 (28)

Hi Hi Hi b/w **C Moon** (M) UK 12/1/72 (5); US 12/4/72 (10)

1973

My Love b/w The Mess (M) UK 3/23/73 (9); US 4/9/73 (1)

Give Me Love (Give Me Peace on Earth) b/w Miss O'Dell (H) UK 5/25/73 (8); US 5/7/73 (1)

Live and Let Die b/w I Lie Around (M) UK 6/1/73 (9); US 6/18/73 (2), Academy Award nom. for Best Original Song, Grammy win for Best Arrangement Accompanying Vocalist, Grammy nom. for Best Pop Vocal Performance and Best Original Score

Photograph b/w Down and Out (S) UK 10/27/73 (8); US 10/5/73 (1)

Helen Wheels b/w **Country Dreamer** (M) UK 10/26/73 (12); US 12/12/73 (10)

Mind Games b/w Meat City (L) UK 11/16/73 (26); US 10/29/73 (18)

You're Sixteen b/w Devil Woman (S) US 12/3/73 (1); UK 2/8/74 (2)

1974

Jet b/w **Let Me Roll It** (M) UK 2/15/74 (7); US 2/18/74 (7)

Oh My My b/w No No Song (S) US 2/18/74 (5); UK 1/9/76 (0)

Band on the Run b/w Zoo Gang (UK) 1985 (US) (M) UK 6/28/74 (3); US 4/8/74 (1)

Whatever Gets You Thru the Night b/w Beef Jerky (L) UK 10/4/74 (36); US 9/23/74 (1)

Walking in the Park with Eloise b/w Bridge on the River Suite (M as the Country Hams) UK 10/18/74 (0); US 12/2/74 (0)

Junior's Farm b/w **Sally G** (M) UK 10/25/74 (16)/ 11/4/74 (3)

Only You b/w Call Me (S) UK 11/15/74 (28); US 11/15/74 (6)

Ding Dong b/w I Don't Care Anymore (H) UK 12/6/74 (38); US 12/6/74 (0)

#9 Dream b/w **What You Got** (L) UK 1/24/75 (23); US 12/16/74 (9)

1975

Snookeroo b/w The No No Song (S) UK 2/21/75 (0); US 1/27/75 (3)

Dark Horse b/w Hari's on Tour (Express) (H) UK 2/28/75 (0); US 11/18/74 (15)

Stand by Me b/w Move Over Ms. L. (L) UK 4/18/75 (30); US 3/10/75 (20)
Listen to What the Man Said b/w Love in Song (M) UK 5/16/75 (6); US 5/26/75 (1)
(It's All Down to) Goodnight Vienna b/w Oo-Wee (S) US 6/2/75 (31)
Letting Go b/w **You Gave Me the Answer** (M) UK 10/18/75 (41); US 9/29/75 (39)
You b/w World of Stone (H) UK 9/12/75(38); US 9/12/75 (20)
Venus and Mars b/w Magneto and Titanium Man (M) UK 11/28/75 (0); US 10/27/75 (12)

1976

This Guitar (Can't Keep from Crying) b/w Maya Love (H) UK 2/6/76 (0); US 12/8/75 (0)
Silly Love Songs b/w Cook of the House (M) UK 4/30/76 (2); US 4/1/76 (1)
Let 'Em In b/w Beware My Love (M) UK 7/23/76 (2); US 6/28/76 (3), Grammy nom. for Best Arrangement Accompanying Vocalists
A Dose of Rock 'n' Roll b/w Cryin' (S) UK 10/15/76 (0); US 10/15/76 (26)
This Song b/w Learning How to Love You (H) UK 11/15/76 (0); US 11/19/76 (25)
Hey Baby b/w Lady Gaye (S) UK 11/29/76 (0); US 11/29/76 (74)

1977

Crackerbox Palace b/w Learning How to Love You (H) US only 1/24/77 (19)
Maybe I'm Amazed (Live) b/w Soily (Live) (M) UK 2/4/77 (28); US 2/7/77 (10)
True Love b/w Pure Smokey (H) UK 2/11/77 (0); US 2/11/77 (0)
Uncle Albert/Admiral Halsey (instr. version) b/w Eat at Home (instr) (M/ Thrillington) UK only 4/77 (0)
It's What You Value b/w Woman Don't You Cry for Me (H) UK 5/31/77 (0); US 5/31/77 (0)
Seaside Woman b/w B-side to Seaside (M as Suzy and the Red Stripes) US 5/31/77 (59); UK 8/10/79 (0)
Wings b/w Just a Dream (S) UK 8/25/77 (0); US 8/25/77 (0)

Drowning in the Sea of Love b/w Just a Dream (S) UK 9/16/77 (0); US 9/16/77 (0)

Mull of Kintyre b/w **Girl's School** (M) UK 11/11/77 (1); US 11/14/77 (33)

1978

Lipstick Traces b/w Old Time Lovin' (S) UK 6/1/78 (0); US 6/1/78 (0)

With a Little Luck b/w Backwards Traveller (M) UK 3/23/78 (5); US 3/20/78 (1)

I've Had Enough b/w Deliver Your Children (M) UK 6/16/78 (42); US 6/5/78 (25)

Tonight b/w Heart on My Sleeve (S) UK 7/21/78 (0); US 7/21/78 (0)

London Town b/w I'm Carrying (M) UK 8/11/78 (60); US 8/14/78 (39)

1979

Blow Away b/w Soft Touch (H) UK 2/16/79 (51); US 2/14/79 (16)

Goodnight Tonight b/w Daytime Nighttime Suffering (M) UK 3/23/79 (5); US 3/19/79 (5)

Love Comes to Everyone b/w Soft-Hearted Hana (H) UK 4/20/79 (0); US 4/20/79 (0)

Old Siam Sir b/w Spin It On (M) UK only 6/1/79 (35)

Faster b/w Your Love Is Forever (H) UK 7/30/79 (0); US 7/30/79 (0)

Arrow through Me (M) US only 8/13/79 (29)

Getting Closer b/w Baby's Request (M) UK 8/16/79 (60); US 6/11/79 (20)

Wonderful Christmastime b/w Rudolph The Red-Nosed Reggae (M) UK 11/16/79 (6); US 11/26/79 (0)

1980

Coming Up b/w Coming Up (Live) + Lunchbox/Odd Sox (M) UK 4/11/80 (2); US 4/14/80 (1), Grammy nom. for Best Rock Vocal Performance for live version

Waterfalls b/w Check My Machine (M) UK 6/13/80 (9); US 7/22/80 (83)

Temporary Secretary b/w Secret Friend (M) UK only 9/15/80 (0)

(Just Like) Starting Over b/w Kiss Kiss Kiss★ (L) UK 10/24/80 (1); US 10/20/80 (1), Grammy nom. for Record of the Year

1981

Woman b/w Beautiful Boys★ (L) UK 1/16/81 (1); US 1/12/81 (2)

I Saw Her Standing There/Whatever Gets You thru the Night/Lucy in the Sky with Diamonds (L and Elton John live Madison Square Garden 1974) UK only 3/13/81 (40)

Watching the Wheels b/w Yes I'm Your Angel★ (L) UK 3/27/81 (30); 3/13/81 (10)

All Those Years Ago b/w Writing's on the Wall (H) UK 5/15/81 (13); US 5/11/81 (2)

Teardrops b/w Save the World (H) UK 7/31/81 (0); US 7/31/81 (0)

Wrack My Brain b/w Drumming Is My Madness (S) UK 11/13/81 (0); US 11/13/81 (38)

1982

Private Property b/w Wrack My Brain (S) US only 1/13/82 (0)

Ebony and Ivory b/w Rainclouds (M) UK 3/29/82 (1); US3/29/82 (1)

Take It Away b/w I'll Give You a Ring (M) UK 6/21/82 (15); US 6/21/82 (10)

Tug of War b/w Get It (M) UK 9/20/82 (53); US 9/13/82 (53)

The Girl Is Mine b/w Can't Get Outta the Rain (M) UK 10/29/82 (8); US 10/25/82 (2)

Wake Up My Love b/w Greece (H) UK 11/8/82 (0); US 11/8/82 (53)

Love b/w Give Me Some Truth (L) UK only 11/15/82 (41)

I Really Love You b/w Circles (H) US only 1982 (0)

1983

Say Say Say b/w Ode to a Koala Bear (M) UK 10/3/83 (2); US 10/3/83 (1)

Pipes of Peace b/w So Bad (M) UK 5/12/83 (1); US 5/12/83 (23)

1984

Nobody Told Me b/w O Sanity★ (L) UK 1/9/84 (6); US 1/9/84 (5)

Borrowed Time b/w Your Hands★ (L) UK 3/9/84 (32); US 5/14/84 (108)

I'm Stepping Out b/w Sleepless Night★ (L) UK 7/15/84 (88); US 3/18/84 (55)

No More Lonely Nights b/w (Playout Version) (M) UK 9/24/84 (2); US 10/8/84 (6)

We All Stand Together b/w (Humming Version) (M) UK 11/12/84 (3); US 11/12/84 (0)

Every Man Has a Woman Who Loves Him b/w It's Alright★ (L) UK 11/16/84 (0); US 10/8/84 (0)

1985

Spies Like Us b/w My Carnival (M) US 11/18/85 (13); US 11/18/85 (7)

I Don't Want to Do It b/w Queen of the Hop (Dave Edmunds) (H) UK 5/85 (0); US 5/85 (0)

Jealous Guy b/w **Going Down on Love/Oh Yoko!** UK only 11/18/85 (65)

1986

Press b/w It's Not True (M) UK 7/14/86 (25); US 7/14/86 (21)

Pretty Little Head b/w Write Away (M) UK only 10/27/86 (0)

Only Love Remains b/w Tough on a Tightrope (M) UK 12/1/86 (34); US 1/19/87 (0)

Stranglehold b/w Angry (M) US only 11/3/86 (81)

1987

Got My Mind Set on You b/w Lay His Head (H) UK 10/12/87 (2); US 10/3/87 (1)

Once Upon a Long Ago b/w **Back on My Feet** (M) UK only 11/16/87 (10)

1988

When We Was Fab b/w Zig-Zag (H) UK 1/25/88 (25); US 1/30/88 (23)
This Is Love b/w Breath Away From Heaven (H) UK 6/13/88 (55); US 7/25/88 (0)
Handle with Care b/w Margarita (Wilburys) UK 10/24/88 (21); US 11/28/88 (45)
My Brave Face b/w Flying to My Home (M) UK 5/8/89 (18); US 5/8/89 (25)
This One b/w The First Stone (M) UK 7/17/89 (18); US 8/1/89 (94)
Figure of Eight b/w Ou Est le Soleil? (M) UK 11/13/19 (42); US 11/14/89 (92)
Ou Est le Soleil? b/w Instr. version (M) US only 7/25/89 (0)
Cheer Down b/w **Poor Little Girl** (H) UK 11/27/89 (0); US 8/24/89 (0)

1989

End of the Line b/w Congratulations (Wilburys) UK 2/20/89 (52); US 2/25/89 (63)

1990–1999

Put It There b/w **Mama's Little Girl** (M) UK 1/29/90 (32); US 5/1/90 (0)
Nobody's Child b/w with a Little Help from My Friends (Live) (Wilburys) UK 6/18/90 (44); US 6/18/90 (0)
Birthday b/w Good Day Sunshine (Live) (M) UK 10/8/90 (29); US 10/16/90 (0)
She's My Baby b/w New Blue Moon (Wilburys) UK 11/5/90 (79); US 11/5/90 (0)
All My Trials b/w C Moon (Live) (M) UK only 11/26/90 (35)
The World You're Coming Into b/w Tres Conejos (M/classical) UK only 9/30/91 (0)
Wilbury Twist b/w New Blue Moon (Wilburys) UK 3/5/91 (0); US 3/25/91 (0)
Weight of the World b/w **After All These Years** (S) UK 5/4/92 (74)
Hope of Deliverance b/w Long Leather Coat (M) UK 12/28/92 (18); US 1/12/93 (83)

C'mon People b/w I Can't Imagine (M) UK 2/22/93 (41); 7/20/93 (0)

Off the Ground b/w Cosmically Conscious (M) US only 4/27/93 (0)

A Leaf (M/classical) UK only 4/24/95 (0)

Free as a Bird b/w Christmas Time (Is Here Again) (Beatles) UK 12/4/95
(2); US 12/12/95 (6), Grammy win for Best Pop Performance by a Duo
or Group with Vocal

Real Love b/w Baby's in Black (Live) (Beatles) UK 3/4/96 (4); US 3/4/96 (11)

Young Boy b/w Looking For You (M) UK only 4/28/97 (19)

The World Tonight (M) b/w Used to Be Bad UK 7/7/97 (23); b/w Looking
for You US 5/6/97 (64)

Beautiful Night b/w Love Comes Tumbling Down (M) UK only
12/15/97 (25)

La De Da (S) UK 1998 (63); US 1998 (0)

No Other Baby b/w Brown Eyed Handsome Man (M) 11/25/99 (42); US
11/23/99 (0)

Fluid b/w remixes (M/The Fireman/experimental) UK only 9/6/99 (0)

Come on Christmas, Christmas Come On (S) 1999 (0)

2000–2011

From a Lover to a Friend b/w Riding into Jaipur (M) UK only 10/29/01
(45)

Freedom b/w **From a Lover to a Friend** (M) UK 11/14/01 (0); US
11/5/01 (97)

My Sweet Lord b/w Let It Down/My Sweet Lord (2000) (H) UK 1/14/02
(1); US 1/14/02 (94)

Vanilla Sky (M) UK 2/4/02 (0); US 12/14/01 (0)

Any Road b/w Marwa Blues (H) UK only 5/12/03 (37), Grammy nom. for
Best Male Pop Vocal Performance (Any Road), win for Best Pop Instrumental Performance (Marwa Blues)

Never without You (S) UK 10/25/03 (0); US 10/25/03 (0)

Tropic Island Hum b/w We All Stand Together (M) UK only 10/20/04 (21)

Fine Line b/w Growing Up Falling Down (M) UK 8/29/05 (20); US
8/29/05 (0), Grammy nom. 2006 for Best Male Pop Vocal Performance

Jenny Wren b/w Summer of '59 (M) UK only 11/21/05 (22), Grammy
nom. for 2007 Best Male Pop Vocal Performance

Fading In and Out (S) UK 7/25/05 (0) ; US 6/7/05 (0)

Really Love You b/w Lalula (M, Twin Freaks) UK only 6/6/05 (0)

Dance Tonight b/w Nod Your Head (M) UK 6/18/07 (26); US 6/18/07 (69)

Ever Present Past b/w House of Wax (M) UK 11/5/07 (85); US 5/15/07 (0)
Nod Your Head (M) download single 8/28/07 (0)
Liverpool 8 b/w For Love (S) UK 12/4/07 (98); US 1/7/08 (0)
Sing the Changes (M/The Fireman) download single 12/16/08 (0)
(I Want to) Come Home (M) download single 12/8/09 (0)
Walk with You (S and M) download single 12/12/09 (0)

Bibliography

BOOKS

Beatles, The. *The Beatles Anthology*. San Francisco: Chronicle Books, 2000.

Bedford, Carol. *Waiting for the Beatles: An Apple Scruff's Story*. Poole: Blandford Press, 1984.

Blaney, John. *Lennon and McCartney: Together Alone*. London: Jawbone, 2007.

Boyd, Pattie, and Penny Junor. *Wonderful Tonight: George Harrison, Eric Clapton, and Me*. London: Headline Review, 2007.

Bramwell, Tony. *Magical Mystery Tours: My Life with the Beatles*. London: Robson Books, 2005.

Brown, Peter, and Stephen Gaines. *The Love You Make: An Insider's Story of the Beatles*. New York: McGraw-Hill, 1983.

Carlin, Peter Ames. *Paul McCartney: A Life*. New York: Touchstone, 2009.

Carr, Roy, and Tony Tyler. *The Beatles: An Illustrated Record*. London: New English Library, 1975.

Cohn, Nik. *Awopbopaloobop Alopbamboom: The Golden Age of Rock*. St. Albans: Paladin Press, 1970.

Coleman, Ray. *Lennon*. New York: McGraw-Hill, 1985.

Cott, Jonathan, and Christine Doudna, eds. *The Ballad of John and Yoko*. London: Michael Joseph, 1982.

Davies, Hunter. *The Beatles: The Authorised Biography*. London: Heinemann, 1968.

Doggett, Peter. *You Never Give Me Your Money*. New York: HarperCollins, 2009.

Gambaccini, Paul, ed. *Paul McCartney: In His Own Words*. New York: Music Sales Corp., 1976.

Gitlin, Todd. *The Sixties: Years of Hope, Days of Rage*. New York: Bantam, 1987.

Giuliano, Geoffrey. *Blackbird: The Life and Times of Paul McCartney*. Toronto: Da Capo, 1991.

Goldman, Albert. *The Lives of John Lennon*. London: Bantam, 1988.

Green, John. *Dakota Days*. New York: St. Martin's Press, 1983.

Guiliano, Geoffrey. *Blackbird: The Life and Times of Paul McCartney*. London: John Blake, 1991.

Harry, Bill. *The Paul McCartney Encyclopedia*. Virgin Books, 2002.

Ingham, Chris. *The Rough Guide to the Beatles*. London: Rough Guides Limited, 2009.

Jones, Jack. *Let Me Take You Down: Inside the Mind of Mark David Chapman, the Man Who Killed John Lennon*. New York: Villard Books, 1992.

Kane, Larry. *Ticket to Ride*. Philadelphia: Running Press, 2003.

Leng, Simon. *The Music of George Harrison: While My Guitar Gently Weeps*. London: Firefly, 2003.

Lennon, Cynthia. *A Twist of Lennon*. London: Star, 1978.

———. *John*. New York: Three Rivers Press, 2005.

Lennon, John. *Skywriting by Word of Mouth*. London: Pan, 1986.

Lewisohn, Mark. *The Complete Beatles Recording Sessions: The Official Story of the Abbey Road Years*. London: Hamlyn, 1990.

Mansfield, Ken. *The White Book: The Beatles, The Bands, The Biz: An Insider's Look at an Era*. Nashville: Thomas Nelson, 2007.

Miles, Barry. *Paul McCartney: Many Years from Now*. London: Secker and Warburg, 1998.

Miller, Jim, ed. *The* Rolling Stone *Illustrated History of Rock 'n' Roll*. (Greil Marcus on Beatles.) New York: Random House, 1976.

Norman, Philip. *Shout! The Beatles in Their Generation*. London: Elm Tree, 1981.

———. *Symphony for the Devil*. London: Penguin, 1984.

———. *John Lennon*. New York: Ecco, 2008

O'Dell, Chris, and Katherine Ketcham. *Miss O'Dell: My Hard Days and Long Nights with The Beatles, The Stones, Bob Dylan, Eric Clapton, and the Women They Loved*. New York: Touchstone, 2009.

Oldham, Andrew. *Stoned*. London: Secker & Warburg, 2000.

Ono, Yoko. *Grapefruit*. London: Sphere Books, 1971.

Pang, May, and Henry Edwards. *Loving John*. London: Corgi, 1983.

Richards, Keith, and James Fox. *Life*. New York: Little, Brown and Company, 2010.

Riley, Tim. *Tell Me Why: A Beatles Commentary*. London: Bodley Head, 1988.

Rodriguez, Robert. *Fab Four FAQ 2.0: The Beatles' Solo Years, 1970–1980*. Milwaukee: Backbeat Books, 2010.

Russell, J. P. *The Beatles on Record*. New York: Charles Scribner's Sons, 1982.

Schaffner, Nicholas. *The Beatles Forever*. New York: McGraw-Hill, 1978.

Schaumberg, Ron. *Growing Up with the Beatles*. New York: Pyramid, 1976.

Seaman, Frederic. *The Last Days of John Lennon*. New York: Dell, 1992.

Shotton, Pete, and Nicolas Schaffner. *John Lennon in My Life*. London: Stein and Day, 1983.

Spitz, Bob. *The Beatles: The Biography*. London: Aurum Press, 2005.

Woffinden, Bob. *The Beatles Apart*. London: Proteus Books, 1981.

ARTICLES

"Beatles George's Pension Plan, DPA January 8, 2001." BeatleCity.com, December 12, 2000. Accessed October 10, 2011, www.beatlecity.com/bnews_harrison.htm.

Blackburn, Robin, and Tariq Ali. "1971 *Red Mole* with Interview John Lennon." *Red Mole*, 1971. Accessed October 10, 2011, http://homepage.ntlworld.com/carousel/pob99.html.

Born, Matt. "Heather Was a High-Class Hooker Paid Thousands." *Daily Mail*, June 12, 2006.

Cameron, Keith. "Coming Up's Invitation to the Dance." *Mojo*, no. 213, August 2011.

Clements, Jon. "Can We Believe Heather This Time?" *Daily Mirror*, October 19, 2006.

Conlan, Tara. "*Sun* Turns Up the Heat on Mills McCartney." *Guardian*, July 25, 2011.

Cott, Jonathan. "The Lost Lennon Tapes." *Rolling Stone*, December 2010.

Couric, Katie. "Interview with Olivia Harrison." *Katie at Night* (transcript), November 26, 2002. Accessed October 10, 2011, http://willybrauch.de/In_Their_Own_Words/oliviaharrison.htms.

Das, Subhamoy. "George Harrison and Hinduism—His Idea of God and Reincarnation." About.com. Accessed October 10, 2011, http://hinduism.about.com/od/artculture/a/harrison.htm.

DeMain, Bill. "When We Was Fab: Nashvillians Remember Paul McCartney and Wings' Working Vacation Here in 1974." *Nashville Scene*, 2002. Accessed October 10, 2011, http://alt.nntp2http.com/tv/ilovelucy/2010/04/bfc220f9a7dfd679f6b6b1a5d2e6fc26.html.

Doyle, Tom. "Starting Over." *Mojo*, no. 203, October 2010.

Ellen, Barbara. "Proper Charlie." *Observer*, July 8, 2000.

"Finance: Diversification at the Vatican." *Time*, January 25, 1971.

Fleischman, Buzz. "Ferdie Pacheco, Cassius Clay, and the Beatles at the 5th Street Gym on Miami Beach, a Back Story." *Miami Pop Culture Examiner*, 2009. Accessed October 10, 2011, www.examiner.com/pop-culture-in-miami/ferdie-pacheco-cassius-clay-and-the-beatles-at-the-5th-street-gym-on-miami-beach-a-back-story.

Friedman, Roger. "Beatles: Lennon Planned to Visit McCartney in 1974." *Fox News*, September 25, 2001. Accessed October 10, 2011, www.foxnews.com/story/0,2933,35067,00.html.

Goodman, Joan. "1984 *Playboy* Interview with Paul and Linda McCartney." The Ultimate Beatles Interview Database, December 1984. Accessed October 10, 2011, www.beatlesinterviews.org/db1984.pmpb.beatles.html.

Harris, John. "I'm Still Standing." *Guardian*, June 10, 2004.

Hynde, Chrissie. "Tears and Laughter." *USA Weekend*, October 30, 1998.

King, Larry. "Interview with Paul McCartney and Ringo Starr." *Larry King Live* (transcript), June 26, 2007. Accessed October 10, 2011, http://transcripts.cnn.com/TRANSCRIPTS/0706/26/lkl.01.html.

Kordosh, J. "December 1987 Interview with George Harrison." Beatlesnumber9.com, December 1987. Accessed October 10, 2011, http://beatlesnumber9.com/creem .html.

"No 3-Beatle Reunion, George Harrison Says." *AP/New York Times*, December 1, 1989.

"Oasis' Gallagher Brothers Go Off on Rock's Old Guard." MTV.com, October 29, 1997. Accessed October 10, 2011, www.mtv.com/news/articles/1425552/oasis -gallagher-brothers-go-off-on-rocks-old-guard.jhtml.

Raz, Guy. "Radio Free Georgetown." *Washington City Paper.com*, 1999. Accessed October 10, 2011, www.washingtoncitypaper.com/articles/16638/radio-free-georgetown.

"Ringo." *Independent*, October 28, 1995.

"Ringo Starr." *TV Guide*, March 11–17, 1989.

Sheff, David. "January 1981 *Playboy* Interview with John Lennon and Yoko Ono." *Playboy*, January 1981. Accessed October 10, 2011, www.john-lennon.com/playboy interviewwithjohnlennononandyokoono.htm.

"The Song Paul McCartney Would Like to Be Remembered For." *Época Magazine*, 2009. Accessed October 10, 2011, http://en.wikipedia.org/wiki/Maybe_I%27m_ Amazed.

"Top 5: Knob-twiddlers." *Washington Times*, October 6, 2010.

Wenner, Jann. "Bob Dylan Hits the Big Themes, from Religion to the Atomic Age." *Rolling Stone*, May 2007.

Wenner, Jann S. "January 1971 *Rolling Stone* Interview with John Lennon and Yoko Ono." *Rolling Stone*, January 21, 1971. Accessed October 10, 2011, www. jannswenner.com/Archives/John_Lennon_Part1.aspx.

Wigg, David. "May 1969 BBC Radio-One 'Scene and Heard' Interview." *BBC Radio 1*, May 1969. Accessed October 10, 2011, www.beatlesinterviews.org/ db1969.0508.beatles.html.

WEBSITES

ABC News.com. "Harrison Attacker Ruled Insane." (November 15, 2000) Accessed October 10, 2011, http://abcnews.go.com/Entertainment/story?id=113210&page=1.

———. "Paul McCartney on Poetry and Lennon." (April 30, 2001) Accessed October 10, 2011, http://abcnews.go.com/GMA/story?id=127011&page=1.

Doggett, Peter. "John Lennon and Money." Beatles Blog by Author Peter Doggett. June 2, 2010, http://peterdoggettbeatles.blogspot.com/2010/06/john-lennon-and -money.html.

Reunion Sessions. "The Beatles Reunion Recording Sessions: The Unofficial Story of the Reunion Sessions." Accessed October 10, 2011, http://reunionsessions.tripod .com/al/faabsessions/1994a.html.

Rock and Roll Hall of Fame + Museum Rockhall's Channel. "Beatles Accept Award Rock and Roll Hall of Fame Inductions 1988." Accessed October 10, 2011, www .youtube.com/watch?v=NO-HK_csGwk.

Spin.com. "Thom Yorke Declines Duet with Paul McCartney." (November 13, 2007) Accessed October 10, 2011, www.spin.com/articles/thom-yorke-declines-duet-paul-mccartney-gallows-map-us-tour.

———. "Dear Yoko." Accessed October 10, 2011, www.beatlesbible.com/people/john-lennon/songs/dear-yoko.

The Beatles Bible.com. "Free as a Bird." Accessed October 10, 2011, www.beatles bible.com/songs/free-as-a-bird.

Vh1.com. "And in the End . . ." Accessed October 10, 2011, www.vh1.com/artists/news/1436073/20000201/beatles.jhtml.

Wikipedia. "Backbeat." Accessed October 10, 2011, http://en.wikipedia.org/wiki/Backbeat_%28film%29.

———. "Jeff Lynne." Accessed October 10, 2011, http://en.wikipedia.org/wiki/Jeff_Lynne.

YouTube. "The Beatles Biographer Bob Spitz Interview (Part 1) with Face Culture." Accessed October 10, 2011, www.youtube.com/watch?v=8BdxR81W34g.

———. "John Lennon on Dick Cavett/2nd Appearance with Live Performance." Accessed October 10, 2011, www.youtube.com/watch?v=31qVGN1gKOE.

Index

About the Author

Andrew Grant Jackson has written for *Yahoo! Movies, Baseline Studio System*, music magazines *Burn Lounge, Mean Street,* and *Dispatch*, and has copyedited the Hollywood monthly magazine *Ingenue*. He directed and cowrote the feature film *The Discontents* (2004) starring Perry King and Amy Madigan and served as actor Jeff Bridges's development associate at AsIs Productions.